U.S. & SOVIET POLICY IN THE MIDDLE EAST 1945-56

U.S. & SOVIET POLICY
IN THE
MIDDLE EAST
1945-56

Edited by John Donovan

FACTS ON FILE, INC.　　　　　NEW YORK

U.S. & SOVIET POLICY

IN THE

MIDDLE EAST

1945–56

Library of Congress Catalog Card No. 78-154633

ISBN 0-87196-200-4

9 8 7 6 5 4 3 2 1

PRINTED IN THE UNITED STATES OF AMERICA

C. J. Chacko

CONTENTS

Page

i

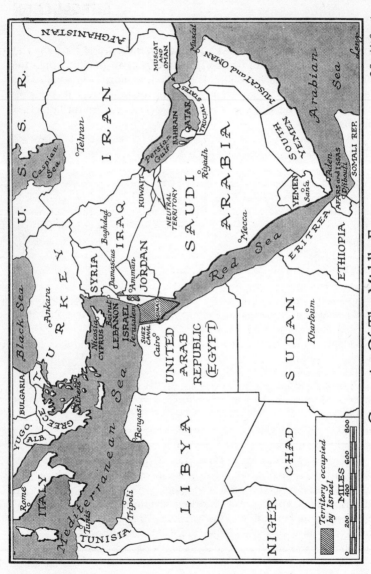

Countries Of The Middle East

INTRODUCTION

GREAT CHANGES HAVE TAKEN place all over the world since the end of World War II. None, perhaps, have been more dramatic than the political upheavals in the Middle East. And, although the Middle East is only one of many areas of crisis and confrontation, recent events indicate that it could become a region of crucial conflict for both East and West.

In 1945 Britain was still the dominant power in the Middle East and France was preeminent in North Africa. The Soviet Union had retained an occupation force in northern Iran but was later prevailed on to withdraw it. The U.S., preoccupied with the many consequences of victory, was encouraging Arab nationalism through the traditional rulers. U.S. commercial groups were undertaking profitable oil investments, and the outlook for a rapport with the Arab world was promising.

Currently, Turkey and Iran are still aligned with the U.S., as is Israel, but most of the Arab nations have become client states—to one degree or another—of the USSR.

The kingdoms of Jordan and Saudi Arabia and the sheikdom of Kuwait continue to have close commercial ties with the West, but these dynasties and the sheikdom have an uncertain future. King Hussein of Jordan has seemed particularly vulnerable because of the growth of the Palestinian commando movement.

The changes in the Middle East came slowly and were the result of both the normal movement of history and the policies followed there by the great powers. By 1945 the wartime alliance between Russia and the Western powers had already turned sour. The meetings at Potsdam and Yalta had revealed basic differences between the Soviet and the West and had provoked mutual suspicion and hostility.

There was almost constant dispute. First it was the disposition of Poland, then the question of German reparations. Next, the USSR colonized eastern Europe and conceived a Communist take-over in Czechoslovakia. Then came a major confrontation over the isolation of West Berlin and a dangerous situation during the Allied airlift to Berlin. (Some years afterward ex-State Secy. Dean G. Acheson told the American people what the dangers had been during the 1948 airlift. "The U.S. was no more than an eyelash away from war," Acheson said.) There were other close calls: in the early 1950s, during the Korean War,

1

when Gen. Douglas MacArthur considered mounting an invasion of Red China; in Oct. 1962, when Pres. John F. Kennedy and Soviet Communist Chairman Nikita S. Khrushchev negotiated an agreement for the removal of Russian missiles from Cuba; and other incidents, some of them during the long-drawn-out Vietnam war.

From the beginning of the post-World War II era, both the U.S. and the Soviet Union were eager to extend their influence in the emerging Arab nations. The colonial powers, France and Britain, were on the way out, and the USSR and U.S., which to some extent ultimately succeeded them, were regarded as the popular victors over Nazi Germany. Both major powers were deeply aware of the strategic and logistical importance of the area, but one of the prime considerations was that both East and West wanted control of the vast oil riches in the Middle East.

At the outset both the U.S. and the USSR resorted to overt diplomacy and covert subversion to obtain their ends. The Russians, more than the Western powers, had to work with underground movements because all of the Arab governments were either royalist or traditionally anti-Communist. In Iran, Russia gave its support to the Tudeh (Masses, or Communist) party, the Azerbaijan nationalists and, later, during an oil crisis, to the lachrymose Dr. Mohammed Mossadeq. The U.S. countered successfully with support for Shah Mohammed Reza Pahlevi.

It is generally agreed that the most crucial event in recent history for the Middle East has been the creation of the state of Israel. As the British mandate in Palestine drew to a close, both the U.S. and the USSR vigorously supported the partition of Palestine and the formation of a Jewish state. There were opponents in the U.S. of the creation of a sovereign and independent Israel. In spite of a powerful pro-Arab oil lobby and strong opposition from his advisers in the State Department, Pres. Harry S. Truman opted for a Jewish state. When the time came, Truman moved with such dispatch that he granted *de jure* recognition to Israel even before notifying the U.S. delegation at the UN. Relations between Israel and Russia were extremely close during this period. For some time before the UN partition of Palestine, the USSR had allowed its satellite Czechoslovakia to ship arms and ammunition to Jewish underground forces in the British-mandated territory. Other countries talked, but the Jews got arms from the Czechoslovaks. In addition, many progressive and leftist-oriented Jews were convinced that the Soviets were, and would be, staunch allies of Israel.

In a short time, however, the Soviet Union withdrew its support of Israel and consistently sided with the Arabs at the UN. Some observers view the Russian decision to abandon a pro-Israel stance as part of a deliberately planned, master chess move. Others feel that Soviet foreign policy has always been coldly pragmatic. It is their feeling that the Russians gave the Jews their support originally because Jewish demands had been a source of difficulty to the British. Accordingly, once the British had given up the Palestine mandate, there remained no need to support the Israelis.

An article written in the Dec. 30, 1970 *N.Y. Times* throws additional light on the Soviet attitude toward Jews. Mrs. Golda Meir, the Israeli premier, wrote: "Nov. 1948, those were the days of the honeymoon, when we Israelis and the Russians were great friends." Israel's first ambassador to the Soviet Union, Mrs. Meir told of having attended an official party given by Vyacheslav M. Molotov, then Soviet foreign minister. At the party she met Mrs. Molotov, who treated her with great cordiality. To the Israeli ambassador's surprise, Mrs. Molotov addressed her in Yiddish and identified herself as "a daughter of Israel." The Soviet foreign minister's wife took evident pleasure in introducing Mrs. Meir (then Myerson) to various dignitaries as her prominent coreligionist. In the weeks after the party Mrs. Meir did not hear from Mrs. Molotov, and this surprised her. Years later, in New York, Mrs. Meir learned why Mrs. Molotov had failed to get in touch with her. The Soviet foreign minister's wife had been sent to prison for 2 years—even though her husband was then one of the most important officials in the USSR.

Over the years, the Soviet Union enlarged its role with Arab states led by leftist military juntas, and the U.S. worked closely with the traditional monarchies. In the past, U.S. strategy had succeeded in Saudi Arabia and royalist Libya despite a fence-straddling position on the Arab-Israeli issue. Even Arab countries that have strong ties with America, however, have condemned the U.S. bitterly for its pro-Zionist policies.

In an attempt to work out a *modus vivendi* with the Arab nations and to demonstrate a sincere interest in the future of those countries, the U.S. for many years made available large sums in grants-in-aid and long-term loans. Before the Egyptians moved into the Soviet orbit and while Col. Gamal Abdel Nasser attempted to play the role of a neutralist, Egypt had received $912 million from the U.S. The largest shares of U.S. aid to the Middle East, however, have gone to 2 Moslem but non-Arab countries: Turkey (over $5 billion) and Iran (almost $2 billion). Even small countries such as Syria and Lebanon, however, have received sizable amounts of U.S. aid, but this largesse in most cases has been curtailed.

Economic aid to Israel from 1946 through 1969 totaled $1.226 billion, but in that time some $411 million has been repaid, so the outstanding figure is $815 million. Since 1968 the amount of military aid to Israel and to Jordan has been classified, but we know that in both cases it has been substantial. During an extended military crisis toward the close of 1970, the U.S. approved a $500 million aid program for Israel. Pres. Richard M. Nixon also indicated that the U.S. would strive to maintain a balance of military power in the Middle East. This was taken to mean that Israel will get armor, aircraft and ammunition required for defense.

U.S. support of Israel continues to infuriate the Arabs to the extent that they overlook many efforts made by the U.S. to help their countries. Almost totally ignored by the Arabs is the fact that the U.S. contributes more to the Palestine Arab Refugee Relief Fund than any other country. The U.S. has donated so far some $478 million and regularly gives $22 million annually to the UN Arab refugee fund.

Arab leaders often angrily denounce the U.S. because it has allowed Zionist organizations to contribute large sums of money to Israel. In a booklet entitled *Jewish Communal Services, Programs and Finances*, S. P. Goldberg estimates that Israel bond sales from 1948 through 1969 amounted to $1,209 billion. In the same period the United Jewish Appeal provided Israel with almost $1,300 billion—a combined total of more than $2½ billion.

From 1946 through 1970 the U.S. made available foreign aid loans and grants amounting to more than $143 billion dollars to countries throughout the world. Some $93 billion was assigned to "less developed countries," and the "developed countries" received approximately $50½ billion. No nation in history has undertaken to finance its friends and allies on such a huge scale.

In recent years the Soviet Union has made available large amounts of military aid, principally to Egypt but also to Iraq, Syria, Yemen, Sudan and to the Yemeni Republican forces.

The Russian investment in Egypt has been enormous. It is estimated that by the end of 1970, $5 billion worth of military aid had been supplied to Egypt by the Soviet Union since 1955, some $2 billion since 1967. The Egyptian army lost hundreds of millions of dollars worth of Russian military equipment during the 6-day war with Israel in 1967. Disregarding the cost, Moscow moved swiftly and set up an airlift of more than 800 planes. In a matter of weeks the Egyptians and Syrians were reequipped with late-model Soviet weapons, planes and missiles. With the new armament came hundreds of Soviet technicians and officers who operated as training cadres.

At the same time economic diplomacy has been accelerated by the

Russians. The one really significant contribution to Egypt was a loan of more than $500 million for the funding and engineering aid in the construction of the Aswan Dam. There have also been considerable economic aid programs undertaken on an annual or 5-year plan basis. Like other Arab nations, Egypt has made several barter arrangements with the USSR as well. Soviet technical aid to industry, agriculture and the social services has been expanded throughout the Middle East.

Paradoxically, the Communist Party is proscribed in many of the Arab countries aligned with the USSR. The Russians apparently have not sought to end this proscription but have worked instead with underground groups—together with such loyal satellites as Bulgaria—in an attempt to unseat governments in conservative Arab countries such as the Sudan, Jordan, Saudi Arabia, Kuwait and, at one time, Yemen.

To some observers, great-power interest in the Middle East is synonymous with the modern world's dependence on petroleum as a source of energy. The oil wealth of the Middle East and North Africa is, of course, of tremendous importance to the entire world, both economically and politically. "Proven" oil reserves in the Middle East, or, more accurately, the Persian Gulf region, amount to 333 billion barrels, 62% of the world total. The reserves in Libya, Algeria and Egypt raise the total for the Middle East and North Africa to 70% of the world supply. With the exception of Iran—Moslem but not Arab—the Mideast's Arab nations possess 60% of the world's known oil.

The major Western companies that produce oil in Arab North Africa (the Maghreb) and the Middle East (the Mashreq) are 5 in number, and they are extremely concerned about the future. U.S. support of Israel has been a red flag to Arabs, who have become more difficult for the West to deal with in recent years. The 5 companies are: Standard Oil of New Jersey, Standard Oil of California, Texaco, Gulf, and Mobil-Oil. The capital investment of these companies in the Maghreb and the Mashreq amounts to about $2 billion. A constant fear of American companies is that Palestine commandos, on their own initiative, may blow up American oil installations as they did in 1969. To minimize that threat, the Saudi Arabian government recently terminated the employment of Palestinians working at Aramco's huge export terminal on the Persian Gulf. In Libya, during recent oil negotiations, industry representatives were warned by the leader of the junta government, Col. Muammer el Qaddafi, that "the U.S. would see its interests threatened as a result of its support for Israel."

A disturbing aspect of the continued turmoil in the Middle East is that if Arab oil is ever curtailed, Western Europe would be in desperate condition. Western Europe is almost totally dependent on Arab oil sources for fuel, lubrication, transportation, industrial power and other energy needs. Europe gets 75% of its petroleum from North Africa and the Middle East (while Japan is almost 90% dependent on Arab sources). The U.S. on the other hand, produces some 78% of its own oil and imports most of the balance of its needs from Venezuela and Canada. A mere 3% comes from Arab sources. In an emergency, the U.S. could do without Arab oil, but its military allies and friends could not.

Under the circumstances, it is obvious that the Russians have altered the strategic military and economic conditions in the Middle East at the cost of the West, particularly of the U.S. As a result of its enlarged role in the Arab world, the USSR maintains a growing naval armada in the Mediterranean and has a military base as far west as Mersel-Kebir, Algeria—only 260 miles from the Strait of Gibralter.

According to some observers, the continued westward movement of Soviet naval power has brought about a precarious naval balance in the Mediterranean. In Oct. 1970 the Soviet fleet in the Mediterranean numbered some 73 ships, including about a dozen submarines. During the same period the U.S. fleet there varied in size from 35 to 40 ships of the line. The strong Soviet presence in the Mediterranean led one U.S. admiral to comment that the U.S. "is walking the 'tightrope' of adequacy in the area." (Recently Vice Adm. Hyman Rickover sounded a warning over the amazing growth of the Soviet navy by pointing out that the USSR's submarine construction program had produced 570 modern submarines in the past 25 years.)

To keep pace with its growing Mediterranean fleet, the Soviet Union has been building and improving naval bases in that area. A major naval base is being built at Mersa Matruh, 155 miles west of Alexandria in Egypt. Soviet surface ships are also serviced at the former French naval bases at Bone and Algiers in Algeria and at facilities at Alexandria and Port Said in Egypt and Latakiah in Syria. Also, since 1967 the Soviets have had an air base at Mersa Matruh at which Egyptian pilots have been trained.

Of major importance is the admission by the Egyptians that 4 Soviet pilots had been killed in dog fights with Israeli fighters and that a 6-man Soviet crew at a SAM missile site had been wiped out by an Israeli attack. (There are precedents for this in the unofficial Soviet participation as combatants in the Korean and Vietnam wars.)

Many concerned people have expressed fear that if both the U.S. and the Soviet Union fail to exert a strong conciliatory and peacemaking influence on the Arabs and the Israelis, there will be no peace in the Middle East, not even a long-term interim peace.

This book is the first volume of a journalistic account of the events that accompanied the clash of U.S. and Soviet interests in the Middle East between the end of World War II and the Suez crisis of 1956—the period in which British and French dominance in the area was being replaced by U.S. and Soviet influence. The contents of this book are adapted largely from the records of FACTS ON FILE and the materials developed by this editor during long years of active journalistic work in Palestine and the other countries of the Middle East before, during and after the creation of the state of Israel. Most of the events recorded in this book are highly controversial, but, as in all books in the INTERIM HISTORY series, great efforts were taken to present all pertinent facts without bias. The objective is to provide a source to which an intelligent reader can turn with confidence when he needs or wants to find out the facts of U.S. and Soviet policy in the Middle East.

RENASCENT NATIONALISM (1945)

Waning Days of World War II

Early in 1945, when it became clear that Germany had lost the war, tides of nationalism began to rise in many parts of the Middle East. In Palestine, Jews and Arabs had observed a temporary truce during World War II. Arabs who had been pro-Axis had either been jailed or intimidated by British troops in the area. For the most part, Arabs curtailed their attacks against Jews, and Jewish defense groups suspended their campaign against the British mandate forces. With the war drawing to a close, however, Arab nationalists and Zionist activists prepared to move. Everywhere in the Middle East the drive toward national independence grew stronger. Egyptians yearned to see the last of the British, and Syrians and Lebanese wished to get rid of the French.

In the course of the war there had been a growth of pro-Soviet and pro-Communist sympathy in many Arab countries. In their hatred of the colonial powers, many Arab nationalists had hoped for a German victory. For a time, Germany had appeared to be invincible, but when the USSR emerged victorious it became the object of much Arab admiration. In addition there were many new converts to communism who had previously been Nazi and Fascist sympathizers. Although ignorant and ill-organized, the peasantry of most of the Middle East was considered ripe for social change. Standards of living were wretchedly low, and Middle Eastern countries were governed by autocratic pashas and venal monarchies.

In retrospect it appears that the Soviet Union gained an important foot-hold in the Middle East during World War II. Diplomatic relations were opened between Arab countries and the USSR during 1943–5 and Communist cadres grew in number among both the intelligentsia and the peasantry. In Iran, the left-wing Tudeh (Masses, or Communist) party grew in size and became more blatantly pro-Soviet despite the political demands made on its country by the USSR with respect to Azerbaijan Province. In Turkey, however, Russian harassment and territorial demands had made the Soviet Union extremely unpopular with the Turkish masses.

It seemed clear to the great powers and to all countries of the Middle East that the area would become a zone of crises for some time to come. Perhaps the most significant fact about the Middle East, politically and economically, was the billions of barrels of oil under the desert. Zionism, Arab nationalism and oil produced a complicated puzzle for the great powers to sort out and argue over.

9

U.S. Diplomatic Initiatives

The White House announced Feb. 20, 1945 that Pres. Franklin D. Roosevelt, after leaving the Yalta Conference in the Crimea, had received King Farouk of Egypt, Emperor Haile Selassie of Ethiopia and King Ibn Saud of Saudi Arabia aboard an American warship. The U.S. ship was anchored in Great Bitter Lake, through which the Suez Canal passes. Ibn Saud had left his country for the first time when he went to meet Pres. Roosevelt. He and his large entourage traveled aboard an American destroyer. At the same time, Prime Min. Winston Churchill conferred separately with Ibn Saud, Farouk, Haile Selassie and also talked with Pres. Shukri al Kuwatly of Syria.

Shortly after these meetings, a development took place that had great influence on the future of the Middle East. The U.S. Mar. 5 invited 39 nations to send delegations to San Francisco in April to attend a conference to draw up a charter of an international organization. It ultimately became the United Nations, or UN, an organization with one main purpose—to maintain peace. China, Britain and Russia joined in extending the invitations but France declined to be an inviting power, although it agreed to participate in the conference.

The voting procedure for the security council of the prospective new international organization, as decided on at the Yalta Conference, was revealed in Mexico City by U.S. State Secy. Edward R. Stettinius Jr. According to Stettinius, this procedure provided that there must be unanimous agreement among the U.S., Britain, Russia, China and France on certain questions regarding use of force. Any of the 5 could veto action to enforce peace.

Zionist & Arab Demands

In the intervening weeks before the war's end and in subsequent months, Zionists and Arab nationalists intensified their drives and behind-the-scenes politicking in London, Paris and Washington over the future of the British mandate of Palestine. What the Zionists wanted as their solution to the problem of Palestine was common knowledge. In May 1942 in New York, world Zionist leaders had prepared a document later known as the Biltmore Program. In it they demanded an end to the British mandate in Palestine, the formation of a Jewish state, the withdrawal of the British White Paper of 1939 (which had banned the further movement of Jews to Palestine) and unrestricted Jewish immigration.

The World Zionist Conference disclosed in London Aug. 13, 1945 that the program laid before the British government in May 1945 by the Jewish Agency for Palestine called for: (1) the creation of a Jewish state in Palestine: (2) empowering the Jewish Agency to settle as many Jews as possible in Palestine and to develop all the country's resources; (3) granting an international loan and "other help" for the transfer of the first 100,000 Jews to Palestine, and for economic development; (4) levying reparations on Germany to repay Jewish losses and to aid in the rebuilding of Palestine; (5) the provision of international facilities for the exit and transit of all Jews who wanted to settle in Palestine. The closing session indorsed this program.

Earlier in 1945, Pres. Roosevelt's death (Apr. 12) had made Vice Pres. Harry S. Truman the President of the U.S. Pres. Truman's first statement on Palestine came Aug. 16, 1945, when he called for the free settlement of Palestine by Jews to the point consistent with civil peace. He then revealed that this was the U.S. position at the Potsdam conference, held from July 17 to Aug. 20.

Reports from London Sept. 23 indicated that the British government planned to refer to the UN the problem of Palestine and Jewish immigration. The cabinet had received from Truman a letter supporting Jewish requests for the immediate admission of 100,000 Jews to Palestine.

William O'Dwyer, executive director of the War Refugee Board, urged his government Sept. 24, in his final report, to take "all necessary steps to effect the reopening of Palestine" to Jewish immigration. O'Dwyer said that he regarded as most pressing the problem of "stateless" Jews.

Abdul Rahman Azzam Bey, secretary general of the Arab League, arrived in London that week for conferences on the Palestine problem. In Washington, Truman denied that the late Roosevelt had made any commitment to King Ibn Saud of Saudi Arabia not to support Jewish claims on Palestine. Earlier, Cairo dispatches had cited Azzam Bey as claiming that the 2 leaders had shaken hands on such a pledge.

The government of Iraq Oct. 4 released in Baghdad the text of a note in which it warned the U.S. that "any support given Zionism is deemed an act directed against Iraq in particular and the Arab peoples in general." The Washington legations of Egypt, Iraq, Lebanon and Syria revealed Oct. 20 that in a memo handed to U.S. State Secy. James F. Byrnes Oct. 12, these 4 Arab countries had warned that there would be war if an attempt were made to set up an independent Jewish political state in Palestine. The 4 countries offered to cooperate on a compromise.

In reaction to the Arab memo, spokesmen for the American Zionist

Emergency Council presented to Byrnes Oct. 23 strong protests against allowing Arab states to be consulted in the internal affairs of Palestine. The Chicago convention of Hadassah, the women's Zionist organization, cabled British Prime Min. Clement R. Atlee protesting "callous" treatment of Jews "by a government [Britain] which has given solemn international pledges to defend their rights."

It was reported from Cairo Oct. 24 that Arab politicians were using the threat of economic sanctions against American oil companies with Middle East concessions. Economic sanctions became an important part of the Arab campaign against opening up Palestine to the Jews. Beirut reported that a subcommittee of the Lebanese Parliament had disapproved a proposed concession for 2 companies to establish refineries in Lebanon at the terminus of the Iraq pipeline.

At a rally of 150,000 persons in New York the evening of Oct. 24, Dr. Israel Goldstein, president of the Zionist Organization of America, called for Britain's fulfillment of the Balfour Declaration—British Foreign Secy. Arthur J. Balfour's assertion of Nov. 2, 1917 that his government favored the establishment of a Jewish national home in Palestine—and for the abrogation of the 1939 White Paper. Goldstein publicly urged Pres. Truman "to keep insisting" on the immediate admission of 100,000 Jews to Palestine. In Chicago that evening Sen. Ralph O. Brewster (R., Me.) urged U.S. government support of a Jewish Palestine as a "listening post" in a "desert of backward and primitive Arab countries." Brewster called Arab threats of force "a myth."

Charge and countercharge passed between Arabs and Jews. Angry threats and accusations were exchanged and led ultimately to new acts of violence. Arab nationalists called a one-day general strike in Egypt, Lebanon, Syria and Palestine Friday, Nov. 2, 1945 in protest against Zionism and the Balfour Declaration. Mobs in Cairo smashed Jewish stores, stoned Jewish families and set fire to a synagogue. Alexandria and other cities reported similar events. 9 persons were reported killed and 520 injured.

British Colonial Secy. George H. Hall Nov. 2 announced the resignation of Field Marshal Viscount Gort as high commissioner for Palestine and Transjordan and warned that violence in Palestine jeopardized the Zionist cause.

British Foreign Min. Ernest Bevin in London and Pres. Truman in Washington Nov. 13 announced a U.S.-British agreement for the creation of a Joint Committee of Inquiry to examine the problem of European Jews and Palestine. Bevin predicted that Palestine would become a trustee state of the UN and in time would have self-government. This amounted in effect to a rejection of Truman's suggestion that 100,000

Jews immediately be admitted into Palestine. Bevin told the House of Commons that Palestine would continue to admit 1,500 Jews a month, beyond the limits of the 1939 White Paper. Truman, however, said that he stood on his previous suggestion. Meantime the joint committee was to investigate conditions in Europe and in Palestine, confer with Jewish and Arab leaders and make recommendations.

The gap continued to widen between Arab nationalists and Zionists, who stepped up their efforts toward increased Jewish settlement of Palestine. In mid-November the Zionist Organization of America approved a $51,700,000 budget for 1946 to be used for the immigration, land acquisition and settlement programs supported through the United Palestine Appeal.

The U.S. Senate Foreign Relations Committee Dec. 11 approved by 17-1 vote a resolution urging U.S. aid in opening Palestine to the Jews and building a "democratic commonwealth." Sen. Tom Connally (D., Tex.) cast the sole vote against the resolution.

CONFLICT OVER PALESTINE'S FUTURE (1946–8)

Violence Intensifies

Statesmen in Washington, London, Paris and New York met in long sessions during early 1946 to discuss proposals for a peaceful solution to the Palestine problem. In Palestine itself, however, the summer of 1946 was a violent one. The British mandatory government reported that 91 persons were killed and 45 injured as a result of the bombing July 22 of the King David Hotel in Jerusalem. Jewish terrorists were particularly active, and Lt. Gen. Evelyn Barker July 28 banned fraternization of British troops with Palestine Jews. Barker's orders said that the Palestine Jews "cannot be absolved of responsibility" for terrorist acts and added that the ban would punish "the race by striking at their pockets and showing our contempt for them." Herbert Morrison, British lord president of the Council, said in London July 31 that Barker's action was justified, but he denounced the language of the order.

Events accelerated throughout the Holy Land. Tel Aviv was subjected to a 22-hour-a-day curfew July 30 as 20,000 British troops began a house-to-house search for terrorists. The city was cut off from the rest of the country by land and sea, and troops were given a "shoot-to-kill" order for curfew violation. A workshop for making bombs was discovered in Tel Aviv, and an arms cache, counterfeiting equipment and almost $1 million in forged government bonds were discovered July 31 in Tel Aviv's largest synagogue.

Grand Mufti 'Escapes'

The French government revealed June 12 that the grand mufti of Jerusalem, Haj Amin el Husseini, supposedly under house arrest, had left Orly Airport at 11:00 a.m. May 29 aboard 'a Trans-World Airlines Skymaster. The mufti debarked in Cairo and disappeared. He carried a false Syrian passport issued to and signed by "Marcus Doualibi." Although he had been technically under surveillance at his villa near Versailles, the mufti had traveled freely. The former Axis collaborator had resided in the Versailles villa since his capture in Germany at the end of the war. New York Zionists blamed the French and British for complicity in his "escape," which Arab leaders hailed throughout the Middle East.

The *N.Y. Post* June 13 published documents, obtained in Germany by Edgar Ansel Mowrer, alleging that the mufti was "party to the murder of nearly 6 million European Jews."

The United Press reported from Beirut June 14 that the mufti was then at the home of ex-Syrian Premier Jamil Mardam some 15 miles from Damascus. (Syria denied the report June 15 as the British Navy continued to stop and search ships at sea in quest of the mufti.) The mufti finally surfaced at the Abdine Palace in Cairo late June 19, where he sought and received asylum from King Farouk of Egypt.

The Trend Toward Partition

Ever since the publication of the Biltmore Program by the world Zionists it had been known that their goal was not merely a Jewish national home but the creation of a sovereign Jewish state in the Holy Land. The existence of Christian and Moslem shrines and the large Moslem majority required that the Jews make their goal the partition of Palestine.

In opposition to the partition trend, the Arab League June 13, 1946 disclosed a 10-point program for Palestine adopted by 32 delegates from 8 Arab countries at a meeting in Bludan, Syria June 8-12. The program included: The creation of a Palestine committee with all Arab states represented to supervise all matters relating to Palestine; the creation of an Arab executive committee in Palestine composed of Jamal el Husseini, Hussein Khalidi, Emile Ghouri and Ahmad Helmi Pasha with the grand mufti of Jerusalem as its spiritual head; recommendations that Zionist forces be disarmed and the sale of land to Jews carry penalties; the creation of an Arab fund for Palestine; the strengthening of the boycott of Jewish goods from Palestine.

The U.S. was urged by the Arab League to withdraw from the Palestine case, and Britain was warned that the Arab League would go before the UN if new talks failed. A secret resolution threatened to arm Arabs unless Britain disarmed the Jews.

Pres. Harry S. Truman June 11 had created a special U.S. cabinet committee consisting of State Secy. James F. Byrnes, War Secy. Robert P. Patterson and Treasury Secy. John W. Snyder to help him with the Palestine problem. Possible military aid was to be discussed with the British, Byrnes said. Byrnes then appointed Henry F. Grady, a shipping line executive and ex-assistant state secretary, as his alternate.

Herbert Morrison told the British House of Commons July 31 that the success of his Palestine partition plan depended upon its approval by the U.S. He said that if the Zionists, the Arabs and the U.S. backed the plan, 100,000 Jews would be admitted to Palestine within a year.

Winston Churchill told the House of Commons Aug. 11 that Britain should turn its mandate for Palestine over to the UN if the U.S. refused to "share the burden of the Zionist cause." He said that the removal of British troops from Egypt left the government open to the accusation that it wanted Palestine as a Middle East military base. His proposal was rejected by the cabinet. (British headquarters in Alexandria had announced July 28 that it would move to the Suez Canal zone before October and that the Empire's general Middle East headquarters would move to Ismailia, 10 miles south of Port Said, before 1947).

Saudi Arabia, Transjordan, Syria and Lebanon Aug. 2 accepted the British invitation for a conference on Palestine. After some hesitation, the Jewish Agency for Palestine refused to authorize its leaders to accept an invitation. The Palestinian Arab Higher Committee having also refused to attend, the conference opened in London Sept. 9 with neither of the principal disputants over the Palestine mandate. The conference ended Feb. 14, 1947, 4 days after the Arab delegations attending had rejected British proposals for Jewish and Arab local self-government within a centralized, British-run framework for the next 5 years.

Meanwhile, the chasm continued to deepen between Arabs and Jews and the partisans of each side over the disposition of the Holy Land. Dr. Emanuel Neumann, vice president of the Zionist Organization of America, declared in London Jan. 1, 1947 that U.S. Zionists would spend "millions" to finance the "illegal" immigration of Jews to Palestine. A Haganah spokesman in Paris claimed that 21,878 Jews had entered Palestine "illegally" during the past 15 months.

Debate on Palestine

The UN had been considering various aspects of the Palestine problem.

The American Council for Judaism (ACJ) Apr. 25, 1947 announced its opposition to the Jewish Agency's request for nonvoting participation in the UN General Assembly. The anti-Zionist ACJ based its stand on the ground that "Jews are citizens of many nations and would be represented by their respective governments." It was believed that American Jews, however, supported Zionist aims. The Political Action Committee for Palestine May 4 ran advertisements in New York newspapers in which it appealed for funds to buy parachutes for young European Jews planning to crash the Palestine immigration barriers by air.

The plenary session of the UN General Assembly in Flushing Meadow Park, N.Y. May 5, 1947 voted, 39–8, against a Polish-Czechoslovak resolution to give the Jewish Agency a hearing before the full Assembly. It then voted, 44-7, in favor of a joint resolution by Argentina, Chile, Uruguay, Byelorussia and Yugoslavia directing the Assembly's 55-nation Political & Security Committee to hear the Jewish Agency on the British proposal to establish a commission of inquiry into the Palestine question. It left to the Political & Security Committee the question of whether the Palestinian Arab Higher Committee and other groups would be heard.

The voting displeased both Arabs and Jews. On the first ballot the losers were Chile, South Africa, Czechoslovakia, Poland, the Soviet Union, the Ukraine, Byelorussia and Yugoslavia. On the 2d vote the losers were Afghanistan, Egypt, Iraq, Lebanon, Saudi Arabia, Syria and Turkey.

The Assembly's Political & Security Committee in Lake Success, N.Y. voted 44-0 May 6 in favor of a U.S.-Argentine resolution to give both the Arab Higher Committee and the Jewish Agency the right to be heard. A U.S. proposal to limit the debate to the point of setting up a Palestine investigating commission was defeated, 23-19. Andrei A. Gromyko of the USSR led the fight for unlimited discussion of the Palestine question.

The Arab states, threatening a boycott because of the May 5 Assembly vote on the Jewish Agency, abstained together with Turkey and France May 6 when the final resolution was passed. The Arab Higher Committee withdrew its application to appear before the group, demanding full Assembly recognition. The Arabs also scored the U.S. State Department for its refusal to let Rasim Khalidi, a member of the Palestine Arab Higher Committee, enter the country because of his pro-Axis war record.

In a move described by some delegates as a "comedy" and a "farce," the Political Committee May 7 adopted, 28-5, an Indian resolution asking the full Assembly to hold a quick meeting and instruct the Political Committee to invite the Arab Higher Committee to its hearings (an action that had been taken May 6).

Then, by the process of changing chairmen (from Lester B. Pearson to Dr. Oswaldo Aranha), the same 55 delegates became the Assembly in the afternoon and adopted the following resolution, 39-11 (Guatemala opposed): "The General Assembly affirms that the decision of the First [Political] Committee to grant a hearing to the Arab Higher Committee of Palestine gives correct interpretation to the Assembly's intention." This action was designed to assuage the hurt feelings of the Arab Higher Committee, which that night cabled Haj Amin el Husseini for instructions. Husseini, grand mufti of Jerusalem, was then in Cairo.

On the 28-5 Political Committee vote, the Arab states ended a sit-down maneuver and supported the measure, as did Britain, France and the U.S. The USSR and China abstained; Czechoslovakia, Guatemala, South Africa, Sweden and Ukraine voted against the resolution. On the Assembly vote, supported by Britain, China, France and the U.S., the dissenters included Colombia, the USSR and the 5 other "Slav states."

U.S. delegate Warren R. Austin urged before the Political Committee May 7 that a "neutral committee" of 7 small nations (Canada, Czechoslovakia, Iran, Netherlands, Peru, Sweden, Uruguay) be named to investigate the Palestine issue. The Big 5 would be excluded. Dr. José Arce of Argentina asked for an 11-nation committee including the Big 5.

Dr. Abba Hillel Silver, 54, Lithuanian-born Cleveland rabbi and chairman of the American section of the Jewish Agency, presented the Zionist case on Palestine before the Political Committee May 8. He made these points: Britain promised the Jews a national home in Palestine through the Balfour Declaration in 1917; the League of Nations mandate turning Palestine over to Britain in 1922 reiterated this promise; such British Empire leaders as David Lloyd George, Winston Churchill, Jan Christiaan Smuts and Lord Robert Cecil had gone on record as favoring such a step—yet since 1939 Britain had restricted Jewish immigration into Palestine.

Rabbi Silver called on the UN to respect "those international commitments of a quarter of a century ago" and grant the Jews an independent state in which they could establish their home. In the interim he urged that immigration restrictions be relaxed. This, he said, would curb the terrorism, which most Jews deplored. As for the proposed inquiry commission, he urged that it visit Palestine to study developments and problems there and also DP (displaced persons) camps in Europe. In Palestine, he continued, it should determine why Jews were restricted to less than 6% of the country, why anti-Jewish laws were tolerated and why Jewish refugee ships were driven away by the British.

Later, Andrei Gromyko rejected U.S., British and Chinese contentions that the Big 5 should remain off the inquiry commission, saying they should shoulder their responsibility.

Henry Cattan, 41, Jerusalem attorney and Christian spokesman for the Arab Higher Committee, in testimony before the Political Committee May 9, called for an end to the "illegal" British mandate and for immediate independence for Palestine while the Arabs still had a majority there. Moshe Shertok, head of the Jewish Agency's political department, had come forward to appeal for Europe's displaced persons before Cattan testified. David Ben-Gurion, chairman of the Jewish

Agency Executive and a leading Zionist, had arrived May 9 by plane in New York from Palestine to head the Agency's UN delegation. U.S. deputy representative Herschel V. Johnson argued May 10 against Gromyko's amendment that the inquiry committee consider immediate independence for Palestine.

An 11-nation subcommittee May 9 submitted a 6-point draft of instructions for the inquiry committee, stressing that independence for Palestine was the "ultimate" goal sought. Gromyko urged that any inquiry committee make an on-the-spot investigation and also consider independence for Palestine "without delay."

Zionists & Arabs Oppose Partition

Jews and Arabs in Palestine reacted unfavorably to the partition proposals being discussed in the UN. Dr. Ariem Altman, president of the United Zionist Revisionists, said at a party rally in Jerusalem July 12, 1947 that the Revisionists would settle for nothing less than an unpartitioned, free Jewish state in Palestine and Transjordan. Palestinian Arab spokesmen, meanwhile, were threatening a *jihad* (holy war) if partition became a fact.

On the other hand spokesmen for the Palestinian Jewish Communist Party July 13 urged the UN Palestine Commission to recommend a "bi-unitarian" Arab-Jewish state. They condemned "Anglo-American imperialists," who, they said wanted Palestine as a base for a 3d world war.

A memo directed July 13 to the UN Special Committee on Palestine (UNSCOP), created earlier, declared that Haganah "unconditionally rejects terrorism" and was strong enough to defend Palestine from Arab attack. *Haganah le Yisrael* ("The Defense of Israel") was the underground military arm of the Jewish Agency.

Hebrew University Pres. Judah L. Magnes, 70, one of Palestine's most influential Jews, rejected partition July 14 and recommended a bi-national state with Jews and Arabs getting equal representation despite the unequal population.

(Aharon Cohen, secretary of the League for Jewish-Arab Rapprochement, reported July 15 that the late Fawzi Darwish el Husseini, relative of Haj Amin el Husseini and a former anti-Zionist, had formed a New Palestine Society and had made an agreement Nov. 11, 1946 to cooperate with the Rapprochement League but was murdered before he could act.)

Several events in the summer of 1947 contributed toward steeling the *yishuv* (Jewish "community" in Palestine) in its determination to achieve separate statehood. One was the *Exodus* affair, which dramatized the issue of immigration—the most serious source of conflict between Jew and Arab. British warships July 18 escorted the American-manned, Haganah refugee ship *Exodus 1947* (formerly the *President Warfield*) to Haifa after a battle in which the American first mate, William Bernstein, 24, and 2 immigrants were killed, more than 30 people aboard injured and the blockage runner and several British vessels damaged. UNSCOP members watched as the remainder of the 4,554 passengers, the largest group of unauthorized immigrants to sail for Palestine in a single ship, were herded aboard British prison ships for removal to Cyprus. The American captain, Bernard Marks, 25, and his crew were arrested. The ship came from France. More violence erupted July 19 when it was learned that the refugees were to be returned to France.

UNSCOP Recommends Partition

The UN Special Committee on Palestine (UNSCOP) concluded its study of the Palestine problem and, at the end of Aug. 1947, published its recommendations, in which the committee's members urged that the British mandate be terminated as soon as possible. The majority report recommended a tripartite partition of Palestine into Arab and Jewish States and an international trusteeship for Jerusalem and its environs.

The Palestine problem continued to overshadow all other issues in the Middle East and at the UN. An Arab Office spokesman said in London Sept. 23 that all of the Arab League states had made a secret agreement 15 months previously to sever all ties with Europe and the U.S. if the UN went ahead with a plan to partition Palestine.

As UNSCOP'S tripartite partition plan took shape at the UN, the fury of Arab nationalists grew. A bomb damaged the offices of the U.S. consulate general in Jerusalem Oct. 13, injuring 2 employes slightly. Similar bombings had occurred at the Polish consulate general the night of Oct. 12 and at the Swedish consulate Sept. 27. Responsibility for the bombing of the Swedish consulate was claimed by an Arab terrorist group, the "Committee for the Arab Holy War."

The Iraq foreign office advised an American House Foreign Affairs Committee group Oct. 13 not to make a projected visit to Baghdad because of "high feeling" over the U.S.' indorsement of the recommendation for partitioning Palestine. The State Department announced the same day that it would issue no passports to American citizens who might want to take part in hostilities on either side in Palestine; Americans so involved would forfeit the protection normally due U.S. citizens abroad.

The Jewish Agency Nov. 24 began registering Jewish youths willing to work for or to defend the proposed new Jewish state. Novelist Louis Bromfield, co-chairman of the American League for a Free Palestine, charged in Washington Nov. 26 that Arab states had obtained $41 million worth of surplus U.S. arms and supplies in preparation for a "pogrom" in Palestine.

UN Votes to Partition Palestine

The UN General Assembly Nov. 29, 1947 adopted UNSCOP'S tripartite partition recommendation by a ⅔ majority. Under UNSCOP'S proposal, there were to be 2 separate states—one Jewish, the other Arab—and a separate enclave for Jerusalem and environs amounting to 289 square miles. The Jerusalem enclave was to be administered by a governor appointed by the UN.

Trouble flared immediately. Syrian demonstrators attacked the U.S., Soviet and French legations in Damascus Nov. 30 because those governments had favored the creation of a Jewish state. Abdul Rahman Azzam Pasha, Arab League secretary general, declared that the UN decision would be "resisted by force." At Acre Prison in Palestine, guards opened fire when Arab prisoners attacked Jewish inmates. Later Nov. 30, 5 Jews were killed in 2 gunfire attacks on buses near Tel Aviv. A general strike was called in the Arab city of Nablus, and police were brought in to break up a protest meeting of 300 Arabs in Jenin.

To many political observers and so-called Kremlinologists, Soviet policy in the Middle East at this time came as a considerable surprise. In the years preceding and just after World War II the Russians had been hostile to Zionism. During the war, the USSR was too busy to undertake extensive attacks against Jewish nationalists, but in 1946 a Soviet publication stated that Zionists did not want independence for Palestine. The Russian journal said that the Zionists wanted a perpetuation of the foreign mandate in Palestine and that their thesis was provocative. According to this article, Arab leaders in the Holy Land were progressive even though there were reactionary, feudalistic elements among them.

When Soviet representatives at the UN finally declared their support for independent Jewish and Arab states in Palestine, they said they would have preferred a united binational Arab-Jewish state. A number of explanations have been set forth for the Soviet *volte-face*; one explanation was that the Russians felt that most Arab governments of record were pro-British. The Zionists, on the other hand, were violently anti-British. Not only did the USSR swing its support to partition, but a high-level foreign policy decision covertly made in the Soviet

Union allowed the Jews in Palestine to buy arms in Czechoslovakia even before the British mandate had terminated. It was pointed out, however, that of the thousands of Russian and Polish Jews then in Israel, it could be presumed that at least some of them were Soviet agents.

After the Soviet Union indorsed Zionist aspirations in Palestine in 1947, hard-core Arab Communists in Palestine such as Tawfig Tubi, Amil Habibi and Fuad Nassar accepted the Soviet position.

Arabs Violently Oppose Partition

Of all the Arab League states, Syria and Egypt had reacted most violently to the partition scheme, demonstrating against the U.S., Britain and the USSR as UN leaders. But the worst communal outbreak outside Palestine occurred in Aden, British colony at the mouth of the Red Sea, where extra British troops were flown in Dec. 5 after 4 days of Jewish-Arab strife in which 50 Jews and 25 Arabs were killed.

Syrian Arab mobs had paralyzed business in Damascus earlier that week. The Soviet cultural center and Communist headquarters there were wrecked in the demonstrations Nov. 30; 4 persons were killed; the Syrian Communist Party was ordered disbanded, and the U.S. and British embassies' flags were torn down. Syria introduced military training in all boys' schools Dec. 1. The parliament enacted a draft law and voted $860,000 for Palestine's Arabs Dec. 2 while a mob attacked the Jewish part of Aleppo. Haj Amin el Husseini, exiled grand mufti of Jerusalem, conferred in Damascus Dec. 1 with Fawzi el Kawukji, leader of the 1936-9 Palestine revolt.

In Egypt the Chamber of Deputies resolved Dec. 1 to help keep Palestine a totally Arab state. The Council of Ulemas, ruling body of 1,000-year-old al-Azhar University in Cairo, called on Moslems Dec. 2 to support and prepare for *jihad,* and Arab League officials promised Cairo students later in the week that they would be trained soon to bear arms for Palestine. There were repeated anti-U.S.-British demonstrations in Egypt's main cities, and the British Institute in Zagazig, 40 miles north of Cairo, was burned Dec. 2. Public demonstrations were banned in Cairo after police clashed Dec. 4 with 15,000 marchers.

In Lebanon, Arab students smashed U.S. legation windows in Beirut Dec. 1, Lebanese Communists declared against Palestine partition and schools were closed to check student disorders. Iraqi students in Baghdad wrecked the U.S. information office Dec. 4, and government leaders in Iraq and Pakistan promised to help fight for an Arab Palestine. Arab attempts to stage anti-American demonstrations in the Saudi Arabian oil fields were restrianed by King Ibn Saud's government.

Jerusalem and the Jaffa-Tel Aviv boundary zone were centers of week-long strife which began when 7 Jews were killed throughout Palestine Nov. 30 and the mayor of Nablus, Arab nationalist center, proclaimed *jihad*, a holy war. British High Comm. Sir Alan G. Cunningham warned the Arab Higher Committee Dec. 1 that Britain was determined to keep order so long as it held its mandate, and police stopped Arab agitators from raising crowds in Jerusalem. But Jewish celebrations there (in which British troops joined) were interrupted and celebrants stoned.

A week of Arab disorders ended Dec. 6 with at least 159 persons killed in the Middle East, 66 of them in Palestine. While Jews in Palestine, Europe and the U.S. celebrated and began planning the new state and the UN moved to implement its plan, war talk was rife throughout the Arab world. The Arab League had announced Dec. 1 that premiers and foreign ministers of 7 Arab states would meet in Cairo the following week to plan strategy against partition.

Jews intensified nationwide recruiting of men and women 17-25 for possible defense duty, and Dr. Chaim Weizmann, Zionist leader visiting the U.S., said in Philadelphia Dec. 1 that Palestine's Jews included 60,000 young men sufficiently armed to prevent major Arab aggression. The Zionist Organization of America's administrative council met in New York Dec. 6 to formulate plans for helping set up the new Jewish state, and ZOA Pres. Emanuel Neumann demanded UN recognition of Jewish volunteer defense units as a Jewish militia. The U.S. State Department Dec. 5 announced an embargo on all American arms shipments to the Middle East, asserting that the quantity sent since 1945 had been negligible, and it reaffirmed that no passports would be issued for Americans avowing a desire to join either Jewish or Arab fighting forces.

The UN Security Council Dec. 9 tabled indefinitely a debate on the partitioning after Syria gave notice that Arab states would challenge the partition plan's legality. Egypt and Lebanon had asked Dec. 8 to be heard when the Council debated the partition plan, and the Jewish Agency for Palestine demanded Dec. 11 that it also be admitted as the Jews' representative. (There was no precedent for the Council admitting an entity other than a state.)

After 6 days of conferences in Cairo, the Arab League Dec. 13 released letters from Imam Yahya of Yemen to the U.S., Britain and the UN, warning that the partitioning of the Holy Land would be considered a "hostile act toward 400 million Moslems." The exiled grand mufti of Jerusalem Haj Amin el Husseini, had been seeing leaders of Arab states while a League military committee held "war councils."

The sessions had begun Dec. 8 with the League promising "immediate measure" to help Palestinian Arabs resist partition; the mufti declared: "When the sword speaks, everything else must be silent." No outside Arab nation, however, had committed itself publicly to send its own army into Palestine. (A Gannett News Service dispatch from Riyadh, Saudi Arabia, Dec. 12 quoted King Ibn Saud as promising to "protect and maintain" American oil operations and expressing hope that the UN would "correct" its "mistake" on Palestine.)

A study of troop strength in the Middle East indicated that the renascent Jewish state was outnumbered by at least 1¾ to 1 in available fighting forces—the Jews enlisting women as well as men. Jews in Palestine had claimed a ready force of 60,000 to combat Arab violence and were registering thousands of others for possible service. Palestinian Arabs had about 10,000 in guerrilla and youth organizations by estimates Dec. 7 and also were recruiting. Strength of Arab states: Egypt, population 18,200,000, army 35,000; Iraq, population 4,150,000, army 25,000; Lebanon, population, 1,170,000, army 5,500; Saudi Arabia, population, 4,750,000, army 5,500; Syria, population, 3,000,000, army 10,000 (but 17,000 volunteers were claimed since the enactment of a new draft law); Transjordan, population 335,000, army 25,000; Yemen, population 1,700,000, no estimate for army.

British Colonial Secy. Arthur Creech Jones had told the House of Commons in London Dec. 11 that Britain wanted to end its Palestine mandate by May 15, 1948 and had appealed for the UN to speed its partition schedule.

At about this time the United Jewish Appeal's national conference in Atlantic City, N.J. estimated that the UJA would need $395,367,000 in 1948 to help the new Jewish state and care for refugees, including 75,000 to be resettled in Palestine. The National Catholic Welfare Conference in New York announced that it would encourage the admission of more displaced persons (DPs) to the U.S.; DP resettlement committees would be set up by a new Resettlement Council in the 118 dioceses and 19,000 parishes in the U.S. to cooperate with Protestant and Jewish groups. The Zionist Organization of America Dec. 11 urged that the U.S. provide ships and other facilities to transfer Jewish settlers to Palestine and see to the adequate arming of Jewish Agency defense forces.

The British army was in action against Arab attackers in northern Palestine during early 1948, and the Irgun Zvai Leumi ("national military organization," an extremist-terrorist group led by Menahem Beigin) threatened Feb. 2, 1948 to start raiding Arabs beyond the borders of Palestine.

Arab terrorist groups claimed responsibility for the Feb. 1, 1948 bombing of the *Palestine Post* building in Jerusalem. (This editor was the last person to leave the building alive following the explosion.)

The British were sensitive as well to Communist activities in the Middle East. London charged that Communist agents were among illegal immigrants from Bulgaria aboard the intercepted ships *Pan York* and *Pan Crescent.* In Milwaukee, Wis., Moshe Shertok, the political director of the Jewish Agency, categorically denied the charge Feb. 1. The British Foreign Office Feb. 6 sent Bulgaria a note rebuking it for "deliberately conniving" with unauthorized Palestine immigrants.

U.S. Proposes Palestine Trusteeship

The UN General Assembly's Palestine Partition Commission Feb. 16, 1948 requested a UN military force adequate to enforce the partition of Palestine over Arab resistance. The U.S. Feb. 24 sidestepped an indorsement of forcible partition and asked the Security Council to continue to seek Arab-Jewish agreement for partition. After Big 5* conciliation efforts had failed, the U.S. Mar. 19 abandoned its partition plan and proposed a UN trusteeship over Palestine. The U.S. proposal of Mar. 19 called for a special UN General Assembly session to create a trusteeship, under which further efforts would be made to reach a Jewish-Arab compromise. Jews denounced the "betrayal" and said that they would fight for a separate state, regardless of the UN's decision.

U.S. Amb.-to-UN Warren R. Austin announced the turnabout in American policy in the UN Security Council in Lake Success, N.Y. His statement climaxed a day of formal and informal talks, which had confirmed that neither the full Council nor its big-power members could agree to carry out partition by force. With the USSR emerging as chief advocate of partition, the U.S.-Soviet-French-Chinese conferences on the problem had ended Mar. 17 with mere agreement that the Council must not let Palestine become a threat to world peace. Austin, who actually first broke word of the new trusteeship plan to other Big 5 members and UN officials at a luncheon with Secy. Gen. Trygve Lie, made a speech to the Council in which he gave these reasons for the policy shift:

● "There seems to be general agreement that the partition plan cannot now be implemented by peaceful means." (The big powers had failed to shake Jewish insistence on partition or the Arabs' all-out opposition to it.)

---

*The U.S., Britain, the Soviet Union, France and China.

● "We believe that further steps must be taken immediately not only to maintain the peace but also to afford a further opportunity to reach agreement" between Jews and Arabs. "To this end we believe that a temporary trusteeship for Palestine should be established under the Trusteeship Council . . . . This would require an immediate special session of the General Assembly, . . . "

An undisclosed putative reason for the U.S. action receiving widespread credence in Lake Success was that it arose from U.S. fears of Soviet infiltration in the Middle East.

Meanwhile, Jews and Arabs readied for war. (Barney Ross, U.S. Marine Corps hero of the Battle of Guadalcanal and former welterweight boxing champion, enlisted in New York Mar. 29 in a George Washington Brigade being recruited by the American League for a Free Palestine. But the State Department reiterated Mar. 30 that it would deny passports for Americans to join either fighting force in the Holy Land.) Moshe Shertok of the Jewish Agency told the UN Security Council Apr. 1: "We have passed the threshold of statehood. We refuse to be thrown back." About 6,000 Palestinian Jews, men and women aged 18-35, were called home from abroad Apr. 4 to register for military service. Arab states redoubled their fight for an independent, unpartitioned Palestine that the Palestinian Arab majority would control. Syria's Faris el-Khouri said Apr 1 that the special Assembly session slated for Apr. 16 would give the UN a chance to reconsider "the blunder which was committed" when it decided in favor of partition.

The U.S. had called for the special General Assembly meeting and for a truce between Palestine's Jews and Arabs after the failure of the Security Council to agree on enforced partition. These U.S. resolutions were adopted by the Council Apr. 1. The truce plea was approved unanimously. The Council then passed, 9-0 (the Soviet Union and Ukraine abstaining), Amb.-to-UN Warren R. Austin's resolution for a special Assembly session to "consider further the question of the future government of Palestine."

With the Soviet Union strongly opposed to giving up on partition, the U.S. did not ask the Council to approve its new plan for a UN trusteeship over the Holy Land. This was saved for the Assembly.

Soviet Amb.-to-UN Andrei A. Gromyko had told the Council Mar. 30 that partition was "a just solution," that he was not convinced that it could not be carried out peacefully and that by "wrecking" it the U.S. would have to take full blame for "a serious blow upon the UN organization." In denouncing the U.S., he charged: Americans were concerned only with "their own oil interests and military-strategic positions in the Middle East"; knowing that the USSR boycotts the UN

Trusteeship Council, the U.S. hoped to obtain a trusteeship and make Palestine "a military-strategic base of the U.S. and England under the pretext of maintaining order in that country."

U.S. delegate Austin Apr. 5 offered the American plan for a Palestine trusteeship at a UN Security Council session that the USSR and Ukraine, as usual, did not attend. The plan provided for the enforcement of the trusteeship by "specified" nations. (The U.S. implied that it hoped that the Soviet Union would not be one of those specified.) The U.S. called for an indefinite trusteeship that would end when the Arabs and the Jews agreed finally on a form of government for the Holy Land. The trust governments, as proposed, would have had a governor general named by the UN Trusteeship Council, a Palestinian cabinet and an elected bicameral legislature. The plan stipulated that: (a) The governor general could call on the "specified" enforcer states for armed assistance, at no cost to Palestine. (b) Palestine should support itself without large UN subsidies. (c) The trusteeship agreement should provide for immigration and land purchases on terms negotiated with Arabs and Jews.

The U.S. plan was rejected by Arabs and Jews. France also protested Apr. 7 that there must be positive decisions before the end of the British mandate May 15 on enforcing order in Palestine and on Jewish immigration. Otherwise, France warned, fighting there would "become more violent and even degenerate into massacres."

Security Council Pres. Alfonso Lopez of Colombia opened truce negotiations Apr. 7 with Jamal el Husseini, Arab Higher Committee vice chairman, and Moshe Shertok, Jewish Agency political director. The talks bogged down Apr. 8. U.S. delegate Austin, however, insisted Apr. 10 that Palestine's Arabs and Jews were "eager enough to solve the question peaceably" and that the possibility of a truce remained.

During the Zionist General Council meeting in Tel Aviv Apr. 6-8, Chairman David Ben-Gurion of the Jewish Agency proposed that a central Jewish governmental authority be created at once. He also advised the Jews not to line up with the USSR or any single bloc of powers.

The U.S. State Department Apr. 9 refused to lift its embargo on arms shipments to the Middle East. Acting State Secy. Robert A. Lovett wrote Rep. Emanuel Celler (D., N.Y.), a pro-Zionist Congressman, that more weapons for either Jews or Arabs would promote violence. Concerned by the threat of an all-out war between Arabs and Jews, the American Association for the UN Apr. 10, 1948 proposed that the UN Palestine Committee be allowed to import American arms and to recruit American volunteers to enforce partition.

For the next 2 or 3 weeks there was sporadic fighting between

Arab irregular forces and units of the Haganah, the Jewish defense force. As the UN meetings continued to drag on, both sides became increasingly restive. Finally, the Arab League declared in Damascus May 13 that a "state of war" existed between its member states and the Jewish "rebels" of Palestine.

IRAN & TURKEY UNDER SOVIET PRESSURE (1945–7)

Crisis in Northern Iran

Although the Palestine problem emerged as the most explosive issue in the Middle East immediately after the end of World War II, there were other trouble spots in the area. The Soviet Union began a war of nerves against both Turkey and Iran. Iran appeared to be in a particularly perilous position because its northern provinces were occupied by Soviet troops.

Iran had been occupied in the summer of 1941 by both Soviet and British troops. This allied invasion had become necessary when Reza Shah, the Iranian monarch, refused to allow his country to be used as a supply route. The shah was deposed and exiled by the British and replaced by his son, the current ruler, Shah Mohammed Reza Pahlevi. Teheran became a neutral capital, Soviet troops occupied 5 northern provinces, and British forces moved into the southern half of the country.

The USSR, Britain and Iran in Jan. 1942 signed a tripartite treaty that gave the Allies the right to establish and use transit and communications facilities in Iran. The treaty emphasized that Iran was not "occupied" and that its sovereignty and independence were not to be infringed. The negotiators agreed on a timetable under which, within 6 months of the defeat of Germany and Italy, Allied troops would withdraw.

Shortly after the U.S. entered the war, some 30,000 American troops were sent to Iran in 1942 as part of the newly created Persian Gulf Command. It was these troops who maintained the vital supply route for U.S. Lend-Lease goods being shipped to Russia. During the war the Russians made heavy-handed use of their occupation troops in Iran, backed a strong Communist press and threw their support behind the Communist-oriented Tudeh party. Most disturbing of all to the Iranian government was that, when the Axis powers were defeated, the Soviet forces made no move to depart.

Soviet intrusion into the internal affairs of Iran was said to be particularly strong in Soviet-occupied Tabriz. For this reason, the U.S. State Department disclosed Nov. 29, 1945 in Washington, Maj. Carl F. Garver and 2 other observers had been dispatched from Teheran to Tabriz to determine whether the USSR was aiding the Azerbaijani rebels. The rebels, with Soviet support, set up an autonomous government in northern Iran in December. British and U.S. forces left the country in Jan. 1946 when the tripartite treaty lapsed. Ahmad Ghavam

Saltaneh formally protested to the UN Security Council Mar. 4, 1946 against the USSR's failure to remove its troops from Iran.

The U.S. State Department Mar. 5 dispatched a note to the Soviet Union protesting against continued Soviet occupation of Iran. The note, delivered in Moscow Mar. 6 and released in Washington Mar. 7, said that Russia's action was a violation of the Anglo-Iranian-Soviet treaty of Jan. 29, 1942 and the Teheran Declaration of Dec. 1, 1943* and that the U.S. "cannot remain indifferent." It requested that the Soviet occupying troops withdraw "immediately" and that Russia reply "promptly."

Although the British had fulfilled their part of the tripartite treaty by removing their troops from southern Iran, the Russians, with their troops still in Iran, backed the Communist rebel movement in eastern Azerbaijan led by Jevadzade Pishevari and supported the establishment of a Soviet-styled Kurdish National Republic (Kurdistan) in Mahabad, Western Azerbaijan. Iranian troops dispatched by the shah in Nov. 1945 to put down these rebellions had been blocked and turned back by Soviet soldiers.

The Issue was debated for weeks at the UN and in several world capitals. The Iranian appeal to the UN came to naught, but world opinion and diplomatic pressures finally led the USSR in April to agree to pull its troops out of Iran. Most important, however, was an agreement signed by Iranian Premier Ahmad Ghavames Saltaneh to establish a Russo-Iranian company and authorize oil exploitation by this company in the northern provinces. The agreement also stipulated that Ghavam would appoint 3 pro-Communists as cabinet ministers. (These 3 did not outlast Ghavam, who resigned as premier Oct. 18, 1946.)

Early in May 1946, the Russians finally moved their troops out of Iran. The Soviet press May 5 denounced the U.S. and Britain for "trampling the independence of small countries" while making an issue of Iran. In Oct. 1947 the Iranian Majlis (parliament) rejected the Russo-Iranian oil agreement and passed laws forbidding concessions to foreign powers. The Russians were furious, since Soviet development of these concessions had already begun.

During all of this time the USSR had continued to keep pressure on the unstable Iranian government by bitter attacks in the Soviet press. Soviet newspapers were also critical of American aid to the Iranians and had become particularly vocal Apr. 10, 1947 when an

*Pres. Franklin D. Roosevelt, British Prime Min. Winston Churchill and Soviet Marshal Joseph V. Stalin had signed the declaration at the conclusion of their 4-day conference there.

Iranian purchasing mission arrived in Washington to seek surplus U.S. military equipment.

A spate of conflicting reports emanating from Teheran added a note of confusion to the situation. U.S. Amb. George V. Allen, in a speech in Teheran Sept. 11, 1947 encouraged Iran to resist alleged Russian pressure to ratify the 1946 Soviet-Iranian oil agreement, which was under fire in the Majlis. Allen said that the U.S. would defend Iran's right to "give away" its own resources or "refuse to dispose of them at any price." A U.S. embassy spokesman also criticized the British for allegedly advising Iran to deal with Russia. (Britain later denied this charge.) Tass Sept. 11 accused Iran of blocking the repatriation of Soviet Armenians. Moscow radio Sept. 12 broadcast a charge that Iran had violated the oil pact of Apr. 1946.

The Kremlin was silent, however, about its withholding of 11 tons of Persian gold deposited with the Soviet State Bank under a safekeeping agreement May 24, 1943. Radio Teheran had reported June 1, 1947 that repeated requests for the money had gone unanswered by the bank and that the Iranian government May 26 had dispatched a note to Soviet Foreign Commissar Vyacheslav M. Molotov expressing "deep concern" over the matter. (Moscow agreed in Dec. 1950 to return the gold.)

The Truman Doctrine

In the early postwar period the USSR continued to attack Turkey in its press. Even before the end of the war the Soviet Union had made demands on the Turks. A few weeks before the collapse of Nazi Germany the Russians had denounced the 1925 treaty of friendship and nonaggression with the Turks. The USSR demanded (a) a revision of the 1936 Montreux Convention (covering passage of Soviet vessels between the Black and Aegean Seas), (b) Soviet bases in the Bosporus and Dardanelles Straits, (c) the return of part of Thrace to Bulgaria and (d) the return of the city of Kars and the town of Ardahan to the Soviet Union. Then and only then could there be a Soviet-Turkish friendship agreement, the Soviets said. News reports from Washington confirmed Mar. 7, 1946 that Russia had demanded the Turkish region of Kars-Ardahan bordering Soviet Armenia as the price of a Soviet defense treaty with Turkey. Soviet Foreign Commissar Molotov had first raised the issue with the West in June 1945 and had done so again at the Postdam Conference in Aug. 1945, according to the reports.

By late 1946 and early 1947 the Turks had begun to fear a Soviet invasion, and neighboring Greece was by then in danger of falling to the Communists as a result of a fratricidal civil war. As a response to this twin threat, Pres. Truman asked Congress to approve what was then in Mar. 1947, a massive economic and military aid program to Greece and Turkey. The amount he requested was $400 million. His action to strengthen Greece and Turkey against Communist threats quickly became known as the Truman Doctrine.

The Russian response to Truman's request was made Apr. 7, 1947. In an appearance before the UN Security Council, at Lake Success, N.Y., Soviet representative Andrei A. Gromyko charged that the U.S. program to aid Greece and Turkey against communism was a "unilateral" action that "by-passes" and "weakens" the UN, "undermines its authority" and constituted direct interference in Greek affairs. Gromyko asked why the U.S. had not brought the matter up before the UN if Greece and Turkey were actually threatened, and he accused the U.S. of first disregarding the UN Balkan Inquiry Commission* and then trying "artifically" to link its program to the inquiry. He admitted that Greece had fought valiantly in the war and needed economic aid, but he said the "major portion" of U.S. aid would be military and would not help the Greek people. As for Turkey, Gromyko scorned its war record and said that "Turkey has no right to receive aid from outside." He urged the Council to create a special commission to keep watch over U.S. aid to Greece.

U.S. delegate Warren R. Austin submitted a resolution proposing that the Balkans Commission maintain a "subsidiary group" in the area during its absence. Gromyko called this a "screen" to "hide the activities of the U.S." Britain's Sir Alexander Cadogan backed Austin, while a Bulgarian and a Yugoslav representative supported Gromyko.

Pres. Ismet Inonu of Turkey said in a telegraphic interview with the United Press May 12, 1947 that Turkey planned to use the $100 million expected in U.S. aid for military purposes. Inonu added that Turkey would seek a World Bank loan for economic development. Further, he said, Turkey would not discuss the granting of a base in the Dardanelles with any power.

The 2 U.S. houses of Congress May 15, 1947 completed action on the amended $400 million Greek-Turkish anti-Communist aid bill and sent it to the President. (The funding itself became part of a $1.66 bil-

---

*The temporary Balkan Inquiry Commission of the UN Security Council was created Dec. 19, 1946 at the U.S. delegation's instance. The commission was authorized to travel freely in Greece, Albania, Bulgaria and Yugoslavia in its investigation of armed strife on the Greek border. It was voted out of existence Sept. 15 after the Soviet Union used its 20th Security Council veto to remove the issue from the Council's agenda.

lion appropriations bill—$1.4 billion of this for foreign aid—passed by Congress July 26.) Senate conferees May 13 had accepted 2 House amendments: (1) to require FBI screening of all personnel sent to the 2 countries; (2) requiring full publicity in the administration of the program. House conferees accepted a Senate amendment requiring Senate confirmation of Presidential appointees to head the missions to Greece and Turkey. Greece would get $300 million, half for the army, half for relief and rehabilitation. Turkey's $100 million was to go entirely for military aid. The UN received the authority to halt the program whenever it saw fit.

FRICTION BETWEEN RUSSIA & THE WEST (1948–52)

Quest for Strategic Advantage

By the beginning of 1948 it appeared clear that no matter what course the UN charted in Palestine, it would be opposed by either the Arabs, the Zionists or both. Relations between the Soviet Union and the U.S. were becoming increasingly strained because of policy clashes all over the world—but particularly in the Middle East, where each power sought either to gain footholds for itself or to deny them to the other. The situation in Iran and Turkey continued to offer opportunities for strategic advantage.

Iranian Premier Ibrahim Hakimi Jan. 14 called off a $25 million Iranian purchase of surplus U.S. war materiel and a $250 million International Bank loan for oil-field development. Iran, he said, needed and could afford only about $10 million worth of U.S. supplies. Hakimi added that Iran would finance oil developments from its $80 million annual royalties from the Anglo-American Oil Co. 6 years of martial law had ended in Iran the previous day, Jan. 13. (The Majlis June 13 elected Abdul Hussein Hajir, ex-interior and finance minister, as premier to succeed Hakimi, who had resigned June 8 under fire for his moderate policies.)

The U.S. State Department informed the Senate Appropriations Committee May 28 that the U.S. would send Iran "nonaggressive weapons," including tanks, guns and fighter planes, that originally had cost $59,995,000 but would take $120 million to replace. The express purpose of this move was to maintain Iran's "international security," the State Department said. Iran July 29 received a $26 million U.S. loan for the purchase and repair of surplus equipment from the U.S. Army.

The British had disclosed Jan. 14 that the U.S. had received "temporary" permission to resume using Mellaha Air Base near Tripoli in British-occupied Libya. The U.S. had built the air base during World War II for military transport flights to Greece and the Middle East. Washington Feb. 3 dismissed a Soviet objection to the American use of the base, saying that the arrangement was legitimate and valid only for as long as Britain administered Libya.

The matter had given rise to a flurry of diplomatic notes between Moscow and Washington. The 3d of these, a Soviet charge that Iran was being militarized by the U.S., was rebuffed by the State Department Feb. 2 with the comment that 40 Americans were helping train the Iranian army at Iran's request. The Iranian government Feb. 4 charged that the Soviet Union was arming and supplying rebels in northern Iran.

34

Iran and the USSR traded accusations at the end of March. The Soviets Mar. 28 accused Iran of having lied about the activities of its U.S. military advisers. Teheran protested Mar. 29 against Soviet propaganda directed at Premier Hakimi. In response to the Soviet charge, Iran Apr. 1 denied that it was under U.S. military influence and accused Moscow of having broken the 1921 Russo-Persian nonaggression treaty by agitating against Iranian authority in Iranian Azerbaijan.

It was reported from Teheran Apr. 4 that the USSR was closing its Caspian Sea shipping line to Iran as a possible prelude to severing diplomatic relations (but it did not break them off). The Soviet Union demanded Apr. 8 that Iran suppress its anti-Soviet press. Arrests of 300 alleged Communists and the declaration of martial law in Mazandaran Province were announced by Iran Apr. 10.

A U.S. State Department report on Turkey Feb. 5 had accused Moscow of maintaining "presistent pressure" for control of the Dardanelles and for Soviet annexation of Turkish territory. "Threat of aggression by Russia," the report said, had compelled Turkey to devote 44% of its budget to defense and had retarded economic development.

Pres. Truman told Congress Feb. 16 that he would seek more military funds for Greece and Turkey. The President was making his 2d report on the $400 million aid program voted in 1947. State Secy. George Marshall and Defense Secy. James Forrestal, in testimony before the House Foreign Affairs Committee Mar. 3, urged the authorization of an additional $275 million in military assistance to Greece and Turkey. The House of Representatives voted to appropriate this amount June 4 for the 12-month period ending July 1, 1949, but the figure was cut to $225 million by the Senate June 16.

Turkey received several U.S. A-26 attack bombers Mar. 26, and the U.S. aircraft carrier *Rendova* left San Francisco Apr. 1 with a cargo of warplanes for Turkey.

A Greco-Turkish foreign ministers' conference in Athens ended Apr. 5 with the reaffirmation by Turkish Foreign Min. Nejmeddin Sadak and Greek Foreign Min. Constantine Tsaldaris of the 2 countries' 1938 pact to resist aggression jointly. (Turkey had failed to live up to this commitment in World War II.)

Turkey joined the European Recovery Program (Marshall Plan) July 4, 1948—a day after the announced deadline for doing so—in order to receive economic rehabilitation aid from the U.S. Turkey had remained neutral during World War II and had suffered none of the wartime devastation that the Marshall Plan was designed to relieve. (The Soviet Union in 1947 had forbidden its east European allies to join the program.)

The Kurdish Question

For the USSR, its policy of pressure on Turkey and Iran south of its Asia Minor borders was made easier by the problems that both these countries had with their nomadic Kurdish minorities. The Kurds in Turkey lived in the highlands east of Anatolia, around Lake Van and near Iraq's northern border. Those in nearby Iran inhabited the northwestern Zagros, the mountainous area near the Turkish and Iraqi borders, and dwelt around Lake Urmia. The Kurds in all 3 countries—Turkey, Iran and northern Iraq—tried to set up an independent state in Iran and Iraq and were willing to enlist the Soviet Union's aid in doing so. Russia provided both sanctuary for fleeing Kurdish rebels and support for the notion that a new Kurdistan, whose people had been submerged for a century and more, could take shape in this area.

Iran had put down one Kurdish rebellion in 1946, and it ended another in 1950. The Iranian government reported Sept. 3, 1950 that its army had overcome a Kurdish revolt near the Iraqi frontier and blamed the uprising on Soviet radio propaganda for a separate Kurdish state. Kurdish nationalists in Paris contended Sept. 10 that the trouble arose from government attempts to appropriate much of the Kurdish harvest, collect high taxes and enforce an old royal decree giving the shah title to lands of the Javanrudi Kurds.

The Turks were anxious to prevent any such emergency. A Turkish military court assisted Ankara in this aim when the retired army Gen. Mustafa Muglali Mar. 2, 1949 received a 20-year sentence for the illegal execution in 1943 of 33 villagers of Oslap on the Iranian frontier. Muglali had said in his own defense that the measure was necessary to quell disorders inspired by Kurdish tribesmen and Soviet occupation forces in Iran.

Quest for Allies

Turkish fears of the USSR led the Ankara government to follow closely the Western moves early in 1949 to forge a North Atlantic security alliance—the Atlantic Treaty (or Atlantic Pact). The Western powers, however, rejected Turkey's request for membership then, arguing that Turkey was geographically too remote from the North Atlantic area to qualify for membership. Undeterred, Turkish Foreign Min. Nejmeddin Sadak in Paris Feb. 17 proposed that the Atlantic security system be supplemented by a Mediterranean area defense agreement.

The Soviet naval publication *Krasnaya Flot* (*Red Fleet*) Apr. 19, 1950 voiced a new Soviet demand on Turkey for special rights in the

Dardanelles. U.S. State Secy. Dean Acheson at a news conference in Washington Apr. 21 termed the Soviet tactic "saber-rattling." Acheson said at the American Society of Newspaper Editors' convention in Washington Apr. 22 that the U.S. was "determined that communism shall not by hook or crook or trickery undermine our country or any other free country that desired to maintain its freedom." Acheson recommended that the U.S. use and expand "the machinery we have"— the UN, the Atlantic and Inter-American pacts—to strengthen the free world politically. The Soviet Communist Party daily *Pravda* Apr. 26 denounced Acheson's recommendations as a "delirious program for the creation of a worldwide American empire."

Foreign Min. Sadak's offer and State Secy. Acheson's recommendation eventually found acceptance with the North Atlantic Treaty Organization (NATO), which invited Turkey to consult with NATO countries on Mediterranean area defense problems. The U.S. government announced Oct. 4, 1950 that Turkey had accepted the NATO invitation.

After a year the Western Big-3 commanders of NATO, U.S. Gen. Omar N. Bradley, British Field Marshal Sir William Slim and French Gen. Charles Lecheres, called on Turkish Premier Adnan Menderes and his leading cabinet ministers in Ankara Oct. 12, 1951 to discuss Turkey's wish to enter NATO. The Menderes government said in a communique issued Oct. 15 that Turkey and the NATO commanders had achieved a "complete identity of views" in their talks and that they had concluded as a "necessary and useful" step that a Middle Eastern command be established. The Menderes government would send a military mission to Washington to continue discussions on this point, the communique said. The 3 NATO commanders, before leaving Oct. 15, indorsed the communique.

Meanwhile, Turkish Amb.-to-Egypt Sayed H. F. Tugay, U.S. Amb. Jefferson Caffery, French Amb. Maurice Couve de Murville and British Amb. Sir Ralph Stevenson had called on Egyptian Foreign Min. Mohammed Salah ed-Din Pasha Oct. 13 with a plan to make Egypt an equal partner with the 4 powers in the projected Middle Eastern command. Egyptian Interior Min. Fuad Sirag ed-Din Pasha Oct. 15 announced that the Egyptian government, after 2 days of deliberation, had decided to reject further consideration of the proposal until Egyptian differences with Britain over other matters (the Suez Canal and the Sudan) had been settled.

Turkish Premier Menderes predicted in a *U.S. News & World Report* interview published Dec. 3 that "reason" would overcome the "emotional" outcry against Britain in Egypt. He expressed confidence that the Egyptians and their Arab allies would eventually join the U.S., Britain, France and Turkey in their plan for Middle Eastern defense. (Syria, one of Egypt's Arab allies, already had given strong indication to the contrary—although Nov. 20 it had denied reports that demonstrators had torn down and burned the flag on the Turkish consulate in Aleppo in anger at Turkey's alliance with the Western colonial powers, Britain and France. Turkey had registered a "very serious" protest in Damascus.)

Turkey and the Western Big 3 proceeded with their plans to establish a Middle Eastern command. The 4 governments Nov. 10 had issued a joint communique outlining 11 guidelines for such a project:

(1) The United Nations is a world response to the principle that peace is indivisible and that the security of all states is jeopardized by breaches of the peace anywhere; at the same time it is incumbent upon the states of any area to be willing and able to undertake the initial defense of their area.

(2) The defense of the Middle East is vital to the free world, and its defense against outside aggression can be secured only by cooperation of all interested states.

(3) The Middle East Command is intended to be the center of cooperative efforts for the defense of the area as a whole; the achievement of peace and security in the area, through the Middle East Command, will bring with it social and economic advancement.

(4) A function of the Middle East Command will be to assist and support the states willing to join in the defense of the Middle East and to develop the capacity of each to play its proper role in the defense of the area as a whole against outside aggression. It will not interfere in problems and disputes arising within the area. The establishment of the Middle East Command in no way affects existing arrangements relating to such matters, notably the armistice agreements and the U.S.-UK-French tripartite declaration of May 1950.

(5) The task of the Middle East Command at the outset will be primarily one of planning and providing the Middle East states on their request with assistance in the form of advice and training. Requests for arms and equipment made by states in the area willing to join in its defense to sponsoring states in a position to assist in this connection will be filled by them to the extent possible, following the coordination of such requests through the Middle East Command.

(6) The Supreme Allied Commander, Middle East, will command forces placed at his disposal and will develop plans for the operations of all forces within the area (or to be introduced into the area) in time of war or international emergency. However, the placing of forces under the command of the Supreme Allied Commander, Middle East, in peace-time is not a prerequisite for joining in the common effort for the defense of the Middle East. Movement of these troops placed under the Supreme Allied Commander, Middle East's command to or within the territories of states joining in the defense of the Middle East will be made only with the agreement of the state or states concerned and in full accord with their national independence and sovereignty.

(7) While details have yet to be formulated, the sponsoring states intend that the Middle East Command should be an integrated allied command, not a national command. The responsibility of the Supreme Commander, Middle East, will be to ensure the effectiveness of the corporate defense enterprise represented by the Command. All states joining in this enterprise will be individually as-

sociated with the Command on the basis of equality through a Middle East defense liaison organization, which will be located in the Middle East Command H.Q. and will be the link between the Command and the countries ready to join in the defense of this area.

(8) Any facilities granted to the Middle East Command by states joining in the defense of the Middle East will be the subject of specific agreements.

(9) The broad mission of the Middle East Command and its cooperative character make it necessary that all states, whether territorially or not part of the area, act in the best interests of the cooperative defense of the area; but the Middle East Command naturally will not further the national interest of any particular state.

(10) A continuing objective of the Middle East Command is to reduce such deficiencies as exist at present in the organization and capacity for defense in a vitally important area so that the peacetime role of the states of the area in Middle East defense will progressively increase, thus permitting the peacetime role of states not territorially part of the Middle East to be decreased proportionately.

(11) Sponsoring states of the Middle East Command do not regard the initial form in which the Middle East Command will be organized as unchangeable; they believe that the Middle East Command, through mutual understanding, should evolve in the manner which will enable it most effectively to provide for the defense of the Middle East area as a whole.

The USSR had apparently become alarmed at these developments, and it dispatched to Ankara Nov. 3 a note expressing its anger at the Turkish intention of joining NATO ("the aggressive Atlantic bloc") and of "allowing Turkish territory to be used for the establishment of foreign military bases on Soviet frontiers." The Soviet government asserted that "a quantity of available data" had shown to the Kremlin's satisfaction that the U.S. was helping establish air and naval bases in Turkey. Large air force bases were being built near Turkey's Soviet border, the note said. The Kremlin interpreted all this as "nothing else than an attempt on the part of the imperialist states to use Turkish territory for the purpose of setting up bases on Soviet frontiers, with aggressive aims—not to mention the fact that Turkey has no connection whatever with the Atlantic." The Soviet Union, "as a state neighboring on Turkey, naturally cannot remain indifferent to these facts," the USSR warned.

Turkey, in its reply Nov. 13, stressed that NATO's aims were not aggressive but defensive. It asserted that it had based its decision on the need "to insure [Turkey's] own national security within the framework of collective security." Turkey disavowed any aggressive aims against any other country in undertaking what amounted to a heavy financial burden. It then referred to the Soviet Union and its Communist allies indirectly as aggressors in the light of "the general policy pursued by them and the military preparations undertaken by them many years under the supervision of Soviet specialists." The Turkish note concluded by observing that "Turkey has been faced with demands intended to imperil its security and territorial integrity." (This was believed to be a reference to the Soviet assertion of claims in 1945 to the Turkish border districts of Kars and Ardahan on the basis of several Soviet historians' allusions to old claims of the Georgian Soviet Socialist Republic on Turkish territory.) "In these circumstances," the note said, "the Turkish Republic is firmly convinced that it bears no responsibility whatever for the deterioration of Turkish-Soviet relations . . . ."

The USSR Nov. 30 sent to Ankara a 2d note denouncing Turkey's projected membership in NATO. The Soviet note referred to Turkey's charges of Soviet aggressiveness as "slanderous fabrications against the Soviet Union's foreign policy."

Turkish membership in NATO won the indorsement (73-2) Feb. 7, 1952 of the U.S. Senate, and Turkish cabinet ministers of foreign affairs, defense and finance attended a NATO ministerial conference in Lisbon Feb. 20.

The U.S. State Department had urged Congress in a statement May 14, 1949 to give Pres. Truman power under the Atlantic Pact and Truman Doctrine arms-aid program to act quickly to meet "changing situations" in the cold war, *i.e.,* new threats of Communist aggression. The statement said that west European defenses had grown so weak as to "invite military aggression."

A clash between Iranian and Soviet troops at a frontier outpost in northeastern Iran had been reported in Teheran Mar. 26, 1949 after a week of bitter quarreling between Iran and the Soviet Union. Iranian military sources said 50 Soviet soldiers had raided Atrek River posts held by the Iranian army in the disputed Gurgan district on the Turkmen USSR frontier—east of the southern shore of the Caspian Sea and 250 miles northeast of Teheran. One Iranian was reported killed and 2 taken prisoner. U.S. State Secy. Dean G. Acheson had taken notice Mar. 23 of a new Russian press and radio campaign against Iran. He issued a statement asserting that Soviet charges that the U.S. had set up military bases in Iran were "demonstrably untrue." But he cited Iran as well as Greece and Turkey as countries in whose security the U.S. had a "continuing interest." Pres. Truman also issued a greeting to Iran Mar. 21 as the "Voice of America" launched a new series of broadcasts to Iran (relayed via BBC and U.S. transmitters in Munich). Iranian military reports Apr. 4 of an "important" Soviet-Iranian frontier battle in Azerbaijan Province were modified Apr. 5 by the Foreign Office in Teheran. The government spokesman said that there had been 3 minor Soviet frontier incidents in 3 months and that a total of 5 men had been wounded on both sides in the latest clash Apr. 2 near Ghandi-boulach, Azerbaijan.

Libya a Free Nation

Libya, which UN economic experts described as the poorest country in the world, became the independent United Kingdom of Libya Dec. 24, 1951. The former Italian colony was the first nation freed entirely under the auspices of the UN.

The pro-Western king of Cyrenaica, Mohammed Idris el Senussi, assumed the Libyan throne as King Idris I in Benghazi Dec. 24 and proclaimed the independence of the new Moslem federation of Cyrenaica, Tripolitania and Fezzan. Britain and France, which had shared in the administration of Libya since Italy lost it in World War II, had already transferred power to King Idris' government. The Libyans adopted a constitution and formed a government under the guidance of a UN commission set up in Dec. 1949 by the UN General Assembly.

King Idris' government allowed the U.S., British and French forces to remain in Libya pending the negotiation of a Libyan defense pact with the West. The U.S. had an air base at Wheelus Field near Tripoli. Britain maintained a brigade of troops in Libya, although it had shifted all but one battalion of the Libyan garrison to the Suez trouble zone. France had 3 airstrips and a company of troops in Fezzan.

Libya's freedom was greeted by Pres. Truman with a message extending the U.S.' "hand of friendship" to the new country.

The Soviet Union Sept. 16, 1952 cast its 53d veto in the UN Security Council to keep Libya from admission to the UN General Assembly. In opposing Libya's entry, Soviet Deputy Foreign Min. Yakub A. Malik said that no other countries would be admitted to the UN until 14 countries—of which 5 enjoyed Soviet sponsorship for their membership applications—had been admitted together. (The 5 were Albania, Bulgaria, Hungary, Outer Mongolia and Rumania.) The Security Council had rejected the Soviet Union's *en bloc* proposal Sept. 8.

Libya did not gain its seat in the General Assembly until Dec. 14, 1955, when it entered as part of a package deal in which Albania, Bulgaria, Hungary, Rumania and Jordan (formerly Transjordan) also were admitted. The Soviet Union and the U.S. both voted for the 6 countries' admission.

The U.S. Woos Arabs

14 U.S. Air Force C-54s on an around-the-clock schedule carried 3,763 Moslems without charge 800 miles from Beirut to Jidda, Saudi Arabia Aug. 25-29, 1952 so that the pilgrims might reach Mecca in

time for the Id Al Adha festival. (Mecca, Islam's holiest city, is 40 miles from Jidda. Moslems believe the Id Al Adha fête, which began Aug. 28, must be attended at least once to achieve salvation.) The U.S. acted on a plea from the Lebanese government when regular air lines and other transportation could not cope with the thousands of pilgrims converging at Beirut from all parts of Islam. Iran's anti-U.S. religious leader and Chamber of Deputies Pres. Ayatollah Kashani was among the airlifted passengers.

The U.S. State Department said that the free airlift was a good-will gesture and would be paid for by funds set aside for pilot training. Among Moslem leaders expressing thanks for the U.S.-aid: Lebanese Pres. Bechara el-Khoury and Premier Sami Solh Aug. 28; Mohammed Alaya, mufti of Lebanon, who ordered Aug. 29 that prayers for Americans be included in all mosque rites during the festival; Saudi Arabian King Ibn Saud, who gave $6,000 worth of Arab costumes to 86 U.S. fliers Sept. 3.

The Saudi Arabian government disclosed Aug. 30 that it had refused visas for the pilgrimage to 16 professors and theologians from Chinese Turkestan (Sinkiang Province), because it was afraid they might spread Communist propaganda.

Jordan had signed an agreement with the U.S. Feb. 16, 1952 to receive $3.78 million in Point 4 technical aid on farming, health, sanitation, water supply, education, transportation and minerals development projects.

Pres. Truman was host at luncheon Aug. 16, 1952 to King Faisal II, of Iraq, who had arrived in New York Aug. 12 for a tour of the U.S. that ended Sept. 18. Prince Abdullah Faisal, Saudi Arabian interior and public health minister, called on Truman Aug. 18 after having made a nationwide tour of the U.S.

WAR IN PALESTINE (MAY 1948-JAN. 1949)

State of Israel Created, Arabs Attack

The new Jewish State of Israel came into existence in Palestine at midnight May 14, 1948. It was unexpectedly recognized by the U.S. 11 minutes later but already knew itself the target of a declaration of war by surrounding Arab countries. 5 of the 7 Arab League states invaded Palestine, mostly in Arab sectors, and began light bombing on Tel Aviv.

Egypt had informed the UN Security Council May 14 that it was ordering its army into Palestine. Jewish Agency spokesmen in Lake Success, N.Y. pleaded with the Council to invoke all of its powers to check this Arab breach of the peace. An Egyptian armed force moved May 14 into the southern coastal strip of Arab Palestine. At exactly 12:01 a.m. May 15, Transjordan's Arab Legion and its Iraqi allies crossed the Allenby Bridge over the Jordan River and occupied Jericho.

Official Soviet comment denounced the Arab attack and called on the Arab governments to desist. As the 25-year British mandate expired, the special UN General Assembly session had adjourned May 14 after merely authorizing an attempt by UN to mediate between Arabs and Jews. The Assembly did not repeal the Nov. 29, 1967 Palestine partition plan nor its proviso for a UN trusteeship over Jerusalem. The Arab invasion of Palestine became a new problem for the Security Council.

Israel, the first Jewish state in the Holy Land since AD 70, was proclaimed at 4:06 p.m. (Palestine time) May 14 at the Jewish National Council meeting in the Tel Aviv Museum of Art. Pres. Truman at 6:11 p.m. EDT astounded the UN General Assembly by making the U.S. the first country to recognize the *de facto* Jewish republic. (The U.S. did not lift its embargo on arms shipments to the Middle East but Truman had this under consideration, it was reported.)

Truman's statement of American recognition said in part: "This government has been informed that a Jewish state has been proclaimed in Palestine and recognition has been requested by the provisional government thereof. The United States recognizes the provisional government as the *de facto* authority of the new State of Israel."

9 minutes earlier, 2 minutes after the British mandate had expired at midnight in Palestine, Iraq's Awni Khalidy paused in UN Assembly debate over the American trusteeship plan for Jerusalem and declared: "The game is up."

Truman in Washington issued the unexpected American recognition of Israel after receiving an appeal from Chaim Weizmann. News of Truman's move threw the Assembly into a turmoil of surprise and indecision. Dr. Philip C. Jessup, acting U.S. delegation chief, admitted to the Assembly that the U.S. delegation had no advance knowledge of the President's intentions. Arabs denounced the U.S. and called the special Assembly session a "fake." Andrei A. Gromyko indicated that the USSR had planned to recognize the Jewish state, but he accused the U.S. of plunging the UN into a "ludicrous situation" by its sudden act. It was widely believed that Truman was especially anxious to recognize Israel ahead of Russia.

The UN General Assembly's final action before adjourning at 8:32 p.m. EDT May 14 was to pass, 31-7 (the Soviet bloc and Cuba opposed, 17 abstaining and 4 absent), a plan to send a UN mediator to Palestine to do his best to obtain a peace and carry on public services. The old Palestine Commission was abolished. The mediator was to be selected by majority agreement among the Big 5. (The mediation plan was based on an American resolution offered in the Political & Security Committee May 12 when it became apparent that the U.S. plan for a Palestine trusteeship was dead.)

The Big 5 powers May 20 agreed on a mediator to seek peace in Palestine under a mandate from the General Assembly. The unanimous choice was Count Folke Bernadotte, 53, president of the Swedish Red Cross and a nephew of King Gustaf V. Bernadotte, whose wife was born in the U.S., had served as an intermediary between the Allies and Germany at the end of World War II. He was paid $26,000 a year by the UN. (Count Bernadotte was assassinated Sept. 17 in Jerusalem by Stern gang terrorists.)

The Assembly's final special-session meeting ended in failure to pass the new U.S. plan for a temporary Jerusalem trusteeship supervised by a UN commissioner. The 20-15 vote for the plan lacked the required 2/3 majority. The Political Committee had referred pending resolutions to the Assembly without recommendation May 14 in a race to get final Assembly action before the 6 p.m. (EDT) deadline for the British mandate's expiration.

The Israeli government was installed in Tel Aviv May 15 and was headed by David Ben-Gurion, 63, a Polish-born veteran Zionist, as premier. Chaim Weizmann, ill in New York, was elected first president of Israel May 16. The independence declaration called for the election of an Israeli constituent assembly by Oct. 1. It was to draft a constitution. Meanwhile the existing 37-man National Council (legislature) and cabinet was to govern provisionally. Israel's declaration offered peace to the Arabs and a guarantee of protection for minorities in Israel. The actual ceremony establishing Israel was held in close secrecy and was carried out May 14 before the beginning of the Hebrew Sabbath (May 15). The declaration was greeted joyously by Jews and well-wishers throughout the world. The new country applied for admission to the UN May 16.

The USSR granted recognition to Israel May 17 in a note implying that it regarded the Israeli government as the *de jure* authority in Jewish Palestine. The International Refugee Organization announced in Geneva May 18 that it would stop helping send refugees to Israel until the new government was recognized by the UN.

Lebanese authorities in Beirut May 20 took 61 Israel-bound passengers, including 41 Americans and 3 Canadians, off the American steamer *Marine Carp*. Those detained, Lebanon said, were "Zionists of military age" and therefore potential recruits for the Israeli army. The U.S. demanded May 21 that the 41 Americans be released from a concentration camp and permitted to leave Lebanon. Lebanon refused May 23. The U.S. announced May 30 that it had made a 2d protest to Lebanon against the detentions, and the 41 Americans were released within a month.

UN Discusses Intervention

While the British-subsidized Arab Legion of Transjordan was seizing most of Jerusalem and Egyptians approached the city from the south, the UN Security Council in Lake Success, N.Y. argued heatedly May 17–22 over whether the Arab states should be threatened with sanctions or force. Advocates of stern action, including the U.S., felt forced to settle May 22 for a mere request that the Arabs and Israelis stop fighting throughout Palestine within 2 days. Britain led the opposition to a stronger UN measure.

Warren R. Austin of the U.S. had submitted a resolution in the Council May 17 to cite the Palestine situation as a "threat to the peace" under Chapter VII (on peace enforcement) of the UN Charter. Austin proposed that the Council order an end to the fighting within 36 hours and question both the Arabs and the Jews of Palestine on their actions. The Soviet Union demanded immediate action on Austin's proposal. Other delegates insisted on delay, but the questionnaires were dispatched May 18. Egypt, Lebanon, Iraq and Syria answered their questionnaires May 22. All vowed that they would never negotiate with Israel.

Britain's Foreign Office declared May 18 that since its Palestine mandate had ended, it was no longer responsible for the Arab Legion. It also said that it would continue its treaty shipments of arms to Arab states unless the UN decided that the Arabs were acting illegally.

Britain and Belgium led an attack in the Security Council May 19 on the American bid for use of UN sanctions or force to stop the war. Sir Alexander Cadogan argued that the Council might commit itself to use a UN police force "which we do not yet possess." (Most Council delegates indicated that they shared this opinion.) He also questioned whether "international" peace was threatened.

Soviet Amb.-to-UN Andrei Gromyko May 21 ridiculed Britain's suggestion that there was no threat to peace in Palestine. Syria's Faris el-Khouri assailed U.S. recognition of Israel and contended that the UN should thank the Arabs for pacifying a local disturbance in Palestine. Arab armies set up civil regimes wherever they advanced in Palestine.

The Council's Consular Truce Commission in Jerusalem had sent a warning May 20, after a member had conferred with King Abdullah of Transjordan, that only "strong diplomatic or military pressure on the Arab states" would stop the war. In the Council, the Ukraine's Vasily A. Tarasenko said May 20 that Britain should be classified as a belligerent for supporting the Arab Legion. Another plea for a "large, powerful" UN police force came from the Truce Commission May 21.

(Thomas C. Wasson, 52, U.S. consul general in Jerusalem and a member of the Consular Truce Commission, was fatally wounded May 22 by a sniper's bullet near the U.S. consulate in Jerusalem. He died in Hadassah Hospital May 23. The Jewish army reported that the sniper was an Arab. Wasson had been a member of the consular service since 1924 and had volunteered for the hazardous Jerusalem post, which he assumed in April. He had sent most of his staff to Haifa. The State Department disclosed May 22 that 2 other U.S. consulate members had been wounded in Jerusalem: Chief Radioman Herbert M. Walker of the naval communication unit [he died May 23] and Thomas J. Gannon, a guard.)

The Security Council May 22 adopted a resolution that omitted the "threat-to-peace" clause and merely requested both sides to cease fire within 36 hours after midnight May 22, EST (or by 7 p.m. May 24, Palestine time). Israel agreed May 23 on condition that the Arabs do likewise. The resolution passed, 8-0, with the USSR, the Ukraine and Syria abstaining and the U.S. voting for it only because it set a cease-fire deadline. At the same time, Austin told the Council that the UN was in duty bound to "help keep Abdullah where he belongs."

U.S.-British Rift; Britain Quits Holy Land

The widening split between the U.S. and Britain over the British defense of the Arabs caused Foreign Secy. Ernest Bevin to summon U.S.

Amb.-to-Britain Lewis W. Douglas in London May 22. Bevin reportedly told Douglas that Britain was maintaining a bulwark against Soviet expansion and communism through its policy in the Middle East and safeguarding oil resources essential to the Western countries.

London was concerned over the possibility that the U.S. would lift its Middle Eastern arms embargo to let Israel import American weapons. State Secy. George C. Marshall had said May 19 that the ending of the embargo would depend on the Security Council's actions on Palestine. Pres. Truman May 21 invited Pres. Chaim Weizmann of Israel to confer at the White House May 25. Huge rallies against the U.S. embargo on arms to Israel had been held in New York, Washington and Chicago May 16. Chairman Styles Bridges (R., N.H.) of the Senate Appropriations Committee stirred up more apprehension May 21 when he announced plans to investigate whether American economic aid enabled Britain to keep sending military supplies to the Arabs, as charged in Zionist advertisements.

Prime Min. Clement R. Attlee denied in the House of Commons May 31 that there was an Anglo-U.S. rift over Palestine, and Foreign Secy. Bevin said June 2 that Transjordan's Arab Legion had been invited into Arab Palestine and had not staged an "invasion."

The last British troops quit Palestine by way of Haifa June 30, 1948. Lt. Gen. G. H. A. McMillan, the force's commander, was the last of 5,000 men to board ship. The Union Jack came down for the first time since Nov. 2, 1917, and the Israeli flag—a blue Magen David in a blue-bordered white field—went up in its place. The British left a month ahead of schedule despite an Arab League protest that it was a violation of the truce.

After the British departure, Premier David Ben-Gurion said: "Today ended a chapter of deceitful and false rule." He warned the Arabs: "If peace does not come, we are ready for war." (A representative of the Israeli government, appearing before the UN July 3, accused Britain of hampering Israel's economic growth by blocking some $400 million in Palestinian sterling balances then in British banks. London had done so without any effort to negotiate, the Israeli representative charged.)

Truce Negotiations

The UN Security Council's efforts to halt the war in Palestine progressed in late May 1948 to the point where both Israel and the Arab League agreed in principle to a 4-week truce. An actual cease-fire, however, was delayed by the issue of Jewish immigration to Israel, and the truce did not start until June 11. Israel issued a cease-fire order to its forces for 3 a.m. June 2, the Council's deadline for answering its truce appeal, in the misunderstanding that this was a cease-fire deadline. The Jews resumed fighting later in the day.

Israel and the Arab League May 29 met the June 1 deadline for replying to the 4-week truce plan advanced by the Security Council. Both sides said that they accepted the plan, but Israel listed 5 "assumptions" as to the meaning of the truce proposal that differed from "explanations" noted by the Arabs. The Council decided June 2 in Lake Success, N.Y., that both replies were "unconditional" acceptances, although they differed as follows:

Israel's reply June 1 "assumed" that (1) the proposed world embargo on arms deliveries to the Middle East would prevent Britain from supplying the Arabs from stores of British equipment in Palestine, Transjordan and Egypt; (2) both sides would hold the lines existing at the moment of the cease-fire; (3) Arabs would give the Jews normal civilian access to Jerusalem; (4) Egypt, Lebanon and Syria would suspend efforts to blockade Israel; (5) Israel would be free to admit immigrants of any age if it did not press them into military service or training during the truce.

The Arab League's supplementary reply filed by Egypt June 2 asserted that (1) efforts must be directed toward unifying Palestine as a single Arab-dominated state instead of making partition permanent; (2) continued Jewish immigration would be a grave threat to Arab countries; (3) Arab League states, as a "regional organization responsible for maintaining security in their zone," wanted to help the UN mediator, Count Folke Bernadotte, and the Council's Truce Commission supervise compliance with the cease-fire. (King Abdullah of Transjordan said in Amman, "We will be patient and help Count Bernadotte's mission. But we will never under any circumstances accept a Jewish state.")

The Security Council June 2 accepted without a vote the ruling by Pres.-for-June Faris el-Khouri of Syria that both acceptances were unconditional, and it granted Bernadotte's request for authority to fix the time when a cease-fire order would become effective. Russia and the Ukraine entered abstentions on the latter point.

Bernadotte had reached the Middle East May 30, and he began to confer with rival leaders in Cairo, Amman and the Holy Land. Bernadotte notified the Council June 4 that only Israeli-Arab differences over immigration were holding up a cease-fire agreement. The Council authorized Bernadotte to interpret the Security Council's May 29 resolution on this point.

Britain accepted Israel's interpretation of the UN arms embargo proposal June 3 by halting all deliveries of war material to Egypt, Iraq,

Palestine, Transjordan, Syria, Lebanon, Saudi Arabia and Yemen. The order affected British stockpiles in Middle Eastern countries. Britain, however, also announced that no Jewish immigrants would be permitted to leave Cyprus during the truce negotiations and cease-fire period. Israel denounced this as illegal.

The cease-fire finally went into effect June 11. During the 4-week truce, Bernadotte worked for a permanent peace between the Arabs and Israel.

(Col. David [Micky] Marcus, 47, an American and a West Point graduate who had played a leading role in the development of Israel's combat forces, was killed while leading Haganah forces in the Jerusalem road battle June 11, a few hours before the cease-fire took effect. His death was ironic in that he was shot mistakenly by an Israeli sentry when he failed to understand the sentry's challenge in Hebrew. As a colonel in the Judge Advocate's Department of the U.S. Army in World War II, he had helped draft Italian, German and Japanese surrender terms and was a member of the U.S. delegations to the Teheran, Dumbarton Oaks, Yalta and Potsdam conferences. Marcus was buried July 1, 1948 with full military honors at West Point, N.Y.)

The Security Council June 15 rejected a Soviet demand that a team of UN truce observers be made up of representatives of all of the Security Council member nations, with the exception of Syria. The USSR wanted to send 5 military observers. The resolution died when only Russia and the Ukraine supported it.

At Bernadotte's request and with the Council's approval, UN Secy. Gen. Trygve Lie asked all UN and non-UN nations June 16 to furnish information on the number of male Jews fit for military service who departed for Israel. The first Jewish immigrant ship since the truce began arrived at Tel Aviv June 13, and men of military age (18 to 45) were ordered sent to an Israeli refugee camp. UN observers held up the landing of 240 motor trucks at Tel Aviv June 14 until it was decided whether they were military imports. With arms imports halted, Israel's arms factories were working overtime.

Lie responded to Bernadotte's request for a token international guard by organizing the nearest thing to a UN military force yet assembled. He recruited 50 volunteers from the uniformed guard and other departments at UN headquarters in Lake Success, N.Y. June 17. All were war veterans and averaged 25 years of age. They included 28 American uniformed guards and 15 Americans, 2 Frenchmen, a Norwegian, a Dane, a Swede, an Australian and a Chinese from other departments. Lt. John Cosgrove, 40, of Jamaica, N.Y., a uniformed guard officer, took charge of the contingent—dubbed "Lie's Legion" and

"Cosgrove's Lancers." The group set out by plane for Palestine June 18. Members carried revolvers, but Bernadotte was to decide later whether they would receive ammunition.

Bernadotte's Peace Plan

With the one-month truce scheduled to end July 9, Count Bernadotte June 28 submitted new peace proposals to the Arab League and the Israeli government. Details were discussed July 4 after both sides had rejected parts of the plan and the Arabs talked openly of resuming warfare. The plan, offered as a "suggestion" only, provided for the following:

(1) The creation of a federal union of an Arab and a Jewish state in the former Palestine mandate including Palestine and Transjordan as well. (In effect, all Arab Palestine would be joined to Transjordan under King Abdullah.) A Council of the Union would promote economic interests of the 2 states, including common services, customs, excises and projects, and would "coordinate" foreign policy and defense. Both states would maintain full control over their own internal and foreign affairs.

(2) Immigration would be free for 2 years, after which either member could request that the Council rule on whether the economic "absorptive capacity" of either state was being exceeded.

(3) Territorial matters: The Negev desert, awarded by the UN to the Jews, would go to the Arabs; Western Galilee, previously awarded to the Arabs, would go to the Jews; Jerusalem would become Arab, "with municipal autonomy for the Jewish community"; Haifa would be a free port; Jaffa's status would be determined later; a free airport would be established at Lydda. Each state would protect religious and minority rights as well as holy places.

Actually, the plan would permit each side to maintain territory it had won during the fighting after the mandate expired May 15. It constituted a return to the federal regime proposed by the minority members of the UN Special Committee on Palestine.

Both sides rejected parts of the plan, the Arabs refusing to recognize the Jewish state in any form, the Jews balking at putting Jerusalem under Arab control or limiting immigration after 2 years.

Bernadotte, flying back to Rhodes July 4 after conferring with the Arab League in Cairo the previous day, said that the door to peace was "still open."

The Arabs, however, left no doubt as to where they stood. King Abdullah announced his rejection of the plan July 3 and said the Arabs were going to "rely on our arms. We are in Palestine for one of 2 things—either permanent glory or honored martyrdom." (In far-off Karachi, the Pakistani Parliamentary Committee agreed June 30 to raise a volunteer corps to fight with the Arabs.)

Israel Begins Diplomatic Exchanges

Pres. Truman announced June 22 that the U.S. and Israeli governments had reached agreement on the exchange of "special representatives." Washington appointed James G. McDonald as head of a U.S. mission in Tel Aviv, and Eliahu Epstein headed an Israeli mission in Washington. It was reported that McDonald and Epstein were to enjoy full diplomatic prerogatives and that the term "special representatives" had been used because Israel was then recognized by the U.S. on a *de facto* basis. (McDonald, an authority on refugee problems, had been League of Nations high commissioner for refugees 1933–5 and had served in 1946 on the Anglo-American Inquiry Commission on Palestine.)

Tel Aviv announced June 25 that Mrs. Golda Myerson (later Meir), a member of the Jewish Agency executive, had been appointed Israeli minister in Moscow and that the Soviet Union had appointed Pavel Yershov, *chargé d'affaires* in Ankara, as its minister in Tel Aviv.

It was announced July 12 that the first Israeli legation would be opened in Prague, where Yehuda Ueberall had been accredited as Israeli minister to Czechoslovakia.

The U.S. disclosed at UN Security Council headquarters in Lake Success, N.Y. Aug. 8 that it would support Israel's application for UN membership. Israel submitted a formal application Nov. 29 for admission to UN. The application was handed to Secy. Gen. Trygve Lie at 6 p.m., exactly a year after the Assembly had passed the 1947 partition resolution, Philip C. Jessup of the U.S. demanded immediate action on Israel's bid in the Security Council Dec. 2, and Yakub A. Malik of the USSR indorsed the application. But Sir Alexander Cadogan of Britain argued that there was no reason for giving the application urgent consideration, and it was referred to the Council's membership committee for study.

Internecine Fighting in Israel

Fighting erupted June 21 between Haganah (by then the regular Israeli forces) and Irgun Zvai Leumi members. The struggle started when Irgunists tried to beach at Nathanya an 1,800-ton tank-landing

craft carrying military equipment, including tanks, ammunition, Bren-
and anti-tank guns, bombs and grenades. The vessel was an ex-
Panamanian ship, the *Altalena*, believed to have been bought for gun-
running purposes by the Hebrew Committee of National Liberation, a
U.S. organization led by Peter Bergson.*

The craft was forced out to sea after a clash in which several
Irgunists were killed, but it came back the next day and was grounded
on the beach off Tel Aviv. Steel-helmeted Irgun members storming
ashore were repulsed by Israeli troops who were rushed to the beach.
Several Irgunists were killed by heavy machine-gun fire. Other Irgunists
reaching the shore conducted a running fight on the shore road.

Haganah units eventually established control, and the Irgunists suffered many casualties. Their craft was sunk by Haganah mortar fire
from the shore.

Israel disclosed July 4 that Bergson was being held on a charge of
"armed resistance . . . and incitement to desertion" following the
Altalena incident. He was released Aug. 26.

Farouk & U.S. Oil Companies Accused

Freda Kirchwey, president of the Nation Associates, publishers of
the weekly magazine *The Nation* (New York), charged in a memo
June 29 to Secy. Gen. Trygve Lie and Pres. Truman that King Farouk I
of Egypt had collaborated with the Nazis during the war. She offered
as proof photostatic copies of documents said to have been captured
from the Nazis. (In Nuremberg July 2 a U.S. war crimes court received
evidence that the German Foreign Ministry had spent $40,000 enter-
taining Haj Amin el Husseini, exiled grand mufti of Jerusalem, and
$52,000 on Rashid Ali el Gailani, Iraqi premier during the war.)

Previously Miss Kirchwey had submitted to Truman "documentary
evidence" that the American oil combine Aramco—Arabian American
Oil Co., consisting of Standard Oil of California, Standard Oil of New
Jersey, the Texas Co. and Socony Vacuum—was "working with the
British Foreign Office, the Arab League . . . and leaders of the Arab
states to destroy the effectiveness of the United Nations and of every
act of the President . . . with respect to the partition of Palestine. . . ."
She said that they "have the active collusion" of the U.S. State Department's Office of Near Eastern & African Affairs, headed by Loy Wesley
Henderson. She named James Terry Duce, Aramco vice president, as an
intermediary between the Arabs and the State Department.

---

*Bergson was also co-president of the American League for a Free Palestine.

Washington had left unexplained the meaning of a shift Apr. 28 that put Maj. Gen. John H. Hilldring, a strong advocate of partition, in the new post of Special Assistant State Secretary for Palestine Affairs. This apparently removed Henderson from supervision of Palestine matters. Hilldring had said in a San Francisco speech Apr. 27 that the Jews should have a separate state and have help in defending it. He had been a principal adviser to the U.S. delegation in Nov. 1947 when partition was put through the UN General Assembly with strong American backing.

Henderson, 56, director of the Office of Near Eastern & African Affairs for 3 years and often denounced by Zionists as pro-Arab, was appointed U.S. ambassador to India by Truman July 14. Joseph C. Satterthwaite, Henderson's deputy, moved up to the directorship July 16.

Truce Expires; New Truce Accepted

The Holy Land truce, which began June 11, expired at 9 a.m. July 9, 1948, and all 3 principal fronts flamed into action. Count Folke Bernadotte's request for an extension of the truce was accepted by the Israelis but rejected by the Arabs. A UN Security Council appeal for an extension of the cease-fire failed to draw a reply from the Arabs. On the day before the truce expired, U.S. and French warships took about 200 UN truce observers aboard at Haifa.

The Arabs renewed the battle despite a strong warning from the U.S. Philip C. Jessup, U.S. representative on the Security Council, had declared July 8 that if the Arabs rejected the truce extension the U.S. would support action against them under Chapter VII of the UN Charter, which calls for economic and diplomatic sanctions and later military action. Syria's Faris el-Khouri replied: The Arabs "are ready to be killed by your atomic bombs" and by the arms of the USSR "if they are willing to join you in this respect."

A new truce took effect July 17–18 on UN prodding. The UN Security Council had held July 15 that the conflict was a menace to world peace and had threatened to use sanctions or force to stop it. This action, recommended by Bernadotte and formally proposed by the U.S., brought about an indefinite truce on Israeli-Arab fronts where the Jews that week had scored some of their biggest gains of the war by capturing Lydda, Ramle and Nazareth. Fighting ceased in Jerusalem July 17. The Arabs then took Britain's advice and joined Israel July 18 in accepting a cease-fire for the entire Holy Land.

The truce was arranged after Bernadotte had arrived in New York from Palestine July 12 and, the same day, had given the Council a report that described the situation as follows:

● Arabs, "bitterly opposed" to "a Jewish state and Jewish immigration," were willing to fight "to the limit of their capacities against what they regard as the injustice inherent in a Jewish invasion supported by the outside world."

● A "Jewish Provisional Government" was nevertheless an established fact. Its people "are intensely nationalistic and apparently fearless in the face of the Arab threat."

● The UN had the alternatives of (1) making it "prohibitively unprofitable" for the Arabs to wage war against the Jews or (2) letting the 2 sides fight it out. Bernadotte recommended July 13 that sanctions or force be used under Chapter VII's Articles 41 and 42 against either side that persisted in waging war.

Dr. Philip C. Jessup of the U.S. July 13 offered a resolution embracing Bernadotte's recommendations. As passed with minor modifications July 15, the measure:

● Declared the Palestine war a "threat to the peace" under Chapter VII's Article 39.

● Ordered an unconditional cease-fire within 24 hours in Jerusalem and a truce within 3 days in all of Palestine. The new truce would last "until a peace adjustment of the future situation in Palestine is reached." Its terms would be the same as those of the 4-week truce that expired July 9.

● Should either side reject the truce or violate it, there would be "immediate consideration by the Security Council with a view to such further action under Chapter VII of the Charter as may be decided upon by the Council."

● Arabs and Jews should resume peace negotiations through Bernadotte in a spirit of "conciliation" and "concession."

The resolution was passed, 7-1, with Belgium, Britain, Canada, China, Colombia, France and the U.S. in favor: Syria opposed; Argentina, the USSR and Ukraine abstaining. The USSR and Ukraine abstained because they disliked the wording of the mediation clause as amended by China; it implied a possible change in the UN's original partition plan. Council Pres. Dmitri Z. Manuilsky of Ukraine criticized Bernadotte for having proposed changes.

Israel and the Arab League Political Committee in Amman agreed July 16 to the cease-fire in Jerusalem, effective July 17. Israel also agreed to stop fighting throughout Palestine whenever the Arabs did likewise. The Arabs had been on the losing end of the warfare all week.

King Abdullah of Transjordan was understood to be in favor of another truce, as urged by Britain, and his Arab Legion did little fighting. (Britain gave the Arabs a foretaste of sanctions July 12 by holding up a $2 million quarterly subsidy payment to the Legion pending the outcome of the Security Council's debate.) Egypt and Syria wanted to continue fighting, and the exiled grand mufti of Jerusalem, Haj Amin el Husseini, said in Cairo July 16 that he was against another truce because the Jews' military successes since July 9 showed that they had benefited from the last one. The Arabs, however, announced from Amman July 18 that they would accept the UN's cease-fire order although they opposed an indefinite truce on the old terms.

U.S. Reenforces Neutrality

The U.S. took several steps early in Sept. 1968 that demonstrated a desire to remain officially—and obviously—impartial and aloof from the conflict in Palestine.

The State Department said Sept. 2 that it had asked Czechoslovakia to stop the delivery of fighter planes and weapons to Israel because such movements violated the terms of the 2d Palestine truce.

The Export-Import Bank announced in Washington Sept. 3 that it was postponing action on a $100 million loan to Israel because of "unsettled political conditions" in the Middle East. The State Department also refused Sept. 4 to permit the emigration of men aged 18–45 to Israel from U.S.-controlled displaced persons camps in Germany and Austria, except in cases approved by Count Bernadotte.

Meanwhile, in Tel Aviv Sept. 3 the World Zionist Organization's action (executive) committee turned down the demands of U.S. delegates that all Israeli cabinet members withdraw from the executive group. But all Israeli minister-members except Finance Min. Eliezer Kaplan then resigned from the action committee.

Bernadotte Assassinated

Count Folke Bernadotte, the UN mediator, and French Col. Andre P. Serot of the UN truce-observer group were murdered Sept. 17, 1948 while riding unarmed in a UN car in Jewish Jerusalem. The driver of the car, Col. Frank M. Begley of Huntington, N.Y., a UN security officer, escaped without injury. (Col. Begley said later that the assassinations took place because of a story in the *Palestine Post* condemning Bernadotte's plan for the internationalization of Jerusalem. "Extremists saw that story," he said, "and decided to take their revenge.")

Events preceding and following the ambush:

● Bernadotte had completed work in Rhodes Sept. 16 on a report to the UN General Assembly, due to convene Sept. 21 in Paris. He then left on a mission to negotiate a reliable truce in Jerusalem, a city he described as "trigger-happy." (An Arab-Jewish artillery duel broke out in Jerusalem Sept. 16 after several days of intermittent small-arms and mortar exchanges. Jews had balked at Bernadotte's insistence on demilitarization of the city for fear that Arab armies surrounding it could not be trusted.)

● After a stop in Damascus, Bernadotte reached Jerusalem by plane at 11 a.m. Sept. 17. He discounted a warning radioed from Haifa that he would be shot at when he reached Jerusalem's Kalandia Airfield and refused to detour around danger areas—on the grounds that he should take the same risks as his truce teams and uphold the UN's authority. A harmless shot struck Bernadotte's car while he drove from Kalandia to a conference with Brig. Norman Lash of Transjordan's Arab Legion in Ramallah.

● Bernadotte's auto convoy was halted at about 5 p.m. in the Katamon quarter, a Jewish suburb in southern Jerusalem, by a jeepload of men taken for Jewish soldiers on roadblock duty. One tommy-gunner ran to Bernadotte's car and fired point-blank through a window. Bernadotte was wounded around the heart; Serot was shot in the head and killed outright. Swedish Gen. Aage Lundstroem, Bernadotte's chief of staff, and U.S. Navy Comdr. William R. Cox, a truce observer, also were in Bernadotte's car but escaped injury.

● Begley, 38, who was driving Bernadotte's car, suffered powder burns when he tried to grapple with the assassins. Begley then sped the car out of the assassins' range and rushed Bernadotte to nearby Hadassah hospital in a vain attempt to get him to a doctor before he died.

● The killers escaped.

Ralph J. Bunche, 44, chief UN aide to Bernadotte and UN Secy. Gen. Lie's personal representative in Jerusalem, was confirmed by the Security Council Sept. 18 as Bernadotte's temporary successor. Bunche had flown from Rhodes Sept. 17 to join Bernadotte in Jerusalem; he arrived an hour after the assassination. Bunche, an American of Negro and Indian ancestry and a grandson of a Negro slave, had been head of Howard University's political science department until 1941, and he had served as secretary to UNSCOP in 1947.

Bunche wired Israeli Foreign Min. Moshe Shertok Sept. 18 that Israel must take "full responsibility" for Bernadotte's assassination, and he called the incident "a breach of the truce." Israeli officials protested against Bunche's placing of responsibility on Israel, but they accepted the terrorists' challenge to Israeli authority. An intensive drive was begun to round up the killers, whom Israel denounced as a "criminal gang." Regular Israeli forces put Jewish Jerusalem under a curfew, sealed it against exit or entry and netted 200 suspects in a house-to-house search for Sternists. The Irgun Zvai Leumi also denounced the assassins.

While Israel's measures in Jerusalem met with no resistance, James G. McDonald, special U.S. representative to Israel, was said to have been warned by terrorists in Tel Aviv that "you are not wanted" in Israel. Arab leaders cited Bernadotte's fate as proof that Israel could not control Jewish extremists.

In an emergency meeting of the Security Council in Paris Sept. 18, UN Secy. Gen. Trygve Lie disclosed that the Palestine problem had been placed on the proposed General Assembly agenda, as requested by Bernadotte in a letter received after his death. Lie also called on the Council to organize a UN guard force to protect truce observers. All Council delegates except Yakub A. Malik of the Soviet Union explicitly condemned the killing of Bernadotte. Malik expressed "sympathy" but said that the UN should enforce its sidetracked 1947 plan for partitioning Palestine.

In Washington, U.S. State Secy. George C. Marshall predicted that the peacemaking efforts Bernadotte started would be "vigorously pursued" and that the world would not permit a new outbreak of general warfare in Palestine. Marshall said the assassination would not affect the U.S. support of Israel. Countless other statements in many countries deploring the assassinations included expressions by Pres. Truman, who sent condolences to Countess Bernadotte.

Responsibility for the Bernadotte-Serot killings was admitted Sept. 18 by a group styled as *Hazit Hamoledet* (Homeland, or Fatherland, Front). It said in notes slipped under the doors of foreign consulates in Jerusalem, "We killed Bernadotte because he worked for the British and carried out their orders." Israel charged that *Hazit Hamoledet* was a terrorist "sham splinter movement" of the Sternists, organized to carry out plots of violence without implicating the Stern Group by name and thus endangering its claim to the status of a legitimate political party. The killings brought down the wrath of the UN, the Israeli government and all other Jewish groups not sympathetic with Sternists on a handful of Jewish fanatics in the Holy Land.

The Stern Group (or gang; formal name: Fighters for the Freedom of Israel) was a fiercely anti-British, well-organized group said to number about 1,000 persons, committed to violence against any opponent of the group's concept of a Jewish state embracing all Palestine and Transjordan. Jewish members were generally of east European, Yemenite and Oriental origin, most of them local leaders, teachers or professionals. The group also had a small Arab wing led by Sheikh Yushef Abu Gosh, 28, a Palestinian. Abraham Stern had founded the group in 1940 when he broke with the Irgun Zvai Leumi because the Irgun gave advance warning of attacks on Britons and Arabs. Stern was killed in 1942; the latest leader of record was Nathan Friedman Yellin, a Polish-born engineer. Sternists had killed Lord Moyne (British resident minister in the Middle East) near Cairo in 1940. The group, with a long record of violent acts—including fund-raising robberies—before and since Israel's establishment, operated secretly in most of Israel but openly in Jerusalem, where Israel's power was limited. The group had hinted that it would kill Israeli leaders if the Jewish state tried to wipe it out. U.S. affiliate: the American Friends of Fighters for Freedom in Israel.

Bernadotte Report

Count Bernadotte's 35,000-word report to the UN General Assembly had been completed Sept. 16, 1948 on Rhodes (the day before he was slain in Jerusalem). The report was based on 2 premises: (1) "Peace must be restored in Palestine by any means possible." (The UN should declare a peace and enforce its terms if Arabs and Jews could not reach an agreement.) (2) "A Jewish state called Israel exists in Palestine, and there are no sound reasons for assuming that it will not continue to do so"; the Arab states were incapable of destroying Israel by force. (On the other hand, there should be guarantees that Israel would not try to annex Arab territory.)

Bernadotte's recommendations for peace terms:

● Recognize Israel and admit it to the UN.

● Rearrange Israel's boundaries by giving Western Galilee (northwestern Palestine) to the Jewish state and the southern Negev desert area to the Arabs. This change in the original partition map was held necessary because it was considered impossible to effect an economic union between Israel and Arab Palestine.

● Bernadotte expressed the opinion—not an outright recommendation—that Arab Palestine should be merged with Transjordan in view of the "historical connection and common interests" of Transjordan and Palestine.

● Make Haifa harbor (Israeli), including the Haifa oil plants, and Lydda airport (Arab) free ports.

● Internationalize Jerusalem under UN control.

• Let Holy Land refugees return home, or compensate them for their dislocation. Meanwhile expand the "inadequate" provisions to care for refugees, especially 300,000 Arabs. (The U.S. ordered its Greek Aid Mission Sept. 22 to send food and DDT to Middle Eastern refugees with voluntary cash contributions raised in the U.S. to replenish the supplies in Greece.)

In the first 7 weeks of the current truce, Bernadotte reported, there had been 288 complaints of violations (183 against Jews, 105 against Arabs), as against 500 during the preceding 4-week truce. The halt to general warfare had provided a "cooling-off period" and had brought about "more moderate and sober counsel in at least some important [Arab and Jewish] quarters."

U.S. State Secy. George C. Marshall announced as the General Assembly convened in Paris Sept. 21 that the U.S. would support the late Bernadotte's "generally fair" plan for the Holy Land. Foreign Secy. Ernest Bevin told the House of Commons Sept. 22 that the plan would receive Britain's "wholehearted and unqualified support"; this was a departure from Britain's previous stand against any Holy Land settlement not mutually agreeable to Arabs and Jews.

Arab League and Egyptian leaders and the exiled grand mufti of Jerusalem said Sept. 21, however, that Bernadotte's plan would be rejected by the Arabs because they opposed the partitioning of Palestine. On the other hand, an Israeli statement in Paris Sept. 22 signified willingness to discuss the Bernadotte proposals but raised 2 main objections: (1) surrender of the Negev would reduce Israel's size by 2/3 and deprive it of "the only available land reserve which offers the prospects of large-scale development"; (2) Jerusalem's 90,000 Jews must have "direct contact with Israel."

Soviet Amb.-to-UN Andrei Y. Vishinsky, addressing the Assembly Sept. 25, was noncommittal on the Bernadotte report. He confined himself to a complaint against the "wrecking" of the Nov. 1947 partition plan and held the U.S. largely responsible.

The International Children's Emergency Fund Oct. 19 voted $6 million for aid to Palestine refugees, and the U.S. and Britain proposed to the UN General Assembly's Social Committee that UN members raise $30 million for the relief of 500,000 Arab refugees in the Middle East.

U.S. Presidential Election

In the U.S., foreign policy with regard to Palestine became a heated campaign issue in the 1948 Presidential election, which Pres. Harry S. Truman won Nov. 2. Truman capitalized on timely information to avert a controversy sure to embarrass his Administration in the closing days of the campaign. *These were the events involved:*

• At an emergency session held in Paris at Egypt's request to consider alleged Jewish aggression, the UN Security Council was told by Israeli spokesman Aubrey (later Abba) S. Eban Oct. 26 that Israel would defy mediator Ralph J. Bunche's directive of Oct. 25 that all Israeli gains in the Negev since Oct. 14 be given up. Israel proposed next day that it negotiate with Egypt on new frontiers between Israeli and Egyptian forces, and Israeli Premier David Ben-Gurion added an appeal Oct. 28 for a separate, permanent peace between Israel and Egypt.

• By Oct. 28, however, Britain and China had won the announced support of France, Belgium and Canada and the implied support of the U.S.' Warren R. Austin for a resolution to create a committee (the Big 5, Belgium and Canada) to determine whether sanctions should be invoked against Israel. The USSR opposed sanctions and won a one-day delay on voting.

• In the Security Council, reportedly on Truman's direct orders, the American delegation reversed itself Oct. 29 on supporting a British-Chinese move for sanctions against Israel if the Jews did not give up gains they had won in the Negev during a truce breakdown earlier in October. The President, campaigning in New York, was said to have dispatched the order as soon as he heard what was afoot in Paris.

• Truman's message arrived in Paris while the Council was meeting Oct. 29 to vote on the threat-of-sanctions measure. Austin, presiding, stalled by resorting to consecutive translation until the Truman communication was clarified. Then, on Canada's motion, a subcommittee composed of Britain, China, Belgium, France and the Ukraine was set up to "study" the resolution. This postponed the issue until after the U.S. elections.

Earlier, Truman had made 2 statements reaffirming his adherence to the Democratic platform plan on Israel (full recognition of the Jewish state and no change in the Israeli boundaries defined by the Nov. 1947 UN partition plan unless Israel agreed to the changes). He also was reported Oct. 25 to have ordered the Export-Import Bank to resume negotiations for a $100 million loan to Israel. (Drew Pearson, a Washington columnist, said Oct. 24 that 2 Republican directors of the bank, William McC. Martin and Lynn Stambough, had been blocking the loan to keep Truman from getting preelection credit for it.) Truman's first statement on Israel that week was issued from Washington Oct. 24. It called the Bernadotte plan merely "a basis for" new negotiations. It also chided Gov. Thomas E. Dewey (R., N.Y.), Truman's principal election opponent, for having made Palestine a campaign issue in the first place. (A GOP reply to the President came Oct. 26 from Sen. Robert A. Taft [R., O.], who said that the statement ambiguously indorsed both the UN partition plan of Nov. 29, 1947 and the Berna-dotte report of Sept. 16, 1948 and was the 5th reversal during Truman's "uncertain and wavering" handling of the Palestine issue.)

Acting State Secy. Robert A. Lovett declined to say Oct. 27 whether there was disagreement on the Israeli question between the President and State Secy. George C. Marshall, who had indorsed the Bernadotte report and its proposed reduction in Israel's territory. But Lovett said that Truman had issued the Oct. 24 statement without prior notification of Marshall.

Truman in New York speeches Oct. 28 again pledged to carry out the Democratic platform promises on Israel. He pleaded with American friends of Israel, however, not to be "emotional" and to understand that U.S. policy toward Israel must be meshed with "our foreign policy throughout the world."

Reports from Paris Oct. 28 said that John Foster Dulles, an American delegate to the UN General Assembly and Gov. Dewey's chief ad-viser on foreign policy, had recommended that Dewey make an imme-diate statement of his views on major issues, for the guidance of the U.S. delegation in the UN, in the event of his election to the Presidency. But Dulles shunned any part in the sanctions-against-Israel confusion.

UN Discusses Palestine Proposals

Dr. Philip C. Jessup, the American delegate to the UN Security Council, gave the council Nov. 20, 1948 this outline of U.S. policy to-wards Palestine:

● The U.S. would oppose any effort to fix the boundaries between the Jewish and Arab states at the current UN General Assembly session. "This raises a vital issue," Jessup said. "We must decide whether we should seek a basis of agreement between the parties or whether we should try to fix boundaries at the session of the Assembly. Our view is that we must continue to seek further agreement between the parties rather than attempt at this time to draw specific boundary lines."
● Jerusalem should receive "special treatment," administratively speaking.
● The Jews should not be asked to abandon any territory to which they were entitled under the original partition scheme of Nov. 1947 without their specific consent. Thus, by implication, the Jews should

retain their gains in the Negev, although the Security Council had recommended an Israeli withdrawal. (The original partition scheme assigned to the Jews almost the whole Negev; this was later withdrawn by
Bernadotte in return for areas that Israel currently occupied in western
Galilee.)
• The U.S. would support Israel's application for immediate admission
to the UN.
• An international guarantee by the entire UN as a whole and not individual states should safeguard the new boundaires and maintain human rights in Arab and Jewish Palestine.
• The U.S. accepted Bernadotte's recommendations on other points,
notably on the right of access to Jerusalem, treatment of Arab refugees
and establishment of a conciliation commission to replace the mediator.

The U.S. envisaged a territorial settlement based largely on the original partition proposals of Nov. 1947. On the other hand, the British
recommended a settlement along the lines of the Bernadotte report.
Jessup supported the Bernadotte recommendations and said the British
proposals contained "many positive and constructive elements," but he
indicated that the U.S. could not fully support them. (The British
Nov. 30 adopted the view that the Arab-Israeli borders should be re-
drawn on a basis of "reciprocity" between Arabs and Jews.)

Simeon Tsarapkin of the Soviet Union held Nov. 22 that the partition resolution of 1947 constituted the only solution for a settlement,
and he said the USSR would continue to give it full support. He
attacked the Bernadotte proposals as tending to "plant discord between
the Jews and Arabs and among the Arabs themselves" and as "obedi-
ently following the instructions to British generals." Tsarapkin strongly
criticized the Bernadotte plan to exchange the Negev for Western Galilee, saying that the Jews were being called on to surrender $2/3$ of the
territory of Israel.

Ralphe Bunche of the UN Nov. 23 listed 7 steps to guide the
General Assembly in its quest of a solution: (1) The affirmation of the
existence of the State of Israel and its admission to UN membership.
(2) A strong appeal to Arabs and Jews to resolve their differences
through direct or indirect negotiations. (3) A conciliation commission
to assist both sides. (4) Clear UN guidance to this commission. (5) An
ironclad international guarantee for the boundaries, adjustable only by
mutual consent. (6) The affirmation of the right of Arab refugees to
return or to receive compensation. (7) Jerusalem to receive a special
international status under UN supervision, with Jewish and Arab communities in the city to enjoy local autonomy.

Negev's Status Delays Armistice

Dispute over the territory Israel had won in the Negev delayed a cease-fire until Jan. 7, 1949.

Israeli Premier David Ben-Gurion had confirmed Nov. 12, 1948 that "there are talks going on" between Israel and "2 Arab governments"—presumably Egypt and Transjordan—on a Jewish-Arab settlement in Palestine. Ben-Gurion declared that Israel was flatly opposed to a new UN proposal whereby Israeli troops would give up their gains in the Negev desert. But he predicted that the Holy Land dispute could be settled "in 4 weeks" if, as he asserted, the U.S. would stop the British from interfering with the Arabs' inclination to talk peace.

According to Tel Aviv reports Nov. 13, Pres. Truman had been won over to the Israeli program of peace by direct negotiation. Truman was said to have informed London that the U.S. would support Arab-Jewish negotiations regardless of how Britain felt about them and would advocate (1) full recognition of Israel and (2) UN responsibility for the relief of 500,000 Arab refugees in the Middle East.

The UN Security Council made a new attempt Nov. 13 to get Israel to give up the Negev territory won from Egypt since Oct. 14. The plan, devised earlier by acting UN mediator Ralph J. Bunche: (1) Israel would withdraw to its Oct. 14 lines; (2) Egypt would stay approximately where it had been forced to retreat to in the Negev fighting. This would demilitarize a large part of the Negev pending further UN efforts to negotiate peace. Beersheba would be placed under the administration of native Arab civilians. Israeli spokesmen had rejected this plan Nov. 12, but it was indorsed 6-0 (the USSR abstaining), by the Council's special committee on the Negev Nov. 13. The committee held that the plan conformed with the Council's Nov. 4 resolution on the Negev situation. Bunche then ordered Israel and Egypt to carry out the new plan. But Israel said Nov. 13 that it would soon begin full-scale colonization of the Negev and make Beersheba the center of the project.

The Security Council Nov. 16 approved by 8-1 vote (Syria opposed and the USSR and Ukraine abstaining) a Canadian resolution, drawn up in agreement with France and Belgium, calling on Jews and Arabs to negotiate for a permanent armistice to replace the truce. Israel Nov. 18 offered the following compromise: Israel would immediately withdraw all troops sent to the Negev since Oct. 14; Israeli troops that had been in the Negev before Oct. 14 would stay there to keep the entire area from falling back into Egyptian hands; Israel was ready to begin armistice negotiations as soon as it was told where and when to meet the Arabs.

Bunche ruled Nov. 19 that the Israeli reply had satisfied, in principle, his order for a Jewish withdrawal to Oct. 14 positions in the desert. Egypt also agreed to establish liaison with Israel through the UN truce mission. As a result, the first preliminary armistice talks were held Nov. 20. Brig. Gen. William E. Riley, chief UN truce observer, met in Tel Aviv with Israeli Foreign Office officials and in Gaza with Egyptian Commander Fouad Sadek Bey.

Despite the uneasy stillness in the Negev, Bunche Dec. 8 informed a special Security Council committee in Paris that he could not persuade the Israelis and Egyptians to comply with the Council's resolutions of Nov. 4 (ordering Jews and Egyptians to withdraw to the positions they had occupied in the Negev before the breakdown of the truce) and Nov. 16 (which called for immediate armistice negotiations). The Israeli government insisted that any military measures taken in the Negev should be considered in the framework of general armistice negotiations. The Egyptian government accepted armistice negotiations "in principle" but argued that the Nov. 4 resolution should be put into operation first.

The Security Council in Paris Dec. 29 adopted, 8-0, with 3 abstentions (the U.S., the Soviet Union and the Ukraine), a British resolution calling for an immediate cease-fire and for the implementation of the Council's Nov. 4 truce resolution. The Soviet and Ukrainian representatives voted for that part of the resolution dealing with the cease-fire, while the U.S.' Dr. Philip C. Jessup abstained from voting on any part of the resolution.

The cease-fire was agreed to by the Egyptian and Israeli governments Jan. 3 and Jan. 6, 1949 respectively. It became effective at 2 p.m. Jan. 7. Ralph Bunche told the Security Council Jan. 7 that the cease-fire had taken full effect. He announced that both Egypt and Israel had agreed to open negotiations in Rhodes within a few days toward signing an armistice and implementing the Nov. 4 and Nov. 16 resolutions.

ISRAEL AFTER INDEPENDENCE (1949–50)

Israel & the U.S.

Pres. Truman Jan. 31, 1949 announced the U.S.' *de jure* recognition of Israel and Transjordan. The disclosures were made in 2 statements issued from the White House.

The first statement: "On Oct. 24, 1948, the President stated that when a permanent government was elected in Israel it would promptly be given *de jure* recognition. Elections for such a government were held on Jan. 25. The votes have been counted, and this government has been officially informed of the results. The U.S. government is, therefore, pleased to extend *de jure* recognition to Israel as of this date."

The 2d statement: "For some time informal and friendly relations have existed between the U.S. government and the kingdom of Transjordan. Consistently with its feeling of friendship for Transjordan, the U.S. government has supported that country for membership in the United Nations. Today the U.S. government has extended *de jure* recognition to Transjordan."

The Export-Import Bank in Washington Jan. 19 had authorized a $35 million credit to Israel to be used in developing the Jewish state's agricultural production. The bank also announced that $65 million more had been earmarked for Israel in 1949, rounding out a $100 million credit.

In New York Jan. 23, ex-U.S. Treasury Secy. Henry Morgenthau Jr. was elected chairman and Henry Montor vice president of the Palestine Economic Corp., formed to promote U.S. investments in Israel. The Israel Corp. of America, formed in New York in partnership with the Jewish Agency for Palestine, had been authorized Nov. 10, 1948 by the Securities & Exchange Commission (SEC) to issue stock.

In Jerusalem, modern Israel's provisional government gave way Feb. 14, 1949 to its first elected legislature, the Knesset Hagdola. Dr. Chaim Weizmann became Israel's first regular president, and an interim constitution was adopted. The U.S., Britain, France and Turkey disapproved of the Jewish Agency Building in Jerusalem as the site of the ceremonies Feb. 14–17 and refused to send diplomatic observers. Their objections were based on the fact that the UN had decided to make Jerusalem an international city.

Israeli Premier David Ben-Gurion Mar. 8 outlined a policy that called for friendship with the U.S., the Soviet Union and all other "peace-loving" nations for neutrality in the East-West cold war. Israel would try to form an alliance with Arab states, but it must not be "directed against any [UN] members" he said. His proposals were submitted to the Knesset in Tel Aviv. Ben-Gurion Mar. 3 had rejected the pro-Soviet Mapam party's demand that he renounce in advance any Mediterranean defense alliance or U.S. aid similar to the Marshall Plan.

Ben-Gurion warned foreign Zionists Nov. 6 that they could not influence Israeli policy through control of Zionist funds or organizations. He spoke at a Tel Aviv convention of the Palestine Foundation Fund, the World Zionist financial agency. (Finance Min. Eliezer Kaplan said at the same meeting that Israel's "war of independence" had cost Israel $300 million, 75% of which had been covered locally.) Ben-Gurion told the Knesset Nov. 8 that Israel had approached the USSR as well as Western countries for financial aid in line with its policy of "peace between East and West." He had said in a speech Oct. 29 that Israel's deficit was increasing by $19.6 million a month and could be offset only by attracting foreign investments, expected to total $240 million in 1949.

Immigration Problems

Harry Greenstein of Baltimore, retiring U.S. adviser on Jewish Affairs in Germany, said in a report released Oct. 25, 1949 that Israel expected about 150,000 more immigrants in 1950. Greenstein's judgement was based on an extensive tour of Israel. Greenstein reported that Israel "was determined to keep the doors open to every Jew in need of a home despite the difficulties of resettling DPs." But the U.S. consulate in Haifa Oct. 6 had reported a backlog of 15,000 persons seeking to leave Israel and emigrate to the U.S. (In Washington Apr. 25, Israeli Pres. Chaim Weizmann had lunched with Pres. Truman and had said that Israel would welcome back Palestinian Arab refugees then in nearby Arab lands if they returned without aggressive intentions.)

The Jewish Agency disclosed Nov. 5, 1949 that the USSR had ignored an Israeli request, through trade union channels, that bans on the emigration of east European Jews be lifted. The agency reported Nov. 10 that in all some 1,800,000 Jews in the Soviet Union and 600,000 in Rumania and Hungary were being prevented from going to Israel. (The American Jewish League Against Communism, Inc. had charged July 24 that the Soviet Union had deported 400,000 Ukrainian and White Russian Jews to forced labor camps in Archangel and Siberia. The league wrote the UN that the deportations were a move to clear the Soviet frontier of pro-Westerners in the event of war.)

At the United Jewish Appeal meeting in Chicago June 8–11, 1950 it was reported that $53,762,000, raised since Jan. 1 in the U.S. as of that date, would be used to aid Israeli immigrants. A long dispute among American Jewish groups over the use of United Jewish Appeal funds had led to the resignations in New York Feb. 16, 1949 of Rabbi Abba Hillel Silver, president of the American section of the Jewish Agency Executive, and of Dr. Emanuel Neumann, president of the Zionist Organization of America. (Silver and Neumann had been upheld Feb. 13 by a national conference of ZOA leaders. They survived attacks on their policies by a new Committee for Progressive Zionism led by Charles J. Rosenbloom of Pittsburgh and including Dr. Stephen S. Wise.) The controversy had first arisen in 1948. It centered on whether the Zionist organization should have a say about Israel's use of UJA funds spent in Palestine. (UJA included the United Palestine Appeal, Joint Distribution Committee to aid Jewish emigrants and displaced persons in Europe and North Africa, and the United Service for New Americans. Their total budget requests in 1949 exceeded $370 million.)

Ben-Gurion appealed in a speech May 23, 1950 for Russia to let its Jews move to Israel. He said the Jews were the only people in the USSR not given national freedom. Russia's estimated Jewish population was 3 million and was the greatest in any country except the U.S. (Rumania's Communist newspaper *Scanteia* charged May 30 that Israel had launched a "campaign of hatred" against Soviet-bloc countries inspired by "American spy [Henry] Morgenthau.")

Mideast Arms Race

Progress toward an Arab-Israeli armistice ran uneasily along with an arms buildup by both sides. The British were the Arab countries' main suppliers. Israel's chief source was Czechoslovakia, the latest member of the Soviet bloc.

U.S. State Secy. Dean G. Acheson Jan. 15, 1950 defended British arms shipments to Iraq, Jordan and Egypt. Acheson said that the West must have the friendship of the Middle Eastern states and see that they got enough arms for "legitimate security requirements." He also said that "there was no cause for alarm" over the possibility that the Arabs might renew their war with Israel. These statements were made in a letter from Acheson to Rep. Jacob J. Javits (R., N.Y.).

A Czechoslovak-Israeli trade pact to run one year was signed and approved by both countries Mar. 20, 1950. The pact called for Israel to buy $9 million worth of manufactured goods and food. The Czechoslovaks would buy $3 million worth of citrus and chemical products.

Much of the manufactures Israel purchased was thought to be arms. A spokesman of the British Foreign Office had declared Jan. 5,

1949 that substantial quantities of war materiel had reached Israel from Czechoslovakia since the initial UN truce had begun June 11, 1948. The Israeli Air Force at that time had consisted of about 40 planes but had since grown to 114 aircraft, including 40 fighters and 22 bombers. These aircraft had been obtained partly through private sources in various countries, but the fighters had almost all come from the state-owned Czechoslovak armaments industry (Skoda Enterprise) and had carried Czechoslovak cannon and machine guns. Other war materiel from Czechoslovakia included high explosive and incendiary bombs, airplane engines, parts, radio equipment and automatic weapons. Skoda technicians had been sent to Israel to convert civilian aircraft.

The British spokesman had also reported that the Czechoslovak air force base at Zatec, 34 miles northwest of Prague, had become the chief distribution center for this materiel and that a small fleet of Curtiss Commandos, C-475 and other transport planes had regularly flown about 80 tons of Czechoslovak arms a week to the Jewish forces in Israel. The air route lay down the Albanian and Greek coasts, with refueling stops in Yugoslavia, and across the Mediterranean to Israel by way of the south coast of Crete. The air crews hired consisted of "experienced airmen of foreign nationality, recruited as mercenaries and highly paid," the spokesman added. (Many of these airmen were Americans.)

Tripartite Declaration

The U.S. embargo on the shipment of arms to Israel was lifted under a new Western Big 3 agreement on a unified policy toward Israel and its Arab rivals. The agreement was announced in a Tripartite Declaration made May 25, 1950 by the U.S. Britain and France.

Revealing a decision taken when their foreign ministers had met in London the previous week, the 3 nations said Israel as well as the Arabs could buy arms from the West if it promised that there will be no renewal of the Palestine war.

Pres. Truman declared that the agreement should "promote the maintenance of peace in the Near East," and the State Department predicted an end to armaments races between Israel and the Arabs once both sides were assured of adequate arms for defense. A British spokesman added that the new policy was set to help the Middle Eastern states arm themselves against Communist penetration. Israel had recently complained about its inability to get American weapons. It charged that Britain's sale of arms to Arab states was letting the Arabs prepare for a new attack on the Jewish state.

The Tripartite Declaration said:

... (1) The 3 governments [the U.S., Britain and France] recognize that the Arab states and Israel all need to maintain a certain level of armed forces for the purposes of assuring their internal security and their legitimate selfdefense, and to permit them to play their part in the defense of the area as a whole. All applications for arms or war materiel for these countries will be considered in the light of these principles. In this connection the 3 governments reaffirm the statements made by their representatives in the [UN] Security Council on Aug. 4, 1949, in which they declared their opposition to the development of an arms race between the Arab states and Israel.

(2) The 3 governments declare that assurances have been received from all the states in question to which they permit arms to be supplied from their countries that the purchasing state does not intend to undertake any act of aggression against any other state. Similar assurances will be requested from any other states in the area to which they permit arms to be supplied in the future.

(3) The 3 governments take this opportunity of declaring their deep interest in, and their desire to promote the establishment and maintenance of, peace and stability in the area, and their unalterable opposition to the use of force or threat of force between any of the states in that area. The 3 governments, should they find that any of these states was preparing to violate frontiers or armistice lines, would, consistently with their obligations as members of the UN, immediately take action, both within and outside the UN, to prevent such violation.

A British Foreign Office spokesman said in London May 25 that both Britain and the U.S. had received similar assurances from Israel that Israel would not commit aggression on its Arab neighbors. The spokesman said that Britain had also received assurances of nonaggression from Egypt, Jordan, Iraq and Saudi Arabia, that France had received such assurances from Syria and Lebanon and that the U.S. had received this assurance from Egypt. State Secy. Dean G. Acheson, Foreign Secy. Ernest Bevin and Foreign Min. Robert Schumann May 13 had declared that "the strength of the free world will never be used for aggressive purposes."

U.S.-Israeli Amity

Signs of increased amity between Washington and Tel Aviv multiplied after the Tripartite Declaration of May 25, 1950. U.S. Vice Pres. Alben W. Barkley said at the United Jewish Appeal's 1950 annual meeting in Chicago June 10 that Israel "is an oasis of democracy in a backward area of the world. Barkley also addressed a Jewish National Fund dinner in Boston June 11, when plans were announced for the establishment near Lydda, Israel of Kfar Truman (Truman Village). The village was established Sept. 4 near Lydda Airport. It was then inhabited by 80 immigrant families from Poland, Rumania and Hungary.

The U.S. and Israel June 13 signed a commercial air agreement under which Trans-World Airlines and Israel's state-owned El Al National Airlines would operate services between New York and Lydda.

50 U.S. Jewish leaders in business and social life met in Jerusalem Sept. 4–6 with Israeli officials and promised to provide $1 billion worth of private American Jewish financing for a 3-year development and immigration program. Israeli sources agreed to supply another $500 million for the program. This decision was confirmed by 1,200 delegates of 44 U.S. Jewish organizations at a meeting of the National Planning Conference for Israel & Jewish Rehabilitation in Washington Oct. 26. Israel will put up another $500 million.

The U.S. Export-Import Bank announced Dec. 26 that it had granted Israel a new loan of $35 million at 3½% interest, repayable over 15 years. The loan enabled Israel to buy equipment, materials and services in the U.S. for agricultural development and irrigation projects, and it also underwrote the promotion of citriculture in Israel. The credit came after earlier loans totaling $100 million made to Israel by the Export-Import Bank over the previous 2 years.

The U.S. attitude on a UN plan for internationalizing Jerusalem appeared to be unclear. Israeli Foreign Min. Moshe Sharett assured the Knesset Jan. 2, 1950 that the U.S. supported Israel's basic contention that modern Jerusalem should be an Israeli city. The Knesset Jan. 23 approved a measure proclaiming Jerusalem as the capital of Israel, and Israel May 28 formally rejected the UN's Jerusalem plan. The U.S., however, abstained Apr. 4 when the UN Trusteeship Council, by 9–0 vote, approved an internationalization statute, under which the UN would rule Jerusalem. The USSR, which had been absent, informed UN Secy. Gen. Trygve Lie in an Apr. 17 letter that it no longer supported the UN plan to internationalize Jerusalem because it satisfied neither the Jewish nor the Arab residents of the city.

The Kem Amendment's restrictions on U.S. economic aid to countries that exported U.S. blacklisted goods to the Soviet bloc were waived by the U.S. National Security Council (NSC) Sept. 15, 1951 for Israel, Egypt and Iran. The NSC reported Sept. 12 that Saudi Arabia had reported compliance with Kem Amendment restrictions. The Kem Amendment had come into being because of the widespread transshipment of strategic goods to the Soviet bloc during the Korean War. It had been sponsored by Sen. James P. Kem (R., Mo.), the only Senator to vote against Pres. Truman's commitment of U.S. troops to South Korea (because the President had not consulted Congress beforehand).

Russia & the Arabs

Some Arabs began to warn that U.S. friendship for Israel might drive Arab states into the Soviet camp.

Arab League Secy. Abdul Rahman Azzam Pasha said in Cairo Apr. 22, 1950 that the Arab countries were ready to "extend the hand to Russia" because the U.S. was "pro-Jewish." He indorsed a proposal by Syrian National Economy Min. Marouf Fawalibi that the Arab League negotiate a nonaggression pact with the Soviet Union.

Lebanese delegate Charles Malik warned the UN in a review of Middle Eastern affairs May 10 that communism was gaining in Arab countries and they might be the targets of the Reds' "next major drive."

EGYPT'S STRUGGLE FOR SOVEREIGNTY
(OCT. 1951 – FEB. 1953)

The conclusion of armistice agreements between Israel and the 4 Arab belligerents before midsummer of 1949 left the U.S. and USSR—both of whom had supported the partition of Palestine—free to resume their early post-World War II attempts at influencing Arab-world policy-making. In the early years of the 1950s, these efforts were focused on Egypt and Iran, 2 countries involved in political and economic disputes with Britain, whose once vast influence in the area was waning rapidly.

Egyptian sovereignty (ostensibly a fact since Feb. 28, 1921) was a problem because of Britain's insistence on reserving for itself control over "the security of the communications of the British empire in Egypt"—i.e., the Suez Canal Zone—and denying Cairo's sovereignty over the Sudan.

Crisis Over Suez & Sudan

Egypt Oct. 15, 1951 rejected a 4-power Western offer to join an Allied defense setup for Suez. It also renounced the 1936 Anglo-Egyptian treaty under which British troops were stationed in the Suez Canal Zone and in the Anglo-Egyptian Sudan (a vast area put under "joint sovereignty" in 1898-9, when Britain was paramount from Cairo to Khartoum).

The U.S., Britain, France and Turkey had offered Oct. 13 to join with Egypt in establishing a Middle Eastern defense command. Egypt would have had charge in the Suez zone with British and other Allied troops stationed there. This system would have replaced Britain's 1936 treaty with Egypt. Australia, New Zealand and South Africa would have been invited to join the new Middle Eastern force. Britain also proposed negotiations with Egypt to establish self-government in the Anglo-Egyptian Sudan.

The Egyptian government rejected these offers, and the parliament in Cairo voted unanimously to abrogate the 1936 Anglo-Egyptian treaty, a move designed to force the British to leave both Suez and the Sudan. Britain responded with a show of force. Its troops battled rioting Egyptians Oct. 16 in the Canal Zone cities of Ismailia and Port Said, and 12 persons were reported killed. British troops also killed 2 Egyptian soldiers in seizing the Ferdan Bridge across the canal. Quiet was restored in the zone Oct. 17 after Egypt sent in several hundred police.

Britain rushed 3,500 paratroops from Cyprus to Suez Oct. 17–18 to bring its Canal Zone garrison up to 60,000 men. It also announced Oct. 18 that 1,000 more infantrymen would be sent to Sudan, where no disorders were reported. Gen. Sir Brian Robertson, British land forces commander in the Middle East, declared Oct. 18 that the British would "maintain our position" in the Egyptian area. He compared the situation with the Berlin blockade of 1948-9, during which he had been British commander in Germany.

In the view of many Western observers, Egypt's real motive for precipitating the crisis was to be found in the contention that Egyptian Premier Mustapha el Nahas Pasha was attempting to divert attention from the incompetence of the Wafdist party by turning to nationalist demands. Earlier in October, 2 Wafdist cabinet ministers had quit in protest against the Nahas government's corruption. Immediately afterwards, Nahas Oct. 8 unilaterally abrogated the 1936 Anglo-Egyptian treaty and the condominium over the Sudan. Nahas then proclaimed Farouk king of "Egypt and the Sudan."

This provocation of the British was soon followed by a program of guerrilla fighting to harass British units in the Suez Canal Zone. Workers in the canal zone were ordered by the Nahas government to abandon their jobs. The British replied by placing numerous villages under marital law.

U.S. State Secy. Dean G. Acheson Oct. 17 expressed "genuine regret" at Egypt's rejection of the 4-power proposals. "This government has noted with surprise that the Egyptian government rejected proposals of such importance without having given them the careful and considered deliberation which they merited," Acheson declared at a press conference in Washington. "These proposals were formulated by the nations interested in the welfare and security of the Middle East, after the most intensive and thorough consideration of the special problems of the area. The invitation to join with the other sovereign nations of the free world in a joint and cooperative effort to make the world safe from aggression was wholly consistent with the independence and sovereignty of Egypt ... It is the hope of the U.S. government that Egypt will carefully reconsider the course of action on which it has embarked, and will recognize that its own interest will be served by joining the other nations of the free world in assuring the defense of the Middle East against a common danger. The U.S. government reaffirms its belief that the action of the Egyptian government with respect to the Anglo-Egyptian treaty of 1936, and the agreements of 1899 regarding the Sudan, is not in accord with proper respect for international obligations. It considers the action of the Egyptian government to be without validity."

But Cairo disregarded the warning and plunged ahead.

The British immediately tightened their control of the canal zone and the Sudan and retaliated against Egypt for trying to oust British forces from both areas. Egyptians staged anti-British, pro-Russian demonstrations.

The British held up all shipments of military equipment to Egypt Oct. 22 and took control that day of the city of Suez at the southern end of the canal zone. They also halted the shipment of goods from the canal zone to Egypt Oct. 23 because Egypt had failed to supply more railroad equipment to the reinforced British Suez garrison. (The request for the equipment was made under the 1936 Anglo-Egyptian treaty.) When Egyptian officials tried Oct. 24 to withhold permits for British ships to enter the canal, the British Navy overrode them.

An Egyptian note to Britain Oct. 21 had protested that British troops in Suez acted as though they were patrolling a "conquered country." Rumors were circulated Oct. 21 that Premier Nahas' cabinet was discussing a possible Egyptian pact with the Soviet Union. Nahas called Britain "the enemy" Oct. 22 and said: "We are about to bring him to a severe accounting."

A pro-Soviet, anti-British demonstration was conducted outside the Soviet legation in Cairo by 3,000 Egyptians Oct. 23 when a half-day holiday was taken in Cairo and Alexandria in protest against the shooting of several Egyptians in the canal zone Oct. 16. There were more minor disorders in the canal zone the next week, and Britain Oct. 22 announced plans to send 3,000 more troops. 4,000 reinforcements had been sent previously.

In Khartoum, capital of the Anglo-Egyptian Sudan, British Gov. Gen. Sir Robert G. Howe had barred 2 Egyptian military and education officials from returning to the territory Oct. 19 after a trip to Cairo. He said that their return might endanger "public order." The constituent commission, which included representatives of all Sudanese parties except the anti-British, pro-Egyptian Ashigga, drafted a message to the UN Oct. 22 asking that an international commission be sent to Sudan pending the establishment of self-rule. The message was held up by Howe until the commission would say it did not want a UN commission to replace the governor general.

The Egyptian government Nov. 3 ordered all Egyptians employed by the British Army in the Suez Canal Zone to quit their jobs by Nov. 30 or face charges of "high treason." Social Affairs Min. Abdel Fatta Hassan Pasha said that more than 40,000 or 45,000 Egyptians already had quit the British payroll there, 21,600 had left the canal zone and 17,000 received new jobs in Egypt. Egypt protested to the UN's International Labor Organization Nov. 4 that Britain was forcing some Egyptians to work in the canal area, thereby violating basic human rights.

The British flew 4,000 troops to Suez from Libya Nov. 2, sent 1,000 British women and children home to Britain from Port Said by ship Nov. 3, seized the Suez custom house from Egyptians Nov. 4 and conducted a weeklong search for weapons hidden by potential guerrillas in canal zone towns.

The crisis over Suez eventually led to serious violence. Clashes between British forces and Egyptian civilians and police in and near the city of Suez took 65 lives and injured many other persons Dec. 3–4, 1951, according to the Egyptian Interior Ministry. British estimates of the death toll were slightly lower. The gunfights broke out after a 6-week strike against the British by Egyptian dock workers in the canal zone had been called off Dec. 2. The British said that Egyptian attacks on their gasoline trucks had touched off the fighting. Egypt estimated that 28 Egyptians and 22 British were killed Dec. 3. Egypt was placed in a state of emergency Dec. 4 after anti-British demonstrations in Cairo and Alexandria in which 19 persons were hurt. All public demonstrations were banned in Egypt Dec. 6.

Returns from a series of student elections under way at colleges in Egypt had shown Nov. 30 that followers of the Moslem Brotherhood, described as a fanatical Islamic organization, were winning. The Brotherhood, outlawed as a terrorist force in 1948, was legalized in 1951 as a "religious and cultural organization."

Gen. Sir Brian Robertson, British Middle East land forces commander, met with Prime Min. Winston Churchill in London Dec. 27. Gen. Robertson said in Fayid (Suez Canal Zone) Dec. 31: "It would be a great mistake for anyone to imagine that pressure and terrorism" will force the British out of Suez.

Cairo made moves in mid-Nov. 1951 to establish an Egyptian hegemony over the Sudan. First, the throne extended its dominion explicitly to include the Sudan. Next, it was proposed that the Sudan be neutralized and allowed to decide on its own fate.

Egypt proposed Nov. 16 that the British withdraw at least temporarily from the Anglo-Egyptian Sudan until the Sudanese decided through a UN-supervised election what their political future would be. The British-controlled Sudanese government in Khartoum dismissed Egypt's proposal Nov. 19 as "completely impractical." British Foreign Secy. Anthony Eden told the British House of Commons in London Nov. 15 that he hoped that the Sudan could achieve "a constitution providing for self-government . . . in operation by the end of 1952," after which the Sudanese might decide whether they wanted a union with Egypt. Meanwhile, Eden said, Britain would "insure the defense and security of the Sudan" and help it prepare for self-government. The U.S. said Nov. 16 that it recognized Farouk I as king of Egypt only. Egypt had notified other countries Nov. 15 that Farouk had taken the title of king of Egypt and the Sudan. Iran under Mohammed Mossadeq recognized Farouk's Sudanese title Dec. 10. Indonesia's recognition of Farouk as king of both "Egypt and the Sudan" was announced Dec. 31.

Mideast Defense Plan

Plans for a Middle Eastern defense system involving the U.S., Britain, France, Turkey, Australia, New Zealand and South Africa would be pushed despite Egypt's refusal to join, the U.S. State Department insisted Oct. 24, 1951. State Secy. Acheson had commented Oct. 21 that Middle Eastern developments must not "jeopardize the security of all the rest of us." On Egypt's renunciation of its British treaty, Acheson took the position that Egypt "can't throw its international obligations overboard."

The Suez-Sudan crisis forced the 4 Western powers most concerned with keeping Soviet influence at a minimum in the Middle East to revise their original areawide defense plan. Their new effort, more generalized in aim and broader in outline, was the principal forerunner of the 1955 Baghdad Pact.

The "principles" of their plan to organize a Middle East defense command were outlined by the U.S., Britain, France and Turkey Nov. 10 in notes to Egypt and the other Arab states and to Israel. They said that the organization would be international in character, concerned with "defense of the Middle Eastern area as a whole" against "outside aggression," and would not further the national interests of any "particular state" or "interfere in problems and disputes arising within the area." Hence it could include regional enemies (Arabs and Israel, Britain and Egypt). The proposed Middle East Command would be devoted at first to "planning and providing the Middle East states, on their request, with assistance in the form of advice and training." Member countries would not have to furnish forces to the Allied "Supreme Army Commander, Middle East" unless they wanted to. The provision of bases would be by special agreements.

Egypt, which said Nov. 8 it would take part in a Near Eastern defense organization limited to Arab states, was unable to line up solid

Arab League support for its policy in Paris talks Nov. 10–12 among Arab UN delegations. (Egypt's main backer was Saudi Arabia.) Syrian Premier Hasan al-Hakim and his cabinet resigned Nov. 10 in disagreement over the Western plan, which Hakim favored but Foreign Min. Faydi el-Atassi opposed. (Communists had clashed with police in Damascus Nov. 7 during Red demonstrations on the 34th anniversary of the Bolshevik revolution in Russia.)

At this point, the Hashemite kingdom of Iraq, the mideastern country considered by some as on the friendliest terms with Britain, came forward with an offer of advice. Iraq's Regent Emir Abdul Illah and Premier Nuri es-Said Pasha submitted to British Foreign Secy. Eden in London Nov. 17 a new plan to solve the Suez-Sudan dispute and set up a Middle Eastern defense organization linked with the West. They were said to have proposed: the evacuation of the British from Suez; a Sudan plebiscite; the creation of an Arab League defense force to be armed by the West; and an Arab alliance with the West that would be sent to Arab countries. The plan found little favor in Britain, where it was held that Arab countries were too weak to defend the Middle East without outside forces to bolster them. (Iraq had announced Oct. 11 that it had asked Britain to negotiate changes in the 1930 treaty [effective until 1955] under which Britain maintained air bases at Habbaniya and Shaiba in Iraq and guarded the bases with British troops.)

The British government said in a White Paper dated Nov. 29 that Egypt had not given the plan for a Middle East Defense Command due consideration before rejecting it. As a result, Egypt risked 2 invasions, as British Amb.-to-Egypt Sir Ralph Stevenson had said: one by the (Communist) aggressor and a 2d by Western liberation forces. The government also asserted that, in reply to Egyptian Foreign Min. Mohammed Salah ed-Din Bey's arguments in July, the British ambassador had told him that the Sudanese wanted genuine self-government, not Egyptian control. It also noted, however, that Amb. Stevenson had doubted the "practical feasibility" of holding a free plebiscite on the matter, as Din Bey had proposed.

Meanwhile it was learned that King Farouk was leaning toward the Western defense alliance. Farouk apparently had split with the Nahas cabinet over the cabinet's refusal to join the anti-Communist defense alliance sponsored by the West. The king appointed 2 advocates of a Western alliance to high court posts Dec. 25: Hafez Afifi Pasha as chief of his personal royal cabinet and Amb.-to-Britain Abdel Fattah Amir Pasha as his adviser on foreign affairs. Student riots in protest against the king's appointees caused the closing Dec. 26 of Fuad and Mohammed Ali Pasha Universities in Cairo and Farouk University in Alexandria. Nahas' cabinet announced Dec. 26 that the king's choice of personal ministers had no effect on its policies.

Britain then adopted what observers described as a carrot-and-stick policy to precipitate matters. The British government announced Jan. 16, 1952 that it would release only $28 million of Egyptian's blocked wartime sterling balances in London in the year's first quarter, not the $42 million that Cairo had requested.

The British cruiser *Liverpool* fired warning salvos off Port Said Jan. 18, while British troops fought off an Egyptian guerrilla attack on a British camp. An American Roman Catholic nun, Sister Anthony, was killed in Ismailia Jan. 19, possibly by a stray bullet, while Britons and Egyptians fought near her convent in a cemetery where guerrillas had stored ammunition. The British intensified their efforts Jan. 21 to round up Egyptian snipers in Ismailia.

Britain disclosed Jan. 23 that King Ibn Saud of Saudi Arabia, a supporter of Egypt in the Arab League, had offered to mediate the Anglo-Egyptian dispute over Suez and the Sudan. His plan was said to call for an alliance between Arab and U.S.-British-French-Turkish security groups, the arming of the Arab states by Western powers and the policing of Suez by Egyptians and small international forces.

U.S. Congress members had expressed almost unanimous opposition to sending U.S. troops to Suez, as suggested in a speech made by Prime Min. Winston Churchill to Congress Jan. 17. The British government said Jan. 19 that the suggestion was meant to apply only after current Anglo-Egyptian strife subsided. Egypt said Jan. 18 that it would appeal to the UN Security Council if other powers moved troops into Suez in support of the British.

Cairenes Riot, Nahas Removed

Cairo's most destructive riots of the 1951-2 Anglo-Egyptian crisis caused King Farouk to dictate a change in Egyptian cabinets Jan. 27, 1952.

Millions of dollars worth of British, U.S. and French property in Cairo had been destroyed Jan. 26 when Egyptian mobs went on a day-long anti-foreigner rampage of looting and burning. At least 67 persons —mostly Britons (no Americans)—were reported killed, nearly all of them when trapped in buildings set afire by arsonists. Rioters started 150 fires and burned out nearly 500 shops and businesses, among them many of Cairo's most famous establishments.

The rioters were stirred up over a battle Jan. 25 between British troops and Egyptian auxiliary police in the province of Ismailia in which 43 Egyptian auxiliary policemen were reported killed and 58 wounded. The outbreak next day in Cairo began when a crowd gathered outside Premier Nahas' residence and demanded an Egyptian march on Ismailia. Then the demonstrators started to apply the torch to places identified with foreigners.

Among Cairo establishments sacked and burned Jan. 26 were Shepheard's Hotel, a luxurious showplace since 1891, often called the most famous hotel in the world; the British-owned Barclays Bank; the élite Turf Club; several department and clothing stores; many airline, oil and other company offices; other clubs, theaters and restaurants operated by or for Europeans and Americans.

Nahas' government called out the Egyptian army to quell the riots. Farouk, who had conferred with U.S. Amb. Jefferson Caffery during the outbreak, signed a decree placing the entire country under martial law. Nearly all business places in Cairo were shut and the city put under dusk-to-dawn curfew. Troops fired into the air to disperse one mob of 20,000 persons.

Nahas said in a radio speech Jan. 26 that the riots had angered him more than the British Army's killing of Egyptian police in Ismailia. He demanded public order during Egypt's "fight for freedom . . . against the occupant" (Britain). Social Affairs Min. Abdel Fattah Hassan Pasha charged that a "5th column, well organized and serving the British," had fomented the riots. It was too late, however, for Nahas' government to save itself.

Nahas yielded the premiership to Aly Maher Pasha, 68, an Independent ex-premier and personal friend of the king. Maher was variously regarded as a staunch nationalist, an ex-Axis sympathizer (he was interned on British orders during World War II) and an advocate of Anglo-Egyptian cooperation. Wafdists, who had been in power since Jan. 1950 and were often reported at odds with the king over how to deal with the West, agreed to support Maher when he said he would continue to press for British departure from Egypt. He won an overwhelming parliamentary vote of confidence Jan. 28 as the Chamber of Deputies and Senate extended martial law for 2 months.

Kremlin Blames U.S., Denounces Defense Plan

The Soviet press, which had been urging Arab countries to shun the West, denounced the cabinet change in Cairo. The Soviet daily *Izvestia*, the unofficial organ of the government, said Jan. 30, 1952 that the shift had been forced on Farouk by U.S. Amb. Caffery.

Soviet Deputy Foreign Min. Andrei A. Gromyko in Moscow Nov. 21, 1951 had handed to the envoys of Egypt, Iraq, Israel, Lebanon and Syria identic notes outlining the Kremlin's position on the 4-power proposal for a Middle Eastern Defense Command sponsored by the U.S., Britain, France and Turkey. Gromyko gave similar notes Nov. 22 to the envoys of Saudi Arabia and Yemen. *The notes said:*

The projected defense command had nothing in common with the interests of maintaining peace and security in the Middle East, nor with the genuine national interests of the states in this area.... The proposals envisage ... the stationing of foreign armed forces on the territory of Egypt and other countries of the Near and Middle East, the accommodation on the territory of Egypt of the headquarters of this command, and the placing at its disposal by Egypt, as well as by other countries in this area, of armed forces, military bases, communications, ports, and other installations.

The setting up of the so-called Middle East Command would lead to the military occupation of the countries of the Middle East by the countries organizing the Atlantic bloc, first and foremost by the troops of the United States and Britain.... The occupation of countries of the Middle East by foreign troops, and the establishment of foreign military bases on their territories in accordance with the plans for setting up the Middle East Command, cannot but lead to the loss of independence and sovereignty by these countries and their subjugation to certain great powers which are trying to use their territories and material resources for their own aggressive ends. All references to the interests of the defense of the Middle Eastern countries are in reality merely a camouflage to disguise the drawing of these countries into military measures of the Atlantic bloc directed against the Soviet Union and the people's democracies.

The Soviet government also declared that, unlike the "powers ... accustomed to regard the countries of the Middle East as their colonies," it had "regarded with understanding and sympathy the national aspirations of the peoples of the Middle East and their struggle for national independence and sovereignty." The Soviet Union said it had "invariably pursued a path of peace." It called "absurd" any notion on the possibility of a Soviet menace in the area and warned that the acceptance of the Western defense project by any Mideastern country would "cause serious damage to the relations between the USSR and those countries, as well as to the cause of maintaining peace and security in the Middle East."

In notes to the U.S., British, French and Turkish envoys to the Soviet Union Nov. 24, Moscow had termed the defense command project "aggressive" and had warned that the Soviet government would not ignore such plans in an area near her borders.

The U.S. denied Jan. 29, 1952 that it was trying in a "formal sense" to mediate the Anglo-Egyptian dispute. But State Secy. Dean G. Acheson said Jan. 30 the 4-power bid to Egypt on the Mideastern defense was not a take-it-or-leave-it proposition but rather, was open to negotiation.

The Soviet government again warned Egypt June 22 to keep out of the proposed Middle East Command.

Anglo-Egyptian Negotiations

In a proposal for Egyptian-British talks, British Foreign Secy. Anthony Eden told the British House of Commons Jan. 29, 1952 that he hoped Premier Maher would join with Britain in efforts to satisfy Egypt's "legitimate national aspirations" without jeopardizing "the security of the free world."

Maher responded Jan. 30 by calling in a British newsman for an interview "as a gesture of friendship with Britain," telling him that Egypt favored a Middle East defense command within the framework of the UN and would "consider any understanding Mr. Eden might propose." Maher also had talks with U.S., British, French and Turkish envoys in Cairo Jan. 30. He was said to have hinted that Egypt might join the Middle Eastern defense setup planned by those 4 countries if the British would first leave Suez and the Sudan.

Agreeing to the Anglo-Egyptian talks, Maher told Eden Feb. 21 that the meetings would open in Cairo Mar. 1 in a "quick and decisive" effort to settle the Suez-Sudan dispute. He said that Egypt would insist that the British leave Suez and permit the union of Egypt and the Sudan. Maher said in a broadcast to the U.S. Feb. 17 that Egypt was "wholeheartedly" in favor of a "remodeled regional organization" for Middle Eastern defense "within the framework of the UN Charter." He compared Egypt's struggle against Britain with that of the American colonies in 1776.

In a gesture of conciliation, the Egyptian cabinet Feb. 16 had ordered that $14,350,000 be distributed as partial damages for the Jan. 26 Cairo riots. A martial law decree Feb. 30 made it a prison offense for Egyptians to spread false rumors that might cause public disorders.

Just as the Cairo talks were scheduled to begin, the Egyptian premiership changed hands Mar. 1 for the 2d time in 5 weeks. Ahmed Naguib al Hilaili Pasha, 60, a jurist famous in Egypt as a foe of government corruption, was named premier by King Farouk after Aly Maher Pasha resigned. Maher reportedly quit because the king wanted to suspend parliament for at least a month to prevent its Wafdist majority from interfering with Anglo-Egyptian talks and plans for economic and political reforms. The suspension was announced Mar. 2.

The new premier, an Independent like Maher, had quit the Wafd party in 1944 because of graft scandals involving the party. He promised Mar. 2 to proceed with the British talks planned by Maher and to speed up reforms promised by his predecessor. He named a non-partisan cabinet whose chief members were holdovers from Maher's regime. The new government retained martial law (decreed after the Jan. 26 Cairo riots), and the Interior Ministry was empowered Mar. 5 to send agitators home if they were stirring up trouble in cities where they did not normally live.

Talks were opened in Cairo with the British Mar. 22 but collapsed May 20 when Egypt rejected British plans for settling the Sudan and Suez disputes.

Hilaili did not last long as premier. King Farouk announced his resignation June 28, and the king June 29 appointed ex-Premier Hussein Sirry Pasha, 60, an irrigation engineer and political independent, as premier. No reason was given officially for Hilaili's resignation, but reports from Cairo indicated that his failure to win concessions from the British and his determination to hold general elections in October had caused a policy break with Farouk. A member of the outgoing cabinet told the press that Hilaili also complained of U.S. interference in Egypt's domestic affairs. U.S. Amb. Jefferson Caffery denied the charge June 29.

Meanwhile, Farouk was recognized as "king of the Sudan" June 23 by Greece, the 11th nation to back Egyptian claims to the Anglo-Egyptian Sudan.

'Free Officers' Seize Power

For years even before the Arab-Israeli war of 1948, Egypt's Free Officers Society had clandestinely plotted to overthrow Farouk and oust the British from Egypt. By 1950 the young officers were of the opinion that some respected senior commander was required as a facade to inspire public confidence. Ultimately, it was decided that the ideal man as their leader was Gen. Mohammed Naguib.

The Free Officers struck July 23, 1952. There was almost no blood spilled, no resistance, and the takeover of the government was remarkably smooth. Aly Maher returned as premier, King Farouk abdicated July 26—after his infant son was proclaimed Ahmed Fuad II, king of Egypt and the Sudan. Titles of the Egyptian nobility (pashaliks and beyliks) were abolished July 30, and a program of radical land reforms soon followed.

The nationalist Wafd party came out in support of Naguib July 28, and he was also supported by the extremist Moslem Brotherhood, the Sudanese Independence Movement and the Arab League.

George Weller of the *Chicago Daily News* foreign staff reported that when the military junta deposed Farouk, the representatives of the U.S. Central Intelligence Agency (CIA) immediately went into action. The CIA's operatives, like many other people, knew that Naguib was only a front for the junta and that the real man in charge was Col. Gamal Abdel Nasser, Weller said. In fact, many Egyptians insist that the CIA encouraged Nasser to mount the coup against Farouk. Years later Weller wrote that "when Nasser came to power in 1952, the CIA had a notion that they had to pay him to keep his friendship and $3 million seemed about right as an opener, when $2,999,990 in $10 bills was delivered to him—a quick-fingered Lebanese middleman took the extra $10—Nasser wondered whether to toss it back at them scornfully. But knowing how stingy the intelligence services of other powers are, Nasser decided to find out more about the lavish Americans. Instead of salting the American bribe away in Switzerland in the customary fashion of African and Latin statesmen, he built a deliberately unfunctional tower. Even today beside the Nile it looks like a missile that aborted and never left the ground. But the tower sometimes does groan out warnings of the rooftop-level window smashing raids of Israeli planes." According to Weller, Nasser did not deport the CIA people because "he, like the Israelis, valued them as a 2d pipeline through which to send Washington his own views, which might be screened too crudely if sent through the State Department."

(In his 1969 book *The Game of Nations,* Miles Copeland 3d, formerly of the CIA, indicated that the CIA had given up on a peaceful revolution in Egypt led by King Farouk. 4 months before the coup, senior CIA representatives were dealing with the "Free Officers Society," Copeland said.)

Naguib asked for military aid from the U.S. or Britain Aug. 7. "I cannot say who will supply us if America and the Western democracies refuse us" arms and other modern weapons of war, he warned. Premier Maher said that he had asked the U.S. for more economic and technical aid and police-force weapons to maintain internal order. The request was made, he said, at an Aug. 26 conference with Naguib and U.S. Amb. Jefferson Caffery. But a U.S. State Department spokesman said Aug. 27 that no new Egyptian request for aid had been reported and that Caffery's conversations with Maher and Naguib centered on Point 4 technical aid to Egypt under a 1951 agreement. The U.S. had made mobile police equipment available to Egypt several months previously, but Egypt had not yet bought any, the State Department added.

Naguib forced the resignation of Maher's cabinet and assumed direct control of the Egyptian government as premier Sept. 7. Maher, who quit after the sudden arrests of 48 top political leaders early Sept. 7, said that "Gen Naguib and myself felt present circumstances made it preferable that the authority should be concentrated in the hands of the armed forces." The army had criticized Maher's "lukewarm attitude" toward proposed reforms. Naguib was the only military man in the new government. Aides said he would resign after elections to be held not later than Feb. 1953.

The U.S. State Department, which foresaw no change in U.S. policy toward Egypt, said Sept. 8 that the U.S. would support the Naguib government. Britain's "moderate optimism" about Naguib's reforms was reported "diluted by anxiety" over the appointment of 3 leaders of the Moslem Brotherhood and other extreme nationalist groups to the cabinet.

In his book, *Nasser: The Cairo Documents,* Mohammed Heikal said that Russians reacted to the Egyptian revolution in "a strictly Marxist fashion." Heikal wrote: "The old guard in the Kremlin saw an army takeover, and for them, since an army is a tool of oppression, the army takeover in Egypt had to lead to an oppressive regime and could not be revolutionary. The Communist Party in Egypt had opposed the revolution from the beginning and tried to whip up more popular opposition by distributing leaflets in the streets. The Soviet Union supported the Communists, and Moscow Radio attacked the revolution bitterly. For the next 3 years the Russians watched Nasser's progress with a mixture of hostility and fascination. They were very slow in absorbing the impact and the meaning of his policies. Even when they signed the arms deal in 1955 they felt they were dealing with a mystery. . . ."

Britain & Egypt Agree on Sudan

Egyptian-British talks on the Sudan and Suez issues were resumed in Oct. 1952. Britain announced 2 concessions to Egypt Oct. 9: the return of the Egyptian army of custody of the El Firdan bridge across the Suez Canal and the release of $14 million from Egypt's sterling balances as "an expression of good will." After months of negotiation, Britain and Egypt reached agreement Feb. 12, 1953 on the future status of the Sudan.

The 2 countries signed an agreement guaranteeing self-determination for the Sudan within a 3-year transition period. Premier Naguib signed for Egypt, and Amb.-to-Egypt Sir Ralph Stevenson signed for Britain. (Naguib had joined forces Oct. 29, 1951 with the Sudanese Independence Movement and had agreed on just such a program.)

The agreement provided for self-determination and self-government for the Sudan. Egyptian and British military forces were to withdraw from the Sudan 3 months after the election of a Sudanese parliament (hence, no later than Aug. 1953) and the formation of a Sudanese government. A British governor general was to exercise supreme constitutional authority during the transition period, which would end whenever the Sudanese parliament decided to proclaim self-determination. An American was to serve on the 7-man international commission set up to supervise the parliamentary election.

IRAN & ITS TROUBLES (1951–4)

Iran faced continuing perils during the early 1950s. It was beset by chronic rebellions in its provinces and on its frontiers. The government was also threatened by the Communist-oriented Tudeh party and by various tribal khans. In the economic sphere, the USSR and the West continued to make demands on the various Iranian governments. Development rights to Iran's vast oil deposits were a coveted prize.

As the years passed, the U.S. tried to buttress the position of the shah against left-wing and tribal threats. The U.S.' main difficulties arose from Iran's occasionally stormy relationship during this period with Britain, a U.S. ally and the Soviet Union's principal rival in the contest for control of Iran's oil developments.

U.S.-Soviet Rivalry

Shah Mohammed Reza Pahlevi, 31, was married in Teheran Feb. 12, 1951 to Soraya Esfandiari, 19, daughter of a once-rebellious Iranian tribal chief and of a German mother. Prior to the marriage ceremonies, a rumour circulated in Teheran that Soviet Premier Joseph Stalin, vying with the West for the shah's favor, had sent the bride a mink coat valued at $150,000. This was denied Feb. 14 by a palace attache in Teheran, who said that the Soviet Union had presented the wedding couple with 2 greenstone, jewel-studded flower pots. Pres. Truman's gift was a $1,250 Steuben glass bowl.

(In 1949 the young shah had begun a policy of distributing inherited royal lands among the peasants living on them or of selling them to landless farmers at low, long-term-payment prices. Iran's big landowners took alarm. Finally, 15 days before his wedding, the shah Jan. 28, 1951 announced the resumption of his program. He said that he would break up his estates—including 1,000 villages surrounded by farmlands—and sell the land in small parcels to the 250,000 peasants who worked it.)

Iran agreed May 18, 1951 to stop letting foreigners (Americans) photograph its Soviet frontier—a practice protested by Moscow—but plans for Iranian broadcasts to Russia over $56,000 worth of Voice of America equipment were announced May 20.

Iran was assured by the U.S. and Britain May 19 that the major Western powers would continue their "interest" in the safety of countries outside the North Atlantic security system. Statements in London by U.S. State Secy. Dean G. Acheson and British Foreign Secy. Ernest Bevin specifically mentioned Iran, Greece and Turkey—the latter 2 later being admitted to the North Atlantic Treaty Organization (NATO). The U.S. followed up these assurances by announcing May 23 that Iran would get help under the U.S. Military Aid Program (MAP) of arms aid.

Shipments of U.S. military aid had continued for several years after the close of World War II. In one of these shipments, 15 Sherman tanks and 18 108-mm. guns were landed at Bandar Shahpur Jan. 25, 1951.

Anglo-Iranian Oil Nationalization Dispute

As early as 1944 Dr. Mohammed Mossadeq, a Persian lawyer and politician who was then a Majlis (lower house of parliament) deputy, had publicly attacked the Anglo-Iranian Oil Co., which still supplied the British Navy with most of its oil. Mossadeq became the leader of a group of Iranian nationalists who resented the presence of the 56%-British-owned Anglo-Iranian Oil Co. and of the government that protected it. Premier Ali Razmara was assassinated in Mar. 1951 by a religious fanatic angered at his failure to move against foreign control of Iran's oil fields. A storm of anti-British feeling finally forced the Iranian Parliament to approve a bill nationalizing the $560 million oil company by Mar. 17, 1951.* The issue became an international dispute involving both the U.S. and the Soviet Union.

Mossadeq had drawn supporters from a cross-section of small parties and had formed them into a national front. With its support, he became the chairman of the parliamentary oil committee that ultimately drafted the 1951 oil nationalization law. Overnight he became an anticolonialist hero to the Iranian masses. Mossadeq had served in the earliest cabinets formed after the sudden accession to power (by *coup d'état*) in 1920 of Reza Khan Pahlevi as shah. Mossadeq had first been justice minister, then finance minister and finally foreign minister. He retired from public life late in the decade—it was said later by his supporters that he left because of a disagreement with the shah over the pace of land reforms that Mossadeq championed. Mossadeq married the Persian Princess Zia Saltaneh in 1930. By 1951, the Associated Press said, he was "reputed to be one of Iran's wealthiest landowners."

Parliament's action in mid-March was followed by a wave of nationalist demonstrations. Tensions in the Iranian capital rose to another peak. Martial law was imposed in Teheran Mar. 20 to curb terrorism after ex-Education Min. Abdul Hamid Zanganeh, a close friend

---

*Razmara had opposed the nationalization plan on the grounds that Iran would thereby lose $\frac{4}{5}$ of its foreign revenues and idle thousands of its workers in the ensuing shutdown.

of slain Premier Ali Razmara, was shot and critically wounded by a Teheran University student Mar. 19. Zanganeh died of his wounds Mar. 25.

The government delayed the implementation of the Anglo-Iranian Oil nationalization measure, and the workers took matters into their own hands. Office employes joined oil-field workers Apr. 1, 1951 in a strike in southern Iran. The Khuzistan Province oil-refinery towns of Abadan, Agah Jari and Bandar Ma'shur were already under martial law, proclaimed Mar. 26 by then-Premier Hussein Ala after the Tudeh party called for a general strike in that region.

British Defense Min. Emanuel Shinwell had warned Iran Apr. 1 against violating its agreement with Anglo-Iranian Oil. Nearby oil-producing Iraq, however, was already profiting from the British-Persian dispute. Baghdad announced Apr. 3 that the Iraq Petroleum Co., owned by an Anglo-U.S. group, had agreed to pay higher royalties to protect its concessions. (The company announced a 50-50 profit-sharing arrangement July 25.)

The strike lasted 4 weeks and precipitated violence causing 11 deaths before the government announced Apr. 24 that the walkout was over and that 17,000 workers had returned to their jobs. Some 250 persons had been arrested. The deaths were of 3 Britons and 8 Iranians, who were killed Apr. 12 in anti-British riots in Abadan. Troops were forced to fire on rioting strikers. Iran accused the company of causing the strike by cutting workers allowances; the company said that Communists were responsible. Britain said it would protect its nationals if Iran failed to do so.

The parliament completed action Apr. 17 on a vote of confidence in Premier Hussein Ala's handling of the oil crisis and his program to nationalize the company. But Ala resigned as premier Apr. 27 on the ground that he lacked sufficient support for his efforts to promote a compromise between Persians backing oil nationalization and British demands for protection.

Mohammed Mossadeq, leader of the National Front, became premier of Iran Apr. 29, 1951, and his forces in parliament enacted measures to implement the nationalization of all of Iran's oil industries then in foreign hands—including Soviet hands. The implemental legislation was passed unanimously by the Majlis (lower house) Apr. 28 and by the Senate Apr. 30. Just before the Senate had completed the legislation, Britain Apr. 30 had sent Iran an offer on the nationalization of Anglo-Iranian Oil providing Iran would agree to supply Britain with oil.

Mossadeq was named premier by Shah Mohammed Reza Pahlevi at the insistence of parliament. Mossadeq was reported then to be 76, although he claimed to be 69 (the age limit for a parliament member was 70). Some Westerners classified him as leftist, even pro-Communist. He contended that he favored Iranian neutrality in East-West confrontations and opposed any outside interference in Iran.

The outlawed Tudeh party, whose Communists allegedly had infiltrated the oil nationalization movement and fomented many strikes, staged a pro-Soviet demonstration by 30,000 persons in Teheran May 1 (May Day). Tudeh demanded in a letter to Mossadeq May 8 that all U.S. military advisers be ousted from Iran.

The Iranian government May 9 rejected an Anglo-Iranian Oil Co. application under the Anglo-Iranian 1933 oil treaty for arbitration of the oil nationalization dispute. (Iran's oil nationalization law provided for the reimbursement of foreign owners of Iranian oil properties.

The U.S. approved the terms of a May 17 note in which Britain proposed to Iran that the 2 countries negotiate on Iran's move to nationalize Anglo-Iranian Oil. Britain hinted May 14 that it might send paratroops from Cyprus to Iran to guard British property. Within a month, Soviet paratroops were engaged in maneuvers on Iran's northern borders. The British note said that Iran's refusal to negotiate a settlement could lead to "the most serious consequences." Iran answered in effect May 20 by turning down Anglo-Iranian Oil's request for arbitration and telling the firm to name representatives to help carry out nationalization. The company was ordered May 24 to do this within a week. A United Press report from London May 27 said that Britain had promised not to use force in Iran without consulting the U.S. in advance.

In reply to an American appeal May 18 for "friendly" negotiation between Iran and Britain, the Iranian government told U.S. Amb. Henry F. Brady May 21 that the U.S. must not meddle in an Iranian "internal" matter. 30,000 Iranians staged an anti-U.S., anti-British demonstration in Teheran May 22 and threatened a Moslem holy war if necessary to nationalize oil. U.S. State Secy. Dean G. Acheson denied May 23 that the U.S. was opposed to Iranian oil nationalization, but he said that a settlement of the Iranian-British dispute by "negotiation between those parties" was of great importance to "the entire free world."

Some of the May 22 demonstrators also voiced death threats against Premier Mossadeq. He had barricaded himself in the parliament building May 13 after he had told parliament of threats against his life and then had fainted.

Britain took its oil nationalization dispute with Iran to the International Court of Justice May 26, but Iran reaffirmed its plan to nationalize Anglo-Iranian Oil. The company and British government asked the International Court in The Hague to rule that Iran would violate international law if it did not accept arbitration under the Anglo-Iranian oil pact. Britain ordered 4,000 paratroops to Cyprus May 25 as a warning gesture to Iran not to molest British citizens or property. The U.S. appealed to Iran again May 26 to negotiate with the British. Foreign Secy. Herbert Morrison said in the House of Commons May 29 that Britain did not oppose Iranian oil nationalization and was willing to negotiate a new pact on that basis.

But Mossadeq told newsmen May 25 that his country's only hope of avoiding economic collapse was to "get rid of Anglo-Iranian agents who have sacrificed the whole nation to satisfy their greed."* He said a world war would result from economic chaos in Iran. His government declared May 28 that it did not intend to use force against Britons but did not recognize the International Court's right to order arbitration. 100,000 Communist-front demonstrators in Teheran May 29 (the 18th anniversary of Britain's 60-year oil-concession pact with Iran) demanded that the government kick out Anglo-U.S. "imperialists." Mossadeq was cheered by parliament when he said May 31 that he would "not budge an inch" on oil nationalization despite British and U.S. appeals and would discuss only oil sales with Britain.

Pres. Truman urged in notes to the Iranian and British governments June 1 that the 2 governments negotiate the oil dispute. But Mossadeq rejected Truman's plea June 11.

The Iranian government and the Anglo-Iranian Oil Co. began a conference in Teheran June 14 on carrying out Iran's oil nationalization program. But the talks collapsed June 19 after both sides rejected each other's proposals. The Iranians had demanded 75% of the company's current revenues; the British countered with a compromise offer of £10 million ($28 million) in advance against an eventual settlement, plus an additional £3 million ($8.4 million) monthly. An Iranian oil commission had already arrived at Abadan, June 11, and the Iranian flag was run up to denote token seizure.

U.S. Amb. Henry F. Grady had tried to delay the expropriation on the grounds that the seizure would stop the flow of Iranian oil and

---

*The *N.Y. World Telegram* reported May 29: Britain collected more in taxes than Iran got in royalties from the Anglo-Iranian Oil Co.; the British government also collected dividends since it owned a 56% interest in the firm, its largest overseas investment. Iran got $44.8 million in royalties in 1950, $37.8 million in 1949. Britain got $63,840,000 in taxes in 1949. The company earned 51^{1/2}$ million in 1949, paid out $19.6 million in dividends and set aside $30.8 million for reserves; it spent about $196 million in Iran in 1950 for operations.

damage both Iran and the West. Britain appealed to the International Court in The Hague June 21 for an injunction to prevent the seizure under an Iranian bill that dissolved the Anglo-Iranian Oil Co. and created the Iranian National Oil Co. in its place. Mossadeq demanded and received June 21 a vote of confidence from parliament for breaking off negotiations with the British and ordering the seizure of the oil properties.

In London, some Conservatives challenged the Labor government's "weak" policy regarding Iran and demanded that troops be landed and the USSR invited to join in partitioning the country on the ground that otherwise Iran would fall anyway and Russia would get all of it. Foreign Secy. Herbert Morrison denounced Mossadeq as a "reactionary" and member of a ruling class that had "diverted" oil profits "from social development to its own ends," then sought to placate the workers by preaching "hatred of the foreigner." But Britain was prepared to withdraw without using force unless 3,000 British employes in Iran were endangered, Morrison said.

Mossadeq appealed by letter to Pres. Truman June 28 for U.S. support against British opposition to Iran's oil nationalization. He accused the Anglo-Iranian Oil Co. of encouraging its employes to leave the oil fields, although Iran had offered to continue their salaries, and of forcing oil tankers to refuse to give receipts for oil received to the Teheran government's Iranian National Oil Co. He promised that Iran would use "all means at its disposal" to prevent any stoppage in the flow of oil and guaranteed the safety of foreign nationals in Iran. Truman again urged both Britain and Iran to settle their dispute peacefully but did not offer to mediate.

U.S. State Secy. Acheson June 27 had rejected U.S. intervention and had denounced Iran's "threat and fear" tactics against the British. 4 U.S. destroyers, however, were ordered from Singapore to the Persian Gulf June 24, apparently "to show the flag." The U.S. government June 28 approved a plan by 18 U.S. oil companies to supply Western Europe with oil if Iranian supplies were cut off.

The 8,000-ton British cruiser *Mauritius* anchored off Abadan, Iran June 28 to cover the evacuation of the 3,000-member British staff, which had unanimously refused to work for the new Iranian firm. The British feared they would be held accountable for any accidents in the oil fields under a drastic antisabotage law proposed to the Majlis by Massadeq. The families of British workers in Iran were flown or shipped out. British oil tankers pumped oil back into storage tanks rather than give the Iranians receipts stating that they owed Iran for the oil. Eric Drake, the British company's manager, went to Basra, Iraq for safety.

The 12-member International Court of Justice July 5 voted 10-2 to grant Britain a temporary injunction. It directed Iran to permit the Anglo-Iranian Oil Co. to continue operating pending a final court decision over the firm's nationalization. Nevertheless, Iran proceeded with its nationalization program by canceling all old Anglo-Iranian Oil Co. contracts July 14 and offering the company's oil to all comers on a cash-and-carry basis.

Mossadeq told U.S. Amb. Grady July 2 that Iran would let the Abadan refinery take a "holiday" unless the British company agreed to pay for the refined oil. He refused to make any more concessions after having told Grady June 29 that he had decided not to press for early passage of the antisabotage law. His decision to reverse himself caused the British government to delay the evacuation of its nationals.

In the U.S., Interior Secy. Oscar L. Chapman July 3 named Stewart P. Coleman, Standard Oil Co. (N.J.) director, to chair a Foreign Petroleum Supply Committee representing 19 oil companies with operations overseas. The committee's task was to make plans to offset the possible loss of Iranian output.

Mossadeq agreed July 11 to let Pres. Truman send W. Averell Harriman, special White House adviser on foreign affairs, to Iran in an effort to mediate the dispute, and within a month Harriman succeeded in bringing the British and Iranians together for talks. His mission, however, provoked some dissension in Iran. 10,000 Tudeh demonstrators staged an anti-U.S. riot in Teheran's Parliament Square July 15 against Harriman's arrival that day. A policeman and 3 civilians were killed, 53 policemen and 35 civilians injured. Mossadeq reluctantly extended martial law to the entire country July 16 to prevent more violence. After meeting with Mossadeq and other Iranian leaders July 15-18, Harriman was said to agree with U.S. Amb.-to-Iran Grady that there was little room for the Iranian government to compromise because of anti-British hysteria in the country. But Harriman, ignoring a reported assassination plot against him, persuaded the Iranian Oil Commission July 19 to resume negotiations with the British.

Harriman's mediation efforts produced a British-Iranian agreement Aug. 2 for a conference between governmental representatives on the Iranian oil dispute. Harriman had flown to London from Teheran July 28 to report to British leaders on Iran's attitude and had returned to Teheran July 31 to consult with Mossadeq. Under the pressure of Iranian nationalists Mossadeq gave no sign of yielding on the enforcement of oil nationalization. Talks began Aug. 6, but the Iranian government refused Aug. 15 to accept a British plan whereby Iran's oil industry would be owned by Iran although operated by a new agency employing mostly British technicians. Harriman backed the British proposal. The talks ended in failure Aug. 22.

The U.S. announced Aug. 30 that it had ended its efforts to mediate in the dispute. Harriman, who had left Teheran for home Aug. 25, met with the British cabinet in London Aug. 27 and was assured that Britain would not provoke war with Iran. He said that it was up to Iran to make the next move towards a compromise. But Iranian officials said Aug. 29 that it was Britain's turn to make new overtures.

The U.S. refused Sept. 17 to forward an Iranian note to London giving Britain 15 days to resume oil negotiations or have its oil technicians expelled from Iran. Harriman told Mossadeq (in a note published Sept. 19) that he would not forward the ultimatum because a British-Iranian oil settlement was "possible and feasible." He recommended (1) an "integrated organization" of Britons and Iranians to operate the Iranian-owned oil industry, (2) adequate compensation to the British for their properties nationalized by Iran and (3) the distribution of Iranian oil through British facilities in a way that would give Britain nearly all of the 30 million-ton annual output.

Economic measure applied by Britain began to tell in Iran's internal politics. So many Iranian deputies opposed to Mossadeq stayed away from the Majlis in Teheran Sept. 6 and 9 that he could not muster a quorum for a vote of confidence on his policies. 14 old-guard oppositionists Sept. 10 issued a manifesto calling Mossadeq's oil nationalization program a failure because "the oil industry has come to a standstill" and "the general situation is steadily worsening." The conservative National Will Party, led by ex-Premier Said Zai ed-Din Tabatabai, was revived in Teheran Sept. 13 to oppose Mossadeq's regime. A parliamentary boycott of Mossadeq Sept. 16 again prevented his winning a vote of confidence.

The Iranian government announced Sept. 17 that it was prepared to negotiate a barter agreement with the Soviet Union to get goods cut off by Britain because of the oil dispute. (British ship cargoes of "scarce" goods to Iran were halted Sept. 13.) Teheran sources said Poland and Czechoslovakia had assured Iran they would buy large quantities of Iranian crude oil. The British asserted that Soviet-bloc countries lacked the facilities for importing a substantial amount of oil from Iran. British Prime Min. Clement R. Attlee had said at the opening of Europe's largest refinery in Fawley, England Sept. 14 that the new plant assured Britain of an adequate supply of oil products and that Iran would be "ruined" unless it resumed "friendly cooperation" with the British. Britain announced Sept. 19 that it had placed an order for 200,000 tons of oil with Rumania, where the USSR had joint control of the oil industry.

Iranian troops seized the Anglo-Iranian Oil Co.'s Abadan refinery Sept. 27 and shut all but 10 of its 300 British technicians out of the plant. When Iran had issued orders Sept. 25 for the British technicians to leave the country by Oct. 4, British Prime Min. Clement R. Attlee had sent Pres. Truman a letter asking what Truman thought should be done. The President appealed to Attlee not to use force to hold the refinery. Britain followed this advice Sept. 27 but was said to plan every possible economic retaliation against Iran. The British Sept. 23 had rejected an informal Iranian request to renew Anglo-Iranian negotiations on Iran's terms.

U.S. Relations

Loy W. Henderson was named Sept. 12 to replace Dr. Henry F. Grady, who was retiring as U.S. ambassador to Iran. Marguerite Higgins reported from Teheran in the *N.Y. Herald Tribune* Sept. 13: Grady quit because State Secy. Dean Acheson had turned down "every important recommendation" by Grady in his last year in the post and had helped Britain put pressure on Iran in the oil crisis despite warnings that "old-style colonialism does not work" in the modern-day Middle East. On the eve of his departure for home, Grady told the French news agency (Agence France-Presse) in Teheran Sept. 18 that Mossadeq was hopelessly stubborn and that it was "quite useless" to talk to him. Grady said Iran was under the rule of terrorists.

The Kem Amendment's restrictions on U.S. economic aid to countries that exported U.S.-blacklisted goods to the Soviet bloc were waived by the U.S. National Security Council Sept. 15 for Iran. Some Persian politicians were reported to have complained that Iran had received much less than its proper share of the U.S. foreign-aid total since the end of World War II. These men had regarded the application of the Kem Amendment to a country with Soviet borders as most discriminatory. The U.S. State Department had said Sept. 8, 1950 that Iran would receive more American economic loans, but Iranian officials had complained that the U.S. was offering only about $25 million immediately through the Export-Import Bank—far short of what the Iranians wanted. Many previously anti-Soviet newspapers were criticizing the U.S. and applauding Russia for its new amicability toward Iran, said the *N.Y. Times* Sept. 10, 1950.

Britain Appeals to UN

The British Foreign Office announced Sept. 28, 1951 that Britain would take the Iranian oil dispute before the UN Security Council.

The Security Council in New York voted 9-2 Oct. 1 to consider the British complaint. Consideration of the case was opposed by the USSR on the ground that the oil nationalization was an internal Iranian matter. After admitting Britain's complaint, the Council postponed further hearings until Oct. 11 so that an Iranian delegation led by Premier Mossadeq could go to New York. It was also hoped that new British-Iranian talks could be arranged during the 10-day interval so that the Council would not have to rule on the case.

Britain had asked that the Council order Iran to (1) obey the July 5 temporary International Court of Justice injunction against going ahead with oil nationalization and (2) rescind the ouster of British oil technicians from Iran. Inasmuch as there was no chance for Council action at once, Britain evacuated its 325 Abadan refinery technicians Oct. 3, a day ahead of deadline set by Iran for them to leave. Iran had ignored a U.S. plea Sept. 27 not to expel the technicians.

Mossadeq told the Security Council Oct. 15 that it had "no jurisdiction" in the dispute and that his country "will not be coerced by foreign governments or by international authorities." He said that Iran was willing to reopen negotiations with Britain on "methods of fixing compensation and the sale of oil to Great Britain" but not on whether Britain could keep a hand in the Iranian oil industry. Mossadeq said that the British had drained off nearly all the profits from Iranian oil for 40 years in company earnings and taxes. Iran's 18 million people had "probably one of the lowest" living standards in the world, he declared. "Our greatest natural asset is oil. This should be the source of work and food for the population of Iran." Mossadeq also said that a Soviet offer to set up a joint Soviet-Iranian company to operate the former Anglo-Iranian properties had been rejected; Iran would not let a new set of foreigners replace the British, he declared. He stressed that Britain, not Iran, threatened international peace with a display of force during the dispute.

British delegate Sir Gladwyn Jebb modified his proposed Council resolution Oct. 15. He asked that Iran enter into a temporary agreement for Anglo-Iranian oil operations pending a full settlement of the dispute. He said that it was no longer practical to ask to resume the *status quo* predating Iranian oil nationalization.

U.S. delegate Warren Austin supported Britain Oct. 17 in asking that the Council intervene. Austin said that Mossadeq's own statement proved that international peace was threatened in Iran and that the dispute involved the Iranian and British governments, not merely Iran and Anglo-Iranian Oil Co.

The Security Council, unable Oct. 19 to adopt a resolution for British-Iranian oil negotiations, adjourned debate on the question indefinitely. It decided to wait for the International Court of Justice to rule on a jurisdictional issue: whether the dispute was international and subject to the court's jurisdiction. A watered-down British resolution asking that Iran negotiate with Britain was abandoned for lack of 7 favorable votes required for adoption. With Britain bound to abstain as a party to the dispute, the resolution had only 6 voting backers: the U.S., Brazil, France, India, the Netherlands and Turkey. Yugoslavia favored a request for British-Iranian negotiations but opposed the British measure because of a controversial clause claiming UN jurisdiction over the dispute. The USSR sought to have the whole issue dropped from the Council's agenda on the ground that it was an internal dispute and the UN had no right to intercede.

Mossadeq in Washington

Premier Mossadeq went to Washington Oct. 23 and conferred with Pres. Truman on the possibility of new Anglo-Iranian talks. Mossadeq took up quarters in Walter Reed Hospital Oct. 24–25 and met there with State Secy. Dean G. Acheson and other U.S. officials. (During a visit to Philadelphia Oct. 22, Mossadeq had reiterated that Iran had thrown out Britons who "seized greedily" on the country's natural riches and that the country would not negotiate on the question of oil nationalization. But he said that Britain was free "to negotiate for the purchase of oil from Iran." Mossadeq remained in Washington into November for talks with U.S. State Department officials, who were also conferring with the British, on a possible oil settlement.

The U.S. State Department said Nov. 13 that it had failed to establish a "new basis" for Anglo-Iranian oil negotiations during 3 weeks of talks with Mossadeq in Washington. Mossadeq dealt mostly with U.S. Asst. State Secy. (for Middle Eastern Affairs) George C. McGhee. He was said to have offered to sell Britain most of Iran's oil but to have refused to let British, U.S., Dutch or any other foreign oil interests help run the Iranian oil industry.

The International Monetary Fund offered Iran an $8¾ million loan Nov. 12 to solve its foreign exchange difficulties for the next 2 months. Mossadeq told the National Press Club in Washington Nov. 14 that Iran needed an "immediate" $120 million U.S. loan to keep it going for a year. He warned that U.S. support of "imperialist" policies in the Near East would intensify the Communist threat there.

Iranian Deputy Premier Hossein Fatemi, aide to Mossadeq in the Anglo-Iranian oil talks in Washington, said there Nov. 17 that Winston Churchill, elected to power again in Britain Oct. 25, was to blame for the lack of an agreement. Fatemi charged that the new British prime minister "does not want" to settle the dispute and was quibbling over oil prices "and other matters" as an "excuse" for not accepting Iran's solution—i.e., to let Britain buy oil from Iran's nationalized resources.

The U.S. State Department had said Nov. 15 that "sympathetic consideration" was being given Mossadeq's plea to Pres. Truman for a S120 million one-year loan to Iran. Britain was said to oppose the loan on the ground that it would probably save Mossadeq's regime, but some U.S. officials deemed Mossadeq easier to deal with than any prospective successor as premier.

The Mossadeq-Fatemi party left New York for home by plane Nov. 18 and was welcomed in Cairo Nov. 20. Egyptians hailed Mossadeq as the "destroyer of Britain" and "enemy of imperialism." Some shouted, "Revolution . . . give us guns!" Fatemi told them that Iran supported Egypt's "sacred struggle for evacuation and unity" in its dispute with Britain over Suez and the Sudan.

Iran Moves Toward Soviet Rapprochement

The settlement of a 31-year-old Soviet-Iranian dispute over the accurate location in 8 areas of Iran's border with Soviet Turkestan opened a new phase in Irano-Soviet relations early in Nov. 1951, at the height of the Anglo-Iranian oil controversy. The demarcation agreement was signed in Teheran Nov. 7 by a Soviet-Iranian joint commission set up 13 months previously. The signing took place 3 days before the 2 countries one-year trade agreement was due to expire.

Under the 1950 trade agreement, the USSR had contracted to buy 35,000 to 60,000 metric tons of rice, 3,000 tons of cotton, 1,000 tons of wool, 300 tons of goathair, 300,000 sheep- and goatskins, 30,000 lambskins, 4,000 tons of oilseed, 4,000 tons of raisins, 2,000 tons of almonds, 2,000 tons of dates, 1,000 tons of pistachio nuts, 500 tons of gum and 1,000 tons of greem cumin from Iran. Iran agreed to buy from the Soviet Union 75,000 tons of sugar, 50 million meters (54.68 million yards) of cotton goods, 30,000 tons of iron rails and railroad material, 20,000 tons of cement, 20 million rials (S500,000) worth of crockery, 10 million rials (S250,000) worth of board lumber and 10 million rials worth of paper.

The Nov. 7, 1951 Soviet-Iranian rapport evoked from Associate Justice William O. Douglas of the U.S. Supreme Court, who had traveled in Iran in 1950, the warning in an interview in New York Nov. 20 that "one of the greatest crises in modern history" was brewing in the Middle East and that the U.S. was trying vainly to "underwrite the *status quo*" for Britain. Britain had "distorted the history of the Near East" in its favor, Douglas maintained. He expressed the hope that "we [the U.S.] will write their history instead of letting Soviet Russia do it." Iranian Premier Mossadeq had left the U.S. Nov. 18 "empty-handed" and believing that Iran's only alternative to bowing to "British colonialism" was to make a deal with the Soviet Union, he said. Mossadeq, in Douglas' opinion, would not bow to Britain; "he knows how to keep from getting shot" by Iranian nationalists who hated the British more than anyone else. (Douglas had urged in a speech at the University of Teheran Sept. 12, 1950 that Iran's big landholders distribute large estates to peasants to combat communism. He said that Iran needed a reform program of "perhaps 10% communism, 15% capitalism and 75% something else." Soviet broadcasts at the time alleged that Douglas was in Iran as a "special Truman spy.")

The USSR's reorganization of the Soviet agency trading with Iran and Afghanistan was disclosed Nov. 20. Soviet trade with those countries was to be handled by the office that also dealt with Outer Mongolia and Sinkiang, not by the Soviet Union's general Mid-Eastern trade agency. The *N.Y. Times* said Nov. 21 that this could indicate a Soviet effort to draw Iran and Afghanistan into Moscow's trade orbit. The Iranian army reported Nov. 16 a lessening of tension on its Soviet frontier. (Example: Russian and Iranian troops did each other the favor of chasing back cows that wandered across the border.)

The next major development in Iran's new policy of Soviet rapprochement became known Dec. 26, 1951, when a Czechoslovak foreign trading delegation to Iran announced in Teheran that Czechoslovakia would buy 500,000 tons of refined oil from Iran and "large" amounts of crude oil for refining in Czechoslovak plants. Iran said that Soviet and Polish tankers would be used to transport the purchase.

Iran Jan. 29, 1952 announced a barter agreement with Hungary under which Hungary would get Iranian oil.

Internal Crisis

Restive students, agitating Communists and Iran's deteriorating economy combined in the last 10 weeks of 1951 to create a severe internal crisis.

Iranian police reported that Communist plans to kill Shah Mohammed Reza Pahlevi and arrange a Soviet invasion of northern Iran had been seized in a raid on the outlawed Tudeh party's headquarters in Teheran Oct. 27. Police and army troops battled 5,000 Communist-led students who marched from Teheran University to Parliament Square in a demonstration Oct. 30 against the Anglo-American plan for Middle Eastern defense and Britain's actions against Egypt over Suez. Another Communist-led demonstration against British policy toward Iran and Egypt was held in Teheran Nov. 2. Teheran University was closed by its officials Nov. 4 because of Communist activity by students, but Premier Mossadeq sent orders from Washington Nov. 6 that it be reopened to forestall riots against the closing. 1,000 Communist-led students seized Teheran University buildings for several hours in a demonstration Nov. 18. Mossadeq's problems with Teheran University prompted the inclusion of the Iranian Education Ministry in a cabinet reshuffle at the beginning of December. Physicist Mahmoud Hessabi was named education minister Dec. 4, succeeding Karim Sanjabi.

Meanwhile, Mossadeq's foes, both right-wing and Communist, denounced him for failing to put Britain in the worst possible light internationally for its actions in the Iranian oil crisis. Iranian opposition leader Jamal Enami had told parliament Nov. 13 that Mossadeq had bungled the oil nationalization program. Enami warned that the Communists were "arming" to seize Azerbaijan Province. He said that Mossadeq's policy of trying to be neutral between East and West was "unrealistic." 5 persons were reported killed and 200 injured in Teheran Dec. 6 when 5,000 Communist-led youths, shouting death threats to Mossadeq, fought a 5-hour battle with 10,000 police troops and anti-Communist Iranian nationalists.

Much of the crisis' rancor arose from its economic aspects. Iran was rapidly going bankrupt, and the country's poor prospects for oil revenues even slightly approximating former earnings caused widespread dissatisfaction, even among the most extreme nationalists. Matters were not improved with the information that the Anglo-Iranian Oil Co., which had extensive holdings outside Iran, Oct. 25 had declared a 5% interim dividend on ordinary stock for 1951—the same as in 1950.

The government Nov. 5 issued an announcement that one major unit of the Abadan refinery, with an annual capacity of 3 million tons, had been put back into temporary operation by Persian engineers and workers. Official plans called for the operation of this unit for just a month to replace stocks and keep the refinery in working order. 2 more refinery sections might be restarted "if buyers are found for our products," the announcement said. The reopened unit was to produce gasoline, kerosene, paraffin and diesel fuel oil.

The National Bank of Iran Dec. 4 temporarily suspended the open-ing of credit abroad for imports to prevent the exhaustion of the coun-try's foreign exchange fund, then down to about £2 million ($5.6 mil-lion). Mossadeq appealed Dec. 22 to the Iranian public to buy $10 million worth of national bonds in the next 2 months to stall off gov-ernmental bankruptcy. Iran Dec. 25 recalled 26 diplomats, including the ambassadors to London, Rome and New Delhi, for lack of foreign exchange to support them abroad. Dr. Henry G. Bennett, U.S. Point 4 aid chief who was killed in a plane crash near Teheran while en route to Iran Dec. 22, was said to have hoped to induce Mossadeq to accept $23 million worth of U.S. technical aid—thus far shunned by Iran so as not to excite Soviet suspicions. The government said Feb. 28, 1952 that it was stripping its offices of Persian carpets and setting aside 1,000 government autos to sell. The government lacked sufficient cash for day-to-day operations because of the stoppage of oil royalties.

Iran's economic misfortune was highlighted by the contrasting suc-cess of contiguous Iraq and of its Persian Gulf neighbor Kuwait with British oil developers. Iraq's parliament was told Dec. 1, 1951, in a speech from the throne by Prince Zaid (for absent Prince Regent Abdul Illah), that there would be a "manifold increase" in Iraq's royalties in 1951 from the Iraq Petroleum Co. as a result of the 50-50 profit split negotiated in August. Other sources estimated that Iraq would get $42 million in 1951, $165 million a year by 1955. Prince Zaid also said that Iraq would press for the revision of its British defense treaty. The Kuwait Oil Co. confirmed in London Dec. 3 that it had signed an agree-ment with Sheikh Abdullah of Kuwait to split profits from Kuwait oil production 50-50. The sheikh's oil income was expected to rise from $28 million to $140 million a year. Kuwait Oil was owned by the Anglo-Iranian (British) and Gulf Exploration (U.S.) companies, the lat-ter a subsidiary of Gulf Oil. Sheik Abdullah had asked the Kuwait Oil Co. Apr. 28 to raise his royalties to $200,000 a day. The Kuwait com-pany was producing ½ million barrels of oil daily.

Britain said in a White Paper Dec. 6 that organized terrorists had forced the Iranian government to nationalize the Anglo-Iranian Oil Co. It said that the Iranian public was not permitted to know that the firm had offered to split its profits 50-50 with Iran.

Britain Dec. 22 rejected a 10-day deadline from Iran for ordering Iranian oil. 4 days later, Iran made its deal with Czechoslovakia. Iran also announced Dec. 26 that it had turned down an International Bank plan for the settlement of the Anglo-Iranian dispute because the bank had proposed rehiring British oil technicians and selling Iranian oil to Britain at special low rates.

U.S. Suspends Arms Aid to Iran

The U.S. State Department announced Jan. 15, 1952 that military aid shipments to Iran had been "temporarily withheld" since Jan. 8 because of the Iranian government's failure to sign the bilateral agreement required by the U.S. Mutual Security Act of 1951. The act stipulated that countries sharing in the military and economic aid programs (a) formally agree by Jan. 8 to the terms laid down in the act, and (b) promise to make a full contribution toward free-world defense and to do their best to develop their own capacity for self-defense. The State Department spokesman added that negotiations between the Iranian government and U.S. Amb.-to-Iran Loy Henderson were continuing and that it hoped that shipments would soon be renewed. The aid suspension was finally ended Apr. 25.

W. Averell Harriman, director of the U.S. Mutual Security Agency, had announced Jan. 23 that because of the continued delay by the respective countries in signing the agreement, all U.S. military aid had been withdrawn from Iran and all economic and technical aid from Afghanistan, Burma, Egypt, Iraq and the Irish Republic. Harriman emphasized that all other nations receiving military aid had fulfilled the requirements of the act, and he said that the U.S. still hoped that Iran would qualify itself.

Premier Mohammed Mossadeq charged Mar. 18 that Pres. Truman had refused to support a U.S. loan for Iran unless Iran accepted British oil terms. The U.S. State Department denied Mar. 20 that it had attempted to trade Iran a $120 million loan for Iranian acceptance of British oil terms. Mossadeq said Mar. 27 that Iran had dropped its request for a U.S. loan to relieve the economic crisis caused by loss of oil revenue.

Teheran was placed under martial law Mar. 30 after Communist youths, denouncing alleged "American germ warfare" in Korea, provoked riots Mar. 28 in which at least 5 persons were killed and attempted Mar. 29 to raid the U.S. Information Service Library.

It was announced in Washington Apr. 15 that agreements on 3 new Point 4 technical assistance projects, covering agriculture, public health and education and totaling $11 million in U.S. aid, had been signed to make available to Iran under the Point 4 program the equivalent of about $6 million in rials. $5 million would cover the supply to Iran of about 34,000 metric tons of sugar, which Iran would sell through commercial channels. $1 million would be used to support Persian exchange students in the U.S. whose funds had been exhausted by the stringent Iranian currency controls. The agreements were based on an exchange of notes, dated Jan. 19, 1952, under which the U.S. government agreed to contribute up to $23,450,000 for technical aid to Iran during the fiscal year ending June 30, 1952.

The State Department announced Apr. 25, 1952 that the U.S. had decided to resume American military assistance to Iran since the Iranian government had assured the U.S. that the use of such aid and Iran's defense objectives would meet the requirements of the 1951 Mutual Security Act. In a note to U.S. Amb.-to-Iran Henderson, Mossadeq declared that his government "supports the principles of the UN Charter to the extent that its economic and general resources permit" and that Iran, attacked from any side, would "defend her freedom and independence with all her might." Mossadeq did not give the pledge to help defend "the free world" ordinarily given by U.S.-arms-aid recipients. Iran became eligible to share in a $396¼ million U.S. arms aid fund for Greece, Turkey and the Middle East. But a State Department spokesman asserted Apr. 29 that the granting of military and technical aid to Iran constituted no change in the U.S. position regarding financial aid to Iran and that the U.S. attitude in the Anglo-Iranian oil dispute also remained unchanged.

Iran was told in a note from the USSR May 22 it had violated the 1921 Soviet-Iranian treaty (permitting the USSR to intervene in self defense if Iran became a base of anti-Soviet military operations) by accepting U.S. military aid. The Russian note was dismissed May 25 by the U.S. State Department as another attempt to "intimidate" the Iranian government. The State Department denied that U.S. aid to Iran violated the 1921 treaty.

Anglo-Iranian Negotiations Fail

Premier Mossadeq issued a bid for new Anglo-Iranian oil negotiations Jan. 27, 1952, when he told British Amb. Sir Francis Shepherd in Teheran that the dispute could "easily be resolved by goodwill" and that Britain should "choose a path so that these differences are resolved." The British Foreign Office, concluding that Mossadeq meant that Britain had to give in on all key issues, said Jan. 28 that Mossadeq's statement did nothing to improve the outlook for a settlement. Iran at that juncture was said to want complete control of the former British oil industries and to be planning merely to sell oil to the British and other foreign countries.

(Mossadeq had forced the closing of British consulates in Iran Jan. 21 on the ground that consulate officials had interfered in Iranian internal affairs during the Anglo-Iranian oil dispute. Mossadeq Jan. 22

rejected Britain's nomination of Robert Hankey, British minister to Hungary and an embassy official in Teheran 9 years previously, to succeed British Amb.-to-Iran Sir Francis Shepherd.)

Negotiations to operate Iranian oil industries broke down in Teheran Mar. 16, 1952. The Iranian government refused to readmit British technicians and disagreed with 5 envoys from the International Bank for Reconstruction & Development on 2 other points: the price of oil to be sold to Britain's Anglo-Iranian Oil Co. and the amount of Iranian oil to be sold to other buyers.

One of the envoys, Hector Prud'homme of the World Bank's loan department, said in London Mar. 23, on his way home to the U.S., that the controversy was "mainly a political problem." Persian officials with whom he spoke admitted this and "said that, while we thought of it as an economic and industrial problem, it was 90% political," Prud'homme said.

The Anglo-Iranian Oil Co. June 9, 1952 reported that 1951 sales were within 15 million barrels of the 288,700,000-barrel total of 1950 despite the loss of about 116 million barrels of Iranian oil. It said that increased production in Kuwait, Iraq and Qatar had almost made up for Iranian losses.

Anglo-Iranian Oil obtained a temporary injunction from a British court in Aden June 18 to prevent the Honduras-registered tanker *Rose Mary,* carrying 1,000 tons of Iranian oil, from leaving the Red Sea port. The ship had put in there June 17 for emergency repairs. The Italian Middle East Oil Co., which had announced June 14 a 10-year contract to buy 2 million tons of Iranian crude oil, had chartered the *Rose Mary* to bring the first shipment to Italy for refinement before delivery to a Swiss company. Iran had sold the oil at 18% below world market prices. Iran had reported the deal May 4 as its first foreign sale of oil since Anglo-Iranian Oil was nationalized.

Iran asked the International Court of Justice in The Hague June 9–11 to declare the Anglo-Iranian oil dispute outside its jurisdiction. The court did so 41 days later. Premier Mossadeq had personally opened Iran's arguments June 9 against Britain's complaint that Iran had violated treaty pledges to negotiate the settlement of any disputes with Britain. Mossadeq said that the oil nationalization was a domestic measure taken by Iran as a "free and sovereign country." He implied that Iran would ignore an adverse World Court decision because the issues at stake in oil nationalization were "too sacred and too vital" to be exposed "even to the theoretical risk of an international decision." The court finally upheld the Iranian position in the matter by deciding, 9–5, July 22 that it lacked jurisdiction because the matter did not qualify as a dispute between 2 governments.

Mossadeq Wins Dictatorial Powers

Mossadeq in the summer of 1952 gambled his political career on the strength of his popularity, and he gained enough power to make his will law in Iran.

Mossadeq resigned as premier July 10 after he had failed to get the backing of parliament and the shah on plans to form a new cabinet, become war minister as well as premier and exercise dictatorial powers for 6 months to cope with the economic crisis. Ahmad Ghavam es Saltaneh, 77, premier during the 1946 crisis over Soviet troops in Iran, was designated July 17 to form a new cabinet, and he received the Majlis' (Chamber of Deputies') preliminary approval. Reports from Teheran said that Mossadeq, as war minister, would have sharply reduced army expenditures to get money for other government functions during the financial crisis brought on by the idleness of the nationalized oil industry.

After 3 days of nationwide rioting in which 300 to 500 deaths were reported, Mossadeq was recalled July 22 to serve as premier. He received a 61-3 parliamentary vote of support, was named war minister and won complete control of the army.

Ghavam resigned July 21 and went into hiding to escape Teheran mobs that demanded his death as a traitor and "servant of the British." Frontier police were ordered not to permit him to leave Iran and to arrest him on sight as a traitor. Iran's parliament July 29 approved the confiscation of Ghavam's properties, valued at $8.9 million. Anti-Ghavam demonstrations had begun with his appointment and had increased July 18 when he pledged to settle the British-Iranian oil dispute. He said that Mossadeq had mishandled the oil affair and had let a dispute with a British company become an unnecessary dispute with the British government. Troops were called out July 19 but failed to quell the mobs despite arrests estimated at 624 by July 20. After Ghavam's resigantion, cheering nationalists marched to the home of Mossadeq, who told them: "Your sacrifice today has saved my country. I wish I had been killed instead of so many innocent persons."

New demonstrations were touched off July 22 when the International Court in The Hague upheld Mossadeq. Nationalists and Communists, who had demonstrated at the British embassy July 21, beat and stoned a U.S. Army officer in Teheran July 24. Communist-led mobs rioted outside American economic assistance offices throughout Iran. U.S. Amb. Loy Henderson closed the Point 4 offices July 24 and instructed Americans to remain indoors.

Mossadeq won his demand for legislative as well as executive powers for a 6-month period of dictatorship when the Senate Aug. 1 reluctantly passed a bill granting him the emergency authority. His government Aug. 13 issued 2 agrarian reform decrees giving peasants democratic rights, ending feudal dues and forced labor charges and cutting landlords' share of crops by 20%, with half of the cut going to the peasants and half to a new rural development and cooperating organization. A decree Aug. 14 providing that government permission must be obtained to hold public meetings and demonstrations was interpreted as a move to suppress disorderly activities of the Tudeh party.

British Dispute Grows, Diplomatic Ties Cut

Armed with his World Court decision, Mossadeq confronted Britain in a test of wills over the oil nationalization issue, and 3 months later the 2 countries severed diplomatic relations.

Shortly after the decision the National Front paper *Bakhtar Emruz* reported July 26, 1952 that Britain had been notified of Iran's willingness to discuss oil property reparations. But British Charge d'Affaires George H. Middleton said July 30 that "no positive proposals for a . . . settlement" had been made in talks he had held with Mossadeq July 25 and 28. Iranian papers, however, continued to emphasize the Mossadeq-Middleton talks and said that U.S. Amb. Henderson was acting as an impartial 3d party. At that point, the British Bank of Iran and the Middle East, in Teheran for more than 50 years, closed July 30, claiming that it was the victim of strict new government regulations.

Meanwhile, anti-U.S. agitation continued. National Front members of parliament demanded July 29 that all U.S. military advisers leave Iran, scoffed at the Point-4 aid program and called for Iran to nationalize U.S. oil holdings on Bahrein Island. American clubs in Teheran closed voluntarily July 25, and Americans were advised to limit parties at home to 12 persons.

Mossadeq Sept. 7 described a proposal offered Aug. 30 by Pres. Truman and Prime Min. Winston Churchill for the Anglo-Iranian Oil dispute as the worst offer that Iran had ever received. He accused Britain of trying to make the dispute a contest between the Iranian and British governments. He said that Iranian courts were the only authorities competent to rule on compensation for seized British holdings but indicated that Iran might agree to take the matter of payment to the International Court if the oil company's claims were limited in advance. The Truman-Churchill proposal had provided for: International Court settlement of compensation; appointment of "suitable representatives" of the company and Iran to arrange the sale of Iranian oil to world markets; British aid in moving oil stored in Iran; relaxation of British currency and export restrictions; $10 million from the U.S. to aid Iran's economic crisis.

Mossadeq's informal counterproposal Sept. 7 took the line that Iran's claims included payment by the Anglo-Iranian Oil Co. of indemnities, customs and back taxes totaling at least £49 million ($137.2 million). The Majlis met Sept. 10 to consider the Truman-Churchill offer but postponed action because of "certain efforts and negotiations which are going on."

The Truman-Churchill plan for settling the oil dispute was officially rejected by Iran Sept. 24 in a note in which Iran also gave Britain 2 weeks to answer a demand for immediate payment of $137.2 million by the Anglo-Iranian Oil Co. The note indicated that Iran would let the International Court decide the compensation to be paid to the oil company for its seized properties. Iran's parliament voted confidence in Mossadeq after he reported on the oil dispute to the Majlis Sept. 16 and to the senate Sept. 17.

Mossadeq Oct. 7 invited Anglo-Iranian Oil Co. representatives to come to Teheran within a week to discuss his counterproposals of Sept. 24. Before the meeting, Mossadeq said, the company should put up £20 million sterling and prepare to credit the balance of £29 million sterling to Iran within 3 weeks. Britain Oct. 15 denounced this counterproposal as "unreasonable and unacceptable."

Mossadeq said Oct. 16 that he would sever diplomatic relations with Britain because Iran had gained nothing through normal relations with the British. He said he hoped that the British would recognize their mistakes so that Anglo-Iranian relations could be resumed in a cooperative spirit.

Iran formally broke diplomatic relations with Britain Oct. 22 with a note in which Mossadeq blamed Britain for the rupture and accused Britain of seeking by intrigue and improper interference to disturb Iran's order and security. Mossadeq expressed hope that the break could be mended. The U.S. State Department called the break "no solution" to the oil dispute. Iranian Foreign Min. Hossein Fatemi said that the break applied only to diplomatic relations and not to economic and commercial activities. Sweden was to look after Iranian interests in Britain, the Swiss to act for Britain in Iran.

Throughout this period Iran had no means to conduct any but the simplest and most tentative trade explorations and little but future oil deliveries to sell. Mossadeq sought financial advice on Iran's predicament from the UN and from a former adviser of Hitler's, Hjalmar Schacht. He received industrial advice on reopening the formerly

British-run oil refineries from W. Alton Jones, president of the Cities Service Corp., an American petroleum processing and marketing company. Schacht had arrived in Iran Sept. 9 at Mossadeq's invitation and left Sept. 14 after a study of Iran's economic condition. He said Iranians were "lazy" and should work more to solve their nation's financial problems. In Hamburg Sept. 16 Schacht praised Mossadeq as "one of the wisest and most far-sighted statesmen I have ever known."

W. Alton Jones said on leaving Iran Sept. 24 that U.S. oil operators would buy Iranian oil and take the accompanying risk of British naval or legal intervention if the oil dispute remained stalemated. Jones said that both sides were to blame in the oil dispute, and he predicted that Iran would "never call in the Russians" to help in oil production. Jones said Sept. 7 he had outlined the exact means of getting the Abadan refinery into operation and that "the rest is up to the premier."

Iranian National Front Party Secy. Gen. Hussein Makki said in Washington Sept. 24 that he had talked with a U.S. businessman who had offered to form a $140 million company to transport and sell Iranian oil to Europe and Asia. Nothing came of the offer, however, and further U.S. oil industry interest dwindled with the subsequent decline in U.S.-Iranian relations. Makki himself, who had become head of Iran's oil nationalization program, said in Hamburg, Germany Nov. 3 that he had rejected an official U.S. invitation to visit the U.S. because of "American support for British economic pressure on Iran."

Mossadeq Challenges the Shah

Shortly after Mossadeq's resumption of power in the summer of 1952 came the first hints of a future power struggle with Shah Mohammed Reza Pahlevi. The contest, perhaps the shah's greatest test, proved to be Mossadeq's undoing.

Observers held that while Mossedeq's loyalty to the shah could perhaps be questioned, the basis of his political support, the National Front Party, controlling nearly 100% of parliament, had remained pro-monarchist. The party, however, called July 27 for "changes in the men surrounding the shah." 10 generals and 2 colonels, including an ex-adjutant to the shah, Lt. Gen. Abdol Hossein Hedjazi, 48, were dismissed from active army service Sept. 8.

The Mossadeq government announced Oct. 13, 1952 that it had quashed a foreign-aided plot against Mossadeq by arresting 4 men and placing a guard around the home of Gen. Fazollah Zahedi who, as a senator, was immune from arrest. The government charged that the men had schemed "in the interest of a certain foreign embassy" (presumably British). Zahedi denied the charge and said Oct. 15 that the charges against him were personal and political. Zahedi finally was arrested Feb. 25, 1953 on charges of plotting with the British to overthrow Mossadeq's government. (Meanwhile, foreign correspondents had been warned Oct. 13 that their messages might be refused transmission if they contained anything considered false news by the Ministry of Posts, Telegraphs & Telephones.)

The Majlis (parliament's lower house) voted parliament's upper house (the Senate) out of office Oct. 23, 1952 in a bill in which the deputies interpreted the constitutional limit on senatorial terms as 2 years and terminated the current Senate session. Foreign Min. Hossein Fatemi denied reports that the act was designed to remove some senators' parliamentary immunity from arrest. 39 of 45 members of the Senate said Oct. 25 that the act was illegal and that future parliamentary acts would be invalid without Senate approval.

Parliament Jan. 19, 1953 extended Mossadeq's power to govern by decree for a full year beginning Feb. 9. The vote was 59 to 1 (with 6 abstentions) despite the opposition of Majlis Speaker Ayatollah Sayed Abolghassem Kashani and other dissidents in Mossadeq's nationalist coalition. Kashani and Deputy Premier Hussein Makki had threatened Jan. 8 to resign if the extension were granted. Kashani said Jan. 20 that the vote did not change his conviction that parliament had no constitutional right to delegate its legislative powers to the premier. During the debate on the extension of power, pro-Mossadeq mobs demonstrated throughout the country and surrounded the parliament building in Teheran, threatening to hold the deputies there until Mossadeq's request was granted.

Sharp differences surfaced in Feb. 1953 between Mossadeq and the shah. Mossadeq, as both defense minister and premier, asserted that the shah had meddled in security matters and had caused confusion among the military commanders. The shah announced Feb. 28 that he would leave Iran that night for an indefinite stay abroad for health reasons and that a regency council had been set up to rule in his absence. Large crowds of royalists, ex-army officers and supporters of Majlis Speaker Kashani converged on the palace. Mossadeq was driven from his home in Teheran by a hostile mob Feb. 28 but managed to retain control of the government Mar. 4 after 4 days of rioting by nationalists, royalists, Communists and religious groups.

These incidents climaxed weeks of tension stemming from Mossadeq's quarrel with the shah over alleged "court intrigues" against his administration. Rumors that it was Mossadeq who was forcing the shah to leave the country apparently touched off the riots. The shah's supporters demonstrated outside the Imperial Palace Feb. 28 until the shah himself promised to remain in Iran. Joined by followers of Mossadeq's chief parliamentary foe, Kashani, the pro-shah forces thereupon marched to Mossadeq's house, smashed the front gates and clashed with government guards as the pajama-clad premier and Foreign Min. Hossein Fatemi fled through a rear door to the U.S. Point 4 Aid office nearby. Later, Mossadeq and other officials took refuge in the parliament building, the traditional political sanctuary. U.S. offices were closed during the outbreak and Americans advised to stay off the streets.

Returning to his home Mar. 1, Mossadeq accused retired army officers and "foreign elements" of inciting the disturbances. He discharged Army Chief of Staff Mahmud Baharmast for failing to subdue the mobs and named Defense Undersecy. Tahgi Riahi as new army chief. In a "victory" broadcast Mar. 2, he thanked his supporters and urged them to refrain from further demonstrations. By Mar. 3, government forces controlled Teheran's main streets, dispersed remaining demonstrators and began rounding up alleged anti-Mossadeq plotters. Business reopened Mar. 4.

Mossadeq renewed his quarrel with the shah Apr. 6 when he demanded that the shah be stripped of his power. In a broadcast to the nation, Mossadeq said that the Majlis must order the shah to "reign constitutionally," not rule. Attempted demonstrations April 7 by supporters of both factions were dispersed in Teheran by police. The shah May 11 issued a royal decree demanded by Mossadeq transferring privately-held royal estates to the government instead of to individual peasants. The decree recommended that plots be rented to peasants on a 99-year lease. 60 million rials ($2 million at official exchange rates, $800,000 at the unofficial rate) was paid the shah for the lands. It was to be spent on charities by the Royal Institute for Social Service under governmental supervision. (Princess Ashraf, twin sister of the shah, was ordered July 26 to leave Iran immediately. She had returned without permission July 25 to raise funds to pay for medical treatment for her son. The princess and Queen Mother Raj Moluk had left Iran in 1952.)

Mossadeq Turns to USSR

Mossadeq's operation of a neutralist, nonalignment policy appeared to suit neither Washington nor Moscow. Rebuffed by Washington, he finally turned to Moscow in search of a financial adjustment and, perhaps, assistance—but too late to save his government.

Mossadeq Mar. 20, 1953 had rejected the latest British-U.S. proposal for settling the Anglo-Iranian oil nationalization dispute. The proposal offered Iran a 20-year payment plan to liquidate the Anglo-Iranian Oil Co.'s claims for compensation. Iranian Foreign Min. Hussein Fatemi announced Apr. 7 that 25% of the proceeds from Iranian oil sales was earmarked for compensation payments.

Mossadeq, in an interview with Homer Bigart published in the *N.Y. Herald Tribune* May 5, appealed for U.S. economic aid to Iran and for the U.S. to buy Iranian oil. He said that his country's economy would decline unless it could sell its oil in quantity. He warned that any violent change in the government, even a rightist coup, would lead eventually to Communist rule.

In an exchange of letters made public July 9, Pres. Dwight D. Eisenhower told Mossadeq that the U.S. could not give Iran special aid to solve economic problems arising from the Anglo-Iranian oil dispute. Replying to a May 28 letter from Mossadeq, the President promised only continued technical and military aid at the 1952 level, and he said that U.S. citizens would oppose the purchase of Iranian oil while the dispute remained unsettled. Eisenhower's letter, dated May 29, advised Iran to reach an agreement with Britain on the large-scale marketing of oil to alleviate "the present dangerous situation" "before it is too late." (In the year ended June 30, Iran had received about $24 million in Point 4 funds from the U.S. and an additional "moderate" amount of military aid. This increased total U.S. Point 4 aid to Iran since 1950 to $47 million.)

Considered desperate for revenues, Mossadeq May 7 signed a bill nationalizing Iran's Caspian Sea fisheries under the Iranian National Fishing Co. Since the Soviet Union shared fishing rights with Iran in the Caspian, the move became an issue in Soviet-Iranian relations. After several months of increased tension, a Soviet-Iranian agreement to hold high-level talks to "remove all differences," including financial and border disputes, was announced in Teheran and Moscow Aug. 10.

Parliamentary Crisis

Mossadeq had decided in July 1953 to shore up his weakening internal political position by forcing countrywide parliamentary elections and—so he apparently hoped—a mandate for constitutional changes.

The resignation of 27 pro-Mossadeq Majlis deputies July 14 ended the effective existence of Iran's only remaining parliamentary body. Reducing active membership to 52, the resignations made opposition deputies ineffective (a 69-member quorum was required for Majlis action) and left Mossadeq absolute ruler under previously-granted decree powers. 29 more pro-Mossadeq and independent deputies quit the Majlis July 15–19, bringing total resignations to 56 and leaving only 23 active members, mostly opposition representatives. Speaker Abdullah Moazami conceded July 19 that there was no hope of further sessions.

The Majlis' dissolution was demanded July 21 at separate Nationalist and Communist demonstrations marking the first anniversary of Mossadeq's return to the premiership. Thousands of Communists, massed in Teheran's Parliament Square, also shouted anti-U.S. slogans and called for the expulsion of Americans from Iran. The smaller, Nationalist meeting was held in the square earlier in the day. The rallies were kept separate to avoid fighting between the 2 groups.

Voting rules decreed by the Iranian cabinet July 25 swept aisde the secret ballot guaranteed by Iran's constitution since 1906. The decree, published July 28, set rules for a forthcoming plebiscite on the dissolution of the Majlis. It provided for 2 polling booths in each election district—one for those voting for dissolution, the other for those against it. Each ballot was to be signed with the voter's name and the number and place of issue of his identity card.

Mossadeq had threatened July 27 that he would resign if the Majlis were not dissolved. He said the Majlis had become "the hotbed and main base of wrecking activities" and accused remaining Majlis deputies of abetting "intrigues and tricks of foreigners." He reiterated a July 20 charge that all Iran's troubles were caused by "plots and intrigues of foreigners."

In the non-secret national plebescite, more than 99.9% of the voters in Teheran Aug. 3 and a similar percentage in cities and towns outside Teheran Aug. 10 approved Mossadeq's proposal to dissolve the Majlis, the government said.

Shah's Supporters Oust Mossadeq

In a brief, bloody revolt, Iranian royalists, led by army troops who turned against their officers, overthrew Mossadeq's government Aug.19, 1953. The uprising climaxed a 3-day contest for power between Mossadeq's Nationalist supporters and forces supporting the pro-Western shah. At least 300 deaths were reported during the revolt, about 200 of them during a tank battle at Mossadeq's heavily-fortified home. After his personal bodyguard was defeated, the mob seized his possessions and sold them on the street to passersby. By mid-afternoon royalist forces made a Teheran radio announcement proclaiming their victory.

Throughout the period during which Mossadeq was prime minister there had been contant rumors of a British invasion. Britain was blockading Iran's Persian Gulf ports, and Britain and the West were boycotting Iranian oil, but Mossadeq had refused to bow to the British. The huge refinery at Abadan was shut down, thousands of workers out of work and a grave financial crisis created. The Teheran press and business leaders had complained of deteriorating economic conditions caused by the lack of oil revenues.

For some time it had been apparent that Mossadeq had been flirting with the Tudeh (Masses, or Communist) party, and Britain and the U.S. indicated concern lest the Soviet Union gain control of Iran's vast oil reserves. (David Wise and Thomas B. Ross wrote in *Invisible Government* of the alleged activities of the Central Intelligence Agency [CIA] in driving Mossadeq out of office. According to Wise and Ross: Communist mobs controlled the streets of Teheran for much of the week after the shah's hurried departure; Mossadeq, however, had failed to line up army support, and with CIA money and influence, the army units moved against the government; CIA money was used to get wave after wave of demonstrators into the streets; Gen. Zahedi came out of hiding, and Anglo-Iranian oil was saved.)

Mossadeq Aug. 16 had temporarily survived a first bid for power by the royalists. He refused to obey a decree of the shah dismissing him as premier. Palace guards who tried to deliver the decree were arrested. Maj. Gen. Fazlollah Zahedi, an old political foe of Mossadeq's who had been in hiding since April, was blamed for the attempted ouster, and a reward was posted for his capture. The shah flew to Iraq from Ramsar, a Caspian Sea resort. Foreign Min. Fatemi denounced the shah as a "traitor," and warned him not to return to Iran. Nationalist and Communist-led mobs celebrated the shah's flight by wrecking all statues of him and his late father in Teheran Aug. 17.

The pro-Mossadeq trend changed after police and army troops, who had been described as loyal to Mossadeq, turned Aug. 18 against the pro-Mossadeq mobs and began forcing them at bayonet-point to shout anti-Mossadeq slogans. The police and troops concentrated their anger on white-shirted youths identified as Tudeh partisans. The troops' boldness in the face of their officers' avowed support of Mossadeq apparently heartened the shah's followers, who previously had staged only one small demonstration. They joined the battle early Aug. 19.

Gen. Zahedi, 56, who had proclaimed himself premier by appointment of the shah Aug. 16, took over the new regime. The shah was in Rome when his followers gained control in Teheran. Mossadeq and 3 of his aides surrendered to Zahedi Aug. 20 and were held under arrest in the Teheran Officers Club. The shah had sent orders for the army to protect the ex-premier. (A military court in Teheran Dec. 21 convicted Mossadeq of treason and sentenced him to 3 years in solitary confinement. The shah had opposed prosecution demands for the death penalty.)

In a broadcast Aug. 19, Zahedi had told the country that he intended to re-establish rule by law, elevate the standard of living and reduce the cost of living, raise workers wages. His regime imposed an
8 p.m. to 5 a.m. curfew, banned public assembly and took other measures to prevent new riots and rebellions. Reports to Teheran Aug. 19
indicated that the Zahedi forces had not yet gained control of some
cities in southern Iran although they had taken charge in Azerbaijan
and other districts in the north near the USSR.

U.S. Aids Iran, Helps Settle Oil Dispute

U.S. financial aid to the new government of Iran was promised by
Pres. Eisenhower Aug. 26, 1953 in a letter to Premier Zahedi. Zahedi's
plea for aid and the Eisenhower answer were made public Sept. 1.
Eisenhower did not name a sum but said the U.S. was "ready to assist"
Iran in rebuilding its economy. The U.S. embassy in Teheran was re-
ported Aug. 31 to have recommended $100 million in emergency aid.

Zahedi told the U.S. President that Iran was grateful for earlier U.S.
aid but that it was "not sufficient in amount and character to tide Iran
over the financial and economic crisis." "The Treasury is empty; foreign exchange resources are exhausted; the national economy is deteriorated. Iran needs immediate financial aid to enable it to emerge
from . . . economic and financial chaos," Zahedi wrote.

Zahedi reported to his countrymen Aug. 27 that the Mossadeq
regime had left a deficit of 17,705,125,040 rials ($544,733,078). He
said that the Mossadeq government had increased the supply of paper
money by at least 50% while dissipating nearly $50 millions of the
dollar and sterling reserves.

Eisenhower granted $45 million to Iran Sept. 5 as emergency eco-
nomic aid under the U.S. Mutual Security Act. The grant was in addition to $23,400,000 announced by the U.S. Sept. 3 for continued
technical and military projects in Iran. The technical aid grant was the
largest U.S. Point 4 annual expenditure in any one country. Both
sums, plus military and technical aid previously pledged, increased the
U.S. contribution to Iran in the fiscal year to $97½ million.

Britain and Iran were reported in London Oct. 26 to have opened
secret talks on the resumption of diplomatic relations. Herbert
Hoover Jr., U.S. State Department oil consultant, completed Oct. 27 a
week of conferences with the Iranian Oil Commission on settling the oil
dispute. Iran proposed in a message to the British Foreign Office (via
Switzerland) the resumption of Anglo-Iranian diplomatic relations and
the settlement of the oil dispute, it was reported Nov. 2.

Britain and Iran announced the renewal of diplomatic relations Dec. 5. Ex-Majlis Speaker Ayatollah Kashani, a *mullah* (influential religious leader), called for a countrywide day of mourning—the closing of all businesses and the wearing of black armbands—Dec. 6 in protest against the resumption, but the capital remained quiet. Teheran University students staged anti-British demonstrations Dec. 7, however, and attempted to disarm the police who came to quell the protests. The police opened fire; 2 persons were killed, and 30 reportedly were injured.

Iran and 8 Western oil companies Aug. 5, 1954 announced the terms under which they agreed to reactivate Iran's frozen oil industry. The agreement, which ended a 3-year battle that had bankrupted Iran, was scheduled to run for 25 years, with 3 5-year extensions. The terms of the pact, covering production, marketing and compensation, were announced in Teheran and London by Iranian Finance Min. Ali Amini and Howard Page of Standard Oil of New Jersey, chairman of the oil firms' negotiators. *The major terms of the pact:*

Production—The 8-firm consortium (Standard Oil of New Jersey and of California, Texas Co., Gulf Oil and Socony Vacuum, all of the U.S.; Anglo-Iranian of Britain, Royal Dutch Shell and Compagnie Française des Petroles) would operate the Abadan refinery and surrounding oil fields. Iran retained title to the fields and refineries.

Marketing—The consortium would buy the oil output from Iran and sell it on the world market.

Compensation—Details of the rate of payment were not announced but it was indicated that Iran and the oil firms would split 50-50. Amini and Page estimated that Iran would get $420 million in direct oil revenue and taxes in the first 3 years. Anglo-Iranian was to get about $85 million for property seized by Iran; the company had originally asked $500 million.

The U.S. had a major mediator's role in the British-Iranian talks, which had begun in Oct. 1953. Groundwork for the pact was credited to Herbert C. Hoover Jr., U.S. State Department oil consultant, who conferred with both sides throughout the negotiations. The agreement was ratified by the Majlis, 113-5, Oct. 21 and by the Senate, 41-4, Oct. 28. The first shipment of fuel oil under the agreement left Abadan Oct. 31 on the Anglo-Iranian company tanker *British Advocate.*

U.S. State Secy. John Foster Dulles Dec. 31 hailed the oil settlement in Iran as a distinct "gain" for Western diplomacy in 1954. The U.S. had announced Nov. 2 that it would give Iran $42.3 million as a grant $85 million in loans to sustain the country's economy until its revived oil industry began to pay dividends.

The shah's hand was considered greatly strengthened by the outcome of the 1951-3 crisis. His chief foes were jailed, exiled or killed by Teheran mobs, and the royalists disposed of the surviving leaders before 1955. (Ex-Foreign Min. Hossein Fatemi, 40, was executed by firing squad in Teheran Nov. 10 for treason in the attempt to dethrone the shah. Fatemi had been convicted and sentenced by a military court Oct. 10, and the shah rejected his appeal Nov. 6. 21 other persons had been executed since the beginning of October for taking part in a pro-Communist conspiracy in the armed forces.)

ISRAEL & THE FOREIGN POWERS (1951–4)

There was turmoil in many parts of the Middle East in the years following the Arab-Israeli war of 1948, but Israel enjoyed a brief period of relative stability. Immigrants flowed into the new country, land was reclaimed, the desert bloomed and the army trained for future battles.

Early in its existence as a state, Israel clearly recognized the pivotal importance of its foreign relations with the U.S. and the USSR. Its relations with the latter, at first apparently cordial, soon fell afoul of ill-concealed anti-Semitism in the Soviet bloc and of the Soviet decision that Russian interests in the Middle East would be better served by supporting Arab nationalism. Israel's relations with West Germany were also prominent in the country's international affairs.

Israel Demands German Reparations

Israel formally asked the British, American, French and Soviet governments Mar. 12, 1951 to support its claim for $1½ billion in reparations from Germany. Israeli notes to the 4 powers pointed out that when reparations had been allocated after the war, the Jewish people had not had a sovereign state, that their claims on Germany had gone by default and that the State of Israel, a principal absorber and rehabilitator of the survivors of Nazism, could speak alone on behalf of the whole Jewish people. The notes referred to the deliberate slaughter of more than 6 million Jews by the Nazis and the confiscation of $6 billion worth of Jewish property. They cited in detail the verdicts at Nuremberg on the Nazi war criminals. Israel declared that indemnification for the heirs of the victims of Nazism and for the rehabilitation of the survivors was within the Germans' capabilities.

Israel also said: Between 1938 and 1950 nearly 380,000 penniless Jews had been taken to Palestine from territory conquered by the 3d Reich. A great deal of support had come from Jewish communities abroad, but most of the cost of resettling and rehabilitating the Jewish immigrants had been paid by financially hard-pressed Israel. The German people, who continued to hold the assets plundered from the Jews, should help pay for the immigrants' rehabilitation, Israel said. $1½ billion—a "minimum claim on behalf of the sufferers of the Nazi regime"—would not be beyond the capacity of the German people to pay over a period of years and partly in valuables other than money. What Israel demanded about equaled the value of West Germany's exports, and West German exports, "in view of Germany's economic recovery, are likely to increase considerably during 1951." Israel urged the British, U.S., French and Soviet governments not to hand over full power to any German government before obtaining an express commitment for the payment of reparations to Israel.

The Israeli Knesset (parliament) Jan. 9, 1952 gave its approval to the opening of negotiations with the West German government on reparations.

Israel Mar. 21 acknowledged at The Hague that it was not in a position to assess accurately the Jewish property confiscated and plundered by the Nazis and could base its claim only on the actual and anticipated cost of resettling Jewish immigrants from former Nazi-controlled territories. Their number was estimated at 500,000, and the cost of their resettlement would amount to $3,000 per person, or $1½ billion. Of this, $1 billion (4.2 billion Deutschemark) was claimed as owed by West Germany. The Conference on Jewish Material Claims against Germany, led at the Hague by Moses Leavitt and Nahum Goldmann, demanded that $500 million (2.1 billion DM) be paid within 5 years. It emphasized that this sum represented only a fraction of the losses sustained.

The Federal (West) German Republic announced from Bonn June 17, 1952 that it was prepared to pay unconditionally 3 billion DM and to settle the total amount in the form of goods in annual installments over a 12-year period. When the negotiations were resumed at The Hague June 19, the Germans affirmed the offer to Israel and subsequently (July 16) extended it to include the payment of 450 million DM to the Conference on Jewish Material Claims. An additional 50 million DM was put aside for compensation payments to Christians of Jewish origin persecuted in the 3d Reich as "racial" Jews.

A draft agreement between the Federal German Republic and Israel, based on the German offer, and 2 draft protocols between Western Germany and the Conference on Jewish Material Claims, were signed at The Hague Oct. 27 by the 3 delegations. The agreement between West Germany and Israel became effective Mar. 27, 1953 when documents of ratification were exchanged at UN Headquarters in New York. The bill approving the agreement was finally passed by the Bundestag Mar. 18 by 239-35 vote, with 86 abstentions. All the Communists in the Bundestag opposed the agreement on grounds that it would only benefit the "industrial magnates" in Israel, Germany and the U.S. and would support the creation of an "imperialist base" in the Middle East. The bill was approved unanimously by the Bundesrat Mar. 20 and was signed Mar. 22 by West German Pres. Theodor Heuss. The Israeli government ratified the agreement Mar. 22

after the Foreign Affairs Commission of the Knesset had approved it by 8 votes to 5, with one abstention. Israel had announced Mar. 3 that it had agreed to waive a clause in the agreement under which goods made available by Germany to Israel could not be carried in German ships. The decision to cancel this clause followed protests by the West German government that the Bundestag could not be expected to ratify an agreement containing a clause discriminating against German vessels.

At a press conference in Tel Aviv Sept. 14, 1952, Israeli Foreign Min. Moshe Sharett disclosed that there had been an exchange of notes with the Soviet Union about Israel's claim for $500 million in reparations from East Germany. He said that the Soviet reply had been unsatisfactory.

The slow growth of Israel's export industries resulted in a huge trade deficit and put a great strain on the country's economy in the first years of its existence. Starting in 1953, the large West German reparations payments to Israel, mostly in the form of goods, greatly eased the situation and reduced the shortage of raw materials for industry and of building materials and food.

Soviet Relations Deteriorate

From the very beginning the USSR's outwardly friendly attitude towards Israel had apparently been not very deep. The relationship between the 2 countries worsened during 1949-52. Russian accusations against the Israelis took the line that the latter had not really established a democratic and truly independent state. According to the Soviets, Israel had become a satellite of the U.S., a partner of a reactionary capitalist regime. Of importance in the Israeli-Soviet estrangement was the normalizing of relations between Israel and Britain. Some observers held that one of the main reasons the USSR had originally supported the establishment of the Jewish state was that in so doing it was opposing British objectives.

At bottom, some analysts said, the Soviet Union's hostility stemmed from fear of Israel's power to divide Soviet Jews' loyalty. According to some experts, Stalin had failed to anticipate the attractiveness of the state of Israel for Soviet Jews. It had long been held in the USSR that Soviet Jews no longer had any interest in a Jewish national movement. It came as a blow to the Russians when this was disproved in the period immediately after the Arab-Israeli war of 1948. In addition, the frequent and strident demands of Israeli government for unrestricted Jewish emigration from Russia proved offensive to Soviet leaders.

Soviet Deputy Foreign Min. Andrei Gromyko Nov. 21, 1951 gave to the Israeli diplomatic representative in Moscow a note warning Israel not to join the Middle East Command sponsored by the U.S., Britain, France and Turkey. The note said that the 4-power "proposals envisage . . . the stationing of foreign armed forces on the territory of Egypt and other countries of the Near and Middle East. . . ."

"The setting up of the so-called Middle East Command would lead to the military occupation of the countries of the Middle East . . . by the troops of the U.S. and Britain," Gromyko's note argued. That "cannot but lead to the loss of independence and sovereignty by these countries and their subjugation to certain great powers . . . trying to use their territories and material resources for their own aggressive ends. All references to the interests of the defense of the Middle Eastern countries are in reality merely a camouflage to disguise the drawing of these countries into military measures of the Atlantic bloc [NATO] directed against the Soviet Union and the people's democracies." The Soviet note said that the USSR had "invariably pursued a path of peace" and that any idea of a Soviet threat to the peace and security of the Middle East was "absurd."

In reply, Israel Feb. 27, 1952 sent the USSR a note assuring the Soviets that Israel would not join any aggressive pact against the USSR and asking that Soviet Jews be permitted to migrate to Israel.

Israel was known to have preferred to remain aloof from all formal alliances. Its relations with the Soviet Union and its east European satellites, however, proved more complex and apparently fraught with more danger to Israel than those with any other area, including the Arab world.

It had been disclosed Jan. 29, 1951 that the Soviet Union had rejected Israel's choice of Salman Shazar (formerly Rubashov), 61, an active Zionist in Czarist Russia, as Israeli minister to Moscow.

The American Jewish Committee reported Feb. 3 that 75,000 Jews had emigrated from eastern Europe in 1950 with the permission of the various governments. 47,000 of these Jews reportedly went to Israel.

The deterioration of relations with the USSR brought additional strains in Israel's handling of its domestic Communists, who were increasingly considered by some Israelis as all but agents of an anti-Israel power. Mrs. Hanna Lamdan, deputy speaker of the Knesset, and David Livshitz, a Knesset deputy, resigned from the leftist Mapam party Feb. 21, 1952 on the ground that it was Communist-controlled. The Israeli Communist Party ended its biennial session in Tel Aviv June 1, 1952 by condemning Zionism and asking for the return of Arab refugees, the expulsion of "American imperialists" and the abandonment of all territories not assigned to Israel in the 1947 UN partition plan.

The U.S. was not slow to underscore the indications of Soviet-bloc hostility towards Israel. For example, after the execution of 8 Czechoslovak Jewish public figures following the Slansky purge trial of late Nov. 1952 in Prague, the U.S. overtly noted the obvious inferences of menace from that quarter for Israel. Western diplomats in Vienna said Nov. 27 that the trial had several aims: (a) to win friends for the Soviets among Arabs by attacking Jews and Israel; (b) to warn Communists that the Kremlin would not permit deviation from its policies; (c) to win over East Germans to whom such events as the Slansky trial furnished confirmation of the correctness of Hitlerism; (d) to warn the 2 million Jews that they could expect to be persecuted; (e) to set the stage for trials in still other satellite states; and (f) to offer a scapegoat for Czechoslovak economic woes and the failure to deliver its quota of goods to Russia.

11 former Czechoslovak Communist leaders were condemned to death and 3 others sentenced to life imprisonment Nov. 27 after the 7-day Slansky trial, in which all 14 defendants had confessed to high treason, sabotage and espionage. The markedly anti-Semitic trial was the biggest purge staged by a Soviet satellite. (Other "show" trials had been conducted by Albania, Bulgaria and Hungary, where the ex-Foreign Min. Laszlo Rajk, also a Jew, was hanged in 1949.) Sentenced to be hanged were ex-Czechoslovak Communist Party General Secy. Rudolf Slansky, 51; Vladimir Clementis, 50; Otto Fischl, 50; Josef Frank, 43; Ludvik Frejka, 48; Bedrich Geminder, 51; Rudolf Margolius, 39; Bedrich Reicin, 41; Andre Simon, 47; Otto Sling, 50, and Karel Svab, 48. Life terms were meted out to Vavro Hajdu, 39; Evzen Loebl, 45, and Arthur London, 37. The Associated Press reported Nov. 27 that all except Clementis, Svab and Frank were Jews. All Western coverage of the trial was through monitored Prague Radio broadcasts. Western newsmen were not permitted in the country.

The indictments of the defendants named a long list of foreigners who allegedly had been associated with Slansky in recruiting "spies" for the West. Among those named were John Foster Dulles, his brother Allen W. Dulles, then the Central Intelligence Agency deputy director; the late U.S. Amb.-to-Czechoslovakia Laurence A. Steinhardt; ex-British Delegate-to-UN Sir Gladwyn Jebb; and even Noel Coward, the British actor-playwright-composer.

Trial testimony indicated that Noel Field, an ex-U.S. State Department employe, and his brother Hermann, who had disappeared in eastern Europe in 1949, were under arrest in a Soviet-bloc country—

Hungary, it later developed. 6 defendants said that they had been recruited as spies by the Field brothers. Another American, Alexander Taub, described as a former General Motors Co. representative in Prague, also was branded a "spy" instrumental in attempts of "American imperialists" to subject Czechoslovak industry to their control. (The U.S. State Department Nov. 20 had rejected as "baseless" the charges that Americans were plotting against the Prague government.)

Mordecai Oren, a leader of Israel's leftist Mapam party who had been arrested in Prague earlier, appeared Nov. 21 as a witness against Geminder and Clementis. Several prominent Czechoslovak Jews reportedly committed suicide during the trial. The deaths of Rudolf Bystricky, 44, ex-ambassador to Britain, and of the Bratislava Communist Party committee leader Dr. Tibor Kovac were reported by Viennese sources Nov. 25. Eric Kohn, the Prague Jewish community secretary, his wife and several high Czechoslovak army officers were reported by Tel Aviv sources Nov. 26 to have taken their own lives.

Israeli Foreign Min. Moshe Sharett Nov. 24 termed the trial "a campaign of desecration . . . calculated to serve as a threat to the Jews of Czechoslovakia and neighboring countries" and described it as "replete with propagandist effects of anti-Semitic incitement" in the Nazi tradition. The Israeli Knesset Nov. 25 expressed its "outrage" at the trial's "affront to Israel." Israeli police guarded the Czechoslovak legation in Tel Aviv after a protest demonstration there Nov. 24.

There was an ironic aspect to Prague's anti-Semitic display, however. Zachariah Shuster, European director for the American Jewish Committee, said in Paris Nov. 27 that the Czechoslovaks accused as "Zionist agents" actually had used their power to harass Jews and destroy Jewish life in Czechoslovakia. He pointed out that Slansky had been in power when measures blocking the emigration of Jewish citizens and capital were enacted. Only 320 Czechoslovak Jews had been permitted to emigrate to Israel in the 2 years after Slansky became the Czechoslovak Communist Party's general secretary. Shuster blamed Otto Fischl for an order allowing emigrant Jews to take with them only a limited amount of clothing and the Czechoslovak equivalent of $1. As a result of the Communist regime's measures, Shuster reported, only the Prague Old-New Synagogue remained open out of the numerous Jewish houses of public worship in Czechoslovakia.

The Soviet "doctors' plot" soon diverted world attention from Czechoslovakia. Tass and Radio Moscow reported Jan. 13, 1953 that 9 doctors and medical specialists—6 of whom were Jews—had been found to have caused the deaths of 2 Soviet leaders and to have plotted to kill others by deliberately incorrect medical treatment. The accused, said to have confessed to the crimes, were described in the accounts as "paid agents" of the U.S. and Britain and as "fiends in human form." They were charged with having killed Andrei Zhdanov, a ranking Politburo member, in 1948, and Col. Gen. Aleksandr S. Shcherbakov, director of the Soviet army's political administration until his death in 1945. Zhdanov had been very influential in Soviet foreign policy and had been reported to be Stalin's most likely heir as Russia's premier. The main details of the plot, according to Tass:

"Some time ago the State Security organs uncovered a terrorist group of doctors who had set themselves the task of shortening the life of Soviet leaders by means of harmful treatment. Among the members of this terrorist group were: Prof. M. S. Vovsi, therapeutist; Prof. V. N. Vinogradov, therapeutist; Prof. M. B. Kogan, therapeutist; Prof. B. B. Kogan, therapeutist; Prof. P. I. Yegorov, therapeutist; Prof. A. I. Feldman, otolaryngologist; Prof. Y. G. Etinger, therapeutist; Prof. A. M. Grinshtien, neuropathologist; G. I. Mayorov, therapeutist.

"The documents and investigations, the opinion of medical experts, and the confessions of those arrested prove that the criminals, secret enemies of the people, subjected their patients to harmful treatment and undermined their health. As a result of investigation, it was established that the members of the terrorist group, utilizing their positions as doctors and abusing the trust of their patients, deliberately and villainously undermined their health; purposely ignored the results of objective examination of the patients; made incorrect diagnoses which did not correspond to the actual nature of the illnesses: and then killed them by means of incorrect treatment.

"The criminals confessed that, having availed themselves of Zhdanov's illness, they made an incorrect diagnosis of his disease and, concealing the myocardial infarction from which he suffered, prescribed a regimen which was contraindicated for this serious illness, and thereby killed Comrade Zhdanov. It has been established through investigation that the criminals also shortened the life of Comrade Shcherbakov by incorrectly applying strong medicines for his treatment, introducing a detrimental regimen, and thus causing his death.

"The criminal doctors tried first of all to undermine the health of leading Soviet military cadres, to disable them and to weaken the defense of the country. They tried to disable Marshal Vassilievsky, Marshal Govorov, Marshal Koniev, Gen. Shtemenko, Adm. Levchenko and others, but arrest thwarted their villainous plans and the criminals failed to achieve their end. . . .

"Most of the participants in the terrorist group (M. S. Vovsi, B. B. Kogan, A. I. Feldman, A. M. Grinshtein, Y. G. Etinger and others) were connected with "Joint," an international Jewish bourgeois nationalist organization set up by the U.S. intelligence service, allegedly to render material aid to Jews in other countries. Actually, however, this organization, under the guidance of the U.S. intelligence service, conducts largescale espionage, terrorist and other subversive activities in a number of countries, including the Soviet Union. The arrested Vovsi stated during the interrogation that he had received a directive from the United States 'to exterminate the leading cadres of the USSR' from the 'Joint' organization through a Moscow doctor, Shimelyovich, and the well-known Jewish bourgeois nationalist [Solomon] Mikhoels.

"Other members of the terrorist group (V. N. Vinogradov, M. B. Kogan, P. I. Yegorov) proved to be agents of long standing [in] the British intelligence service. . . ."

Tass reported Jan. 20 that the Order of Lenin had been conferred on Dr. Lydia Timashuk "for assistance given to the government in uncovering the doctor-murderers." One of the 9 accused doctors (Prof. V. N. Vinogradov) had also received the Order of Lenin—in Feb. 1952 for "outstanding services in the development of Soviet medical science."

With the Jan. 13 announcements of the "doctors' plot" came the Soviet journalistic attacks on Zionism. The Soviet press accused Israel of "espionage" and launched a particularly sharp attack on the American (Jewish) Joint Distribution Committee (also known as the "Joint"), which the press accused of having conducted "undermining activities [in the Soviet Union] under the orders of the American intelligence."

Edward M. Warburg, chairman of the "Joint," Jan. 13 denied the Soviet press' charge. He said: "The American Jewish Joint Committee has been engaged in the relief and rehabilitation of Jewish victims of war and persecution since 1914.... It has operated at one time or another, according to need, in some 60 countries.... It has never engaged in political activities or deviated from its principle of exclusive adherence to its humanitarian role. The charges ... that the Joint Distribution Committee has engaged in espionage or has participated in plots against the Russian government, or any government, are fantastic. We categorically deny that there is any truth whatsoever in any of these charges."

Michael MacDermott, the U.S. State Department's official spokesman, issued this statement Jan. 13: "The reported Soviet arrest of a number of Jewish doctors with the accusation of 'medical sabotage' seems to be another step in the recent Soviet campaign against the Jews revealed in the anti-Zionist aspects of the Slansky trial. The Soviets have had recourse again to an old technique of theirs. The real motivation for the present charges is not yet known, but the Soviets have used this technique of the accusation of 'medical sabotage' before. For example, it was claimed during the 1947 'purge' trials that Maxim Gorki, the writer, had been the victim of medical sabotage by opponents of Stalin. It is becoming increasingly clear that the current Soviet allegations of Zionist plots are indicative of an extraordinary and growing sense of internal insecurity."

Israeli Foreign Min. Moshe Sharett declared in the Knesset Jan. 19 that the intrinsic falsity of the Soviet allegations, like those made in Prague, was obvious and that the charges against those accused were "utterly inconceivable to any normal human being." He said that the whole affair was intended exclusively for consumption in the Soviet bloc for the purpose of frightening the Jewish communities in the Soviet Union and the "satellites" and of preparing the populations of those countries for possible "reprisals" against the Jews. "Any attempt by persons and public bodies in Israel to justify or defend campaigns of anti-Jewish instigation which imperil the safety of Jews in any land will be regarded by the government of Israel as a hostile act against the State, from which all necessary consequences will be drawn," he declared. "The government of Israel will expose in the United Nations and on every platform the campaign of instigation against the Jewish people now going on in countries under Communist rule, and will raise its voice in warning of the danger which threatens millions of Jews living there."

Sharett's statement was supported, with one exception, by all parties in the Knesset, including the hitherto pro-Soviet Mapam. The exception was the Communist Party and its 5 deputies, whose leader, Shmuel Mikunis, provoked anger in the chamber when he asserted that there was no anti-Semitism in the Communist countries and that the arrested Jewish doctors had been "traitors to their country." (Mapam expelled the Knesset deputies Moshe Sneh [once a "security member" of the Jewish Agency Executive], Jacob Berman and Tustum Bustani from party membership Jan. 20 for their defense of the Soviet Union's treatment of the "doctors' plot.")

Histadrut, the Israeli General Federation of Labor, voted Jan. 16—with only one opposing vote—to ban Communist Party members from all union posts. It adopted a resolution denouncing the Communist Party as "an enemy of the nation, traitorous to the state and serving the interests of foreign powers." Histadruth's secretariat voted Feb. 8 to suspend all current Communist officers and to seek court sanction for the ouster of all Communist members from its unions as "avowed enemies of the Jewish nation."

The Soviet foreign affairs weekly *Novoe Vremy (New Times)* charged Jan. 21 that Premier David Ben-Gurion and other Israeli and Zionist leaders, by "supporting the policy of American imperialists," were working for the establishment of "bloody fascist regimes permeated by a spirit of racial bigotry, including anti-Semitism." The weekly, in denouncing Jewish "enemies of the Jewish working people," said: Ben-Gurion and Foreign Min. Sharett were servants of the U.S. State Department; Dr. Reuben Shiloah of the Israeli Foreign Office was chief of Israeli intelligence; Amb.-to-U.S. Abba S. Eban was an agent of British intelligence; the late Pres. Chaim Weizmann was a British sympathizer; the American Joint Distribution Committee operated an espionage-diversionist network in eastern Europe; Zionist leaders, hostile "toward the Soviet Union and the entire camp of peace," had "sold out" to U.S. intelligence and were helping to create a "5th column" in the "People's democracies" in return for American support of Israel.

The Israeli consulate in New York commented that "anti-Semites have accused Jews of many things" but that the Russians, through *New Times* were the first to have "accused Jews of Israel of anti-Semitism."

Jewish communities and organizations throughout eastern Europe became targets of a continuing campaign against alleged Western agents in the Soviet bloc. Police raided Jewish homes and business places throughout East Germany Jan. 18, 1953 in a search for "Zionist spies." West Germans reported Jan. 22 that 383 Jews had fled East Germany since the beginning of 1953. Among them, it was reported, was Julius Meyer, head of the Federation of Jewish Communities in East Germany and a Socialist Unity (Communist) member of the Volkskammer (parliament). The East German Interior Ministry also began taking a census of all church buildings in the state Jan. 19 with a view to converting "unnecessary" church buildings to other uses. *Taegliche Rundschau (Daily Review)*, the Soviet army newspaper in East Berlin, indicated Jan. 18 that the East German moves were under the direction of 3 Moscow-trained Communists: Deputy Premier Walter Ulbricht, the Socialist Unity Party leader; Wilhelm Zaisser, the secret police chief; and Deputy Foreign Min. Anton Ackermann.

The arrest of Lajos Stoeckler, president of the Hungarian Jewish community, had been announced in Budapest Jan. 17. He was said to have been caught with "substantial amounts of American dollars and Swiss francs" in violation of Hungarian law. Stoeckler's Communist-approved organization was understood to have administered funds of the American Joint Distribution Committee since it had been banished from Hungary in 1950. The Communist organ *Esti Budapest (Evening Budapest)* commented Jan. 17 that Hungary had to "take a lesson from Moscow revelations" of alleged Zionist conspiracy against Soviet leaders and "unveil hidden enemies in our own country." The replacement of Hungarian Justice Min. Gyula Decsei, a Jew, by Bela Kovacs was announced in Budapest Feb. 8.

A search for "enemy elements—bourgeois nationalists and Jewish Zionists"—in Lithuanian Republican government organizations was announced in Kaunas Jan. 20.

Nikolai A. Mikhailov, a Soviet Communist Party secretary speaking in Moscow Jan. 21 on the 29th anniversary of Lenin's death, demanded a merciless drive against "degenerates or double-dealers" within the Soviet Communist Party.

A new volume of the *Soviet Encyclopedia*, as described in dispatches from Moscow Feb. 6, said that the Jews did not constitute a nation because they were not a "historic, concentrated, stable community of people." It denounced Zionists as "agents of American and

British imperialists" and called Israel a reactionary state and a war base for the U.S.

The Soviet Union broke diplomatic relations with Israel Feb. 12, 1953, giving as the reason the bombing Feb. 9 of the Soviet legation in Tel Aviv. Foreign Min. Andrei Y. Vishinsky said that the "terrorist" incident gave "evidence of the contempt of Israel for the elementary conditions for normal diplomatic activities of the representatives of the USSR." He called in Israeli Amb.-to-USSR Shmuel Eliashiv at 1 a.m. Moscow time and announced the severance, at the same time demanding the immediate withdrawal of the Israeli legation from Moscow. The Israeli Foreign Office later Feb. 12 called the break a "mere pretext" for further steps toward the "utter isolation and intimidation of Soviet Jewry, for whose fate grave anxiety is felt."

The Feb. 9 explosion, caused by a missile thrown into the Soviet legation garden in Tel Aviv, injured the wife of Soviet Min.-to-Israel Pavel Ivanovich Yershov and 2 legation employes. Israeli Premier David Ben-Gurion Feb. 10 denounced anti-Communist extremists held responsible for the bombing and offered full compensation to the victims and restitution for all damage done to the legation. Israeli police arrested 30 to 50 suspects, many of them members of the Young Hebrews Association and the Anti-Communist League, who had conducted demonstrations against anti-Jewish acts in the Soviet bloc.

Ben-Gurion told the Knesset Feb. 16 that Moscow's break with Israel was the culmination of a "campaign of defamatory propaganda against the State of Israel, the Zionist movement and world Jewry." His statement was indorsed, 79-16, by the Knesset Feb. 17.

(Soviet Communists had staged a huge ceremonial funeral in Moscow Feb. 15 for Col. Gen. Lev Zakharovich Mekhlis, one of 2 Jewish members of the Soviet Communist Party Central Committee, whose death had been announced Feb. 13. Foreign observers in Moscow regarded the unusual tribute to Mekhlis as an attempt to offset effects abroad of Soviet measures against Jews.)

In Washington Feb. 17, U.S. State Undersecy. Walter Bedell Smith received diplomatic representatives of 7 Arab states (Egypt, Syria, Jordan, Lebanon, Iraq, Saudi Arabia and Yemen), who urged the U.S. not to extend aid to Israel because of its dispute with the USSR. (Israeli Amb.-to-U.S. Abba S. Eban had called on all free countries Feb. 13 to give Israel increased moral and material support "because, of all the governments in the Near East, we have shown our devotion to democratic causes.") Egyptian Amb. Kamil Abdul Rahim told Smith that Israel was trying to "exploit" the Soviet diplomatic break and that Western "help of any sort" for Israel would fan the "smoldering fire" of Jewish-Arab enmity.

The Moscow *Literaturnaya Gazeta (Literary Gazette)* charged Feb. 17 that 140,000 Arabs in Israel were living under "intolerable conditions" in "a ghetto." (The first of many villages for Arabs displayed by the 1948-9 war to be established by the Israeli government had been formally opened near Ramle Feb. 11. Each of 50 Arab families received a one-room concrete house, 2½ acres of garden and farm land and an interest in 125 acres of cooperative olive and orange groves.)

Stalin's death Mar. 5, 1953 brought the Soviet anti-Zionist campaign to a standstill before the 9 accused Soviet doctors had been forced to stand trial. The new Soviet Interior Ministry announced Apr. 4 that 15 prominent Soviet doctors, including the 3 Slavs and 9 Jews previously accused, had been freed because the charges against them had been proven false. The 6 other doctors implicated with the original 9 were named in the announcement, but no details of any charges against them were made available. A former deputy minister was accused of trumping up the case, and a Communist Party secretary was dismissed for having let the ex-deputy succeed with his scheme.

The doctors' exoneration erased one of the chief reasons offered for an anti-Zionist campaign begun in the USSR during the last weeks of Stalin's life. Israel called on the new Soviet regime Apr. 4 to complete its "redress of injustice" by the "termination of the anti-Jewish campaign" and the "resumption of normal relations" with Israel.

The Soviet announcement by Deputy Premier Lavrenti P. Beria's Interior Ministry Apr. 4 acknowledged that the confessions and other evidence against the doctors had been obtained through "the use of impermissible means of investigation which are strictly forbidden" under Soviet law. The Communist Party newspaper *Pravda* Apr. 6 singled out a deputy chief of the old State Security Ministry named Ryumin as the instigator of the miscarriage of justice. It said that he and several of his colleagues, who had sought to inflame "nationalist hostilities" in the USSR, had been arrested. *Pravda* reported Apr. 7 that Semyon Diesovich Ignatiev had been dismissed from the new 5-man Communist Party secretariat because, as State Security Minister when the doctors were arrested, he had been guilty of "political blindness and gullibility."

Solomon Mikhoels, director of the Jewish State Theater before his death in 1948, had been named as a link between the doctors and the American Joint Distribution Committee. An article in *Pravda* Apr. 6 cleared Mikhoels as well as the doctors. It said that Ryumin and his associates had concealed from an investigating commission certain facts about the medical treatment of Zhdanov and Shcherbakov. *Pravda* promised everyone in the Soviet Union that "his citizen's rights are under the reliable protection of Soviet socialist legality" and that each

Soviet citizens' constitutional rights "will be sacredly observed and secured by the Soviet government."

Diplomats and U.S. officials in Washington expressed varied opinions Apr. 4 on why the Russians had reversed the case against the doctors. Some thought that it was done to end the anti-Jewish campaign, which had damaged Soviet prestige throughout the world. Others believed that it signified a struggle for power among Soviet politicians and a feeling of insecurity on the part of the Malenkov regime.

The Soviet Union resumed diplomatic relations with Israel July 20, 1953 and named Aleksandr Abramov as minister. Abramov presented his ambassadorial credentials to Israeli Foreign Min. Moshe Sharett in Jerusalem Dec. 2 in recognition of Israel's right to relocate its foreign ministry there from Tel Aviv. (Foreign Min. Sharett had written to Soviet Foreign Min. Vyacheslav Molotov July 6 and had renewed Israel's offer of full compensation for the injuries to personnel and restitution for Soviet property damaged in the bomb explosion Feb. 9 at the Soviet legation in Tel Aviv.)

Large-scale commodities trading ultimately developed between Israel and the USSR. The Israeli embassy in Moscow announced Nov. 3, 1955 that the Soviet Union had agreed to sell Israel 350,000 to 400,000 tons of crude and fuel oils and buy 15,000 tons of Israeli fruit.

Israel's relations continued bad, however, with Rumania, another Soviet-bloc country and, before World War II, home to the 2d-largest Jewish population in eastern Europe. For half a year beginning in the fall of 1953, leading Rumanian Jews, most of them Zionists and many already in jail for several years, were tried—some secretly—and sentenced for treason, espionage and "Zionist crimes." 150 Rumanian Jews reportedly were in detention, and at least 73 of them stood trial between Oct. 1953 and May 1954. Among those tried, and their sentences: Dr. Mishu Benvenisti, ex-chairman of the Zionist Federation of Rumania, tried in Mar. 1954, life imprisonment; Mrs. Mishu (Susanne) Benvenisti, a leader of the World Jewish Congress' Rumanian section, tried in Oct. 1953, 15 years; Ion Cohen, chairman of the World Jewish Congress' Rumanian section, tried in Mar. 1954, life imprisonment; Dan Eshanu, Poalc Zion (Zionist Labor Party) chairman, tried in Apr. 1954, sentence not published; Leon Itzcar, ex-chairman of Rumania's Jewish National Fund, tried in Apr. 1954, sentence not published; Dr. Cornel Jancu, deputy chairman of the World Federation of General Zionists, tried in Apr. 1954, sentence not published; his wife, Mrs. Cornel Jancu, tried in Mar. 1954, 20 years; Ion Littmann, a leader of the World Jewish Congress' Rumanian section, tried in Nov. 1953, 10 years; the Jewish historian Dr. Theodore Loewenstein, tried in Apr. 1954, sentence not published; M. A. Mark, leader of Hashomer Hatzair, a leftist Rumanian group, tried in Mar. 1954, 20 years; Dr. Bernhard Rohrlich, ex-chairman of the Zionist Federation of Rumania, tried in Apr. 1954, sentence not published; Moshe Weiss, Rumanian Zionist youth leader, tried in Mar. 1954, 20 years; and A. L. Zissu, editor and Jewish anti-Nazi resistance hero, tried in Mar. 1954, life imprisonment.

(The Rumanian news agency Agerpres reported July 4, 1954 that Mrs. Susanne Benvenisti and Ion Littmann's sentences had been reversed and that they would be retried. Agerpres also reported that several other imprisoned Jewish figures had been released.)

The trials had provoked a strongly adverse reaction in Israel. Premier Moshe Sharett told the Knesset May 24, 1954 that Israel was convinced from the reports it had received of the trials that Rumania had conducted them merely to punish Rumanian Jews attempting to emigrate to Israel. Sharett declared that Israel would "unceasingly protest against this injustice" and continue to urge the victims' release and their right to relocate in Israel.

Rumania June 3 dispatched a note of protest to Israel over a "campaign of calumnies against the Rumanian People's Republic" conducted by "certain press organs and leading elements of political organizations in Israel known to be hostile to the Rumanian People's Republic." The note termed the attitude of some Israeli leaders toward the alleged campaign "an inadmissible attempt at interference in the internal affairs of another country." Israel would have to accept "the consequences arising from such actions," the note warned.

Later in June, Rumanian Chief Rabbi Moses Rosen and 37 colleagues in the Rumanian Rabbinate denied the existence of any racial discrimination in Rumania and declared that "for the first time in the country's history" Rumanian Jews could hold responsible posts in public life.

The World Jewish Congress early in July asked the UN Economic & Social Council (ECOSOC) to consider the trials of Rumanian Jewish leaders in its deliberations over Rumania's application for ECOSOC membership.

Israeli-U.S. Relations

Relations between the U.S., the world's most powerful country at midcentury, and Israel, one of the world's most diminutive, proceeded slowly but steadily on a basis of solid mutual respect. The principal differences in the first years of their mutual relations arose from Israel's preoccupation with neutrality and its problems with neighboring Arab countries.

(A special difference in another area stemmed from U.S. policy in reviewing the Nazi war crimes. John J. McCloy, the U.S. high commissioner in Germany, drew down on the U.S. an unfavorable reaction from Israel after announcing Jan. 31, 1951 that the U.S. occupation administration had decided to reduce or commute the sentences of 89 German war criminals detained in the U.S. Zone—including 21 persons previously under the death sentence. The U.S. occupation administration confirmed 7 remaining death sentences and 5 other prison sentences. Foreign Min. Moshe Sharett Mar. 12 informed the U.S. of Israel's feeling that the U.S. move "has in large measure undone the great achievement of the Nuremberg trials." Israel felt "profound pain" at the high commissioner's statement, Sharett said. He added: McCloy's step "will inevitably be interpreted as having introduced the consideration of political expediency into what was regarded throughout as a judicial and humanitarian issue, and that the deterrent effect of the sentences has therefore been gravely impaired.")

What was intended as a firm basis for good mutual relations took shape as Israel and the U.S. concluded in Washington Aug. 23, 1951 a treaty of friendship, commerce and navigation—the first of its kind for Israel with another country. The treaty was signed by U.S. State Secy. Dean G. Acheson and Israeli Amb. Abba S. Eban. The agreement set forth principles of nondiscriminatory treatment in trade and shipping between the 2 countries, contained provisions for private investment to promote the economic development of Israel and declared that both governments would accord to citizens and corporations of one another equally privileged treatment on a par with that extended by each to its own citizens and corporations. This provision represented an economic relationship far more mutually advantageous than the extension of most-favored-nation treatment.

The U.S. remained Israel's major trading partner for the first 3 full years of Israeli independence. The value of trade between the 2 countries amounted to $76.8 million in 1949, more than $105½ million in 1950 and more than $109.3 million in 1951.

A new factor entered into the bilateral trade after the U.S., Britain and France announced May 25, 1951 that all 3 Western countries would lift their joint embargo on the shipment of arms to Israel. The 3 countries' foreign ministers had decided in London the previous week that Israel (as well as Arab countries) could buy arms from the 3 if it promised that there would be no renewal of the Palestinian war. Pres. Truman said that he expected the agreement to "promote the maintenance of peace in the Near East." The State Department saw the agreement as a force for deterring an Arab-Israeli arms race. A British spokesman said that the new policy was aimed at helping both sides guard against Communist penetration.

The U.S. National Security Council Sept. 15, 1951 waived for Israel, Egypt and Iran the Korean-wartime restrictions on U.S. economic aid to countries exporting U.S.-blacklisted goods to the Soviet bloc. The restrictions had been imposed by Congress late in May 1951 under an appropriations bill rider later known as the Kem Amendment, after Sen. James P. Kem (R., Mo.), a leading sponsor. The National Security Council Sept. 12 had announced that Saudi Arabia had reported compliance with the Kem Amendment's restrictions.

U.S. economic assistance to Israel took several forms over the first few years of their mutual relations. The 2 countries Feb. 26, 1951 announced the conclusion of a "Point 4" agreement to provide Israel with technical assistance. 14 agreements implementing the $800,000 U.S. Point-4 program for Israel were signed June 11, 1952 in Jerusalem. (This was the first U.S.-Israeli pact signed in Jerusalem, not officially recognized by the U.S. as the Israeli capital.)

The U.S. Aug. 17, 1952 granted Israel $73 million in foreign aid for the fiscal year 1953. More than $70 million of it was earmarked for the relief and resettlement of immigrants to Israel; the rest was for technical cooperation projects. U.S. foreign aid to Israel in the 1954 fiscal year amounted to $52½ million.

The U.S. Foreign Operations Administration Apr. 21, 1954 alloted $13,125,000 in economic aid for Israel in the last quarter of fiscal 1954 (to June 30), thus increasing total U.S. economic aid to Israel in the fiscal year to $52½ million.

The U.S. Export-Import Bank extended a number of longterm loans to Israel—$135 million by 1951—at low interest rates for the purchase of American equipment, supplies and services for irrigation, citriculture and general agricultural purposes.

In the private sector, apart from the numerous Israel bond drives conducted by American Jews, organized generosity took the form of such offers as that by the Zionist Organization of America (ZOA) Jan. 18, 1953 to see to the mass transfer to Israel of 1½ million Jews left in eastern Europe if the Soviet-bloc lands would release them. (The ZOA's national administrative council met in New York shortly after the Soviet Union had announced the "discovery" of the Soviet "doctors' plot.") The United Jewish Appeal (UJA) conducted annual fund-raising campaigns for the new country's development. (UJA's goal for 1952, for example, was set Feb. 23 at $151½ million.)

Israel depended heavily on such private support in the first years of its existence. After moves to borrow $75 million to $111 million from the U.S. in 1953 came to nothing, Premier Ben-Gurion Nov. 13 wired the United Israel Appeal (the United Jewish Appeal's fund channel to the Jewish Agency for Israel) for $100 million to discharge Israel's "crippling short-term indebtedness." United Israel Appeal pledged Nov. 15 to borrow $75 million immediately for this purpose and appealed to American Jews to provide $125 million in UJA contributions and Israel bond subscriptions in 1954. Israeli Finance Min. Levi Eshkol Dec. 13 seconded this appeal and, 11 months after having announced a $35 million deficit in Israel's operating budget, pronounced his country as half-way toward its goal of economic self-sufficiency.

Despite the rank of American trade and the size of its aid contributions, both public and private, Israel showed no compulsion to consult U.S. interests before proceeding in international affairs. "Even the U.S. does not have enough money to buy" Israel's subservience, Ben-Gurion told the Knesset Nov. 5, 1951 after the Knesset had indorsed (63-16) his moderately pro-Western foreign policy. Nevertheless, he said, Israel enjoyed better relations with the West than with the Communist world, where Israel could deal only with governments and not directly with citizens, as in the West.

As outlined by Ben-Gurion, Israeli policy gave no consideration to taking any role in the Middle Eastern security organization planned jointly by the U.S., Britain, France and Turkey. Israel Nov. 19 denied reports that it had decided to join the projected defense command and asserted that its abiding concern involved instead the state's defense against another Arab attack. With the failure of Israel's position to gain wide recognition in the West, however, the American Zionist Council, coordinating and public relations arm of the American Zionist organizations, urged State Secy. John Foster Dulles Mar. 1, 1952 to withhold arms from the Arab League states unless they made peace with Israel.

The Soviet bloc's anti-Zionist campaign of late 1952 and early 1953 evoked a formal expression of sympathy from the U.S. Senate, which Feb. 27, 1953 adopted (79-0) a resolution condemning the Soviet Union and other east European governments for "vicious and inhuman campaigns" against Jews and other minorities in their lands. 15 absent Senators later asked to be recorded as voting affirmatively on the resolution. (*Izvestia,* the Soviet government's unofficial newspaper, had charged Feb. 24 that 3 American Jewish public figures had elaborated plans to make Israel the principal anti-Communist base in the Middle East. Izvestia listed the 3 as ex-Treasury Secy. Henry Morgenthau, Jr., Rep. Emanuel Celler [D., N.Y.] and Rep. Jacob J. Javits [R., N.Y.].)

U.S. State Secy. Dulles and Director Harold E. Stassen of the U.S. Mutual Security Agency visited Israel during a 20-day Mideast fact-finding tour May 10-30, 1953. Israeli economists asked Dulles and Stassen May 14 to help Israel borrow $75 million in the U.S. to convert expensive short-term credit into long-term obligations. The economists said that Israel had to meet $111 million in short-term debts by Mar. 31, 1954; they estimated that Israel could save $10-$15 million annually by the conversion.

When the 2 Americans visited Premier Ben-Gurion in Jerusalem, they discussed Mideast defense, compensation and resettlement of Arab refugees, Jordan Valley development, Jerusalem, other aspects of Israel's finances and world issues. Israeli Pres. Itzhak Ben Zvi made public May 18 a letter from Pres. Eisenhower, delivered by Dulles, in which the U.S. President said he was "most anxious . . . that the tensions" between Israel and the Arab states "be overcome so that real peace may return to the Near East." Eisenhower also expressed the hope that Israeli-American friendship would "continue at full tide in the future."

On his return from the Middle East June 1, State Secy. Dulles commented obliquely on Israel's long-standing intention of relocating its Foreign Ministry in Jerusalem, to which Israel 3½ years earlier had moved all its other ministries. "The world religious community has claims in Jerusalem which take precedence over the political claims of any particular nation," Dulles said.

Israel July 10 notified all foreign diplomatic missions (except the Netherlands' which had already moved) that it would officially transfer its foreign ministry from Tel Aviv to Jerusalem within 2 days. The geographical separation had prevented the Foreign Ministry from playing its full role in current affairs, Israel maintained, but the transfer in no way implied any governmental pressure on foreign embassies to move with the Foreign Ministry.

Dulles July 28 described the Israeli decision as "inopportune" and said that it added to "tensions in the Middle East" and "embarrassed" the UN in its aim of making Jerusalem an international city. Dulles also said that the U.S. government had twice asked Israel—in July 1952 and in Mar 1953—not to move the ministry.

Israeli Foreign Min. Moshe Sharett July 29 replied to Dulles with a public assertion that "full opportunity had been taken of Mr. Dulles' recent visit to Israel to acquaint him with the views and intentions of Israeli government." Sharett suggested that "the institution of some suitable form of UN supervision over the holy places"—most of which lay on the Jordanian side of the divided city—was "the only practicable way in which the international community can give expression to its interest in Jerusalem."

Eric A. Johnston, an official American visitor to the Middle East in Oct. 1953, reported to Pres. Eisenhower Nov. 17 on discussions that he had held with Israeli, Egyptian, Jordanian, Lebanese and Syrian governmental figures as the President's personal representative. The talks concerned UN Relief & Works Agency proposals, drafted by the Tennessee Valley Authority (TVA) on the basis of a study by the consulting engineering firm of C. T. Main, Inc., for developing the Jordan River's power and irrigation potential at a cost of $121 million. Johnston reportedly told the President that Israel, Jordan, Syria and Lebanon would probably accept the plan "after serious scrutiny."

But Jordanian Premier Fawzi el-Mulki had already said Nov. 14 at an interview in Amman that his government stood "fully prepared to continue bearing economic hardships rather than take part in any project leading to cooperation with Israel, either directly or indirectly." Premier Mulki denied that the Jordanian government had even promised Johnston to consider the plan. Johnston Nov. 23 denied that any of the Arab governments to which he spoke had rejected the plan.

Meanwhile, Israeli representatives to the UN had argued Nov. 17 that their country's prior plan to divert water from the upper Jordan for a hydroelectric power project was in no way incompatible with the TVA proposals. Israeli Amb.-to-UN Abba S. Eban asked the UN Security Council Nov. 18 to speed its decision on Israel's plan, which Israel Oct. 28 had agreed to suspend temporarily on the complaint of Syria, in order to facilitate the Security Council's deliberations.

The TVA project envisaged the irrigation of a 230,000-acre area— ⅔ of it in Jordan, Lebanon and Syria—through 2 power dams. The advantages of such a project, as Johnston saw them, were 3: (a) it would provide land and, hence, a living, for more than 300,000 of the 875,000 Palestinian Arab refugees living on a UN dole; (b) it would thereby remove the chief impulse for the continual border raids fueling the Arab-Israeli rancor; and (c) it would finally decide the perennially dangerous issue of the Jordan's water rights. UN sponsorship of the project was designed to obviate the necessity—professedly odious to the 3 adjacent Arab lands—of entering into a treaty with Israel over the matter.

Eastern Border Problems

The uneasy peace between Israel and its eastern Arab neighbor Jordan underwent several severe tests involving armed raids in both directions across their common border. The first major incident occurred shortly before mid-Oct. 1953, and the violence continued sporadically until Apr. 1954.

The Johnston mission to the Middle East had been spurred by the sudden crisis resulting from a night raid of 500 armed Israelis on the Jordanian village of Qibya Oct. 14-15, 1953. At least 42 Arab villagers perished in the raid. The village school and reservoir were destroyed, and the nearby villages of Shuqba and Badrus were shelled by a supporting party. The raid was in reprisal for repeated attacks from Jordan in which 421 Israelis had been killed since 1950. In the latest of those, the night of Oct. 12-13, a woman and her 2 children had been killed in the Israeli village of Yahud by a grenade thrown into their home. The attackers were believed to have come by Qibya.

Premier Ben-Gurion, in a radio broadcast Oct. 19, denied that Israeli regular forces had taken any part in the Qibya raid. He said that a "searching investigation" had left it "clear beyond doubt that not a single army unit was absent from its base on the night of the attack." "While the [Israeli] government deplores the shedding of innocent blood at Qibya," Ben-Gurion said, "all responsibility for it rests with the Jordanian government, which for years has tolerated and thereby encouraged acts of murder and pillage against inhabitants of Israel. . . . The government of Israel declares before the world that . . . we do not wish any circumstances to base our relations with our neighbors on force and the use of arms."

The U.S. State Department Oct. 19 declared that "those who are responsible should be brought to account." The U.S. government had grown "increasingly concerned" at the heightening tension on Israel's borders, it said. State Secy. Dulles Oct. 20 confirmed reports that the U.S. would withhold $60 million allocated for economic aid to Israel. He did not cite the Qibya raid as the cause but gave as the reason Israel's failure to comply with a ruling by Maj. Gen. Vagn Bennike, head of the UN's Palestinian truce supervision team, that Israel halt all work on its Jordan River hydroelectric project.

Pres. Eisenhower, at a press conference Oct. 28, expressed satisfaction with Israel's decision to comply with Gen. Bennike's request and announced that U.S. economic aid would resume at once. Dulles thereupon announced that the U.S. had set aside $26 million for economic aid to Israel in the July-Dec. 1953 period.

Events precipitated by the Qibya raid provoked some questions in Israel about U.S. interest in promoting Arab-Israeli conciliation. Dulles had been in London Oct. 16 conferring with the foreign ministers of Britain and France, and he had joined his Western Big 3 colleagues in urging the UN Security Council to look into the Qibya matter and to take up the whole problem of Arab-Israeli border violence. Israel took this as an opportunity to make overtures to Jordan for direct talks on their border strife problem.

Israeli Foreign Min. Sharett asked U.S. Charge d'Affaires Francis H. Russell Oct. 17 to use his good offices to help bring about high-level border security talks between Jordan and Israel. Israeli Amb.-to-U.S.-&-UN Abba Eban Nov. 12 urged that such talks take place immediately within the UN. Eban made the proposal 3 days after the UN Security Council had opened a formal debate on the Qibya raid and the general matter of border tensions between Israel and its neighbors. The Israeli government Nov. 16 finally addressed to the U.S., British and French governments identic notes repeating Eban's request for support for Israel's proposal of talks in New York between Israeli and Jordanian representatives on the functioning of the 1949 Palestine armistice agreement between the 2 countries.

Opinion within the U.S. Senate's influential Foreign Relations Committee seemed divided on the subject. Sen. Alexander Wiley (R., Wis.), the committee chairman, said at a United Israel Appeal seminar in Chicago Nov. 15 that the U.S. government wanted to establish a Middle Eastern defense command against Communist penetration and would "do everything feasible to encourage the Arab leaders to sit down with Israel around the peace table." But Sen. Guy M. Gillette of Iowa, the committee's ranking Democrat, said that the Eisenhower Administration was showing signs of attempting "to appease the war parties in the Arab states by kicking Israel in public." Gillette argued that such a policy would only serve to "strengthen those who yearn for a '2d round'" in Palestine. Gillette's view subsequently came to be shared in many quarters.

Jordanian Min.-to-U.S. Yusuf Haikal Nov. 16 rejected Israel's invitation for talks in New York and said that Jerusalem was the only likely site for them. Haikal also rejected Israel's suggestion that Jordan's Arab Legion (commanded by British Ltd. Gen. John Bagot Glubb) guard the Israeli-Jordanian border and demand that Israel withdraw its troops from the border.

At UN headquarters Nov. 18, the U.S., Britain and France submitted to the Security Council a joint resolution expressing "the strongest censure" of "the retaliatory action at Qibya taken by armed forces of Israel." The Western Big 3 powers said they regarded the Qibya raid as "a violation of the cease-fire provisions of Security Council resolution of July 15, 1948" and as "inconsistent with" Israel's "obligations under the General Armistice Agreement [of 1949] and the [UN] Charter."

Israel Nov. 18 rejected the censure resolution (from which the Soviet Union remained silently aloof). It berated British Amb.-to-UN Sir Gladwyn Jebb Nov. 21 for having supported Jordan's refusal of talks with the Israelis at the UN. Jebb Nov. 20 had indorsed Haikal's suggestion of Jerusalem as a site for such talks. Jebb had also indorsed UN truce chief Bennike's report on which the censure motion was based—in particular the charge that Israeli military forces had played a role in the Qibya raid.

U.S. Amb.-to-UN James J. Wadsworth defended the resolution Nov. 20 when it came up for a formal motion of consideration. Wadsworth emphasized the importance of bilateral observation of the Israeli-Jordanian armistice agreement of Apr. 13, 1949 as a necessary prerequisite for enduring peace in the area.

When the Security Council Nov. 24 voted to adopt the resolution (9-0), the Soviet Union and Lebanon abstained. Soviet Amb.-to-UN Yakub Malik broke his silence Nov. 25 by hailing the adoption of the Western Big 3's censure resolution and deploring the UN General Assembly's failure to demand that Israel comply with its resolutions on the matter of border strife. No talks between Israel and Jordan were forthcoming in 1953, either in New York or Jerusalem, despite a letter from Amb. Eban urging UN Sec. Gen. Dag Hammarskjold's intercession. The Israeli Knesset Dec. 8 indorsed Israel's stand of regretting the Qibya raid but denying any military part in it; the vote was 58-22.

Israeli Foreign Min. Moshe Sharett, who also became premier after David Ben-Gurion's retirement early in Dec. 1953, again pressed for Hammarskjold's intercession. Finally, shortly after mid-Feb. 1954, Israel and Jordan received invitations from Hammarskjold to meet in Jerusalem under his chairmanship for talks on "concrete and limited issues" involved in implementing their Apr. 13, 1949 truce agreement. The Israeli government Feb. 23 accepted the invitation, but Jordan, after consulting the Arab League Feb. 24, asked Hammarskjold to refer the subject of such talks to the Israeli-Jordanian Mixed Armistice Commission.

The next major incident in the Israeli-Jordanian border-area violence came Mar. 17, 1954, when 2 men with submachine guns ambushed an Elath-Beersheba bus in the Negev Desert's Scorpion Pass 12 miles east of the Jordanian border. The attackers killed the bus driver and

9 men and 2 women on the bus and seriously wonded a woman and a child. 3 passengers escaped. Israel charged Jordan with responsibility. Jordan denied the charge and offered to help find the murderers. Israel accepted the offer, and investigators from both countries tracked the killers to a point 6 miles from Jordan before the trail was lost.

Israel put the matter before the Israeli-Jordanian armistice commission, which Mar. 23 rejected Israel's motion to condemn Jordan for the Scorpion Pass attack. After an equal number of Israeli and Jordanian representatives had deadlocked the vote, U.S. Navy Commander Elmo H. Hutchison, the commission's chairman, abstained from the voting, and the Israeli motion failed to carry. Hutchison maintained that the evidence for Israel's contention was inconclusive and later noted that the suspects named by Israel had not been found.

Israel, openly disgusted, began boycotting the commission and warned that the government and Israeli authorities might not be able to prevent reprisals. (UN Secy. Gen. Hammarskjold said Mar. 25 that he had given up efforts to arrange direct high-level Israel-Jordan peace talks because Jordan insisted that the Armistice Commission was the only "appropriate" channel for negotiations.) Premier Sharett told the Knesset Mar. 24 that the Israeli government had urgently requested that the U.S., Britain and France put the matter before the UN Security Council. He justified Israel's boycott as a withdrawal from an organization "incapable of preventing bloodshed" and standing convicted of "complete moral bankruptcy."

Ex-Premier Ben-Gurion advised Israelis to rely for protection not on the UN but on their own strength. In an article in the Histadruth daily *Davar* of Tel Aviv Mar. 26, in which he explained his decision to retire from public life, Ben-Gurion wrote that the UN great powers' vote was determined by their own interests and not by justice.

The next round of violence came soon. An Israeli watchman was murdered Mar. 27 in the village of Kisalon, near Jerusalem. Jordanian officials reported Mar. 27 that an Israeli patrol had fired on Arab farmers inside Jordan. Israel asked the Mixed Armistice Commission Mar. 28 to look into 10 incidents of Arab infiltration; in these incidents, an Arab was killed and 2 Arabs captured. On the night of Mar. 28-29, a group of armed Israelis raided the village of Nahhalin, 3 miles inside the Jordanian border. There they encountered a force of Arab Legionaries and Jordanian national guardsmen and withdrew. Another Arab Legion unit cut off their retreat. The number of Israeli casualties was not published. Jordanian casualties included 5 national guardsmen and one woman villager killed and 14 villagers wounded in Nahhalin and 3 Legionaries killed and 4 wounded in a truck that struck a land mine.

The Israeli-Jordanian Mixed Armistice Commission Mar. 30 unanimously condemned Israel for the raid, which Premier Sharett deplored and called a "local affair" in reaction to the Kisalon watchman's murder. Lt. Gen. Glubb, commander of the Arab Legion, estimated the numerical strength of the raiders Mar. 30 as 240 men.

(The Egyptian-Israeli Mixed Armistice Commission censured Israel Apr. 4 for 2 attacks on Egyptian military posts in which 3 Egyptian soldiers were killed and one wounded. Boycotted by Egyptian members, the commission condemned Egypt Apr. 11 for 4 truce violations near Gaza Apr. 8-9 in which an Israeli was killed and 5 wounded. Israel and Egypt were censured by the commission Apr. 29 for clashes along the Gaza strip Apr. 25 and 26. The Israel-Jordan Mixed Armistice Commission, boycotted by Israel, condemned Israel Apr. 28 for an all-day siege of Budrus village Apr. 26 during which an Arab girl was wounded. Israel, apologizing for the incident Apr. 26, blamed it on stray bullets fired during Israeli army maneuvers near Budrus.)

British Foreign Secy. Sir Anthony Eden in a speech in the House of Commons Mar. 29, announced that the British government was consulting with the U.S. and French governments on a joint request for a UN Security Council review of the entire Palestine situation. On Jordan's behalf, Lebanon put before the Security Council Apr. 1 a request for formal debate on the Nahhalin raid. Israel complained to the Council Apr. 5 that Jordan had repudiated the UN truce agreements.

Israeli Amb.-to-UN Eban contended Apr. 7 that the Israeli-Jordanian truce machinery had suffered "a complete organic breakdown." He said recent Soviet vetoes of Security Council resolutions criticizing Arab states indicated that the Council could take only actions "congenial to Arab opinion." Eban told newsmen that since 1949, Arab raiders had killed 500 Israelis and that Jordan's Arab Legion and National Guard had killed or wounded 39 and abducted 28 since Nov. 24. He said Israelis were becoming less willing "to suffer . . . without response."

The Security Council reopened its discussion of Middle Eastern tension Apr. 8, 1954 as Israeli-Arab clashes increased. The session had been called Apr. 5 by Soviet Deputy Foreign Min. Andrei Y. Vinshinsky, Council president for April, to consider Israeli and Lebanese charges.

Delegates of the U.S., Britain, France, the Netherlands and Turkey expressed support in the UN Security Council Apr. 8 for Israel's demand that the Council review the entire question of Middle Eastern tension. Lebanon, supported by the USSR and Nationalist China, demanded that the Council confine itself to Jordan's complaint against the Israeli attack on Nahhalin. The Council Apr. 27 delayed for a 3d time a decision on procedure in considering cross-complaints of Israeli and Jordanian armistice violations. Britain proposed a new agenda item: "Compliance with and enforcement of the general armistice agreement."

The Security Council ended a month of procedural argument May 4 by voting to permit general debate on the Israel-Jordan border situation. The vote on the Brazilian-Colombian resolution was 8 for, Lebanon and the USSR opposed, China abstaining. The Arab nations had threatened to quit if full debate were permitted but after the Council voted, Dr. Charles Malik of Lebanon said the Arabs would not withdraw. He later introduced a resolution condemning Israel for the Nahhalin attack and calling for a UN economic and diplomatic boycott of Israel.

Jordan's lower house of parliament Apr. 20 had voted thanks to Soviet Deputy Foreign Min. Vishinsky, Security Council chairman for April, for his support of the Arab cause in the UN. Jordan said Apr. 22 that Britain had given "satisfactory" assurances that it would defend Jordan in the event of an Israeli attack without waiting for UN consultation.

The Jordan government headed by Premier Fawzi el-Mulki resigned May 2, apparently in a dispute over British attempts to get Jordan to modify its policy toward Israel. Britain allegedly had advised Mulki to agree to bilateral talks and to accept a general UN debate on the situation. A new Jordanian government was formed May 4 by Twefik Abul Huda, 65, a Palestine native who had been premier during the war with Israel.

Jordan withdrew May 28 from UN Security Council discussion of disorders in Palestine after Israel had demanded that Jordan commit itself to a peaceful settlement under terms prescribed by the UN Charter. Jordan contended that accession to the Israeli demand could eventually lead to direct talks between the 2 countries and that this would imply recognition of Israel—a step Jordan would never take.

Confidence in U.S. Friendship Wanes

Israel was reported to be increasingly worried, as 1954 progressed, over U.S. policy in the tense Middle Eastern situation. This concern mounted after a ranking U.S. State Department official made a speech to an anti-Zionist American Jewish organization in Philadelphia. The address seemed to many to indicate a definite "pro-Arab" shift in U.S. policy-making.

Assistant State Secy. Henry A. Byroade told the national conference of the anti-Zionist American Council for Judaism in Philadelphia May 1 that the U.S. was concerned lest continued turmoil in the Middle East cause the area to fall under "the control and influence" of the Soviet Union. Bryoade maintained that there was "no inspired formula" to "erase the underlying causes for the mutual feeling of hostility and distrust." He said, however, that these factors might help establish a climate of peace: (1) limitation of immigration into Israel and assurances by Israel that it had no expansionist intentions; (2) abandonment of Arab "negativism" toward Israel; (3) acceptance by both sides of a "realistic" approach to the Arab refugee problem, whereby a majority of Palestinian refugees would be resettled in the Arab countries with Israel compensating them for abandoned property. (The American Council for Judaism ended its conference May 2 with a strong indorsement of the Eisenhower Administration's "impartiality" between Israel and the Arab states.)

Israel protested May 3 that Byroade's comment on immigration was "unjustified interference" in Israel's internal affairs and was "liable to impose a severe strain" on U.S.-Israeli friendship. The Israeli objection reaffirmed "the right of every Jew to emigrate to Israel" as "a fundamental part" of Israeli policy. Israeli Prime Min. Moshe Sharett, in a speech marking Israel's 6th independence anniversary (May 8), charged May 5 that "the great powers" were vieing with each other for Arab friendship "by injuring Israel." (Sharett and Finance Min. Levi Eshkol May 2 lauded U.S. aid for Israel's economic development. Their praise was given in letters to Bruce McDaniel, retiring director of the U.S. operations mission to Israel.)

Sharett said in a foreign policy debate in the Knesset May 10 that "only a complete lack of insight into the way Israel came into being, how she has grown, and her fundamental articles of faith for the future" could have led Byroade to propose that Israel announce an end to the "great historic process of the gathering-in of exiles" and "close the gates of the country in the face of fellow Jews who might at any time knock at them." Acknowledging that there were "isolated verities" in Byroade's remarks, Sharett said that their effect was undone by language that gave the Arabs new excuses for avoiding peace. He held that Byroade had expressed "the recent tendency of the U.S. to show greater lenience to the Arab states while turning a stern face toward Israel." This tendency might have been aggravated by signs from the USSR, in the Security Council and elsewhere, of a Soviet policy of "wooing" the Arabs, Sharett said.

Another area of concern for Israel involved the prospect of U.S.

arms shipments to the Arab states. First in this connection came a military aid deal between the U.S. and Iraq, but Israel also noted a likelihood of some form of U.S. military aid to Egypt, too. In a note to Washington Mar. 25, Israel had expressed "grave concern" at the negotiations then going on for U.S. military aid to Iraq. The note charged that Iraq was a leading force behind the Arab countries' attacks on Israel and quoted remarks by Iraqi cabinet members to indicate the permanent role of hostility toward Israel in Iraqi foreign policy.

Iraq announced Apr. 25 that the U.S. had agreed to strengthen the Iraqi Army with unconditional military aid. Israeli Amb.-to-U.S. Abba Eban Apr. 26 protested to the State Department over the move. The Israeli Foreign Ministry Apr. 27 issued a statement terming the agreement "prejudicial to the prospects of peace in the Middle East" and "bound to endanger Israel's security." The Knesset May 17 adopted a motion deploring the U.S.-Iraqi agreement. The motion ended a week-long foreign policy debate during which Sharett May 17 put the U.S. on notice that the agreement would be considered in his country as having been aimed against Israel.

The issue of Western arms for Egypt opened, rather ironically, with Britain July 18 disclosing that another Western country—Spain—had been selling arms and munitions to Egypt. Britain had forbidden its own munitions makers to market weapons there during the Anglo-Egyptian dispute over the Suez Canal. The U.S. State Dept. said July 19 it had inquired in Madrid about Spanish exports of arms to Egypt and other countries and expressed "concern" that such export might violate terms of the U.S.-Spanish military aid pact. Britain revealed the same day that it had asked Spain several times to stop sending arms to Egypt. Spanish arms manufacturers had been reported July 18 to have contracted for the delivery to Egypt of $3½ million worth of mortars, shells and machine guns. The British government announced July 22 that Spain had pledged to export no more to Egypt. the N.Y. Times reported July 23 that Spanish customs agents in Bilbao had been ordered to halt all such shipments.

The likelihood of an Egyptian arms deal with one or more of the Western Big 3 powers arose right after the initialing July 27 of an agreement between Britain and Egypt for British troops to evacuate the Suez Canal Zone. 2,000 British troops sailed from Port Said Aug. 17 in the first big withdrawal of British forces from the canal zone under the Anglo-Egyptian agreement. (The agreement was signed Oct. 19 in Cairo by Britain and Egypt.)

The initialing of the Suez agreement was heartily welcomed in Washington July 28 in such a way as to arouse in Israel fears that the

West would soon supply Egypt with weapons. Pres. Eisenhower said at his press conference that he was convinced that the Suez agreement encompassed both Egypt's legitimate national aspirations and the West's defense requirements. The President expressed the hope that Egypt would proceed to improve both its economic and its defense-and-security situation. State Secy. Dulles welcomed a British-Egyptian agreement to guarantee freedom of navigation in the canal and said that the agreement supplied "a new and more permanent basis . . . for the tranquility and security of the Near East." The Egyptian government Jan. 25 had imposed a blockade on all ships passing southward through the canal bound for the Israeli port of Eilat (Elath) in the Gulf of Aqaba. Israel had taken the matter before the UN Security Council, but the Soviet Union had joined Lebanon Mar. 29 in voting against a New Zealand resolution of "grave concern" at Egypt's blockade.

Premier Sharett said at a press conference Aug. 20 that he did not "consider [U.S. State Secy. Dulles'] verbal assurances [of Western control over an Arab arms buildup] satisfying." Egyptian Premier Gamal Abdel Nasser had declared in Cairo Aug. 3 that Egypt would welcome U.S. military aid in strengthening its armed forces and that he assumed the U.S. would aid Egypt in the event of attack "by some other power."

British Quartermaster Gen. Sir Ouvry L. Roberts revealed in Cairo Aug. 15 that talks were under way on equipping Egyptian forces with modern British arms. The British Foreign office announced Aug. 30 that Britain had lifted the embargo imposed in Oct. 1951 on the export of arms to Egypt. The Foreign Office said that the British government would license the sale of military supplies to Egypt once it had received assurances from Egypt that the arms would not be used for aggressive purposes.

Sharett denounced the Anglo-Egyptian Suez agreement during a 2d foreign affairs debate that took place in the Knesset Aug. 30 and Sept. 1. He condemned the U.S. for what he construed as a policy of arming Egypt and Iraq. Observers inferred from Sharett's remarks that Israel considered Washington responsible for Britain's plans to sell arms again to Egypt. Sharett held that Britain had "completely ignored" Israel's interests in reaching the Suez agreement. The British government should either have made Britain's evacuation of the canal zone dependent on Egyptian recognition of an obligation to make peace with Israel or else have offered Israel enough special aid to counterbalance Egypt's new advantage, Sharett declared.

The Knesset Sept. 1 adopted a resolution expressing official anxiety over U.S. and British arrangements to arm Arab states opposed to

Israel, condemning Britain's lack of consideration for Israel's vital interests when concluding the Suez agreement with Egypt and advocating that the Israeli government strengthen Israel's armed forces.

The Egyptian Revolutionary Council Sept. 2 issued to foreign newsmen—but not to Egyptian journalists—a "background paper" in which the Council asserted that Egypt had decided to cast its lot with the West but was not ready to adhere to a formal defense pact, because the Egyptian people would regard such a pact as a form of colonialism. The council insisted that Egypt was opposed to communism and regarded the Soviet Union as the only major threat to the Near East. When the paper's contents became known to Egyptian journalists and were reported in the Egyptian press Sept. 3, Nasser issued a denial that Western observers took as intended for domestic consumption only. Egypt had reportedly been warned Mar. 23, 1954 that any Western-sponsored Middle East military pact with Arab states would be considered "unfriendly and even hostile" by the USSR.

MIDDLE EASTERN DEFENSE ALLIANCES (1954–6)

Egypt's refusal to join the Western-sponsored Mideastern defense project left the Western Big 3 and Turkey in Sept. 1954 without a solid North African anchor to their long-projected areawide command. The U.S. had a strategic air base in Libya but no troops. Neither Britain nor France had bases in Libya, which late in 1953 did admit a British military mission to train a Libyan army. Libya, according to a N.Y. Times report Jan. 2, 1954, turned down a French offer of financial aid in exchange for permission to establish military bases there. A nationalist uprising in Algeria, France's principal base of operations in North Africa, began Nov. 1, 1954 in the Aures Mountains, just as 3½ years of nationalist guerrilla disturbances were subsiding in neighboring Tunisia.

Birth of the Baghdad Pact

The prospects of North African cooperation having dimmed, Western military planners looked once again further east, where allied efforts to effect a Mideastern defense command had begun. Those efforts had become merely mechanical after the onset of the Suez and Iranian oil crises in 1951. It had remained for Turkey, the Western Big 3's Mideastern partner, to take the initiative in reviving the Arab world's interest in such a scheme. This it succeeded in achieving by first concluding—over strenuous Soviet objections—a friendship-and-military assistance pact with Pakistan in Apr. 1954.

The Soviet Union had warned Turkey Mar. 18 that the proposed friendship pact harmed Soviet-Turkish relations and was closely connected in Russian minds with plans of the "aggressive Atlantic bloc" to set up military bases in the Middle East. In its note to Pakistan Mar. 28, the Soviet government deplored "the granting of military bases on the territory of Pakistan in a military bloc which is a tool of the aggressive forces of imperialism." The British Commonwealth country's step would harm Soviet-Pakistani relations, and Pakistan would be to blame for it, the note said.

The Iraqi ambassador to the Soviet Union had received in the Kremlin Mar. 26 a Soviet note declaring that any Arab country becoming party to an areawide defense pact would be regarded by the Soviet government as having performed an "unfriendly and hostile act."

Turkey and Pakistan signed their mutual defense and economic cooperation pact in Karachi Apr. 2 and invited neighboring states, particularly Iran and Iraq, to join their alliance. The 2 new partners agreed to set up a joint defense system against an "unprovoked attack" on either, to supply each other with arms and to exchange information for mutual economic advantage. The treaty was automatically renewable every 5 years unless either party gave one-year notice of termination.

The U.S. said the Turkish-Pakistani pact would bolster the free world's defenses. India and the USSR opposed the alliance, and Egypt assailed it as a "conspiracy" to lure the Arab states into the Western defense network. The 8 Arab League nations, including Iraq, reassured one another in the League's Political Committee in Cairo Apr. 1 that they had no intention of joining Western-sponsored defense pacts or military aid agreements.

U.S. State Secy. John Foster Dulles said Dec. 31, 1954 in an end-of-year statement on the Middle East that he regarded the Turkish and Pakistani moves toward defense of the Mashreq (the Islamic east) as a "gain" for the West in 1954.

A change of government in Iraq early in August paved the way for that country's entry into a bipartite defense agreement with Turkey that grew into the Baghdad Pact (the Middle Eastern Treaty Organization [METO], later known as the Central Treaty Organization [CENTO]).

Gen. Nuri es-Said, then 66, head of Iraq's Constitutional Union Party and a friend of the British, became Iraq's premier Aug. 4 for the 14th time since 1930. He named as his foreign minister Mousa el-Shabandar, then Iraq's ambassador in Washington. With the support of the Iraqi branch of the Hashemite dynasty and the cooperation of Britain, Nuri made Iraq the cornerstone of the Mashreq's regional defense setup, of which he became, in the words of the Arab historian Philip Hitti, the "local architect."

Turkey and Iraq Feb. 24, 1955 concluded a military alliance, signed in Baghdad by Nuri, Turkish Premier Adnan Menderes and Turkish Foreign Min. Fuad Koprulu, both of whom had visited Baghdad Jan. 6-14. Nuri and Menderes Jan. 14 had first announced their intention of concluding a mutual defense arrangement. Menderes had also visited Damascus and Beirut en route home but failed to induce either country to join Turkey and Iraq in the project. Anti-Turkish demonstrations in Damascus and Aleppo had preceded and coincided with his visit.

The Turkish-Iraqi announcement also drew opposition from Egypt, where the government of Premier Gamal Abdel Nasser, Nuri's chief rival for the honor of leading spokesman of the Arab world, denounced the forthcoming treaty as a "serious blow to Arab unity."

Nuri excused himself from attending the opening in Cairo Jan. 22, 1955 of an emergency meeting of Arab League premiers summoned by

Nasser and sent in his stead ex-premier Fadhil el-Jamali with Iraq's deputy foreign minister and the director of propaganda. An Egyptian Foreign Ministry spokesman said Jan. 24 that Egypt had rejected a Turkish invitation to join the Turkish-Iraqi defense pact.

A delegation comprising Lebanese Premier Sami Solh, Syrian Foreign Min. Faydi el-Atassi, Jordanian Foreign Min. Waleed Salan and Egyptian Propaganda Min. Salah Salem was named to call on Nuri in Baghdad. Before the conference in Cairo closed, the Egyptian government threatened to withdraw from the Arab League's security pact and abandon Egyptian plans to unify the Arab countries' armies unless Iraq dropped its projected pact with Turkey.

The Arab League delegation visited Baghdad Feb. 2. Nuri refused to postpone the signing of the Iraqi-Turkish pact. Nasser Feb. 3 refused to meet Nuri in Beirut unless Nuri promised in advance to abide by a majority decision of the league's members in the matter. Nuri rejected any preconditions, and the proposed meeting did not take place. Syria, Lebanon and Jordan Feb. 6 rejected an Egyptian resolution that the Arab states should not conclude defense pacts with countries outside the league.

The Turkish-Iraqi Middle Eastern defense plan excluded Israel. This exclusion was protested to the U.S. and Britain by Israel, it was disclosed in Washington Mar. 3. Deputy Assistant State Secy. John D. Jernegan, addressing a conference of U.S. Jewish organizational leaders in Washington Mar. 6, said that it was "out of the question" to try to include Israel and Arab states in "plans involving military cooperation" for the time being.

Syrian Foreign Min. Khaled el-Azem announced Mar. 6 that Saudi Arabia, Syria and Egypt had agreed to join in a new Arab defense pact forbidding alliances with non-Arab countries.

Egypt indicated Mar. 20, through a press conference statement by Propaganda Min. Salah Salem in Cairo, that it might be brought into a Western alliance for Middle-Eastern defense if given the Negev (held by Israel) as a land connection with Jordan and Saudi Arabia. Israel denounced the suggestion Mar. 21 as attempted "blackmail at the expense of Israel's territorial integrity."

British Foreign Secy. Sir Anthony Eden announced in London Mar. 30 that documents linking Britain to the Turkish-Iraqi defense pact had been initialed in Baghdad that day. They included: a new pact giving Britain's Royal Air Force both Iraqi bases and the right to help train Iraq's air force; and an accord on close Anglo-Iraqi defense collaboration in peace or war. Eden told the House of Commons that the accords could serve as the base of a general Middle East defense plan.

Pakistani Premier Mohammed Ali Jan. 27, 1955 had proposed a tripartite defense alliance to Iraq and Turkey. Ali announced July 1 that Pakistan had decided to accede to the Turkish-Iraqi pact, which meanwhile had gained another adherent when Britain Apr. 4 joined Iraq and Turkey in the project.

Iran was the next to join the alliance. As early as July 18, 1954 Iran had indicated its willingness to do so by informing the USSR that Iran had the right to join any regional alliances safeguarding Iranian independence and territorial integrity and denying Soviet charges that Iran was gravitating toward an "aggressive military bloc." (The Soviet Union July 8, 1954 had demanded an explanation of reported Iranian talks with the U.S. and other Western countries on possible entry into the Turkish-Pakistani defense accord. The Kremlin had maintained that any such move by Iran would violate the Soviet-Iranian friendship pact of 1927.)

Iran's final decision was announced in Teheran Oct. 11, 1955, and a one-clause bill clearing the way for Iran to join in the Baghdad Pact was passed by the Iranian Senate Oct. 19 (36-4) and by the Majlis unanimously Oct. 23. The U.S. joined the pact's members in welcoming Iran's move, but the Soviet Union, in a strongly worded protest from Soviet Foreign Min. Vyacheslav M. Molotov Oct. 12, denounced the move as "incompatible with the interests of consolidating peace and security in the Middle and Near East" and "in contradiction to good-neighborly relations between Iran and the Soviet Union." Iran Dec. 5 rejected the Soviet protest. Iran asserted that membership was "essential to Iran's prosperity" and that the Soviet protest was "interference in Iran's internal affairs." (Awni Khalidy, permanent Iraqi representative to the UN, announced Dec. 15 that he had been named METO secretary general.)

Jordanian Premier Hazza Majali announced Nov. 20 that Jordan would remain outside the Baghdad Pact for the time being, despite strong requests to join from Turkey and Iraq. The Jordanian government was reported to feel that its current treaty arrangements with Britain already linked Jordan to the pact. Egyptian opposition was cited as another reason for Jordan's non-membership.

Only Turkey, Pakistan, Iraq and Iran of the countries of the Islamic east moved into the joint military alliance despite repeated Soviet warnings. Afghanistan, Jordan, Lebanon, Saudi Arabia and Syria remained aloof from the Baghdad Pact. An evidence of Kremlin feelings was a Soviet Foreign Ministry statement of Apr. 16, 1955 that called Western-sponsored military alliances in the Near East a threat to Soviet security and spoke of bringing up the matter in the UN.

Jordanian Premier Said el-Mufti resigned Dec. 14 after 4 ministers quit his cabinet in protest against British insistence that Jordan join the Baghdad Pact to obtain continued British arms aid. The British conditions had been presented by Field Marshal Sir Gerald Templer, Imperial General Staff chief, during week-long talks in Amman on the continuation of economic aid and Britain's annual subsidy of £11 million ($30.8 million) to Jordan's 20,000-man Arab Legion. Jordanian King Hussein asked Deputy Premier Hazza Majali to form a new cabinet Dec. 14. Pro-Western Majali had been expected to bring Jordan into the pact. But anti-pact demonstrations broke out almost immediately, a general strike was held Dec. 17 in Amman, and crowds stormed the Turkish consulate in the Jordanian sector of Jerusalem Dec. 19. Hussein agreed Dec. 19, at Majali's request, to dissolve parliament in preparation for elections based on the METO issue, and Majali resigned to make way for a caretaker government. Senate Pres. (and ex-Premier) Ibrahim Hashim was sworn in as caretaker premier Dec. 21.

Anti-pact demonstrators tore down a U.S. flag outside the U.S. consulate in the Jordanian sector of Jerusalem Dec. 20 after funerals for 3 persons killed by Arab Legionaires in the Dec. 19 demonstrations. It was estimated that 10 persons had been killed and 100 injured during nation-wide rioting in the previous 5 days.

Khrushchev Attacks METO

Soviet Premier Nikolai Bulganin and the Soviet Communist Party leader, Nikita S. Khrushchev, reported on their visit to India, Burma and Afghanistan during a 4-day session of the Supreme Soviet (parliament) Dec. 26-29, 1955. Khrushchev went on to criticize Iran, Turkey and Pakistan for their participation in the Baghdad Pact. He said:

Even before the ink with which our joint statements on the results of the Geneva conference was signed had dried, our partners in the conference had begun to involve more countries in the aggressive Baghdad Pact. They have dragged Iran into the pact and are forcing other countries to follow suit.... We cannot remain silent about the fact that, in spite of all the efforts the Soviet Union has made to ensure friendly relations with Iran, the government of that country has joined the Baghdad military pact, thus placing Iran's territory at the disposal of aggressive forces who are plotting attacks against the Soviet Union.

This is true not only of Iran but of Turkey as well. When Kemal Atatürk and Ismut Inönü held the reins of power in Turkey, our relations with that country were very good, but those relations have subsequently become clouded. We cannot say that this happened through Turkey's fault alone. We, too, made some improper declarations that cast a cloud over those relations. But subsequently we took steps to retrieve the situation and to restore friendly relations with that country. Unfortunately, these steps have not been reciprocated by Turkish statesmen. American generals and admirals are travelling to Turkey, making bellicose speeches, and making a parade of their forces through visits of naval squadrons....

Pakistan, which is also a party to the Baghdad Pact, has found herself in a similar position in relation to her neighbors. It is a fact that Pakistan's relations with India, and also with Afghanistan and the Soviet Union, leave much to be desired. One cannot, for instance, fail to notice that the American Adm. Radford visited Pakistan, and subsequently Iran, quite a short time ago. It was evidently purposes entirely different from those of promoting economic and cultural contacts that he had in mind when he went to those countries. . . .

In connection with the Baghdad Pact, a few words should be said about the situation in the countries of the Near and Middle East. The sponsors of the Baghdad Pact are moving heaven and earth to inveigle the Arab nations into this aggressive bloc. But they are coming up against the mounting resistance of the peoples of those nations. Soviet public opinion has been following sympathetically the valiant struggle of the people of Jordan against the attempts to force their country to join the Baghdad Pact.

We understand the yearnings of the Arab nations who are fighting for their complete liberation from foreign dependence. One cannot, at the same time, fail to recognize as deserving of condemnation the acts of the state of Israel, which, ever since it came into being, has been threatening its neighbors and pursuing a policy hostile to them. It stands to reason that such a policy does not conform to the national interests of Israel and that imperialist powers stand behind those who are carrying out this policy. They are seeking to use Israel as their instrument against the Arab peoples, with an eye to the ruthless exploitation of the natural wealth of that area.

U.S. Role in METO

The U.S. both promoted and supported the Middle Eastern Treaty Organization (METO), but apparently deemed it more judicious to play an indirect role within the areawide alliance itself. Accordingly, it never joined either METO or its successor group, the Central Treaty Organization.

U.S. State Secy. John Foster Dulles told representatives of the American press at a news conference in Washington Jan. 11, 1956 that he had developed the Baghdad Pact as an idea during his visit to the Middle East in May 1953 with Mutual Security Agency Director Harold Stassen. In answer to a question, Dulles said that the U.S. would consider joining the pact whenever it seems that such a step would contribute to peace and stability in the area—but not as an isolated act.

British Prime Min. Anthony Eden visited Pres. Eisenhower in Washington Jan. 30–Feb. 1, 1956, and the 2 leaders reaffirmed the Baghdad Pact's importance to them. Eisenhower pledged: "The U.S. government will continue to give solid support to the purposes and aims of the pact, and [U.S.] observers will play a constructive part in the work of its committees."

Eden told a joint session of the Canadian Parliament in Ottawa Feb. 3 that Britain "welcome[d this support], and here our views are alike." "The pact has economic purposes and aims which fully match its military provisions and importance," Eden said. "We have considered the kind of help which each member-country needs, and we are determined to make a success of the pact. All this does not exclude help to other countries in the area," he added. "An example is Jordan, to whom we shall continue to make substantial payments under [Britain's 1948] treaty [with Jordan, as revised Dec. 22, 1955]."

SOVIET-ARAB RAPPROCHEMENT (1954–6)

Soviet cooperation with Arab governments in the Middle East increased at a deliberate pace. In the opinion of some historians, Soviet feelings toward the Arabs warmed considerably after Stalin's death Mar. 5, 1953. The first Soviet moves toward closer cooperation with the Moslem world were made toward Afghanistan, Egypt and Syria. In Syria, the Communists were growing in strength and favored a national front. This development did not come about in Egypt until 1955, and Egyptian Communists were frequently jailed even thereafter. According to some observers, Egypt's Gamal Abdel Nasser frequently pitted the U.S. against the USSR in a successful scheme to get improved aid and trade offers from both rivals.

Although Soviet leaders continued to utter critical comments–denunciations, even–on the subject of Arab nationalist movements and even twitted Nasser on this score, they made it clear that they regarded the Arabs, not the Israelis, as the "great progressive force" in the Middle East. Soviet relations with Israel deteriorated once again, while Moscow's prestige with the Arab countries by and large increased.

Economic & Aid Arrangements with Egypt

Egypt had signed an agreement as early as Jan. 17, 1951 to buy 50,000 tons of Soviet wheat. Early in 1952, Egypt bought the same amount of wheat, this time from the U.S. Shortly thereafter (Feb. 23), Egypt concluded a barter agreement with the Soviet Union for nearly 200,000 tons of Soviet wheat in exchange for more than 21,200 tons of Egyptian cotton. Egypt then announced Feb. 28, 1952 that it had promised political, economic and social cooperation with the U.S. in exchange for a promise of more U.S. Point 4 aid.

The Egyptian government disclosed Apr. 28, 1955 that it had concluded a trade agreement with Sovrompetrol, the joint Soviet-Rumanian oil company, for about $9 million worth of kerosene and crude oil in exchange for Egyptian cotton and cotton yarn.

The Egyptian Finance Ministry had announced Apr. 27 that a trading mission from Communist China was en route to Cairo for talks on the purchase of Egyptian cotton. Egyptian Propaganda Min. Salah Salem had said in Bandung, Indonesia, Apr. 21, during the 3d-world conference there, that "the question of closer relations with China may grow out of the trade talks." But Premier Gamal Abdel Nasser told Chinese Premier–Foreign Min. Chou En-Lai that he was not then willing to discuss Egyptian diplomatic recognition of Communist China.

Egyptian Commerce Min. Abu Nusseir opened a Chinese Communist trade fair in Cairo Apr. 1, 1956. The Chinese were reported Apr. 2 to have bought $17½ million worth of Egyptian cotton since Aug. 1955 and to have shipped iron and oils to Egypt. Reports from Hong Kong Apr. 16 said that Egypt and China had signed an $11.2 million trade agreement involving Egyptian cotton and Chinese machinery.

It had been reported from Cairo Mar. 28, 1956 that the Soviet Union had offered Egypt uranium and aid in building an atomic reactor and was training Egyptian scientists in Moscow under the terms of a Feb. 1956 agreement for the construction of an Egyptian nuclear laboratory.

A United Press survey published Apr. 15 showed Egypt to have received $165 million in Soviet-bloc aid to underdeveloped countries already in 1956. The survey, based on U.S. government sources, also showed Afghanistan to have received $115 million, Syria $8 million, Turkey $4 million, Iran $3 million and Lebanon $2 million.

Contest to Finance Aswan Dam

Egyptian officials confirmed Oct. 13, 1955 that the Soviet Union had offered to help finance the construction of a $1.3 billion high dam project on the Nile River near Aswan in return for cotton, rice and other commodities. The offer created a stir and evoked many newspaper headlines.

Egyptian Amb.-to-U.S. Ahmed Hussein told U.S. State Secy. John Foster Dulles Oct. 17, however, that Egypt would rather have the International Bank for Reconstruction & Development (World Bank) and the U.S. finance the dam. Hussein said in Washington that the Soviet Union had offered Egypt a loan of $200 million toward the construction cost, repayable in the form of Egyptian commodities over a period of 30 years at 2% interest. Hussein said that the loan would cover about ⅓ of the project's estimated cost. He did not know what action his government would take on the offer and had not discussed with Moscow the possible transfer of Soviet technicians to Egypt to assist in the project, Hussein said.

Egyptian Finance Min. Abdel Moneim el-Kaissouni opened talks in Washington Nov. 21 with representatives of the World Bank to seek financing of the 15-year dam project. Egyptian officials said that the construction of the dam was a "matter of economic life or death."

The U.S. and Britain told Egypt Dec. 17 that they would finance the start of the project. The U.S. and Britain would, "subject to legislative authority," consider granting "further support toward financing the later stages to supplement World Bank financing," the State Department said. State Secy. Dulles said at his news conference Dec. 20 that "this dam is something which goes back 2 years and more and is not attributable at all to the Soviet proposal." First phase details of the Anglo-American offer had been drawn up in Washington Dec. 16 by U.S. State Undersecy. Herbert Hoover Jr., British Amb.-to-U.S. Sir Roger Makins, World Bank Pres. Eugene R. Black and Egyptian Finance Min. Kaissouni. The U.S. and Britain offered Egypt an initial $70 million grant, of which the U.S. was to contribute $56 million and Britain $14 million in blocked sterling (money Britain owed Egypt for goods and services during and since World War II). This would be used to build 3 coffer dams and the foundations of the main dam and bore 7 tunnels, each more than a mile long. The World Bank had not yet made a firm commitment on the project.

Soviet Amb.-to-Egypt Daniel S. Solod said in Cairo Dec. 18 that the USSR intended to help in the project "unless there is something in Egypt's agreement with the West which specifically excludes us." (Solod later returned to Moscow to head the Middle East desk in the Soviet Foreign Ministry.)

Dulles said at his Dec. 20 press conference that U.S. grants to Egypt for the Aswan dam would amount to $15-$20 million a year and come, in fiscal 1957, from a $100 million "flexible Presidential fund for use in the Near and Middle East." Commenting on Soviet aid offers in various parts of the world, Dulles said: The U.S. "seeks no monopoly in rendering economic assistance. We welcome any grants of economic aid which invigorates less-developed countries and makes them more free and more independent.... If the Soviet Union were to follow our example [in giving such aid], that would be gratifying.... But there is likely to be a question as to whether the Soviet really seeks to promote the vigorous independence of free nations. That question arises because of the long Soviet record in absorbing other countries.... We hope that Soviet economic aid is not offered as a Trojan horse to penetrate and then take over independent countries." (An agreement to coordinate Western policies to meet Soviet penetration in the Middle East had been reached in Paris Dec. 15, 1955 by Dulles, British Foreign Secy. Harold Macmillan and French Foreign Min. Antoine Pinay, who were attending a North Atlantic Council meeting.)

An Egyptian communique Feb. 9, 1956 said that "substantial agreement" had been reached with the World Bank on a $200 million loan to help build the Aswan High Dam. The announcement came after 2 weeks of talks in Cairo between World Bank Pres. Eugene Black and Premier Nasser and other Egyptian officials.

Reports from Washington Apr. 9 brought word that the Soviet Union had informed Egypt that Moscow was prepared to help Egypt obtain Sudanese permission for backing up the Nile. Such permission was an essential precondition for progress on the Aswan dam project. Nasser said in Cairo Apr. 1 that he had "not rejected" a Soviet offer of long-range credit for the project and that talks on U.S. and British offers were continuing. Reports from Cairo Apr. 24 said that Egypt had given the Sudanese Republic $1½ million in arms after talks with Sudanese Premier Ismail el-Azhari, who before going to Egypt had disclosed Apr. 15 that arms talks with a Czechoslovak military delegation were in progress in Khartoum and that the Sudan had accepted an offer of Soviet technical assistance. (According to reports from Hong Kong Apr. 14, a Communist Chinese trade delegation also had completed talks in Khartoum.)

Opposition to U.S. aid for the Aswan dam was developing in the U.S. Senate. Sen. Walter F. George (D., Ga.), chairman of the Senate Foreign Relations Committee, reiterated his objections to long-term U.S. foreign aid commitments and, in speeches Apr. 27 and 29, singled out for attack the proposed U.S. financial support for the dam project. George called such proposals "ill-advised" and "wholly inconsistent" in the situation currently existing between Israel and the Arab states, among whom Egypt was "at the spearhead," he said. George asserted Apr. 27 that the Aswan Dam would make 2 million acres available for cotton growing and thereby cut into U.S. cotton exports. He opposed seeking an Egyptian stipulation that the land would not be used for cotton because this would be "tying strings" to aid and, therefore, wrong in principle. George Apr. 29 expressed doubt that a large Middle Eastern-aid expenditure would help settle Arab-Israeli disputes.

The Senate Appropriations Committee disclosed July 16 that it had asked State Secy. Dulles to spend no Mutual Security funds on the dam without the committee's "prior approval." The State Department, discerning an Egyptian trend toward rapprochement with the world's Communist countries, had meanwhile attempted to ease the U.S. out of its verbal commitment to help finance the dam. State Secy. Dulles at a press conference May 22 had termed Egypt's recognition May 16 of the Peking regime as China's legitimate government "an action that we regret." Dulles said that if Egypt accepted Soviet aid for the Aswan project, "it would be unlikely . . . that we would find it practical" to join in funding the project.

The Kremlin soon afterward sent Soviet Foreign Min. Dmitri Shepilov on a Middle Eastern tour. He arrived in Egypt June 16, 1956 and told Egyptian farm workers and government officials in the Nile

Valley village of Bernesht June 18 that "the Arab countries may rely on the Soviet Union as their unselfish, faithful and reliable friend." Shepilov, who attacked the "aggressive Baghdad [METO] military bloc," said in his June 18 speech that the USSR wanted "to improve relations and establish friendship [with] the U.S., France, Britain, Greece, Turkey, with all our neighbors," but it "cannot go on at the expense of our good relations with the Arab countries, with our friends in the East."

Shepilov, invited to Cairo to attend celebrations centering on British evacuation of the Suez Canal Zone, conferred with Premier Nasser, Min. Mahmoud Fawzi, War Min. Abdel Hakim Amer and Soviet Amb.-to-Egypt Yevgeni D. Kiselev June 16 and reportedly presented Egyptian Trade & Commerce Min. Abu Nusseir June 17 with a list of industrial goods that the USSR was ready to trade for Egyptian cotton. Soviet embassy spokesmen in Cairo confirmed June 18 that Shepilov and Nasser had discussed Soviet-Egyptian trade and Soviet aid for Egyptian atomic plans and the Aswan dam June 17. Egyptian sources said June 18 that the USSR had offered £400 million Egyptian ($1.112 billion) for the Aswan project, with repayment in 20 years at 2%).

World Bank Pres. Eugene Black arrived in Cairo June 19 following a 3 day visit with King Saud of Saudi Arabia. Egypt was reported June 19 to be continuing negotiations with the World Bank, the U.S. and Britain on Western financing for the Aswan project. Reports from Cairo June 19 said that the U.S.-British offer was based on an initial gift of $70 million and later loans of $80-$150 million.

The U.S.-Soviet foreign aid contest over the Aswan dam and Egypt ended July 19, 1956, when the U.S. government officially withdrew its offer of a $56 million grant for its construction. The State Department said that the grant had been contingent on "Egyptian willingness and ability to concentrate its economic resources" on the project, but that "developments have not been favorable" and the "U.S. government has concluded that it is not feasible in the present circumstances to participate" in the project.

Egyptian Amb.-to-U.S. Ahmed Hussein was informed of the aid withdrawal when he called on State Secy. Dulles to discuss the Aswan program July 19. Hussein had returned from Cairo July 17, reportedly under orders from Egyptian Pres. Nasser to "reach agreement as soon as possible" on the Dec. 16, 1955 U.S. and British Aswan offers.

State Department officers July 19 stressed economic factors behind the U.S. reversal and said that a heavy "mortgage" had been imposed on future Egyptian cotton crops by Egyptian-Soviet bloc arms and industrial pacts. U.S. Congressional opinion was said in Washington reports

July 16 to have been turned against the aid program by Nasser's increasing anti-Western policies and adverse effects that the Aswan grant might have among U.S. allies in the Middle East and Asia. The State Department July 19 also cited Egypt's failure to reach agreement with the Sudan on the division of the Nile's waters.

The cancellation of the proposed $14 million British grant for the Aswan dam was announced July 20 by a British Foreign Office spokesman who said that the decision had been made after "continuous consultation" with Washington. The Foreign Office said that the withdrawal had been made for substantially the reasons given by the U.S. and had not been affected by the July 19 meeting between Hussein and Dulles because "nothing new was revealed in the Dulles-Hussein talks."

World Bank officials in Washington said July 23 that the Bank's $200 million loan offer to aid the Aswan project had been contingent on the U.S. and British grants and had "automatically expired" when they were withdrawn. The World Bank denied Egyptian Finance Ministry claims July 23 that Bank Pres. Eugene Black had termed Egypt's economy sound in a July 9 letter to Finance Min. Abdel Monneim el-Kaissouny.

Soviet Foreign Min. Dmitri T. Shepilov told reporters at a Belgian embassy National Day reception in Moscow July 21 that he did not consider Soviet aid for the Aswan project "a live question." Shepilov said that "there are now more vitally important problems for the Egyptian economy," particularly "industrialization," although he did "not minimize the importance of the Aswan dam." Shepilov said that "if the Egyptian government considers Soviet help" necessary, the USSR would "consider favorably any Egyptian requests."

A *N.Y. Times* dispatch said July 22 that Western observers in Cairo had long believed that Egypt was using "inflated reports of Soviet aid offers to obtain more liberal Western terms" for the Aswan project. The *Times* reported July 20 that a "gasp of surprise and anger" had swept Cairo at news of the Western withdrawals but that officials had refused comment despite violent press attacks on the reversal.

Soviet Amb.-to-Egypt Yevgeni D. Kiselev told reporters in Cairo July 24 that the Western press had "exaggerated" Shepilov's remarks on Aswan dam aid and said that "we are ready to finance the Aswan high dam if Egypt asked for it." Kiselev reportedly joined Nasser for talks July 24, accompanied by 2 Soviet planning experts identified as Pirovsky and Napalkov. A Reuters dispatch said that the Soviet embassy in Cairo had denied July 24 that Kiselev had offered Aswan aid if requested by Egypt.

Nasser spoke July 24 at inauguration of a new refinery and pipeline on the outskirts of Cairo and attacked the U.S. for "lies" about Egypt. Nasser said that "if an uproar in Washington creates false and misleading announcements, without shame," that "the Egyptian economy is unsound," then "I look at Americans and say: May you choke to death on your fury!" Nasser claimed July 24 that Egypt's national income had increased 32% since the army-led revolution of 1952.

A report by the U.S. Senate Foreign Relations Committee's subcommittee on technical assistance July 22 estimated foreign aid credits currently offered by the USSR at more than $1 billion. The study, revealed by Sen. Mike Mansfield (D., Mont.), said that Soviet aid, formerly aimed at Afghanistan and India, had shifted "in the short space of 13 months" to programs in Asia, Africa, the Middle East and Latin America. The report quoted Egyptian National Production Min. Hassan Trahim as having said that the USSR had offered a $300 million 26-year loan to finance the Aswan dam. Egyptian Amb.-to-U.S. Ahmed Hussein was quoted as having reported the Soviet offer at $200 million for 30 years, repayable in rice and cotton.

The study listed these other Egyptian-Soviet bloc trade negotiations and agreements: Bulgaria—negotiating to build oil processing and food plants since March; Czechoslovakia—offered rubber and shoe plants in June 1955 and a pact to aid a ceramic factory in Dec. 1955, and agreed in March to build cement plant; Communist China—a 3-year Egyptian trade and barter pact was signed in July 1955; East Germany—negotiating since February to build an Alexandria shipyard, chemical, auto and sugar plants and a power station; Hungary—a pact to build 7 bridges was reported made in June 1955 and an agreement to aid power station construction in Dec. 1955; Poland—contracted to aid and equip an enamelware plant.

Moscow Cultivates Afghanistan & Syria

A rapprochement in Soviet-Afghan relations came about in 1954 and pivoted about the 2 countries' mutual disagreement with the policies of Pakistan, Afghanistan's southern neighbor and rival among Pashtun tribesmen in the Wakhan region of Afghanistan's northeastern Badakhshan Province. Soviet coolness toward Pakistan came about as the result of Pakistan's signing of the U.S. Mutual Defense Assistance Agreement in May 1954 and its admission to the South-East Asian Treaty Organization in Sept. 1954.

Afghanistan was reported Apr. 11 to have received an offer of Soviet military support in the event of "aggressive interference" by Pakistan and its Western allies to prevent a plebescite demanded by Afghanistan in Pakistan's North-West Frontier Province. Afghan Premier Sardar Mohammed Daud Khan had broadcast a warning to Pakistan Mar. 29 against a projected merger of all West Pakistani provinces and princely states into a single administrative area. Daud demanded a plebiscite first among 7 million Pashtun tribesmen (of Afghan descent) on whether they preferred an independent state. A mob of demonstrators invaded and damaged the Pakistani embassy in Kabul Mar. 30. Daud was said to have held several talks with Soviet Amb. Mikhail V. Degtyar between Mar. 30 and Apr. 11. Afghan Shah Mohammed Zahir Khan was revealed Apr. 11 to have offered to restore ex-Premier Mahmoud Zahir (replaced by Daud in 1953) if the U.S., Britain and Turkey promised to support Afghanistan against attack by Pakistani government or guerrilla forces.

Soviet Premier Nikolai Bulganin and Nikita Khrushchev, the Soviet Communist Party leader, visited Kabul Dec. 15-18, 1955 and conferred with the shah, Afghan Premier Daud and Afghan Foreign Min. Sardar Naim Khan. Bulganin and Daud signed 3 documents Dec. 18: a joint statement on international affairs (including an announcement that Afghanistan and the USSR intended to expand their mutual political, economic and cultural ties); a 10-year extension of the Soviet-Afghan neutrality treaty of 1931; and an economic agreement providing for a long-term Soviet credit of $100 million to Afghanistan for development purposes.

Afghanistan and the Soviet Union Mar. 1, 1956 concluded an agreement for the USSR to furnish materials and equipment for 2 Afghan hydroelectric power plants, 3 auto repair factories, airfields at Kabul and Bagram, a road over the Hindu Kush mountain chain, irrigation works and a science laboratory. Soviet experts were to participate in these projects.

Soviet relations with Syria had become important enough by 1955 for the 2 countries to agree Nov. 16 to elevate their legations in Damascus and Moscow to embassy status. They also concluded in Damascus a one-year trade agreement that provided for Syrian exports of cotton, wool, vegetables, dried fruits and tobacco and Soviet deliveries of tractors and other agricultural machinery, motor vehicles, wood pulp and some nonindustrial products.

Soviet Foreign Min. Shepilov visited Damascus June 23-25, 1956 while touring the Middle East. It was then announced that the USSR and Syria had decided to expand their economic cooperation and to negotiate further trade accords and cultural agreements. Shepilov announced that Syrian Pres. Shukri al-Kuwatli had accepted an invitation to visit the Soviet Union. Shortly afterwards, Syrian Premier Sabry Assali announced in Damascus July 3 that Syria had decided to extend diplomatic recognition to Communist China.

Jordan Keeps Western Ties

Soviet efforts at penetrating the Middle East made relatively little headway in Iraq and Jordan in the early postwar years. In Jordan, the chief barrier was King Abdullah, whom the British had placed in nominal control of Transjordan, the state they had created in 1920 to connect their mandates over Palestine and Iraq. British Colonial Secy. Winston Churchill had confirmed Abdullah as the area's *de facto* ruler in the spring of 1921—provided that Abdullah accepted British financial assistance and military protection and gave up his designs on French-mandated Syria.

Abdullah coexisted well enough with the British to retain his hold over Transjordan through World War II. The British declared the state to be independent in a treaty signed in London in Mar. 1946, and Abdullah became its king May 25. Abdullah Apr. 24, 1950 annexed Arab Palestine, thereby more than doubling his young state's population, considerably increasing its surface area and greatly changing its character. In fact, Abdullah's country henceforth became known as Jordan and abandoned the name Transjordan. By the Jordanian parliament's annexation measure, eastern Palestine from Hadera in the north to below Hebron in the south passed under Abdullah's control. So also did the northeastern quarter, or Old City, of Jerusalem.

Jordan's early postwar course did not attract the interest of Russia, which Sept. 13, 1949 vetoed for the 3d time Jordan's attempt to gain entry into the UN. In a joint statement with Gen. Francisco Franco, whom he was visiting at the time in Spain, Abdullah Sept. 19 recorded in the city of Seville his complete agreement with the Spanish chief of state on what both leaders construed as the Communist menace in the postwar Middle East.

Abdullah had already traveled east to Iran, in whose capital Aug. 7 Jordan and Iran had concluded a treaty of friendship, economic cooperation and mutual assistance. Both parties to the treaty pledged that they would "not refuse to accept any proposition that has been approved by Islamic countries and tends to create closer harmony between them."

Abdullah's ventures in foreign diplomacy and other plans ended abruptly July 20, 1951 when a 21-year-old Arab tailor shot him to death as he was entering Jerusalem's El Aqsa Mosque for Friday prayers. The assassin, himself immediately killed by the king's bodyguard, had belonged to the Holy War Organization, an extremist group founded in 1948 by Haj Amin el Husseini, the exiled grand mufti of Jerusalem. It was afterwards argued that the deed had been plotted out of anger with Abdullah for his relative lenity toward Israel, but this was never satisfactorily indicated in the testimony of other members of the organization at the 11-day conspiracy trial that opened before a military court Aug. 18, 1951 in Amman. After the trial, Egypt refused (on the ground that there was no extradition treaty) Jordan's request for the extradition of 2 of the 6 men convicted of the assassination conspiracy. Both men had been living in Cairo since before the assassination and were convicted of having planned the conspiracy there.

(The assassination was witnessed by Abdullah's grandson, who a year later became King Hussein. In *Uneasy Lies the Head,* an autobiography published in 1962, Hussein reported that the U.S. ambassador to Jordan had visited Abdullah in Amman 2 days before the assassination and had urged him not to go to Jerusalem because "I have heard there may be an attempt on your life.")

Abdullah was succeeded by his elder son Talal, who was sworn in Sept. 6, 1951 as a constitutional monarch. Within a year, the Jordanian parliament had deposed Talal as mentally unfit and proclaimed his son Hussein, 17, as king.

Jordan took one significantly divergent path from Abdullah's policies during his son Talal's brief reign. Shortly after Talal's accession, Jordanian Premier Abdul Tewfik Huda Pasha announced Sept. 18, 1951 that his government did not contemplate a union between Jordan and Iraq, the 2 branches of the Hashemite dynasty, and would cooperate with other Arab countries in attempting to retrieve Arab rights in Palestine. Relations between Jordan and Egypt, Saudi Arabia and other foes of the late King Abdullah's cherished goal of a "Greater Syria" at once improved.

Jordan encouraged Western aid to continue, nonetheless. Jordan Dec. 20, 1951 signed a Point-4 aid agreement with the U.S. for $1 million worth of U.S. wheat and $3.2 million worth of technical assistance. The 2 Feb. 12, 1952 signed a Point-4 matching-funds agreement on economic development providing for a U.S. contribution of $2.78 million and a Jordanian matching contribution of $1 million in dinars. The 2 countries Apr. 7, 1953 signed a 3d Point-4 agreement for joint development. This agreement provided for a U.S. contribution of 110,000 Jordanian dinars and of land and buildings to the value of 223,690 dinars, and for a Jordanian pledge of $1.95 million from a $3 million U.S. allocation fund. British Foreign Undersecy. Anthony Nutting had announced Mar. 9, 1953 that Britain would contribute £1¼ million ($3½ million) in the fiscal year 1953-4 toward the realization of a 5-year plan of Jordanian economic development. Nutting said that ⅖ of the contribution would be recorded as an interest-free loan toward the cost of development and the other ⅗ as part of the budgetary assistance provided for under the Anglo-Jordanian alliance treaty of Mar. 1946.

The British Treasury announced Dec. 30, 1955 that economic aid to Jordan would be increased by £500,000 ($1.4 million), bringing total 1956 aid to $3,350,000 ($9,380,000) "to make Jordan economically as well as politically independent as soon as possible." The aid increase was to speed development of a deep-water port at Aqaba, near Eilat (Elath), where Israel was completing a port.

The U.S., France and Great Britain had announced simultaneously Aug. 27, 1952 that they had raised their legations in Amman, Beirut and Damascus to embassy status and that the Jordanian, Lebanese and Syrian legations in their countries would thenceforth enjoy ambassadorial status.

Jordan's improved standing with the Western Big 3 enhanced its economic prospects. Although not yet a UN member, Jordan received and accepted a UN offer of assistance. The Jordanian government and the UN Relief & Works Agency for Palestine Refugees in the Near East (UNRWA) signed in Amman Mar. 31, 1953 an agreement under which UNRWA would earmark ⅕ of its $200 million refugee "self-support" funds for a large-scale Jordan River Valley irrigation-and-power project planned by U.S. and British engineers. The project was designed to double the amount of land then under irrigation in the region between the confluence of the Jordan and Yarmuk Rivers and the Dead Sea and to provide a living for 20,000 Arab refugee families. The project's construction cost was estimated at $50-$60 million, 95% of which Jordan would amortize.

The development scheme envisaged the construction of a 400-foot-high dam across the Yarmuk River, which formed the western end of the border between Jordan and Syria. Syria would pay 5% of its cost. The dam was to supply the motive force for 2 5,000-kilowatt power stations and the irrigation source for 95,000 acres in the Jordan Valley. The Jordanian government had approved the plan July 2, 1952 as an acceptable alternative to an earlier one, based on Israeli-Jordanian co-operation, that would have involved the use of the Sea of Galilee (Lake Tiberias, or Lake Kinneret) as a reservoir.

Subsequent developments, however, sharpened Jordan's suspicions of Western intentions. When U.S. State Secy. John Foster Dulles conferred in Amman May 15, 1953 with Jordanian Premier Fawzi el-Mulki, Fawzi reportedly informed Dulles that Jordan would entertain no discussion on the subject of Middle Eastern defense until each of the Arab states' major problems could be settled. Fawzi ascribed his own country's plight to the dislocations brought about by the influx of Palestinian Arab refugees. Jordanian Foreign Min. Hussein el Khalidi told Dulles that Jordan's British-led military force, the Arab Legion, had made up its mind that there could be no peace between Jordan and Israel. When Eric Johnston arrived in Amman in October as Pres. Eisenhower's special emissary for serious talks on the Jordan River Valley development plan, Jordan's King Hussein and government had assumed a politely noncommittal position.

(At the close of his 4th trip to the area, Johnston announced in Beirut Sept. 6, 1955 that he had made new concessions to the Arabs to win approval for the U.S. plan to develop the Jordan River Valley. He said the revised plan provided for greater water storage than earlier planned in the Yarmuk basin of Jordan and Syria. A decision on water storage in Israeli-controlled Sea of Galilee would be put off pending a neutral study. But after an Arab League meeting in October on the matter, Jordan and the other Arab states affected again deferred a decision on whether to accept the U.S. project.)

Throughout the first postwar decade, Jordan remained within the British—and therefore Western—sphere of political and economic influence. In *Uneasy Lies the Head,* King Hussein explained his frustration at the extent of this influence: "Our political leaders tended to turn . . . to the British embassy before making the slightest decisions. A classic example of this occurred when the Soviet Union, wishing to establish diplomatic relations with Jordan, approached our charge d'affaires in Cairo and requested him to transmit a message to me. The message reached Jordan through diplomatic channels to the prime minister. When he received it, the prime minister did not consult me but took the message, without informing me, to the British embassy first!" Hussein listed no dates for this incident. Jordan and the Soviet Union did not establish diplomatic relations until late in Aug. 1963.

ISRAELI-EGYPTIAN BORDER STRIFE (1952–5)

Clashes in the Negev

Armed attacks occurred sporadically on Israel's Negev desert frontier with Egypt from Aug. 1952 until Feb. 1954, when the reports of truce violations began numbering several each month.

The principal series of events as reported from the area in 1953 is illustrative. Egypt complained Jan. 26 that an Israeli armed force had violated the truce line near Gaza and killed 5 Arab refugees. Israel Feb. 20 reported an encounter in which Israeli forces killed 3 Arabs and captured one. Israel complained Apr. 19 that the Egyptians had attacked 5 Israeli fishing boats off the coast of the Gaza Strip and Apr. 29 that Egyptians had mined a bridge and attacked an Israeli truck near Aujz el Hafir. Egyptian press reports Aug. 30 spoke of a Gaza Strip raid in which armed Israelis had killed 15 and injured 22 persons in the El Boreign Arab refugee camp.

Israel Feb. 25 rejected Egyptian editorial "demands" for a road through the Negev to Jordan. In what at first seemed to Israel a sufficient response, its general staff Sept. 29 fully denied an allegation by Egyptian Propaganda Min. Salah Salem that Israeli military forces had occupied El Auja in the demilitarized zone near the Egyptian border. The Israeli government Sept. 29 also denied that Israeli military forces had entered the area but acknowledged that a new *kibbutz* (farm commune) had been established there. Egypt announced Oct. 2 that it would protest to the UN Security Council against the alleged military occupation.

Israeli Amb.-to-U.S. Abba S. Eban Oct. 1 had denounced the Egyptian charges as propaganda and, having learned of Egypt's intention of complaining to the UN Security Council, described the step as an abuse of the UN. Egypt, meanwhile, moved troops into the area. Egypt complained to the UN Security Council Oct. 3 of Israeli fortifications in the area but requested no Council action. Israel found itself the object of Britain's official disapproval, and U.S. State Secy. John Foster Dulles and Egypt's Abdel Gamal Nasser exchanged notes over the affair.

By 1955, the Negev and Gaza-Strip frontier area had become an embattled zone.

Egypt complained to the Egyptian-Israeli Mixed Armistice Commission Feb. 28 that Israeli military forces had launched an attack in the Gaza Strip. The target of the attack was an Egyptian army camp. It soon came to light that 38 Egyptians and 8 Israeli soldiers had been killed and 31 Egyptian and 13 Israeli soldiers wounded in this most serious clash between the 2 countries since their 1949 truce. Egyptian Col. Salah Gohar reported to the commission that 2 platoons of Israeli soldiers had penetrated 2 miles into Egyptian-held territory, demolished an Egyptian army post and a water-pumping station supplying residents and refugees and hurled grenades into the Gaza railroad stationmaster's house, injuring his young son. Gohar added that an Israeli army unit further south had ambushed a truck carrying Egyptian reinforcements.

Israeli authorities asserted that the Israeli units were in hot pursuit of an Egyptian unit that had crossed the frontier and ambushed an Israeli patrol. An Israeli spokesman Mar. 1 listed 40 armed encounters, 27 Egyptian raids into Israel (in which 7 persons died and 24 were wounded), 26 condemnations of Egypt by the commission for these raids, several instances of sabotage (including the destruction of Israeli water pipelines) and no Israeli incursions into Egypt since Sept. 1954.

The Egyptian-Israeli Mixed Armistice Commission in Jerusalem asserted by 2-1 vote Mar. 6 that the Israeli army had committed an act of "brutal aggression" by what it described as the "prearranged and planned attack ordered by Israeli authorities" in the Gaza Strip Feb. 28. The commission's UN chairman, Francois Gicomaggi of France, and Egyptian delegates outvoted the Israeli delegation in adopting the resolution to condemn Israel. Gicomaggi's abstention on Israel's countercharge that the Gaza battle grew out of an Egyptian ambush of an Israeli patrol had the effect of defeating it. Israel announced an appeal to UN Truce Supervision headquarters in Jerusalem.

The UN Security Council in New York agreed unanimously Mar. 4 to recall Canadian Maj. Gen. Eedson L. M. Burns, chief Palestine truce supervisor, from Jerusalem to report on the Gaza incident. All Council delegates except the USSR's indicated in statements Mar. 4 their belief that Israel was to blame for the battle. Selim Sarper of Turkey, Council president during March, called on the Israelis and Egyptians to abstain from further fighting so as to avoid a possible major flareup of violence in the Middle East.

The Egyptian-Israeli armistice commission Mar. 7 then upheld Israeli complaints against Egypt's alleged provocation of 2 incidents that preceded the Gaza raid: the killing of an Israeli in Rehovot Feb. 25 by 3 armed Egyptian border violators and Egyptian troops' firing Feb. 22 on an Israeli patrol that was questioning Arab civilian grass-cutters who had crossed the Gaza Strip frontier. An Israeli patrol was rebuked by the commission for having opened fire on an Egyptian army post across the border Feb. 22.

Gen. Burns Mar. 11 rejected the Israeli appeal of a Mixed-Armistice Commission decision that Israel was to blame for the Feb. 28 attack near Gaza. U.S. State Secy. Dulles indicated Mar. 15 that the Gaza incident had caused the U.S. to postpone a pledge of aid to Israel in the event of an Arab attack.

Israel was condemned by unanimous Security Council vote Mar. 29 for the Feb. 28 attack. The U.S. joined other Council nations in rejecting Israel's argument that the attack was a justifiable retaliation for harassment by Egyptian infiltrators. Council members also deplored a raid Mar. 24 on an Israeli wedding party in Patish, for which the armistice commission had held Egypt responsible Mar. 27.

A Negev farmhouse 7 miles from Egyptian-held territory was bombed Mar. 15 and one man wounded by attackers thought to have come from the Gaza Strip.

Israel charged before the Security Council Apr. 6, 1955 that Egypt had started a series of border incidents that threatened the 6-year truce. Israeli authorities charged that Egyptian forces had loosed a 2-hour mortar barrage on the Israeli Negev settlement of Nahal Oz Apr. 3, killing 2 Israeli soldiers and wounding 16 (2 Egyptian soliders were also killed). But the Egyptian-Israeli Mixed Armistice Commission condemned both Israel and Egypt Apr. 9 for the battle.

Burns warned both countries Apr. 10 that the Gaza incidents had "resulted in a deteriorating situation [that] can and should be ended." Israel asked the UN Security Council Apr. 11 to speed consideration of its complaints against "Egyptian assaults." The Council had suspended consideration of Israel's latest complaint pending a report from Burns.

Mortal violations of the Israeli-Egyptian truce continued to occur, and the 2 sides fought a 2-hour battle near Kifsoufim May 21.

Efforts to Stop the Fighting

Israel and Egypt were urged by UN Secy. Gen. Dag Hammarskjold in appeals he sent June 5, 1955 to exercise restraint in their Gaza frontier zone and to support Burns' efforts to reduce tension. Egypt announced June 6 its rejection of a UN proposal that Egyptian and Israeli officials negotiate directly, instead of through the UN armistice agency, to end Gaza clashes. U.S. Amb.-to-UN Henry Cabot Lodge Jr., acting as UN Security Council president for June, sent letters to both countries June 7 urging that they cooperate "promptly" with efforts by Gen. Burns to restore order in the Gaza district.

Israeli Premier Moshe Sharett June 17 proposed the establishment of a mined zone along the Gaza Strip, fenced in by barbed wire and patroled by joint Israeli-Egyptian units (as Burns had recommended Mar. 17 to the Security Council). Sharett maintained that only such a drastic arrangement could interdict the area to Arab marauders. His statement represented a reply to a proposal by Egyptian Premier Nasser June 5 that a demilitarized zone be established around the Gaza Strip.

Egyptian-Israeli meetings were begun in Gaza June 28 in an effort to negotiate an end of Gaza-Strip fighting, but the talks were suspended June 29 in failure to reach agreement on an agenda. Burns was chairman of the talks. The talks were resumed July 6 on the Egyptian-Israeli border after the conferees agreed on an agenda proposed by Burns. An Israeli delegate said that the agenda was similar to the one rejected the previous week before by the Egyptians. Egypt and Israel reached agreement on a preamble for a security arrangement July 14, and a joint communiqué June 15 expressed hope for a final draft within a week.

Egypt announced Aug. 24 that it was quitting the talks with Israel because of Israeli "aggression" against an Egyptian post near Mefalsim in the Gaza Strip Aug. 22. Egypt's decision was given to Burns, who was visiting Cairo to discuss details of the deadlocked talks. Israel and Egypt accused each other of provoking the Aug. 22 incident in order to sabotage the Gaza talks. Israeli officials said their troops had crossed the armistice line and stormed the Egyptian post after Egyptians had attacked a routine Israeli patrol-convoy of 3 vehicles. One Egyptian was killed.

The breakdown of Gaza Strip peace talks Aug. 24 was followed by a week of Israeli-Egyptian fighting. Jet fighters clashed over Gaza Aug. 29 in what was believed to be the first such incident since the 1949 armistice. Israel said 4 Egyptian planes were driven off after entering Israeli air space, while Egypt said 2 Israeli planes dived over an Egyptian town in the Gaza zone.

Egypt agreed Aug. 31, 1955 to a cease-fire proposed by Gen. Burns. This happened nearly a day before an Israeli army unit raided the Khan Yunis military camp 4 miles inside the Gaza Strip, killing 25 *fedayin* (commando irregulars), 10 Egyptian soldiers and 19 others and wounding 50 persons in reprisal for terrorist raids. Israeli casualties amounted to one soldier killed and 8 wounded. 2 Israeli jets intercepted 4 Egyptian ones north of the Gaza Strip Sept. 1 and shot down one. The Israeli Foreign Ministry asserted that Israeli troops had attacked an Egyptian military camp that had been a base for terrorist squads that had killed 15 Israelis since Aug. 25. Israel called on Burns to "obtain the assurance of the Egyptian government that it accepts full responsibility for these acts and that it is ready to give guarantees" for an immediate end to hostilities.

The U.S. Sept. 1 indorsed calls for a cease-fire. State Secy. Dulles and State Undersecy. Herbert Hoover Jr. said they expected both sides to be able to reach an understanding—which they did Sept. 4. The UN Security Council Sept. 8 approved, 11–0, a U.S.-British-French resolution directing both sides to cooperate on achieving the tighter border controls recommended by Gen. Burns. The 3 powers acted after Burns Sept. 5 had submitted a report to the UN on 10 days of clashes that caused at least 70 deaths. Burns recommended establishment of a 1-kilometer-wide (1,100-yard) "effective physical barrier" between Israeli and Egyptian forces as the "only" way to avoid further clashes.

The U.S. had already made unilaterally an important demarche toward a general peace settlement in the Middle East. It was spurred by the mounting Gaza Strip crisis but looked beyond that and included other problems. Dulles in New York Aug. 26 had proposed a 3-point program to further "stability, tranquility and progress in the Middle East." Dulles said, in a speech before the Council on Foreign Relations, that a solution of the 3 "principal remaining problems" left from the 1949 Palestine armistice agreements seemed possible and could pave the way for solution of other problems that obstructed the "aspirations of the Middle Eastern peoples." One of these problems was the status of divided Jerusalem, for which Dulles recommended a UN review. Dulles said that he spoke "in this matter with the authority of Pres. Eisenhower." *He made these proposals for pacifying the Middle East:*

Refugees—Money was required for "practical projects for water development" to create more arable land for 900,000 Arab refugees from territory occupied by Israel. Compensation also was "due from Israel to the refugees." If Israel could not make adequate compensation, "there might be an international loan to enable Israel to pay the compensation which is due." "Pres. Eisenhower would recommend substantial participation by the U.S. in such a loan" and "would recommend that the U.S. contribute to the realization of water development and irrigation projects which would, directly or indirectly, facilitate the resettlement of the refugees." These projects would "enable the people throughout the area to enjoy a better life," and the solution of the refugee problem "would help in eliminating the ... recurrent incidents which have plagued and embittered" Israelis and Arabs. Countries through which the Jordan River flows "have shown an encouraging willingness to accept the principle of coordinated arrangements for the use of the waters. Plans for the development of the valley are well advanced." Special U.S. Amb. Eric Johnston was making his 4th visit to the area "in an effort to eliminate the small margins of difference which still exist." (Johnston opened talks with a special Jordanian government committee in Amman Aug. 25.)

Fear—"The nature of this fear is such that it is hardly within the capacity of the countries of the area, acting alone, to replace the fear with a sense of security." Security "can be assured only by collective measures which commit decisive power to the deterring of aggression." "Pres. Eisenhower has authorized me to say that, given a solution of the other related problems, he would recommend that the U.S. join in formal treaty engagements to prevent or thwart any effort by either side to alter by force the boundaries between Israel and its Arab neighbors." Dulles hoped "that other countries would be willing to join in such a security guaranty and that it would be sponsored by the UN."

Boundaries—As fixed by the 1949 armistice agreements, Israel's boundaries "were not designed to be permanent frontiers in every respect." They partly "reflected the status of the fighting at the moment." "In spite of conflicting claims and sentiments, I believe it is possible to find a way of reconciling the vital interests of all the parties. The U.S. would be willing to help in the search for a solution . . . " "At a time when a great effort is being made to ease the tension which has long prevailed between the Soviet and Western worlds, can we not hope that a similar spirit should prevail in the Middle East? That is our plea."

Dulles said at his news conference Aug. 30 that he had received unofficial reports that the USSR had offered military equipment to Egypt and other Arab countries. He said such action would not contribute to the easing of tension discussed at the Big 4 summit meeting in Geneva. He said that the U.S. and Britain had urged Israel and Egypt within the past 48 hours to avoid force in the Gaza area.

The Middle East's reaction to Dulles' proposals took a month to become clear. The first Arab comment came in a Radio Cairo broadcast of Aug. 29 that denounced the "Dulles plan" as an attempt "to deliver the Arabs to the mercy of Israel." The Egyptian foreign ministry announced Aug. 31 that representatives of the Arab states would meet in Cairo to discuss the U.S. plan after special U.S. Amb. Johnston, then in Cairo, had completed his Middle Eastern tour.

Israel's first official reaction to the U.S. proposals came Sept. 6, when Israel asked the U.S. State Department for an explanation of "frontier adjustment" and other details. Israel called the U.S. plan "constructive."

Israeli Premier Moshe Sharett said in an interview with the British United Press Sept. 11 that Israel was willing to discuss certain mutual border adjustments with its Arab neighbors but not prepared to make unilateral concessions of territory, particularly in the Negev. In Sharett's view, Dulles had appeared to "make the fixing of boundaries a condition that must come before the conclusion of the defense treaties, which he himself regards as urgently needed." But the existing armistice lines, "whatever technical or other demerits they possess, have at least the inestimable advantage of being agreed upon, whereas any agreed correction of these lines in the near future is highly problematical, if not illusory," Sharett observed. He said "the Negev was of particular importance to Israel both for its mineral wealth and for the "supreme value" of Eilat, its southern port. "That foothold on the Red Sea is of far-reaching significance to Israel and invests with the same quality of decisive value any part of the land bridge between it and the main body of the state's territory," Sharett declared.

Israeli Amb.-to-U.S. Abba Eban Sept. 11, with the authority of Premier Sharett, warmly commended Dulles' "realistic and imaginative approach" to the Middle Eastern problem but said that it was "acutely discouraging to read Mr. Dulles' paragraph on frontiers." Eban maintained that the Israeli government considered the existing truce lines between Israel and the Arab states as having "more solid attributes" than Dulles' speech had indicated. The lines had existed by international agreement and arrangement for 7 years "in recognized integrity" even though hostilities had occurred from time to time; they were "vastly superior to any imaginary line which does not have the tradition of stability or the virtue of reality," he said. Both Israel and the Arab states had agreed not to change the lines except by agreement. None of the parties had invoked the armistice procedure for change; all were more likely to prefer the existing lines to a quest for a new agreement, Eban said. Anyhow, "there can be no question of unilateral concessions by Israel to the Arab states. . . . "

Eban argued that what could be "a fitting subject for the tripartite agreement in 1950 cannot be an unfitting subject for a treaty engagement today." Moreover, even the advocates of a new boundary agreement did not propose any drastic alterations. "How, then, could an adjustment, which admittedly would be only minor in character, be so momentous as to make all the difference between the application of a treaty solution and its denial?" Eban asked. There was "nothing intrinsically tense" about the shape of the existing truce lines; tension would result rather from the relationship between the governments on either side of the line, he maintained.

It was "the foundation of Israel's position," Eban said, that "we will explore every road of progress towards the liquidation of conflict between the Arab states and Israel. While being ready for mutual adjustments of the boundary line, we shall accept no unilateral territorial concessions for ourselves, just as we have demanded nothing from our neighbors. Mr. Sharett's statement on the Negev is an absolutely fundamental and immutable part of our policy. Now that there is an important willingness in principle for the leaders of the United States to engage themselves by a treaty to thwart aggression in our area, we urgently advocate that this priceless stability be conferred upon our region now and not be lost through association with unattainable conditions." Eban concluded by saying that Israel and the U.S. had drawn closer together in this "memorable discussion" but that much work remained to be done before the promise incorporated in Dulles' statement could effect a lasting peace and genuine security for the Middle East.

Syrian Premier Said Ghazzi told Syria's parliament Sept. 26 that Syria rejected any plans or attempts for the conclusion of peace with Israel, including Dulles' proposals.

Israeli Foreign Min. Sharett told Dulles Dec. 6 that Israel was willing to discuss some "minor mutual adjustments" of borders but that Israel took an "irrevocable stand" against making territorial concessions. Sharett told newsmen later that he had told Dulles he saw no improvement of peace prospects in the Middle East, but "if there is willingness on the Arab side then there will be peace."

Israeli sources in Washington disclosed Dec. 19 that Israel, in response to State Department urging, had recapitulated previous offers of concessions to draw up a 7-point peace plan: (1) Israel would open natural lines of communication between Egypt and Lebanon to all forms of Arab traffic. (2) Jordan would be offered a free port at Haifa, transit rights across Israel. (3) Israel would consider establishment of communications across the Negev between Egypt and Jordan. (4) Arab planes could fly across Israel. (5) Israel would compensate Arab refugees for property left behind in Israel. (6) Israel would join in unified development of the Jordan and Yarmuk valleys. (7) Israel would accept minor frontier adjustments.

The events of the preceding several months had determined for Israel the maximum limits of the latitude of its stand. Israel, in a letter to the UN Security Council Sept. 28, 1955, had protested Egyptian shipping restrictions as violating international law, the 1949 Egyptian-Israeli armistice and previous Council resolutions. Israel said it would protect its right to free passage "at whatever time and by whatever methods" it deemed necessary. Israel was building a port in the southern end of the Negev at Eilat on the Gulf of Aqaba to stimulate trade with East Africa and the Far East. Israel, Egypt, Jordan and Saudi-Arabia bordered on the gulf. Egyptian guns dominated its only navigable entrance.

Israeli Premier-designate David Ben-Gurion declared Sept. 25 that Israel would seek talks with Egypt on Aqaba when Eilat port facilities were nearing completion. He said the completion of the port would be the "first job" of his new government. (Ben-Gurion, called on to form a government by Israeli Pres. Izhak Ben-Zvi Aug. 18, had said he would seek a coalition of the same parties that were in Israel's first government in 1948. But he was reported Sept. 11 to have virtually abandoned such hopes because of political demands by the religious groups.)

Israel and Egypt withdrew their forces from the demilitarized zone of El Auja in the Negev Oct. 2 in compliance with an agreement worked out by UN truce chief Burns. Israel had entered the 95-square-mile triangle Sept. 21, charging that Egypt had 2 military positions in the zone. 2 Egyptians were wounded as the Israelis moved in. Israel claimed sovereignty over the area; Egypt said neither side had sovereignty.

Continued Clashes

An Egyptian force Oct. 26, 1955 had driven Israeli border police from the zone, killing one Israeli, wounding 3 Israelis and capturing 2. An Israeli army unit Oct. 27 raided Kuntilla on the Sinai Peninsula well inside the Egyptian frontier, killing 10 Egyptian soldiers, taking 20 prisoner and destroying 17 army trucks.

In New York Nov. 3, UN Secy. Gen. Hammarskjöld expressed "grave concern" to Israel over its action in the outbreak. He submitted truce proposals to both sides without disclosing them publicly. The proposals were submitted after Hammarskjöld conferred with representatives of the U.S., Britain and France and with UN truce chief E. L. M. Burns of Canada, who then returned to Jerusalem.

U.S. Asst. State Secy. George V. Allen conferred separately in Washington Nov. 5 with Israeli Amb. Abba Eban and Egyptian Amb. Ahmed Hussein, both of whom assured Allen that their respective countries had no aggressive plans. A State Department statement issued after the talks deplored the "resort to force for the settlement of disputes" and declared that the U.S. "strongly supports the UN's efforts to achieve settlement by peaceful means, especially the current proposals of Gen. Burns." The State Department noted reports that UN observers under Burns had been "prevented from carrying out their assigned functions." The U.S. asked that these observers "have full liberty to perform their peaceful functions."

Adlai E. Stevenson, the 1952 Democratic Party candidate for President, said Nov. 11 that "a major effort of statesmanship is required . . . to avert a political disaster" in the Middle East. "We have shown little initiative within or outside of the UN in devising measures to prevent these border clashes," he declared. Stevenson suggested that UN guards might patrol the critical areas. He made the proposal in a speech sponsored by the Woodrow Wilson Foundation at the U. of Virginia.

Pres. Eisenhower said Nov. 15 that the U.S. "will play its full part" in working for a peaceful settlement of Israeli-Arab disputes. He repeated offers of "formal treaty engagements" to guarantee "boundaries upon which Israel and its immediate neighbors agree." Eisenhower's statements were made in a letter to Rabbi Abba Hillel Silver, who read the Presidential message at a New York mass meeting organized by the American Zionist Council and other Jewish groups.

The most severe Israeli-Arab fighting since the 1949 armistice broke out at the strategic El Sabha post in the El Auja-Nitsana demilitarized frontier zone during the night of Nov. 2-3. The post had been claimed by both Israel and Egypt. The Egyptians said the post changed hands twice during the night, and both sides claimed they were in control of it Nov. 3. The Israelis said they had killed 50 Egyptians and captured 40; the Egyptians said 70 of their men were killed or missing. An Israeli spokesman denied an Egyptian claim of 200 Israeli dead. (Israeli casualties were put later at 5 killed and 8 wounded.) Mortar and artillery fire continued through Nov. 4, but a UN official said that "nothing serious happened," Israeli and Egyptian forces also clashed along the Gaza Strip border Nov. 4 and 5, but no casualties were reported.

Egyptian Premier Nasser told a *N.Y. Times* reporter in Cairo Nov. 3 that Israel's forces "attacked ours, thus determining the answer" to Israeli Premier-designate Ben-Gurion, who had asked Nov. 2 for Israeli-Arab negotiations. Nasser said: "Hardly 10 hours passed since . . . [Ben-Gurion] posed to the world as a peace-loving man before he ordered his troops to march on El Sabha inside Egyptian territory."

Israel's resources were further strained during this period because of border tensions with Syria, which had signed a mutual defense pact with Egypt in Damascus Oct. 20 and had set up a joint military command with Egypt Nov. 29. Syrian shore batteries fired on an Israeli police boat in the Sea of Galilee Dec. 10. Israel responded Dec. 11 by raiding Syrian fortifications northeast of the Sea of Galilee, killing 56 Syrians and capturing 30 while losing 6 dead and suffering 12 wounded. Syrian delegate Ahmad el-Shukhairy urged the UN Security Council Dec. 16 to impose economic sanctions against Israel for the Israeli attack on Syria. Israeli delegate Abba Eban replied that Israel had raided Syria after a year of "persistent" Syrian attacks on Israeli fishing boats on the Sea of Galilee, which "lies within Israeli territory" and where Syria "has no political or geographical status." Eban quoted an Israeli communiqué of Dec. 11 that said the Israeli raid was made "to silence the batteries responsible" for an attack on Israeli fishing boats Dec. 10 "and to insure the security of Israeli citizens engaged in their lawful occupations." Eban said: "Either peaceful activity on the lake would have to be stopped in deference to Syrian guns, or Syrian guns would become silent in order that the conditions for work and development might be restored."

10 of the 11 Security Council members (Brazil was scheduled to speak later) criticized Israel Dec. 16 for the raid. U.S. Amb.-to-UN Henry Cabot Lodge expressed the "shock" of the U.S. government

which opposed "such acts of military violence." Regardless of whether or not there were provocations, he said, "the UN have undertaken not to resort to the use of force in the settlement of their disputes. Israel has specifically undertaken not to resort to force." Soviet delegate Arkady A. Sobolev criticized Israel in harsher terms than the U.S., Britain or France. He said that the Council should take steps to forestall recurrences. The Council deferred action pending a report from the UN truce chief in Palestine, Gen. Burns.

In his report Dec. 21, Burns called the Israeli raid "a deliberate violation" of the Syrian-Israeli armistice agreement of 1949. "Such actions may well produce a violent reaction by the ... attacked country, and what had been conceived as a limited raid develops into full-scale hostilities," Burns warned. "In the present atmosphere of tension and military activity, this possibility must be faced." Burns suggested an informal arrangement under which Israeli police boats that protected fishing vessels would keep a "certain distance" from Syrian guns. He said that the Syrian firing on Dec. 10 was directed at a patrol boat and that no fishing vessels were fired upon since the fishing season had begun in November. He reported that 56 Syrians and 6 Israelis had been killed in the Israeli raid Dec. 11.

Egyptian Premier Nasser Dec. 15 sent a letter warning UN Secy. Gen. Hammarskjöld Dec. 15 that further Israeli attacks on Arab countries would force Egypt "to take matters into her own hands." Egypt would "not hesitate to use her land, sea and air forces to insure her security and maintain peace in the area, as the Security Council has shown itself incompetent to prevent repeated occurrences of such incidents." Nasser said. He listed 6 incidents starting with the Israeli attack on Gaza Feb. 28. Nasser accused Israel of a "barbarous attack" on civilians as well as military positions Dec. 11. He said that future attacks on Syria or Egypt would bring "immediate retaliation" which would be "joint not individual."

Egypt announced Dec. 26 that Saudi Arabia had agreed Dec. 24 to bring its armed forces into the joint Egyptian-Syrian command. Maj. Gen. Abdel Hakim, Egyptian war minister, was commander of the joint forces. Nasser and Saudi Arabian Crown Prince Emir Faisal reportedly had agreed on a joint defense pact in Cairo Oct. 25.

Czechoslovak-Egyptian Arms Deal

Israeli-Egyptian border strife took on a new dimension in the late summer and early autumn of 1955 when it became known that the Soviet bloc's leading armaments maker, Czechoslovakia, had agreed to supply Egypt with the amount and variety of arms the latter sought. And Deputy Egyptian Premier Gamal Salem, arriving in Calcutta from Rangoon Sept. 4 for a 17-day tour of India, confirmed that the USSR had offered arms to Egypt. He said Egypt had not received any Soviet arms so far but would have to accept them if European countries did not honor promises and contracts to supply arms.

Egyptian Premier Nasser announced Sept. 27 that Czechoslovakia had signed a barter agreement the previous week to exchange all kinds of Czechoslovak arms in return for Egyptian cotton and rice. Egypt, meanwhile, informed Britain that Egypt had decided to accept a Soviet offer of arms aid. Speaking at a military exhibition in Cairo, Nasser said the Czechoslovak agreement was on "a purely commercial basis" and "will not create Russian or Czechoslovak influence in the Middle East or Egypt." "We will never attack or threaten anyone else," he declared, "but the Western powers have refused to give us arms for defense." Nasser said that Egypt had applied to the West, "but all we got were demands." (U.S. sources at UN headquarters said Sept. 27 that the U.S. had rejected an Egyptian request in June for jet bombers, heavy tanks and artillery and naval craft because the U.S. feared that such heavy equipment would alter the balance of forces in the Middle East. In 1954 Egypt had declined to sign a mutual-security agreement with the U.S. under which U.S. arms could not be used for aggression.) Nasser said that Egypt had rejected offers of Western arms "at the expense of our freedom" and that the U.S. and Britain were annoyed "at our success in procuring arms."

Mohammed Heikal, publisher of *Al Ahram* and Nasser's intimate, describes the prelude to the Russian arms deal with Egypt quite differently than does Miles Copeland 3d, ex-consultant to the CIA and State Department. In *Nasser: The Cairo Documents*, Heikal wrote: "The report that finally opened [John Foster] Dulles' eyes came from an Egyptian who was in the CIA's pay. In September this man telephoned the top CIA agent at the embassy, John Eichelberger, and told him that the arms deal with Russia had been signed. Eichelberger reported to Washington and then the explosions started. At 3 o'clock in the morning a very agitated Eichelberger telephoned me and pleaded, asking me to beg Nasser not to fall into a Communist trap. Tell the President to 'keep his pants on' he said, there was a special messenger on his way from Washington . . . ."

In *The Game of Nations,* Copeland wrote: ". . . In mid-September Kermit Roosevelt [U.S. State Undersecretary for Middle Eastern & Communist Affairs] received a personal message from Nasser to the effect that he was about to sign an agreement with the Russians and that if he, Roosevelt, wanted to try talking him out of it he was welcome to do so." Copeland and Roosevelt arrived in Cairo and met with Nasser. ". . . Nasser was in a teasing 'I told you so' mood, very cheerful and all set to enjoy hearing the famous Roosevelt persuasion grapple with his own unanswerable arguments. But Roosevelt surprised him. Instead of arguing that Nasser should not accept the arms (the CIA had convinced us that this would be futile, since they had been reliably informed that Nasser had *already* concluded the deal), Roosevelt said, 'If the deal is as big as we hear it is, it will worry some people but in general it will make you a big hero . . . .'" Roosevelt went on to suggest that Nasser announce that he was obtaining the Russian arms only for defensive purposes and to adopt a "statesmanlike" attitude by calling publicly for a common effort with the Israelis for a lasting peace in the area.

The immediate public reaction of the Western Big 2 leaders was a noncommital statement issued by Dulles and British Foreign Secy. Harold Macmillan in New York Sept. 28. They said: The U.S. and Britain "have for some time been in close consultation with each other [and] with other governments" regarding "arms supply policies in the Middle East." The U.S. and Britain were in "complete harmony" on the subject and based their policies "on the desire, on one hand, to enable the various countries to provide for internal security and for their defense, and on the other, to avoid an arms race which would inevitably increase the tensions in the area."

A British spokesman said the USSR was included in the reference to "other governments" and that the joint statement was made "to correct the false impression that the U.S. is going to offer arms to Egypt to forestall the USSR in supplying them." The spokesman also denied reports that Britain had protested "such action by the U.S." Dulles said in Washington Sept. 28 that he had discussed the sale of arms to Egypt in a talk with Soviet Foreign Min. Molotov in New York Sept. 27 "as part of a general review of world matters."

George V. Allen, U.S. Assistant State Secretary for Near Eastern, South Asian and African affairs, left Washington by air for Cairo Sept. 28 for talks with Nasser. He also was scheduled to visit Lebanon and Greece "to discuss current problems." Dulles, who returned to

Washington from New York that day, said that Allen's trip was "only
a more or less routine visit." Allen in Cairo Oct. 1 joined British Amb.-
to-Egypt Sir Humphrey Trevelyan and the French ambassador in expressing to Nasser their "grave concern" at the arms deal.

Nasser, in an interview Oct. 1 with the Cairo correspondent of the
London *Times*, stressed that the Czechoslovak arms arrangement would
not open the door to Communist influence in Egypt. Nasser said that
the sole reason for the Czechoslovak agreement was Egypt's "genuine
fear" that Israel was planning to extend its borders. Nasser said that he
had been "feeling insecure" since the Gaza incidents in February and
that this feeling of insecurity had been heightened in subsequent
months by the speeches of Ben-Gurion during the Israeli election campaign and of other Israeli "extremist leaders" who had spoken of the
expansion of Israel. Nasser also professed to have been alarmed by arms
supplies that, he said, had been received by Israel—"Sherman tanks from
Britain and fighters, tanks and medium artillery from France"—and by
the "constant threats against the Egyptian position at Gaza." He said
Egypt feared that it could not rely on external aid or protection because the UN was "impotent" and the British-U.S.-French tripartite
agreement of 1950 was "useless." Therefore, he declared, Egypt had
sought arms wherever it could get them. Egypt had been trying "from
the first day of [its] revolution" to obtain arms from the Western countries without prior conditions being attached but had been "rebuffed,"
Nasser continued. He said he would have preferred to buy arms from
Britain since the Egyptian army had formerly been equipped with
British material, but Britain had not supplied enough arms. France had
agreed to supply planes, aircraft, guns, and tanks. Nasser said, but had
delivered only a few tanks before cancelling the agreement on the
ground that Egypt was meddling in North African affairs. The U.S. had
at first been prevented from selling arms to Egypt by "British influence"
and later had insisted that membership in a mutual security pact was a
prerequisite for the supply of arms, Nasser said. In June, he asserted,
he had warned the British and U.S. ambassadors that Egypt would have
to get arms from the "Iron Curtain" countries if it could not obtain
them from the West. Shortly afterwards, Nasser had approached both
the Soviet Union and Czechoslovakia, and an agreement had eventually
been concluded with Czechoslovakia. There was no agreement with the
Soviet Union although the USSR knew of and approved the
Czechoslovak-Egyptian agreement, Nasser said.

Nasser emphasized that the receipt of arms from an "Iron Curtain"
country would not mean any expansion of Communist influence in
Egypt. He declared: "We are strong enough to cope with all internal

subversion, including communism. Communism is banned in Egypt. We have 5 or 6 underground Communist organizations, but we know all about them. They have no able leadership. Many other Communists are in prison."

When asked whether the deal would lead to an arms race in the Middle East, Nasser said that there was already "a one-sided arms race, with Israel getting all the armaments." The aims of his policy, Nasser declared, were defense against external aggression and security against internal subversion. Nasser insisted that he had "no aggressive intention at all." Egypt's foreign policy had 2 objectives, "to be completely independent ourselves and to help others to self-determination," he said. Egypt's purchase of arms from Czechoslovakia did not mean that the Egyptian army would ultimately be entirely equipped by the "Iron Curtain" countries. Egypt had no fixed policy on this, he said, "because these decisions do not lie with us but with the great powers who control arms production."

The Soviet government Oct. 2 supported Czechoslovakia's right to supply arms to Egypt. The Soviet news agency Tass distributed this Soviet government statement: "It appears from foreign press reports that pressure has been exercised of late upon some Middle Eastern countries to make them buy their defense requirements exclusively from the Western countries and on terms imposed by the Western countries. It also appears that the Egyptian government regards such pressure as an intolerable interference detrimental to the independence of Egypt and to the interests of her legitimate defense. The Soviet government holds the view that every state has the legitimate right . . . to purchase arms for its defense requirements from other states on the usual commercial terms and that no foreign state has the right to intervene. . . . The Soviet government has expressed this point of view to the Egyptian and Czechoslovak governments and also to the British and U.S. governments."

At an emergency meeting of the Israeli cabinet Oct. 3, Premier Moshe Sharett reported on the "steps taken with the powers to prevent an arms race and to ensure the security of Israel." Sharett had met with the British and U.S. ambassadors on the previous day, after an earlier meeting with the Soviet charge d'affaires. The Israeli charge d'affaires in Prague Oct. 4 informed the Czechoslovak government that Israel regarded the sale of arms to Egypt as an "unfriendly act" and as tantamount to abetting agression.

An official Israeli statement issued after the cabinet meeting described Egyptian reports of Israel's superiority in armaments as "without foundation" and termed the figures given by Nasser a "ridiculous exaggeration." It declared that Israel was far behind Egypt in military equipment and pointed out that Israel's military budget was $1/3$ that of Egypt's. The Israeli government expressed Israel's "grave concern" at the prospect that the existing military balance might be altered substantially in Egypt's favor and at the likelihood that this might encourage Egyptian aggression against Israel. If reports on the arms to be supplied to Egypt proved to be accurate, the statement added, Israel must "take every step at her disposal to improve her defensive power, including the purchase of increasing quantities of armaments."

Efforts to Curb Arms Race

Israeli Amb.-to-U.S. Abban Eban, speaking in the UN General Assembly's general debate Oct. 3, 1955, called on the big powers to avoid disturbing the military balance in the Middle East. Quoting from a statement by Soviet Foreign Min. Vyacheslav M. Molotov in the UN Sept. 23 that the UN's primary objective must be the ending of arms races, Eban said: "It is unfortunate that a few days later an armament race was stimulated in the Middle East." Eban said that the purchase of arms was a sovereign nation's right but that there also were political and moral implications. He asked whether "Israel, or indeed any state in like circumstances," would be expected to "wait passively while a hostile neighbor, asserting or practicing a state of war, strengthened himself for the decisive blow."

Eban was followed to the UN rostrum by Syrian chief delegate Ahmad el-Shukhairy, who declared: "We accept no intervention, no observation, from any side in the exercise of our right to build up our defense." Conceding that excessive arms threatened peace, he said that to be underarmed invited aggression. He suggested an international arms pool, under UN control, to effect a just distribution of arms among the "haves" and "have-nots."

U.S. State Secy. Dulles said at his news conference Oct. 4 that he had discussed the selling of Soviet arms to Egypt during 2 talks with Molotov in New York. (Molotov had left New York for Moscow Oct. 1). Dulles said he had told Molotov that, "from the standpoint of U.S. relations with the USSR, such delivery of arms would not contribute to relaxing tensions." He declined to say whether the U.S. might provide arms to Israel to balance Soviet-bloc arms to Egypt. In a press statement, Dulles said: "It is difficult to be critical of countries which, feeling themselves endangered, seek the arms which they sincerely believe they need for defense. On the other hand, I doubt very much that, under the conditions which prevail in the [Middle East] area, it is possible for any country to get security through an arms race." There was a "better understanding" between Egypt and the U.S. as the result of talks in Cairo between Nasser and U.S. Assistant State Secy. George Allen. But "we have no reason to believe" that Egypt would not carry through its arrangement with Czechoslovakia.

Weapon Maneuvering

Nasser, in an interview with Kennett Love of the *N.Y. Times* Oct. 5, said Egypt had informed the U.S. in June that it would seek Soviet-bloc arms if the U.S. would not supply them. (U.S. State Department officials said they had heard of no such alternative in June.) Nasser said that the U.S. apparently thought Egypt was "bluffing," but "I needed the arms and I had no alternative but to supply myself from the East." Nasser said he had learned through sources in Western capitals of the arms Israel had "contracted to receive in the next 10 months." Remarking that Israel had bought French Mystère jet fighters, Nasser said: "So now we will be meeting Mystères with MiGs. This is better than meeting Mystères with nothing." (The French Foreign Ministry denied Nov. 25 that licenses had been granted for the export of Mystère jet fighters to Israel but said that slower Ouragan jets had been shipped to Israel.) The Egyptian government announced in Cairo Oct. 7 that the arms to be supplied by Czechoslovakia would include MiG fighters.

Saudi Arabian Crown Prince Emir Faisal, arriving in Cairo Oct. 7 for an Arab states foreign ministers' conference opening the next day, reported that the USSR had offered arms to his country. He said the offer had been made by the Soviet ambassador to Iran during King Saud's visit to Iran in August.

Egyptian Amb.-to-U.S. Ahmed Hussein said in Washington Oct. 17 that he had assured State Secy. Dulles that Egypt's arms supplies from Czechoslovakia were being acquired as a "single commercial deal" and that they would be used solely for defensive purposes. Hussein told reporters that he had told Dulles that Egypt had "no intention at all of using these arms to attack Israel," and that the decision to buy Czechoslovak arms would not affect U.S.-Egyptian relations.

Israeli Premier Sharett told the Knesset in Jerusalem Oct. 18 that Egypt's purchase of Czechoslovak arms had cast "a deep shadow over the entire scene of Israel's foreign and defense affairs" and was "liable to bring about a revolutionary and ominous change in Israel's security situation." Sharett held that the arms deal implied a political and military tie between Egypt and the Soviet bloc. He therefore appealed to the Western powers to arm Israel and called for an Israeli security pact

with the Western powers, particularly with the U.S. Sharett emphasized, however, that such a security pact would not be regarded as a
substitute for arms. He said: "The ability for defense when war breaks
out, the ability to deter an enemy from attacking and so to avoid war,
depends first and foremost on the military strength of the country
which is the target for aggression."

Sharett accused the USSR of instigating the Egyptian-Czechoslovak
arms deal. He rejected the Soviet characterization of the arms agreement as merely a "commercial transaction." Neither Egypt nor Czechoslovakia had pretended that the arms were not intended for use against
Israel, Sharett noted. How does the USSR justify the sale of such quantities of weapons to Egypt?" he asked. "What is all this about a financial transaction, cotton and rice, 'modest means of self-defense,' and all
other whitewash of which the Tass agency's statement is compounded?
This Soviet initiative in the strife-torn Middle East, this dangerous disturbance of the balance of armed forces, this vehement spur to an arms
race giving free reign to fierce aggressive instincts—what relation does it
all bear to a policy of lessening international tension, progressive disarm-
ament, and working towards stable world peace which the USSR at
present avows?"

Sharett said: "What is the truth about the relative strength of Israel
and the Arab nations which surround her, maintain a state of war
against her, and are constantly vowing to wipe her off the face of the
earth? The truth is that the strength of the military manpower of the
Arab states—regulars and reserves—is more than twice as great as
ours.... The military budgets of Egypt, Syria, Lebanon, Jordan, Iraq
and Saudi Arabia amount to £140 million [$392 million] annually to-
gether, or £700 million, while Israel's entire budget—ordinary and
development, including defense—amounts to £631 million. The military
budget of Egypt alone is almost equal to the entire Israeli budget.
Egypt's army alone is superior to the Israeli defense forces in all cate-
gories of heavy weapons for use on land, sea, and in the air. The truth
is that there are Arab states which possess heavy arms which we do not
have—they are sold to them, but not to us. Our strength is in quality,
in the morale of the army, in its organizational and technical superiority. But quality, even the highest, can never serve as a full substitute
for the vast quantitative advantage." Although, Israel had always
opposed an arms race in the Middle East, "faced with an alarming and
decisive increase in the armed power of Egypt, our first demand has
become 'Arms! Arms in quantity and of quality, and cheap!' This
claim is directed first and foremost towards the great powers who
undertook publicly to keep the military balance between us and states

hostile to us. . . . Let the call go out to all Israeli citizens, to the dispersed Jewish people and to the whole world—arms for Israel!"

Sharett disclosed Oct. 19 that he had asked the Soviet ambassador in Israel to outline his country's Middle East policy but had received no reply. The Israeli government had information that the initiative for the Czechoslovak-Egyptian arms deal had come from Russia, whose representatives were trying to arrange similar deals between other Arab states and the Communist countries, Sharett declared. He added that if war resulted from the new crisis, "it would be perfectly clear who struck the match which started the conflagration." Sharett ruled out the idea of preventive war, as proposed Oct. 18 by Menahem Beigin, leader of the Herut party (an outgrowth of the terrorist Irgun Zvai Leumi).

In a speech in Jerusalem before leaders of the United Jewish Appeal Oct. 20, Sharett repeated Israeli requests for a U.S. security treaty. He said the idea had been affirmed in principle during discussions with the U.S. Sharett appealed Oct. 21 for Israeli public contributions to defense funds to match Egypt's public funds campaign.

All Israeli political parties except the Communists backed a resolution passed Oct. 24 by the Knesset, 84-5, calling on "the powers" to supply "defense arms to Israel." The 5 Communist deputies asked for an end to negotiations with the West. The resolution expressed anxiety at the big shipments of arms to Egypt and at the continued flow of arms to Iraq and other Arab countries, "which declare themselves to be still at war with Israel and which are plotting against this country's existence."

The U.S. State Department asserted Oct. 12 that it had received reports of Communist offers of arms to Israel. Such an offer was denied by Israeli officials in Washington, and the USSR's Tass news agency Oct. 23 called the reports "pure fabrication." But the State Department said Oct. 26 that it had received "further information" of the alleged offers.

U.S. State Secy. Dulles had said at his news conference Oct. 18 that he "would be disposed to" resume discussions of the Middle East with Soviet Foreign Min. Molotov during a forthcoming Big 4 foreign ministers' conference scheduled to open in Geneva Oct. 27. "I have done it twice, and the 3d time might have more luck than the first 2," Dulles said. He pointed out that the Middle East was not on the Big 4 agenda, "although it is always permissible, I suppose, for the foreign ministers to put a new item on the agenda if all of them want to do so." Dulles said he thought it "quite likely" that the Middle East would be discussed in "informal talks which take place as a by-product of these conferences." He said he had not heard of suggestions that the USSR might ask to subscribe to the U.S.-British-French declaration of 1950 on the Middle East.

Commenting on Israel's request for U.S. arms aid to balance Soviet-bloc aid to Arab nations, Dulles said that the 1950 declaration had "2 broad concepts" regarding arms: "One, that it is desirable to avoid a serious imbalance of power; the other is that it is desirable to avoid an armaments race." "We do not yet know . . . the military significance" of the Czechoslovak-Egyptian arms agreement, he said, because "we do not know yet the full quantity or the kinds or the quality. . . . Second-hand arms is a business which is very difficult to appraise accurately. . . . Countries with large armaments are constantly discarding the old types, and . . . the actual value of the discards is . . . not always easy to judge." Dulles concluded that it was too soon to say "whether what is taking place is going to increase the military potential of Egypt."

The first shipment of Czechoslovak material to Egypt arrived in Alexandria aboard a Soviet ship Oct. 20. It consisted of 133 crates of unspecified arms.

Israeli Premier-Foreign Min. Sharett left Israel Oct. 23 for talks with the Big 4 foreign ministers. An Israeli announcement Oct. 22 said he would warn of "danger which looms over Israel as a result of the Czechoslovak-Egyptian arms deal." Sharett conferred first with British Foreign Secy. Macmillan and then with U.S. State Secy. Dulles in Paris Oct. 26, just before they left for the Big 4 meeting in Geneva. Sharret was understood to have asked for weapons to balance Soviet-bloc aid to Arab nations and for a guarantee of Israeli frontiers. He met with French Min. Antoine Pinay on arriving in Geneva Oct. 27 and conferred with Macmillan again Oct. 31.

Sharett conferred with Soviet Foreign Min. Molotov in Geneva Oct. 31 after having told newsmen that he would ask Molotov to halt the shipment of Soviet-bloc arms to Egypt and other Arab countries. After meeting with Molotov, Sharett told newsmen he would leave Geneva Nov. 1 "with the feeling that the views of the Israeli government have been fully and authoritatively represented" to the Big 4 powers. He urged the Big 4 to "restore the arms balance in the Middle East." He said Israel would strive for peace but was "ever determined to fight back if attacked.

In a speech at the annual Lord Mayor's Banquet in London Nov. 9, British Prime Min. Sir Anthony Eden expressed his regret that the Soviet Union had injected into the "delicate" Middle Eastern situation "a new element of danger" by delivering weapons "to one side only." "It is fantastic to pretend that this deliberate act of policy was an innocent commercial transaction," Eden said in reference to Soviet Foreign Min. Molotov's characterization of the Czechoslovak arms deal to his American and British counterparts during talks in Geneva in September. The Soviets "must have known well enough in advance what the effect ... of these large quantities of arms must be," Eden maintained. He asserted that the Soviet-bloc arms deals had "brought a sharp increase of tension with very dangerous possibilities." (The U.S. State Department Nov. 18 issued a statement saying that the U.S. agreed with Britain on the need for a settlement of the Middle Eastern crisis.)

Israeli Premier-designate Ben-Gurion, presenting a 5-party coalition government to the Knesset Nov. 2, had said that Czechoslovakia had known that the arms it sold to Egypt were "intended [not] for the improvement of conditions of labor and life of the masses" but "to destroy the state of Israel." He charged that Czechoslovakia acted "not of its own volition but on the initiative and decision of the USSR."

It was reported in Washington Nov. 7 that the U.S. had decided to sell Israel "significant" quantities of arms.

U.S. State Undersecy. Herbert Hoover Jr., at a press conference in Denver Nov. 9, read a statement on the Middle East by Pres. Eisenhower. It said in part that "recent developments have made it ... imperative that a settlement be found." The statement reaffirmed support for the UN's truce efforts, which had "already contributed so markedly to minimize violence in the area." "I hope that other nations of the world will cooperate in this endeavor, thereby contributing significantly to world peace," it continued. Recent hostilities "inevitably retard our search for world peace. Insecurity in one region is bound to affect the world as a whole." Eisenhower also said: "While we continue willing to consider requests for arms needed for legitimate self-defense, we do not intend to contribute to an arms competition in the Near East because we do not think such a race would be in the true interest of any of the participants." The U.S.-British-French declaration of May 1950 "still remains our policy."

The State Department disclosed Nov. 10 that it had warned Israel and Egypt that it would "be strongly opposed to the side which starts a war and would be very favorably disposed to the side which convinces us that it desires to maintain peace."

Israeli Foreign Min. Moshe Sharett arrived in New York Nov. 10 to begin a tour for the Israel Bond campaign. He told newsmen that Israel would accept arms from any country if its security were threatened but said that he knew of no Soviet offer to sell arms to Israel. Moshe Sharett told the National Press Club in Washington Nov. 21 that Israel, like "any other nation," would take arms from the Soviet bloc if its survival were at stake in "a very tight corner." But, he added, the question "hardly arises," since the U.S. was under a "moral obligation" to counterbalance Communist arms sales to Egypt. Sharett pledged that Israel would not "launch an offensive war no matter what the provocation might be." Peace in the Middle East must be based on "maintenance of the *status quo*," he said.

Israeli Amb.-to-U.S. Abba Eban had formally asked the U.S. Nov. 16 to sell Israel specified arms "under the most lenient conditions" to offset the "massive" shipment of Soviet-bloc arms to Egypt. He said that the weapons he asked for amounted to "considerably less": than the $70–$100 million worth Egypt reportedly was buying from Czechoslovakia. (Israel's request for U.S. arms was reported in Washington Nov. 17 to amount to less than $40 million. Israel reportedly had asked for at least 40 late-model jet planes, antisubmarine vessels, heavy tanks, antitank guns and antiaircraft weapons.) The State Department said that it would "consider" the Israeli request, as well as an Egyptian warning that Cairo would buy more arms "wherever we can get them" if Israel got U.S. weapons.

Egyptian Premier Nasser warned Nov. 16 that the sale of U.S. weapons to Israel would touch off a Middle East arms race.

U.S. State Secy. Dulles said at his news conference Nov. 29 that the U.S. "very distinctly" had the initiative in the Middle East despite the Soviet effort "being made there for the first time." "When a person has not been making any particular effort and he starts to make it, that . . . in a certain sense, gives him an initiative," Dulles observed. "But if you want to take the total situation on a comparative basis, I believe that what we are doing . . . is of incomparably greater importance and significance than these tentative proposals that the Soviets are now making." Dulles said that "we don't yet see clearly how much solid substance there is behind the smiles" Russia was directing toward the Middle East and South Asia. He said that he had observed no "developments which require us to alter the general magnitude of our programs."

An agreement to coordinate Western policies to meet Soviet penetration in the Middle East was reached in Paris Dec. 15 by Dulles, British Foreign Secy. Harold Macmillan and French Foreign Min. Antoine Pinay, who were attending the North Atlantic Council meeting.

The British Foreign Office announced Dec. 31 that "no further licenses are now being granted for the export of surplus war material," following "urgent investigation" of some British press reports that surplus material sold as scrap had been overhauled in Belgium and sent to the Middle East. (190 Valentine tanks exported to Belgium as tractors reportedly were equipped with guns and shipped to Egypt. Bren gun carriers and scout cars reportedly were overhauled and sent to Egypt and Israel.) The British statement said that no "significant quantities" of surplus war exports and no exports of tanks had been licensed for several months.

Israeli Foreign Min. Sharett had made a strong verbal protest Dec. 30 to Soviet Amb. Aleksandr N. Abramov in Tel Aviv over Soviet Communist Party leader Nikita S. Khrushchev's references to Israel in a speech to the Supreme Soviet Dec. 29. The Israeli press reported that the Israeli government took particular exception to Khrushchev's statement that Israel had adopted a "hostile and threatening" policy towards its neighbors since the state came into existence, and that it had allowed itself to be used by "imperialist powers" as their "instrument against the Arab peoples." Sharett was believed to have warned Abramov that Khrushchev's remarks could be construed as a direct encouragement to the Arab states to attack Israel.

Israeli Finance Min. Levi Eshkol presented Dec. 5 a supplementary budget of £113 million ($65 million) for the fiscal year ending Mar. 31, 1956, mostly "for the acquisition of arms and equipment and increasing our preparedness." The budget request provided for stockpiling of food and raw materials. The Mapai party gave Israeli Premier Ben-Gurion a vote of confidence Dec. 29 on his firm "line of action" in dealing with Arab states.

MIDEAST DOMINANCE SHIFTS TO U.S. & USSR (1956)

The border-and-navigation dispute between Israel and Egypt led to a showdown in 1956, a pivotal year in Middle Eastern and world history. British and French influence in the Middle East came to an end after Britain and France participated in an invasion of the Suez Canal Zone that proved to be a military success but a dismal political failure. Britain's protege Jordan underwent a severe test of its internal cohesion. (Early in 1957 Jordan renounced its 10-year-old alliance with Britain.) Syria threw off all remaining traces of its former connection with France. The Soviet Union and the U.S. became the political heirs of France and Britain and acquired the major portions of direct foreign influence in Middle Eastern affairs largely as a result of the Suez invasion and of the other developments that followed World War II. Henceforth both states exercised political sway that neither power had ever successfully exerted previously in the area.

Jordan Moves Toward 'Neutralist' Stance

Britain's influence over Jordan had placed the Hashemite kingdom in an embarrassing position in the Arab world. Matters reached the danger point with an outbreak of popular disorders early in 1956. The Jordanian government declared a state of emergency in the Old City of Jerusalem Jan. 8 following the outbreak. Arab Legion troops opened fire on rioters, killing several of them. Demonstrators marched to the U.S. consulate and tore down the American flag. Personnel from the consulate and their families withdrew from the city. Radio Cairo asserted Jan. 8 that towns and villages in north and south Jordan had threatened to secede and join Syria and Saudi Arabia, respectively.

U.S. State Secy. John Foster Dulles summoned the Jordanian charge d'affaires in Washington Jan. 9 and requested that he ask his government to take proper measures to protect U.S. citizens and property from mob violence. A State Department spokesman said that it was obvious that the measures taken by the Jordanian government to prevent mob action had been inadequate.

Calm prevailed again by Jan. 14, when the royal government lifted the curfew imposed on Amman and other towns. The government also lifted news censorship. It then came to light that a mob in El Zerqa, where the Arab Legion had its headquarters, had killed a lieutenant colonel—one of the Legion's 60 or so British officers, whom many Jordanians wanted dismissed.

The riots appeared to be a recurrence of the mid-Dec. 1955 disorders that had resulted in at least 14 deaths and the injury of more than 100 persons in Amman. The 1955 disorders had erupted Dec. 15, a day after the resignation of Premier Hazzah Majali and the remainder of Jordan's government. 4 cabinet ministers had begun the resignation procession Dec. 13 after a 3-hour cabinet session attended by Gen. Sir Gerald Templer, chief of the British imperial general staff, who reportedly had gone to Jordan with proposals for closer Anglo-Jordanian cooperation. One of these proposals was for Jordan to join the Baghdad Pact.

Samir el-Rifai took from King Hussein the oath of premier Jan. 9, 1956 and pledged in a radio broadcast to his countrymen: "My government will give full details of its internal and foreign policies in the ministerial statement which I shall shortly deliver to parliament, but meanwhile I wish to declare that adherence to any new pacts is not the policy of my government and that we shall continue our endeavors to strengthen cooperation and consolidate our friendly and fraternal relations with Arab countries . . . . "

The king, in a letter approving Rifai's cabinet choices, gave priority to the "preservation of friendly and brotherly relations with all Arab countries" over the much-desired "preservation of good relations existing between our country and friendly and allied countries."

Egypt, Syria and Saudi Arabia had violently opposed the trend towards Jordan's possible adherence to the pact, and Radio Cairo, even before the January rioting, had urged Jordanians to overthrow their government. Egypt, Saudi Arabia and Syria Jan. 11 gave to the Jordanian charge d'affaires in Damascus "a memo . . . expressing the desire of the 3 Arab states to negotiate with the Jordanian government on the manner in which those states can offer the Jordanian government help and financial aid," a joint Egyptian-Saudi Arabian-Syrian statement said.

The 3 states suggested "a conference of the 4 heads of the Arab states" (them and Jordan), "either in Damascus, Cairo or Riyadh" with the aim of "render[ing] Jordan strong enough to withstand possible Israeli aggression." "The 3 states are prepared to give Jordan aid in substitution for British aid for the Arab Legion and the [Jordanian] national guard," the statement added.

Britain had already arranged to finance Jordan in fiscal 1956-7 to the amount of £12,550,000 (about $36 million)—an increase of £950,000 over 1955-6. This sum would provide £9.2 million for the Arab Legion, £2¼ million as an interest-free loan for economic development and £1.1 million in budget aid—£350,000 of that for the national guard.

Jordan was reported Jan. 17 to have rejected any conference on its economic ties with Britain and to have proposed instead a pan-Arab conference. 6 days later, however, Jordan reportedly did agree to confer some time in 1956 with Egypt, Saudi Arabia and Syria.

Jordan's internal affairs resumed a semblance of normality, but 200 Jordanian students stormed the U.S. embassy in Cairo Feb. 12 during a demonstration against the Baghdad Pact.

Jordan's relations with Britain, meanwhile, were reaching a critical stage over Britain's role in Jordan's military affairs. In an initial act of military independence, King Hussein asked the Jordanian parliament Feb. 28 to double the previous expenditure of $700,000 on a Jordanian air force. Britain had never provided Jordan with anything more than assurances of British air cover in the event of hostilities, and Britain had not indicated that it planned any policy change.

A more daring assertion of military independence was made Mar. 1 when King Hussein, 21, dismissed Sir John Bagot Glubb, nearly 60, as commander of the Arab Legion. Glubb Pasha, as he was called, was ousted after 26 years of service to the Hashemite monarchy in Jordan and was asked to leave the country at once. The West was amazed at the act, and Britain's Prime Min. Sir Anthony Eden cabled Hussein, asking him to reconsider the step. Arab nationalists, however, celebrated by displaying anti-imperialist banners in Jordan's towns.

According to the British diplomat Anthony Nutting, Eden, insisting that "the whole business reeked of [Egyptian Premier Gamal Abdel] Nasser's intrigues," wanted to sever Britain's relations with Jordan completely. "With the greatest difficulty I managed to dissuade . . . [Eden] from making such a threat, on the grounds that it would force Hussein to turn to Egypt—the one thing Eden wished to avoid," Nutting wrote in his 1967 book, *No End of a Lesson.* "To gain this point I had to concede that every British officer serving with the Jordan army should be ordered home."

King Hussein gives the following account of the incident in his 1962 autobiography, *Uneasy Lies the Head:*

. . . My main motive in dismissing him [Glubb] was . . . [that] we were in disagreement on 2 issues: the role of Arab officers in our army and strategy in the defense of our country . . . .

It was my express desire to have more of Jordan's officers in high army posts, to take over gradually all commands. . . . But this was against the prevailing British policy, and their counterproposals were . . . ridiculous . . . .

Glubb, . . . despite his love for Jordan and his loyalty to my country, was essentially an outsider, and his attitude did not fit at all into the picture I visualized. Yet, since the Arab Legion was the single strongest element in Jordan, he was, paradoxically, one of the single most powerful forces in our country. . . . He was serving as my commander-in-chief yet could not relinquish his loyalty to Britain . . . .

It did seem to me that . . . I had won one small battle, when the British authorities finally agreed to submit a plan of Arabization. . . . but my elation was short-lived when I was gravely informed that the Royal Engineers of the Arab Legion would have an Arab commander by 1985!

I disagreed . . . above all . . . [with Glubb's] military line of defense against Israel . . . . Jordan has a longer frontier with Israel than any Arab state—nearly 400 miles our of 670 . . . . If war came, I argued, we should plan to start our defense right on our 400-mile frontier with Israel and accept death with honor if we could not hold it . . . We began to train some of the civilian population . . . [as] 'National Guards' . . . to defend the area in depth, giving the . . . Arab Legion the opportunity to attack selected points in Israel if we were attacked . . . . [But] to my way of thinking, a purely defensive strategy invited disaster . . . .

In vain I pointed all this out to Glubb. To all my pleas he advised cautious patience. He advocated at first a withdrawal that, in the event of attack would end up on the East Bank [of the Jordan], pending the arrival of reinforcements, before we could develop a counterattack. This meant Jewish occupation of the Palestinian territory Jordan occupied. . . . It was unthinkable, and though in the end, as military capabilities improved, a line of defense was drawn in the West Bank area, nearer Israel than Glubb had previously planned, it still meant losing a lot of territory before a battle even started.

. . . There were other arguments when I learned that we were short of ammunition. I realized he had some justification for his theory; this was the margin that separates the honor and the shame of a nation.

. . . In his book *A Soldier with the Arabs* . . . [Glubb] mentions . . . 'The British refused to give us ammunition but they agreed to send barbed wire.' . . . If Glubb could not stock our ammunition depots, . . . he was in no position to advise me to fight an honorable battle . . . .

I also tried to build for Jordan its own air force. What good was an army against a powerful air-minded foe like Israel when we were at the mercy of another country for air support? . . .

This state of affairs, which he was powerless to rectify, naturally led Glubb to encourage his officers . . . to accept the view that we must yield territory in the case of attack. . . .

All these problems came gradually to a head. I was determined to build up strong, well balanced armed forces, . . . and since this was not possible with Glubb, our self-respect demanded that we fight our battles alone.

. . . Glubb had to go. . . . There was no other course but to carry out my decision. It was a surgical operation which had to be done brutally. . . .

To make his motives even clearer, Hussein in 1962 decided to publish his directive of Mar. 6, 1956 to Premier Rifai:

You are no doubt aware that our action in depriving Gen. Glubb of his post was due to loss of confidence in his judgment and the fact that his presence had become a troublesome factor in our country. But at no time did it occur to us that this matter should lead to any change in the relations between Jordan and her Britannic majesty's government, which are governed by treaty, or that the traditional friendship between our 2 countries should be affected.

With regard to British officers serving in the Arab Legion, kindly note that Jordan will honor her obligations towards them according to their contracts and to the treaty. After proper consideration it is our aim that these officers should continue to serve in the Legion, to raise its standard to the level we hope for.

With reference to rumors that we intend to replace the British subsidy by an Arab subsidy, your excellency is no doubt aware of the existence of a treaty with Great Britain which confers certain benefits on both parties. Payment of an Arab subsidy, assuming it were to be made, does not in any way annul the effectiveness of the Anglo-Jordanian treaty. Nonetheless, Jordan welcomes every form of Arab assistance of a kind she can use to improve her position along the armistice lines where she faces a perfidious enemy and to fill in gaps in her military defence system following the recent transfer of command into Arab hands.

In views of the above I trust your excellency will do the utmost to emphasize and expound these facts in the interests of the country.

British Prime Min. Eden had already received assurances on the king's intentions from the British ambassador in Jordan when Eden Mar. 5, 1956 told the British House of Commons that the British government was immediately withdrawing the top 15 British officers from service in the Arab Legion and bringing them home because of Glubb's ouster. Eden said:

The House will have heard with resentment and regret of the summary dismissal of Gen. Glubb and 2 other senior British Officers of the Arab Legion. The lifetime of devoted service which Gen. Glubb has given to the Hashemite Kingdom of Jordan should have received more generous treatment. ... The king of Jordan and the Jordan prime minister have told her majesty's ambassador that they do not want any change to take place in Anglo-Jordanian relations and that they stand by the Anglo-Jordan treaty.

It is clear from the treaty that its whole spirit is based on the need for consultation to ensure mutual defence, and in this sense Gen. Glubb's dismissal is, in view of the government, against the spirit of that treaty.

Her majesty's government have given due weight to the Jordan Government's statement regarding the officers. They feel that in view of the treatment meted out to the British officers who have been dismissed, it would be wrong for British officers in the Arab Legion to be left in an uncertain position. In our opinion officers in executive commands cannot be asked to continue in positions of responsibility without authority. We have, therefore, asked that such officers should be relieved of their commands.

According to an Arab Legion spokesman Mar. 6, there were at the onset of the crisis 71 British officers besides Glubb in the Legion. Col. Sir Patrick Coghill was ousted as the Legion's intelligence officer, and Brig. William Hutton was dismissed as the Legion's chief staff officer, leaving 17 British officers under contract with the Legion and 51 others on loan from the British army.

The British government Mar. 7 permitted a public airing of hints that it was reconsidering its $36 million annual subsidy to Jordan in the light of Glubb's ouster. In a letter appearing in the London *Times* Mar. 8, Glubb himself urged the British government not to "get tough" with Jordan over his ouster and to forgo halting its subsidy.

Hussein let it be known Mar. 9 that he had rejected an offer carried to him by Syrian Premier Said el-Ghazzi from Egyptian Premier Gamal Abdel Nasser, King Ibn Saud of Saudi Arabia and Syrian Pres. Shukri al-Kuwatli to replace the current British subsidy with contributions of their own. Hussein's step was interpreted as an earnest of his intention not to disrupt Jordan's relations with Britain.

In an interview with the Old Jerusalem independent daily *Al Difaa* Mar. 19, Hussein stressed that Jordan would continue to pursue a policy of neutrality. Jordan would not join either the "Iraqi-Turkish" (Baghdad) pact or the Egyptian-Saudi Arabian-Syrian axis, Hussein said. Jordan, however, would "always endeavor to strengthen cooperation and union between the Arab countries," he declared. He said that the command changes in the Arab Legion would produce "no effect whatsoever" on Jordan's resolve to fulfill its duties under the Anglo-Jordanian alliance.

The command of the Arab Legion May 24 devolved on Lt. Col. Ali Abu Nuwar, an opponent of Glubb and close friend of the king, who promoted Nuwar to the rank of major general. Nuwar moved at once to enlarge the Legion, establish closer coordination between it and Jordan's national guard and discharge all but 15 of the Legion's British officers. Jordanian Defense Min. Mohammed Ali Ajlouni May 26 revealed plans approved by Nuwar to merge the 17,000-to-25,000-man Legion with the Jordanian national guard to form the Jordanian army.

King Hussein, meanwhile, had named Said el-Mufti to succeed Premier Rifai, who resigned May 20 after returning from Syria. Rifai reportedly had angered Hussein while in Syria by aligning Jordan May 19 with other Arab League states in an anti-French strategy on North Africa. Mufti was reported May 21 to have said that he would seek a revision of Britain's subsidy arrangement so that Jordan would henceforth control all British subsidy funds earmarked for the Legion.

Syrian Defense Min. Abdel Hassib Raslan revealed Aug. 19 that Egypt, Saudi Arabia and Syria had agreed to extend permanent financial assistance to Jordan in equipping its border defense force. Raslan said that the offer was made unconditionally and separately from the 3 Arab states' Jan. 11 offer—which they had not withdrawn, though Hussein had rejected it.

Jordan's relations with Syria had become a matter of increasing interest to Western observers. King Hussein and Premier Rifai paid a 3-day visit to Damascus Apr. 9 and conferred with Pres. Kuwatli. A communique issued jointly in Amman and Damascus Apr. 12 announced that the 2 countries had agreed to coordinate their defense plans and cooperate militarily with respect to their frontiers with Israel in the event of an Israeli attack. Jordan and Syria agreed to strive for an over-all coordination of Arab military plans and forces in defense against any Israeli attack. The 2 countries also pledged not to join any "foreign" pacts, the communique said. On another level, Jordan and Syria announced an agreement of collaboration toward closer economic and cultural cooperation.

Kuwatli returned the visit May 28–31, accompanied by his premier and military chief-of-staff. Before Kuwatli left Amman, the 2 governments concluded 4 agreements: (a) abolishing the need for passports and visas by citizens of either country for travel between Jordan and Syria; (b) elevating the status of the 2 countries' respective legations to embassies; (c) granting freedom of transit for truck traffic through Syria from Lebanese ports to Jordan; (d) setting up active military cooperation between the 2 countries through a projected permanent agency for joint consultation and strategy in times of war. Syria also reportedly pledged 62,500 Jordanian dinars (then about $175,000, since the dinar was pegged to the British pound sterling and supported by Britain) toward the Arab League's Dead Sea potash production scheme.

Hammarskjöld's Peace Mission

A sequence of Middle Eastern developments in Mar. 1956 alarmed the Western Big 3 enough to prompt the dispatch to the area of a top-level UN peace mission led by Secy. Gen. Dag Hammarskjöld. These were the major events:

● Israel Mar. 6 lodged a strong protest with the UN Security Council over 2 truce violations for which it blamed Syria. In the first, Syrian troops Mar. 4 killed at least 3 Israeli policemen and wounded and captured a 4th policeman in a patrol vessel on the Sea of Galilee as the Israeli police attempted to salvage an Israeli vessel that had run aground. In the 2d, Syrian antiaircraft fire Mar. 5 downed an Israeli light plane in Israeli territory, wounding the pilot.

● An Israeli soldier and an Egyptian sapper were killed Mar. 6 one mile inside Israeli territory in a land-mine incident.

● Syrian Pres. Shukri al-Kuwatli and Saudi Arabian King Ibn Saud met with Egyptian Premier Nasser in Cairo Mar. 6–11 and drew up a "comprehensive plan to safeguard Arab security and defend it against the dangers of Zionist aggression and foreign domination." The 3 leaders agreed on means "to counteract attempts exerted through the Baghdad Pact to bring pressure to bear upon Arab countries, thus endangering Arab unity." They also offered Jordan "all possible support in the event of any foreign pressure or Zionist aggression." (Jordan's King Hussein had tried in Feb. 1956 to convene an Arab summit conference, but Cairo refused to go unless all Arab countries beforehand unconditionally repudiated the Baghdad Pact.)

● Armed Jordanians crossed into Israeli territory Mar. 10–12, killed an Israeli policeman and wounded 2 other Israeli policemen in the borderline village of Karkur and killed an Israeli settler 4 miles inisde Israel. Israeli forced killed one of the raiders, and the others escaped back into Jordan.

● The Israeli government asked the UN Truce Supervisory Organization Mar. 11 to investigate an alleged Egyptian troop buildup in the Gaza Strip and northern Sinai area. Israel claimed that the number of Egyptian troops there was far more than necessary to defend the area.

● Israel in mid-March intensified the digging of fortifications in the area bordering the Gaza Strip and in the Negev desert opposite Israel's border with Egypt. Israeli Premier David Ben-Gurion Feb. 21 had appealed for 150,000 volunteers to assist in the project.

The U.S. Mar. 20 asked Sir Pierson Dixon of Britain, UN Security Council president during March, to call an "urgent and early" Council meeting to discuss Arab-Israeli tension. The American note to Dixon said border violations were recurring at a dangerous rate" and "the buildup of armed forces on either side of the armistice demarcations lines" raised doubt as to whether Israel and its Arab foes were "fully complying with . . . armistice agreements." The U.S. requested that the Council discuss compliance in Palestine with armistice terms and resolutions on their observance adopted by the Council the past year.

(Reports from UN Headquarters in New York Mar. 20 said the U.S., Britain and France were prepared to ask that Secy. Gen. Hammarskjöld be sent on a fact-finding mission to Palestine. The 3 Western powers also were said to have discussed plans for possible military action to maintain present boundaries of Middle Eastern states.)

Pres. Eisenhower said at a press conference in Washington Mar. 22 that any major outbreak of hostilities in the Middle East would be a worldwide "catastrophe." The President emphasized the need to convince both Israel and the Arab countries that mediation was the only road to a peaceful solution of their differences. The U.S. fully supported the UN in such efforts, he stressed, and took "very seriously" its own obligations under the Tripartite Declaration of May 25, 1950 with Britain and France.

U.S. Amb.-to-UN Henry Cabot Lodge requested Mar. 26 that the UN Security Council consider a U.S. resolution on the Middle East that described the situation there as "likely to endanger the maintenance of international peace and security" if it went on much longer. The U.S. proposed "as a matter of urgent concern" that Hammarskjöld visit the area, confer with Israeli and Arab leaders and Canadian Gen. Eedson L. M. Burns, the UN truce team chief, survey on the spot all means of strengthening the truce team's machinery and of relieving the tension there and report back to the Security Council within a month of the resolution's adoption. Lodge accompanied his resolution with the plea that the UN exert its full authority to confront the budding crisis.

British Amb.-to-UN Sir Pierson Dixon, French Amb. Herve Alphand and the Australian and Peruvian representatives on the Security Council supported the U.S. resolution. The delegate of Iran, however, asked for a formal adjournment of the debate so that the Arab countries involved and Israel would have a chance to tell the Security Council their views on the matter. (Israel, Egypt, Jordan, Lebanon and Syria had already asked for permission to take part in the Council's discussions.)

Soviet Amb.-to-UN Arkady A. Sobolev supported the adjournment proposal. He was joined in this by Yugoslavia and Cuba, and the debate was put off until Israel and the concerned Arab countries' representatives could be present.

Meanwhile, Eisenhower had invited Mexican Pres. Adolfo Ruiz Cortines and Canadian Prime Min. Louis Saint-Laurent to confer with him at a precedent-setting meeting of North America's 3 heads of government in White Sulphur Springs, W. Va. Mar. 26–28. None of the countries issued a communique on the talks, but the Canadian prime minister told Canada's House of Commons Apr. 9 that the 3 leaders and their foreign ministers had conducted "considerable discussion" on the Middle Eastern situation, "the seriousness of which everyone recognized," and concluded that only an agreed political settlement between Israel and its Arab neighbors could guarantee peace in the area. Nevertheless, all present indorsed the policy of taking all possible steps through the UN to reduce the existing tension in the Middle East. Canadian External Affairs Min. Lester B. Pearson, Mexican Foreign Min. Luis Padilla Nervo and U.S. State Secy. John Foster Dulles accompanied the 3 leaders to the conference.

The Security Council reassembled Apr. 3, 1956. Sobolev, who reportedly had met that day with Syrian Rep.-to-UN Ahmad el-Shukhairy, charged that "certain Western powers" had planned armed intervention in the Middle East on the "pretext" of preventing war and proposed in the Council amendments that would restrict Hammarskjold's freedom of inspection in Palestinian armistice zones and require him to obtain the "concordance" of both the Arab governments and

Israel before arranging any improved armistice compliance. Sobolev asserted that the ambassadorial talks in Washington (he presumably meant White Sulphur Springs, W. Va.) had led to a worsening of the situation. The Soviet ambassador condemned French Foreign Min. Chistian Pineau's proposal (Mar. 22 during talks with U.S. State Secy. Dulles and British Foreign Secy. Selwyn Lloyd at a South East Asian Treaty Organization conference in Karachi, Pakistan) for a Western Big-3 conference on the Middle East. He also denounced the dispatch of 1,500 U.S. Marines to the Mediterranean area (Mar. 7 to replace a battalion withdrawn in the spring of 1955) as an aggravating factor.

U.S. Amb. Lodge in the Security Council Apr. 3 introduced minor changes in his resolution for a Middle East peace mission by Hammarskjöld. The changes were intended to offset Sobolev's proposed amendments. Lodge, who opposed Sobolev's amendments, changed his resolution to emphasize that it applied to areas delineated in the Arab-Israeli armistice pacts. Lodge said that the purpose of the U.S. resolution was to enable Hammarskjold to carry out his discussions with the concerned parties "entirely within the framework of the armistice agreements."

The Arab and Israeli representatives welcomed the U.S. initiative and assured Hammarskjöld of their cooperation. Shukhairy and Egyptian delegate Omar Loufti had asked Mar. 28 for "clarification" and limitation of the resolution specifically to the armistice agreements. They had warned that their governments would oppose any attempt to give Hammerskjöld power to suggest solutions for broader Middle Eastern problems. Israeli Amb.-to-UN Abba Eban said Apr. 3 that he favored the U.S. resolution, but he called attention to the "limited task" given Hammarskjöld under the proposal.

The Security Council Apr. 4 rejected the Soviet amendments to the U.S. resolution and unanimously adopted the original resolution. Sobolev said that he would vote for the resolution because it had been "accepted by the interested parties" (Israel and the concerned Arab countries). Hammarskjold immediately accepted the mission, asked for complete cooperation and appealed for the restraint of the Middle Eastern countries in dispute.

Eisenhower said at his press conference Apr. 4 that he would "never be guilty" of sending U.S. troops "into anything that can be interpreted as war, until Congress directs it." The President, referring to reports that British Prime Min. Sir Anthony Eden had been urging a firmer U.S. Middle East policy, said that "they haven't pressed me" and that his constant communication with Eden had not brought him any urgent appeals for Middle East action. (The British Foreign Office Apr. 4

issued a statement denying reports that Eden had written a personal letter urging Eisenhower to adopt a strong anti-Egypt line along with the British government.)

At his Washington news conference Apr. 3, U.S. State Secy. Dulles had said that Eisenhower would prefer to have Congressional approval before committing troops in any war crisis but might do so in an emergency arising while Congress was not in session. Dulles added that he saw no current emergency such as would create the need for U.S. troops.

A statement issued by White House Press Secy. James C. Hagerty Apr. 9 with "the full approval of the President" said that the U.S. would support Hammarskjöld's peace-making efforts fully and "observe its [UN Charter] commitments within constitutional means to oppose any aggression in the [Middle East] area." The statement added that Eisenhower and Dulles viewed the Arab-Israeli crisis "with the utmost seriousness" and that the U.S. was "determined to support and assist any nation which might be subjected to such aggression." (The U.S. statement was praised by diplomatic officials of the British and French governments. Ex-Prime Min. Sir Winston Churchill said in London Apr. 12 that should Israel be attacked by Egypt, it would become "a measure of honor to make sure that they are not the losers.") Hagerty said in Augusta, Ga. Apr. 12 that Eisenhower had sent personal messages to both Premier Ben-Gurion of Israel and Premier Nasser of Egypt urging restraint and outlining the current U.S. policy of aid for either side should it be the victim of aggression.

Hammarskjöld left New York Apr. 8 for the Middle East, consulted in Rome Apr. 9 with Henry Vigier, political adviser to Gen. Burns, the UN truce chief, and with Henry R. Labouisse, head of the UN Relief & Works Agency in Palestine, and flew Apr. 10 to Beirut. Hammarskjöld met Burns and senior officials of the Israeli Foreign Ministry in Lydda, Israel later Apr. 10. Still later Apr. 10 he and Burns flew to Cairo. Hammarskjöld and Burns conferred Apr. 11 with Egyptian Premier Nasser and Foreign Min. Mahmoud Fawzi.

Henry Cabot Lodge, president of the UN Security Council during April, announced Apr. 12 that Nasser and Israeli Premier Ben-Gurion had each assured Hammarskjöld in face-to-face meetings that their governments would comply unconditionally with their 1949 armistice agreement's prohibition of any recourse to warlike actions. Both Israel and Egypt, however, reserved the right to act in self-defense. Lodge released to his Council colleagues the text of Hammarskjöld's correspondence with Ben-Gurion and Nasser—all of it relating to Israel's and Egypt's records of truce observance. In his correspondence, Hammarskjöld deplored the current truce breakdown in the Gaza Strip area and urged both leaders to reapply the armistice there. Ben-Gurion Apr. 12 sent Hammarskjöld another letter asking what, in the light of fresh examples of raiding activity by Egyptian-backed *fedayin* (guerrilla irregulars), Nasser could offer as convincing assurances that Nasser would "put an end to the raiders' activities ... and ... refrain from all other acts of aggression and violence." (Tension in the Gaza Strip area had flared again Apr. 5. A 10-hour artillery duel caused the deaths of 59 civilians and 4 Egyptian soldiers in the City of Gaza. Each side blamed the other for starting the barrages. Arab *fedayin* Apr. 7 killed 2 Israelis and wounded 12 in sorties up to 15 miles inside Israel from the Gaza Strip.) In still another letter, dated Apr. 13, Ben-Gurion asked Hammarskjöld to take up the matter of Egypt's longstanding blockade—made total in Jan. 1954—of Israeli shipping from the Suez Canal.

(UN sources said Apr. 16 that Hammarskjöld had rejected Israeli requests for consideration of the Suez Canal blockade, citing the Apr. 4 Security Council resolution delineating his peace-mission powers.)

Hammarskjöld continued negotiations in Cairo through Apr. 14 in an effort to win firm cease-fire pledges from both Israel and Egypt. Cairo reports said Apr. 13 that Egypt had "virtually accepted" an 8-point UN peace plan and that Hammarskjöld had answered Israel's Apr. 12 charges and requested Israeli assurances against Gaza Strip attacks. Accompanied by Gen. Burns, head of the UN Palestine Truce Organization, Hammarskjöld left Cairo Apr. 14 for a tour of the Gaza zone, stopped briefly at Lydda and continued on to his peace mission headquarters in Beirut. Hammarskjöld left Beirut Apr. 7 for negotiations with Ben-Gurion in Jerusalem.

Meanwhile, attacks by Egyptian *fedayin* continued sporadically Apr. 11-16 throughout the Gaza-Beersheba-Tel Aviv area: An Israeli rabbi and 3 children were reported killed Apr. 11 near Tel Aviv. The Israeli air force reported that a British-built Vampire jet of the Egyptian air force had been shot down over the central Negev Apr. 12 after a 4-plane Egyptian formation was intercepted by Israeli jets. The Egyptian air force claimed to have downed a French-made Israeli Ouragen jet in the same clash.

Hammarskjöld announced in Jerusalem Apr. 19, 1956 that both Israel and Egypt had agreed to the enforcement of a Gaza Strip ceasefire effective at 6 p.m. Apr. 18. Hammarskjöld said that Israeli Premier Ben-Gurion and Foreign Min. Moshe Sharett had agreed in talks Apr. 17-19 to greater freedom for UN Truce Supervisory Organization observers and to the construction of fixed UN posts on the Israeli side of the Gaza frontier. The cease-fire bound Israel and Egypt to the observance of Article II, Paragraph 2 of the 1949 Egyptian-Israeli armistice agreement forbidding shooting or passing across the truce lines by either side's forces.

It was reported from Cairo Apr. 19 that Egyptian forces had received cease-fire orders and that charges had been filed listing 12 minor Israeli violations of the truce.

Israel agreed Apr. 20 to restrict its patrol boats along the Sea of Galilee border with Syria and to give Syrian farmers access to water from the Sea of Galilee. Hammarskjöld said that, despite Israeli threats to renew work on the disputed Jordan River irrigation plan in the demilitarized Israeli-Syrian border zone, he was "sure we are on the right road," and "personally I don't see any reason why we should lose it." Hammarskjöld ended his talks with Israeli leaders Apr. 20 and flew to Beirut, where Lebanese Foreign Min. Salim Lahoud reportedly rejected a UN request Apr. 21 to reopen talks on political aspects of the Palestine question. Hammarskjöld flew to Damascus Apr. 23 for talks with Syrian Premier Said el-Ghazzi, who agreed Apr. 24 to observe the terms of the UN cease-fire plan for Galilee. (Israeli reports said Apr. 23 that Syrian guns had fired on 15 Israeli fishing boats on the Sea of Galilee.) Hammarskjöld conferred with Jordanian King Hussein and Premier Samir el-Rifai in Amman Apr. 25–26 and with Lebanese Pres. Camille Chamoun and Foreign Min. Lahoud in Beirut Apr. 27.

(It was reported from Israel Apr. 24 that 4 Israeli surveyors had been killed in the Negev Apr. 23, apparently by 8 *fedayin* infiltrators from Jordan. Israeli Foreign Min. Sharett Apr. 24 protested the killings in a telegram to Hammarskjöld in Damascus. The Israeli-Jordanian Mixed Armistice Commission voted 2–1 Apr. 26 to condemn Jordan for the 4 deaths. Israel had charged Apr. 19 that one Israeli soldier and a Jordanian guardsman had been killed when a Jordanian patrol fired on Israelis near Nehusha.)

Hammarskjöld met with Israeli Premier Ben-Gurion and Foreign Min. Sharett in Jerusalem Apr. 30–May 1 to discuss a reported deadlock on cease-fire enforcement by Israel and Syria. UN informants said May 1 that Syria had demanded that Israel not resume work on its irrigation project in the demilitarized zone. Hammarskjöld reportedly told Ben-Gurion and Sharett May 3 that a resumption of work on the project would violate a 1953 Security Council resolution asking for the suspension of the work. The Israeli leaders were said to have replied that the 1953 resolution, which promised "urgent examination" of the dispute, had not been acted on and no longer was binding.

Hammarskjöld talked in Cairo Apr. 28–30 with Egyptian Premier

Nasser and Foreign Min. Fawzi about general cease-fire provisions. Israeli Foreign Min. Sharett protested Apr. 29 against renewed violence in the Gaza Strip area, where 2 Israelis were killed and one wounded Apr. 29. Israel reported that an investigation of one incident, with UN observers participating, showed that an Israeli settler had been killed and mutilated by Gaza border infiltrators guarded by Egyptian troops.

Hammarskjöld, in a "progress report" from Jerusalem May 3 on his peace mission, said cease-fire "assurances" given him by the Israeli and Egyptian governments had "served to relieve the threatening situation in the Gaza area." He said conditions there had "considerably improved as a result of strict orders issued by the 2 governments." Apr. 10. He reported also that his negotiations on observance of the Israeli armistice agreements with Jordan, Syria and Lebanon "have in all cases been concluded with positive result." Hammarskjöld said previous cease-fires had been "established locally, or between military commanders," whereas he had secured "a reaffirmation by the governments to comply unconditionally with the fundamental clauses of the [armistice] agreements."

Hammarskjöld talked with Israeli Premier Ben-Gurion in Jerusalem and Syrian Premier Said el-Ghazzi in Damascus May 2, and with Egyptian Premier Nasser in Cairo May 3 en route to Rome, where he worked until May 5 on his final report.

Hammarskjöld returned to UN headquarters in New York May 6, one month after leaving on his mission.

Hammarskjöld issued his final report to the Security Council May 10. He said that a cease-fire and compliance with armistice agreements had been reestablished between Israel and Egypt, Lebanon, Syria and Jordan. Hammarskjöld said: "The final settlement is probably still far off, but even partial solutions to the harassing problems of the region would be a contribution to the welfare of the peoples concerned and to the peace of the world." A lasting cease-fire would depend on the willingness of the 5 states concerned. He had urged Israeli compliance with a 1953 Security Council resolution asking Israel to delay work on the Jordan River plan and had told the Arab states that Israeli non-compliance was a matter for the UN. He had not been able to settle Israeli and Egyptian refusals to enforce the El Auja (Nitsana) demilitarized zone. He had obtained specific commitments on local armistice compliance between Israel and Egypt in the Gaza area but only partial pledges on keeping the truce between Israel and Syria on the Sea of Galilee.

On the question of "Egyptian interference with Israeli shipping through the Suez Canal," Hammarskjöld said: "My attitude has been that the Suez question, as adjudicated by the Security Council [in its resolution of Sept. 1, 1951, whose first article Israel invoked], is not a question of compliance with the armistice agreement in the sense of my mandate. For that reason I have not, within the framework of my mandate, discussed the issue with the Egyptian government. For the same reason I have found that I should not in this report evaluate the legal reasons presented by Israel in support of the view that the blockade represents a case of non-compliance ... [with] the armistice agreement. My mandate is directly concerned with the state of compliance or non-compliance with the armistice agreement as a cause of ... tension. In an approach looking beyond the immediate problems it is obvious that the question raised by the government of Israel should come under consideration in the light of the Council's finding, in its resolution of Sept. 1, 1951, that the blockade is incompatible with the armistice regime, as the regime put an end to a state in which Egypt could avail itself of belligerent rights."

Soviet Diplomatic Initiatives

Soviet Premier Nikolai A. Bulganin and Nikita S. Khrushchev, the Soviet Communist Party leader, visited Britain for 10 days in Apr. 1956 at the invitation of British Prime Min. Sir Anthony Eden. While they were en route to England, Soviet Foreign Min. Vyacheslav Molotov in the Kremlin Apr. 17 issued a statement in which the Soviet government offered its support for "UN measures directed toward ... strengthening peace in the area of Palestine and [toward] the implementation of the corresponding decisions of the Security Council."

Molotov's statement put the blame for the Middle Eastern crisis on "military alignments which serve the aims of colonialism," but it called on both Israel and Arab states to "refrain from any kind of action" that might increase tension and to "make the necessary efforts to alleviate the difficult position of hundreds of thousands of Arab refugees deprived of their homes and means of subsistence." The Soviet government "considers it essential, in the interests of strengthening peace and security, to direct efforts towards a stable, peaceful settlement of the Palestine question on a mutually acceptable basis, taking due consideration of the just national interests of the interested parties," the statement said. It added:

A great achievement of the peoples of the Middle East since the 2d World War has been the establishment of the national independence and sovereignty of a number of states which, until recent times, were colonial or mandated territories. The Soviet Union regards with sympathy and ardent support the attempts of the

Near Eastern countries–Egypt, Saudi Arabia, Syria, Lebanon, Yemen, Jordan, Sudan, Iraq, Israel and others–to strengthen their independence. The Soviet Union has assessed in the same manner the actions of Britain and France, which facilitated the solution of urgent Near Eastern problems by recognizing the independence and sovereignty of these states. . . .

While striving to ensure the consolidation of peace and the development of international cooperation, with due regard for the rightful national interests of the peoples of all countries, the Soviet government is unswervingly opposed to the violation of peace in the Near East and to any actions which might lead to the outbreak of armed conflict or be used as pretexts for precipitating such conflicts. It considers that it is possible and necessary to avoid an armed conflict in the Near East and that it is in the interests of all Near Eastern states not to allow themselves to be provoked into becoming involved in military operations. At the same time the Soviet government considers that it is illegal and inadmissible to use the Arab-Israel conflict as a pretext for outside interference in the internal affairs of independent Arab states or for introducing foreign troops in the territory of the Near East.

Molotov affirmed Apr. 17 that the statement could serve as a basis for the Soviet leaders' talks with Eden on the Middle Eastern situation. The statement had avoided criticism of Israel and had expressed the Kremlin's "appreciation" of the role played by Britain and France in the Middle East.

Speaking for the Eisenhower Administration, State Secy. John Foster Dulles in Washington Apr. 17 welcomed any "truly genuine" Russian support for UN Middle East peace moves. A White House statement said in Washington Apr. 18 that "the Administration is of course still studying the Soviet statement, but if it demonstrates a real desire . . . on the part of the Soviet Union to back the UN effort, the President welcomes this support." Sen. Mike Mansfield (D., Mont.) urged in the Senate Apr. 18 that the U.S. call a new "summit conference" to act on the Middle East problem.

Pres. Eisenhower, addressing the American Society of Newspapers Editors in Washington Apr. 21, said that a Soviet government "genuinely devoted" to a peaceful order "can have friendly relations with the U.S. and the free world" but that he saw no essential divergence from the Kremlin's policy of subjugating "once free nations." The President suggested the creation of a committee of highly qualified citizens that could recommend ways to meet "the Soviet shift in economic assistance and trade."

It was reported in a United Press news agency survey Apr. 15 that Soviet-bloc aid to underdeveloped nations had totalled $506 million in 1956. The UP said that U.S. government statistics showed Egypt getting the largest share of any single country: $165 million. (Other shares listed in the survey: Afghanistan $115 million, Iran $3 million, Lebanon

$2 million, Syria $8 million, Turkey $4 million. Soviet Foreign Trade Min. Ivan G. Kabanov told the UN Economic Commission for Europe in Geneva Apr. 9 that current Russian aid credits to Communist and non-Communist countries totalled $5 billion. Kabanov said that the USSR was ready to trade heavily with Europe when "extraordinary" U.S. expenditures there ceased.

The U.S. State Department Mar. 23 had confirmed reports that between 200 and 300 Egyptian commissioned and non-commissioned officers were receiving training at Soviet bases in Poland—on the Hel Peninsula near Gdynia, according to the London *Times* Mar. 24—and that Czechoslovak military cadres were training domestic army forces in Egypt. The *Times* article also reported that Polish ports had for some time been used in the shipment of Czechoslovak arms to Egypt.

Reports from Cairo Apr. 21 said that Egyptian reception of the Soviet statement on peace moves had cooled with the announcement that British and Soviet leaders were discussing the Middle East in London. The Cairo weekly *Akhbar El Yom* said Apr. 21 that "Middle East problems are for Middle East peoples to solve. . . . We want no guardians. . . . We are not defendants being tried in absentia." (Moscow newspapers had renewed attacks on the Baghdad Pact Apr. 19 and had expressed sympathy "with Arab aspirations.")

According to dispatches from Jerusalem Apr. 23, the initially hopeful Israeli reaction to the Soviet statement of support for UN peace moves had been tempered by Foreign Min. Moshe Sharett, who told the Knesset Apr. 23 that, while he saw "innovations" in the Soviet statement that could "herald a change for the better," he "doubted that the authors of this declaration have given the necessary attention" to the "striking contradiction" between the sale of Soviet-bloc arms to Egypt and Soviet protestations of peace.

According to dispatches from Cairo Mar. 28, the USSR had offered Egypt uranium and aid to build an atomic reactor and was training Egyptian scientists in Moscow under terms of a Feb. 1956 pact for the construction of an Egyptian nuclear laboratory. Washington reports said Apr. 9 that the USSR had informed Egypt that it was ready to help obtain Sudanese permission for the backing up of the Nile, a procedure essential to the Aswan High Dam project.

Reports from Cairo Apr. 24 said that Egypt had given the Sudanese Republic $1½ million worth of arms after talks with visiting Sudanese Premier Ismail el-Azhari. (Azhari had disclosed Apr. 15 that arms talks were then under way in Khartum with a Czech military delegation and that the Sudan had accepted a Russian technical assistance offer.)

Both Khrushchev and Bulganin reportedly indicated in talks with

British Prime Min. Eden Apr. 18–20 that the Soviet Union would maintain its current Middle Eastern policy and not restrict the sale of Czechoslovak weapons to Egypt because it would be "inconsistent" to change the Soviet policy of arms sales to any who wanted to buy them. Khrushchev had said in London Apr. 27 in answering a news conference question on the possible halting of Soviet-bloc arms shipments to the Middle East: "If it were possible to agree, through the UN or otherwise, that [arms shipment to the Middle East] would not take place, we . . . would be prepared to take part in such an undertaking which would help to bring about peace in troubled areas of the world." Khrushchev said that, "as a matter of fact, our own country does not ship arms to anybody. We would like it if there were no shipments at all, but such shipments are taking place."

In a joint communique issued in London Apr. 26, Britain and the USSR had said they both would take steps to end "the armaments race in all parts of the world" and bring peace to the Middle East and would support UN efforts "to secure a peaceful settlement, on a mutually acceptable basis, of the dispute between the Arab states and Israel."

Khrushchev said at Moscow's Central Airport Apr. 30, as he and Bulganin returned from Britain, that Pres. Eisenhower's Apr. 21 speech contained "many valuable statements about the possibility of friendship" between their 2 countries. He asserted that all disputes between the U.S. and Soviet Union could be resolved with "good will from both sides." Bulganin said that Anglo-Soviet agreement to support UN peacemaking efforts in the Middle East "opens up [great] possibilities for the 2 countries to give an example of joint work for the cause of peace in such an important area." But he also said: "In the Soviet government's view, the main source of friction in the Middle East, the reason for the deterioration of relations between the Arab states and Israel—as well as between other countries—is the creation of military groupings such as the Baghdad Pact. The British side does not share our views on this question. We in turn could not recognize as correct the British view on this question. As you see, here we take different stands."

Soviet diplomats had been active on the fringes of the Arab world attempting to counteract the attractions of the METO (Baghdad Pact) alliance. They explored the possibilities of closer economic relations with Libya but were rebuffed. Libyan Amb.-to-Egypt Khalil el-Gallah had said in Cairo Mar. 21 that Libya would never be used by the U.S. or Britain as a base against the Arab states. The Libyan parliament Mar. 30, however, indorsed the Libyan government's rejection of an offer of Soviet aid. (The Libyan government reported Apr. 7 that it had received $9 million worth of U.S. aid in fiscal 1956 and had arranged to receive $11 million worth in fiscal 1957. It was also reported that the U.S. planned to increase grain relief to Libya and to provide enough equipment to raise the strength of Libya's army to 2,600 men.) The Kremlin had better luck with Yemen. The Soviet Union Feb. 27 had announced the ratification of a 2d treaty of friendship with Yemen, which had been concluded in Cairo in Oct. 1955. A Soviet economic mission had gone to Yemen early in 1956.

The Yemeni crown prince, Emir Seif el-Islam Mohammed el-Badr, visited the Soviet Union June 11–25. Badr, who was also Yemen's foreign minister, joined Premier Bulganin June 24 in issuing a communique that announced a trade agreement calling for the exchange of Yemeni coffee for "a number" of Soviet commodities. The 2 countries accredited their ambassadors in Cairo to each other as ministers.

Soviet Foreign Min. Vacheslav M. Molotov, 66, resigned without explanation in Moscow June 1 and was succeeded by Dmitri Trofimovich Shepilov, 50, who for 4 years had been the chief editor of the Soviet Communist Party daily *Pravda*. The change was generally interpreted as a conciliatory gesture toward Marshal Tito, the Yugoslav president, due shortly to visit Moscow. Shepilov ½ month later began a tour of the Middle East, visiting Egypt June 16–22, Syria June 22–25, Lebanon June 25–28 and Greece June 28–29 (the last stop being for informal talks with Premier Constantin Karamanlis and Foreign Min. Evangelos Averoff on the Cyprus question and the improvement in the 2 countries' economic and political relations).

Israeli sources said June 17 that no reply had been received to an invitation extended to Shepilov to visit Israel. The invitation had been given by Israeli Foreign Ministry Director Walter Eytan. But Soviet Premier Bulganin told Israeli Amb.-to-USSR Joseph Avidar at a French embassy reception in Moscow June 18 that "we believe that you want peace." (André Philip, member of a French Socialist delegation to Moscow in May, had said in Paris June 5 that Nikita S. Khrushchev had denied anti-Semitic feelings and had told the group "there is still a cold war between us and Israel, but we expect to get it over quickly.")

Shepilov had been invited to Cairo as a guest at official Egyptian celebrations of the final British military evacuation of the Suez Canal Zone. (The evacuation took place June 14 with the departure from Port Said for Cyprus of Brig. John H. S. Lacey and 91 officers and men.) Shepilov conferred with Egyptian Premier Gamal Abdel Nasser, Foreign Min. Mahmoud Fawzi, War Min. Abdel Hakim Amer and Soviet Amb.-to-Egypt Yevgeni D. Kiselev in Cairo June 16 and reportedly presented Egyptian Trade & Commerce Min. Abu Nusseir June 17 with a list of industrial goods that the USSR was ready to trade for

Egyptian cotton. Soviet embassy spokesmen in Cairo confirmed June 18 that Shepilov and Nasser had discussed Soviet-Egyptian trade, and Russian aid for Egyptian atomic plans and the Aswan dam June 17. Egyptian sources said June 18 that the USSR had offered £400 million Egyptian ($1.112 billion) for the Aswan project with repayment in 20 years at 2%.

Shepilov told Egyptian farm workers and officials in the Nile Valley village of Bernesht June 18 that "the Arab countries may rely on the Soviet government as their unselfish, faithful and reliable friend." He attacked the "aggressive Baghdad [METO] military bloc." The USSR wanted "to improve relations and establish friendship [with] the U.S., France, Britain, Greece, Turkey, with all our neighbors," Shepilov said, but it "cannot go on at the expense of our good relations with the Arab countries, with our friends in the East."

Nasser June 20 reviewed the newly equipped Egyptian army units in Cairo celebrations marking the withdrawal of British troops from the Suez Canal Zone. Western observers said that the display, attended by Shepilov and British Gen. Sir Brian Robertson, included: Stalin, Centurion and Czechoslovak T-34 tanks; MiG-15, Ilyushin-28, Meteor and Vampire jets; Soviet ABC troop carriers and artillery and Soviet trailer-borne torpedoes. The paraders, estimated at 11,000 men, included units of the Jordanian Arab Legion, Saudi Arabian, Lebanese, Libyan and Yemeni armies and troops of the newly formed Palestine Army recruited by Egypt from among Gaza Strip refugee camps.

A Soviet-Egyptian communique issued June 22 said that the 2 countries had reached "complete agreement on the questions discussed." It stressed "Soviet-Egyptian relations in all the fields of political, economical and cultural cooperation" but did not mention any Soviet commitment on the Arab dispute with Israel.

Shepilov arrived in Damascus June 22 for talks with Syrian Foreign Min. Salah el-Bitar and Pres. Shukri al-Kuwatli, who accepted an invitation to visit the Soviet Union. Shepilov flew to Beirut June 25 for meetings with Lebanese Pres. Camille Chamoun, Premier Abdullah Yaffi and Foreign Min. Salim Lahoud June 26–28. Reports from Damascus June 23 and Beirut June 28 said Shepilov had failed to issue a "clear statement" on Palestine demanded by Lebanese leaders.

Western observers interpreted Shepilov's tour as a clear sign of Soviet support for the Arab states in their dispute with Israel. The Soviet Communist Party leader seemed to confirm this view. Nikita Khrushchev, in an interview published by the Cairo newspaper *Al Ahram* July 1, said that "war between Israel and the Arab states would mean World War III." *Al Ahram* quoted Khrushchev as having said that

Israel, "an imperialist creation," was "launching aggressive attacks" against its Arab neighbors but that "all the results will be in their [the Arab neighbors'] favor."

Israel Shops for Arms

Egypt's Oct. 1955 deal for Soviet-bloc weapons had precipitated an escalation of the Middle Eastern arms race. Israel strove above all to obtain U.S. bombers and fighter jets and, achieving no initial success, turned to Canada and France. In the U.S., Democratic Party candidates and spokesmen during the election year 1956 took stands in support of Israel's requests for U.S. arms. The controversy had been heated since the disclosure in mid-February that the U.S., apparently with Eisenhower Administration approval, was shipping tanks to Saudi Arabia, under Ibn Saud an outspoken foe of Israeli independence.

An American shipment of light army tanks to Saudi Arabia was halted, then released by the U.S. government over Israeli objections Feb. 17–18, 1956. Press reports Feb. 16 that 18 M-41 Walker Bulldog tanks were being loaded aboard the Liberian-flag freighter *James Monroe* in Brooklyn for shipment to Saudi Arabia caused the U.S. State Department to order a temporary suspension of all arms shipments to the Middle East early Feb. 17. The suspension was announced simultaneously by the State Department and by White House Press Secy. James C. Hagerty in Thomasville, Ga., where Pres. Eisenhower was vacationing.

Following protests from Saudi Arabian Amb.-to-U.S. Sheikh Abdullah al-Khayyal,* the State Department lifted the embargo Feb. 18, after Acting State Secy. Herbert Hoover Jr.† conferred by phone with Eisenhower. (State Secy. John Foster Dulles was vacationing off the Bahamas.) The State Department announcement Feb. 18 said the U.S. had agreed to sell the tanks, for training purposes, to Saudi Arabia Aug. 25, 1955, before "the massive shipment of arms by the Soviet bloc was confirmed in September," clearly signalling "an arms race that would increase the danger of war in the area." The State Department

---

*Sheikh Abdullah told newsmen Feb. 17 that the U.S. embargo would create "an unfortunate impression" in the Arab world, but he said that there was no necessary connection between the tank shipment and the renewal in June of the 5-year agreement concerning the U.S. air base at Dhahran in Saudi Arabia.
†As acting State Secretary while Dulles was on vacation. Dulles told newsmen in Washington Feb. 22 he had not heard of the tank controversy until he saw Miami newspapers that day on his return from an 11-day holiday.

said Saudi Arabia had paid for the 18 tanks Nov. 26, 1955 and had been promised shipment in mid-February.

State Secy. Dulles and Undersecy. Hoover, appearing Feb. 24 before the U.S. Senate Foreign Relations Committee, explained the temporary suspension Feb. 17 of American arms shipments to the Middle East. The committee had arranged for Dulles and Hoover to answer charges that the one-day embargo signified confusion in the Eisenhower Administration over Middle Eastern policy.

Hoover gave the Senators details of the embargo and its revocation after Dulles had discussed policy in an opening statement. Hoover said in reply to questions by Sen. J. William Fulbright (D., Ark.): "The suspension was entirely my decision"; it "was fully concurred in by the President—and I do not believe that I should discuss my relations with the Executive." Hoover said that the suspension was ordered "primarily" due to press and radio "charges" that the shipment of 18 tanks to Saudi Arabia "was not in compliance with the laws and export regulations of the U.S." "We had no way of being able to find out, late on the night of Feb. 16 . . . that all of the laws and regulations had been complied with," so the *James Monroe's* scheduled sailing with the tanks early Feb. 17 was held up. Hoover "made the decision to reinstate all shipments" Feb. 18 after an investigation was completed and "the facts were brought to me."

Dulles stressed to the Senate committee that the U.S. had no intention of becoming involved in an arms race in the Middle East. Because of Soviet-bloc munitions shipments since the autumn of 1955, "conditions for an arms race [there] now exist," Dulles said. "Certain countries of the Middle East vie with one another in the purchase of military items." He noted that Israel naturally wanted to increase its striking capacity under the existing circumstances, and he added: "However, Israel, because of its much smaller size and population, could not win an arms race against Arabs having access to Soviet stock. It would seem that Israel's security could be better assured, in the long run, through measures other than the acquisition of additional arms in circumstances which might exacerbate the situation."

Dulles said that in its position the U.S. relied on the UN, "by which Israel was created," on the Tripartite Declaration of May 25, 1950 and on arrangements made by Pres. Eisenhower and British Prime Min. Eden at the beginning of February for consultations with France. Together, these measures amounted to "a more effective deterrent than additional quantities of arms," he said.

(Dulles also spoke in his opening statement to the committee of the need to seek universally acceptable borders in the disputed areas of

Palestine. He said: "The present border arrangements were not designed to be permanent frontiers in every respect. A more permanent and agreed line is necessary. In spite of conflicting claims and sentiments, I believe the achievement of such a line is possible, and the U.S. remains willing to assist in the search for a solution.")

During questioning by Sen. H. Alexander Smith (R., N.J.), Dulles said that the tank shipments were not involved with Israeli-Arab problems "because things like tanks cannot get across the desert." In reply to Sen. Wayne Morse (D., Ore.), Dulles said the 18 tanks did not increase Saudi Arabian war potential "in any appreciable degree." Dulles told Sen. Hubert H. Humphrey (D., Minn.) that the tanks would help "maintain internal security" in Saudi Arabia, where "there have been large-scale riots and disturbances at various points." Dulles said that if the U.S. failed to give Saudi Arabia "its reasonable requirement in this area, it is probable, at least possible ... that our air base agreement would not be renewed."

Humphrey asked for verification of reports that "American personnel of the Jewish faith" were not stationed at the U.S. base at Dhahran at the request of Saudi Arabia. Dulles replied: "It may be. I think that for many years ... there has been a prohibition on Jews in Saudi Arabia." Dulles denied that the U.S. had agreed to a Saudi Arabia ban on "American businessmen who may be of the Jewish faith." While "we do have to recognize the fact that Saudi Arabia is an ally," that does not mean "we approve of all its practices at all," Dulles said.

A shipment of 18 U.S. light tanks was reported to have been unloaded at Dammam, Saudi Arabia Mar. 28, 1956. There matters rested until the controversy was revived by the confirmation in Washington May 16, by the U.S. Defense Department, that a shipment of ammunition and other material bound for Saudi Arabia was being loaded at a North Carolina port. Sen. Herbert H. Lehman (D., N.Y.) demanded an immediate inquiry by the Administration, but the State Department minimized the value of the shipment.

The controversy seemed to have the effect of warning off prospective arms purchases by Syria. Cairo Radio reported Feb. 27 that Syria had called off 4-month-old negotiations with the U.S. on the supply of American weapons because Syria had found unacceptable the condition that Syria sign a mutual security pact with the U.S.

In his testimony before the Senate Foreign Relations Committee Feb. 24, Dulles had gone to some length to describe the Administration's reaction to and analysis of the Czechoslovak-Egyptian arms deal. He told Sen. J. William Fulbright (D., Ark.) that the U.S. had not received "what we regarded as really firm information about it" until

Sept. 1955, when the State Department had learned that the deal was being made. Dulles said that the Egyptians had approached the U.S. for arms in July 1955 and that "we gave them prices," but the Egyptians had "found that they could get arms from the Soviet bloc more cheaply"—for a barter of cotton. The U.S., although "not in the business of selling [arms] for a profit," had Defense Department-fixed prices higher than those of "various countries of Europe . . . also selling arms," Dulles said.

Uncertainty over the strength of the Czechoslovak arms shipments ordered by Egypt was a factor in delaying action on Israel's application to buy $50 million worth of American weapons, Dulles conceded in answer to a question by Sen. H. Alexander Smith. But Dulles said the U.S. also was holding up arms sales to Israel "because we do not believe that . . . the shipment would be conducive to . . . a permanent peace between Israel and the Arab states." "We are doing everything we can to try to limit this particular Egypt-Czechoslovak deal to a one-shot operation," Dulles declared.

Washington sources said Apr. 2, 1956 that a final decision on Israeli requests to buy $63 million worth of U.S. arms had been delayed again by Pres. Eisenhower, State Secy. Dulles and Assistant State Secy. George V. Allen at a White House meeting Mar. 28. Israeli Amb. Abba Eban, who called at the State Dept. Mar. 30, reportedly was told that the U.S. government still was studying Israeli requests to buy purely defensive radar equipment and that active arms might be released at a later date; Israel would have more success directing requests to Britain and France (tacitly approved by the U.S. as Middle East arms suppliers).

Rep. Kenneth B. Keating (R., N.Y.), leader of a special 5-man committee representing a bloc of 50 GOP Congressmen formed to win Administration approval for arms shipments to Israel, had said Apr. 1 that the group was studying plans to add specific funds for Israel to the Administration's $4.9 billion foreign aid appropriations bill.

Israeli Amb. Eban said in New York Apr. 1 that Egypt would soon have 250 jets within 12 minutes flying time of Israel and that the U.S. held the key to the Israeli defense effort. Reports from Paris Mar. 30 had said that France had begun the shipment of 12 Mystère-4 jet fighters bought by Israel, whose fighter command was said to have fewer than 40 aircraft.

Dulles, at a press conference in Washington Apr. 3, said that there was no change in U.S. policy towards the shipment of arms to Israel. The Israeli request for munitions had not been rejected, he said. It was still under consideration. Dulles said he believed that the public statements of Egyptian Premier Nasser were actuated by a desire to maintain the genuine independence of the area. He indicated that he saw no reason to think that Egypt had made an irrevocable decision to repudiate its ties with the West and "accept Soviet vassalage." Dulles said that the basic U.S. objectives in the area were to avoid war and to support the independence of the countries there.

Israeli Foreign Min. Moshe Sharett summoned U.S. Amb.-to-Israel Edward B. Lawson in Tel Aviv Apr. 4 and reportedly expressed Israeli dismay over U.S. refusal to release $63 million worth of defensive arms requested by Israel. Social Welfare Min. Moshe Shapiro said in Tel Aviv Apr. 3 that "a country which we had regarded as a friend has deceived us."

Presidential Press Secy. James Hagerty said in Augusta, Ga. Apr. 12 that Pres. Eisenhower had sent personal messages to both Premier Ben-Gurion of Israel and Premier Nasser of Egypt urging restraint and outlining the current U.S. policy of aid for either side should it be the victim of aggression.

Israel, however, refused to be put off. Eisenhower had said at his news conference Mar. 7 that he did not favor the shipment of additional U.S. weapons to Israel because it was necessary to avoid "the initiation of an Arab-Israeli arms race" and Israel, with 1,700,000 people, could never "absorb" as much armament as the Arab world's 40 million. This position had been supplemented Apr. 9 by a White House statement pledging the U.S. to oppose any aggression in the area by all means "within the Constitution" and in accordance with the U.S.' responsibilities under the UN Charter. Nevertheless, Israeli Amb.-to-U.S. Eban reportedly renewed requests for U.S. arms in a call on the State Department in Washington Apr. 23.

Premier Ben-Gurion had told the Israeli Knesset Apr. 22 that the U.S.' Apr. 9 statement on Middle Eastern policy and the 1950 British-French-U.S. Tripartite Declaration on Israeli-Arab frontiers were not a "substantial guaranty of Israel's security or any deterrent to the aggressors who are planning war against us." The "only thing that might deter war against Israel is the supply . . . of sufficient defensive arms," Ben-Gurion said. Referring to Hammarskjöld's peace mission, Ben-Gurion said that the new cease-fire "does not reduce in the slightest" the danger of war in the area. He asserted that when Arab armies attacked Israel in 1948, no UN member "could be found willing to lift a finger in Israel's defense."

Ben-Gurion said at an emergency session of the 24th World Zionist Congress in Jerusalem Apr. 24 that the U.S. and Britain had imposed an embargo on Israel and must bear "terrible responsibility" for what might happen. Jewish Agency Executive Co-Chairman Nahum Goldmann said Apr. 24, however, that the U.S. State Department had used "transparent subterfuge" in urging U.S. allies to arm Israel. Dr. Goldmann's charge gained some support 2 weeks later. Reports attributed to Washington diplomatic sources May 8 said Dulles had told the NATO Council in Paris that the U.S. would not sell arms to Israel but would permit allied nations to divert off-shore procurement program materiel to fill Israel's weapons requests.

The French Foreign Ministry, meanwhile, had announced Mar. 6 that Israel had commissioned private French armament makers to supply "certain antitank weapons." Reports from Paris Apr. 16 said the Israeli government had applied to buy 12 more Mystere-4 jet fighters. The French government was said to have previously sold Israel 12 Ouragan jets. Israeli Amb.-to-Britain Eliahu Elath told reporters in London July 6 that since the Czechoslovak-Egyptian pact of Oct. 1955, France had supplied Israel with 24 Mysteres and some (reportedly at least 12) Ouragan jets but that Israel had no jet bombers.

Canadian External Affairs Secy. Lester B. Pearson said in Ottawa May 8 that there was "no foundation" to reports that Canada had agreed to sell Israel 36 F-86 Sabrejets. Pearson had said in Ottawa Apr. 17 that Israel had asked permission to buy "between 20 and 36 F-86 jets" from Canada and that the U.S. had stated that it had no objection to the sale. Pearson reported Aug. 2 that Canada would delay a decision on selling jets to Israel until it had investigated the relationship to the Palestinian conflict of a crisis brought about by Egypt's nationalization of the Suez Canal. By the summer's end, Canada decided to sell 24 Sabrejets to Israel. It was announced Sept. 21 that Israel had assured Canada that the jets would be used only for defensive purposes and to help offset the accumulated sales of Soviet MiGs to Egypt. (Prime Min. Louis Saint-Laurent had reported to the Canadian House of Commons Mar. 16 that Canada had approved the shipment to Israel of 1,754 rounds of 25-pound artillery ammunition, worth about $30,600; some Sherman tank parts replacements, worth about $136,300; and some electronics equipment.)

Israel's desire to buy American arms had become the concern of both major U.S. political parties early in 1956, and the Administration quickly realized the domestic political significance of the issue. State Secy. Dulles had said Feb. 6 that the U.S. "recognizes that current developments could create a disparity in armed forces between Israel and its Arab neighbors," but the U.S. was "not convinced that the disparity can be adequately offset" by additional Israeli arms purchases. However, he added, "we do not exclude the possibility of arms sales to Israel."

Dulles made these statements in a message replying to 40 Republican Congressmen who had urged in a letter Feb. 3 that the U.S. grant Israel's request for arms to offset Arab purchases from the Soviet bloc. Dulles said that U.S. foreign policy "embraces the preservation of the State of Israel" and the principle of "maintaining our friendship with Israel and the Arab states." Israel's possession of "equal or superior arms is not the only deterrent to aggression," he said. The UN "is capable of providing many forms of protection," and the U.S.-British-French declaration of 1950 outlined a policy "to deter aggression by either side against the other." Middle Eastern security "cannot rest upon arms alone but rather upon the international rule of law and upon the establishment of friendly relations among neighbors, for which the U.S. was "actively working," Dulles said.

Prominent figures in the Democratic Party had already been expressing their views on the matter. Mrs. Franklin D. Roosevelt Jan. 28 had issued in her own name as well as on the behalf of ex-Pres. Harry S. Truman and the labor leader Walter Reuther a statement urging the U.S. to sell weapons to Israel and thus restore the power balance that they believed had been upset the previous autumn.

The first recognizable potential Presidential candidate to take a stand was ex-Gov. Adlai E. Stevenson (D., Ill.), who said Feb. 4 that the U.S. and other Western powers should immediately "restore an equitable balance of armed strength" in the Middle East by shipping arms to Israel. Stevenson's Feb. 4 statement was made in a message read at the opening, in Miami Beach, Fla., of a national drive to sell $75 million in Israeli bonds. In Daytona Beach, Fla. Apr. 11, Stevenson said that the U.S. should give Israel, an endangered state, defensive arms "to prevent aggression" rather than merely pledge "support to Israel if that state should be subjected to aggression." "We should make it clear that we will not tolerate aggression," he stressed. Stevenson elaborated Apr. 22 in a televised interview on the National Broadcasting Co.'s program "Meet the Press." He said that his program for the Middle East would be to reaffirm the Tripartite Decision of 1950 and to arm Israel to offset Czechoslovak weapons to Egypt and thereby "enable the Israeli to prevent war by defending themselves." These things should have been done earlier, and it should have been made clear that they "are only conditions . . . to establish . . . that Israel is a permanent historical fact," he said. In a speech in Los Angeles May 11, Stevenson urged that the U.S. send weapons to Israel and restore the military balance to what it had been before Egypt's deal with the Soviet bloc. He proposed that when this point was reached, a UN call be issued for an arms embargo in the area to ensure the balance. Stevenson also urged the U.S. to declare that Israel was "here to stay" and to promise to intervene against armed aggression by either side.

Sen. Estes Kefauver (D., Tenn.), campaigning in Presidential preference primaries of several states, suggested Apr. 4 in Miami, Fla. that if Israel's leadership and the leaders of the neighboring Arab countries would sit down and frankly discuss the "very dangerous situation" in the Middle East with U.S., French and British leaders, the talks "might bring the understanding and peace we seek." Kefauver charged the Eisenhower Administration with failing to make clear to the U.S. public that the preservation of peace in the Middle East depended on the success of U.S. efforts to help Israel obtain arms and redress the imbalance brought about by Egypt's deal with the Soviet bloc. The U.S. should tell the world that "we will not sit idly by and see a brave little democratic nation suffer aggression," Kefauver said. In a speech at Occidental College in Los Angeles Apr. 20, Kefauver brought up the new menace of direct Soviet influence in the area. He said that U.S. delay had enabled the USSR "to take another giant step" by becoming "a party of interest in the Middle East," where "it appears likely now that no effective settlement can be made . . . unless the Soviet Union is a party to the agreement."

Gov. W. Averell Harriman of New York did not campaign in Presidential primaries but still sought the Democratic Party's Presidential nomination. Harriman, at an American Jewish Congress convention in New York Apr. 12, assailed the Eisenhower Administration for refusing to sell defensive weapons to Israel after the Communists had given arms Egypt. He attributed the current Middle Eastern crisis directly to this failure. Harriman, Sen. John F. Kennedy (D., Mass.) and Mayor Robert Wagner of New York joined at a New York political rally in urging the U.S. to supply arms to Israel to keep a military balance in the Middle East.

Sens. Hubert H. Humphrey (D., Minn.) and Paul Douglas (D., Ill.) charged in the U.S. Senate May 19 that a U.S. government curb on the shipment of 21 surplus Army half-tracks to Israel clearly exposed the Eisenhower Administration's favoritism toward the Arabs. The U.S. State Department had disclosed May 18 that the shipment had been halted by the U.S. Customs Bureau in New York May 10. Although the export license for the shipment covered half-track spare parts only, the vehicles were discovered fully assembled, customs officials had reported. Humphrey urged June 19 that the U.S. sell weapons to Israel to counteract the effects of the Soviet bloc arms sales to Egypt.

Adlai Stevenson won the Democratic Party's Presidential nomination, and Sen. Kefauver became his Vice Presidential running mate. The party in Chicago late Aug. 15 adopted a campaign platform that devoted more attention to the Middle East than to any other area of foreign policy. It said: "We will urge Israel and the Arab states to settle their differences by peaceful means" and "assist Israel to build a sound and viable economy" for its own people and Jewish refugees given sanctuary in Israel. "We will assist the Arab states to develop their economic resources and raise the living standard of their people." "We will assist in carrying out large-scale" programs for Arab refugee "resettlement in countries where there is room and opportunity for them." "We support the principle of free access to the Suez Canal under suitable international auspices." Eisenhower Administration policies toward the Middle East were "unnecessarily increasing the risk that war will break out in this area"; a Democratic administration would "faithfully carry out" the Western Big 3 declaration of 1950 to prevent use of force in the Middle East. "The Democratic Party will act to redress the dangerous imbalance of arms . . . created by the shipment of Communist arms to Egypt, by selling or supplying defensive weapons to Israel . . . " "We oppose . . . the practice of any government which discriminates against American citizens on grounds of race or religion" and would make no "arrangement or treaty" on this basis.

The Republican party in San Francisco Aug. 21 published a campaign platform pledging support for Israel against aggression and recognizing Israel's preservation as an important tenet of American foreign policy. The platform also included a vow of continued friendly relations with both Israel and the Arab countries. The GOP, insisting that it had used "every honorable means at our command" to "alleviate the grievances and causes of armed conflict among nations," promised to "maintain our powerful military strength as a deterrent to aggression and guardian of the peace."

Stevenson's stand on the issue of U.S. arms for Israel appeared somewhat vaguer after his nomination. In an interview published in the *N.Y. Times* Sept. 18, Stevenson maintained that he was still in favor of a Middle Eastern arms balance to help Israel deter aggression, but he said he doubted whether an imbalance existed any longer. In a message to the Zionist Organization of America Oct. 20, Stevenson asserted that the course of wisdom would be for the U.S. to base its Middle Eastern policy on the recognition that Israel had become a permanent state there and that aggression against it must be prevented. He urged the Administration to arm Israel and restore a military balance to the area.

U.S. Cancels Aid for Aswan Dam

The U.S. State Department informed the Egyptian government July 19, 1956 that the U.S. had decided not to help finance the Aswan dam. After 7 months of negotiations with the World Bank, the British and the Egyptian governments, the State Department said, the U.S. government had "concluded that it is not feasible in present circumstances to participate in" the project. The British government July 20 also canceled its aid for the dam. Egypt thus lost outright grants of $56 million from the U.S. and of $14 million from Britain as well as a World Bank loan of $200 million that had been contingent on the U.S. and British grants.

The State Department message, handed by State Secy. Dulles to Egyptian Amb.-to-U.S. Ahmed Hussein July 19, attributed the decision to (a) "developments within the . . . 7 months" following the opening of negotiations (during which period Egypt had formally recognized the government of Communist China), (b) Egypt's increasingly "uncertain . . . ability . . . to devote adequate resources to assure the project's success" after having mortgaged its cotton crop to pay for Soviet-bloc arms, and (c) Egypt's failure to reach agreement with the Sudan, Ethiopia and Uganda (then a British protectorate) on the division of the Nile's waters.

Egyptian Pres. Nasser (he had been elected president June 24, 1956) made a bitter attack on the U.S. as part of his address just outside Cairo July 24 at the opening of a new oil refinery and pipeline to Suez. He ridiculed the argument that Egypt's economic prospects were the U.S.' and Britain's real motive for withdrawing the offer of financial assistance. "If rumor in Washington tries to represent that the Egyptian economy is not strong enough to warrant American aid, then I say: 'Choke on your fury, but you will never succeed in ordering us about or in wielding your tyranny over us, because we know our path—that of freedom, honor and dignity. . . . We shall yield neither to force nor to the dollar.' "

Soviet Foreign Min. Dmitri Shepilov had told reporters at the Belgian embassy during a National Day reception in Moscow July 21 that he did not consider Soviet aid for the Aswan dam "a live question." Shepilov said that "there are now more vitally important problems for the Egyptian economy," particularly "industrialization," although he did "not minimize the importance of the Aswan Dam," Shepilov said that "if the Egyptian government considers Soviet help" necessary, the USSR would "consider favorably any Egyptian requests."

A *N.Y. Times* dispatch said July 22 that Western observers in Cairo had long believed that Egypt was using "inflated reports of Soviet aid offers to obtain more liberal Western terms" for the Aswan project. The *Times* reported July 20 that a "gasp of surprise and anger" had swept Cairo at news of the Western withdrawals but that officials had refused comment despite violent press attacks on the reversal.

Soviet Amb.-to-Egypt Yevgeni D. Kiselev told reporters in Cairo July 24 that the Western press had "exaggerated" Shepilov's remarks on Aswan Dam aid and said that "we are ready to finance the Aswan high dam if Egypt asked for it." A Reuters dispatch said that the Soviet embassy in Cairo July 24 denied that Kiselev had made the offer. The embassy then said July 27 that Kiselev's offer was not official.

Nasser Nationalizes Suez Canal

Nasser announced in a speech in Alexandria July 26, 1956 that the Egyptian government had nationalized the Suez Canal Co. and would use its revenues (annually about $100 million) to build the Aswan dam. Nasser also said that Egypt had "frozen" all Canal Co. funds in Egypt and would pay off the company's shareholders at the final closing prices of the company's stock on the Paris Bourse (stock exchange), where it had been listed for daily sale for at least 85 years.

Egyptian Commerce & Industry Min. Abu Nusseir July 27 issued a statement accusing the Suez Canal Co. of having "failed to comply with its obligations" to maintain the canal properly—*e.g.*, to provide a suitable harbor at Ismailia for the largest ships and to furnish the adequate equipment for transit trade at Port Said. Nosseir also declared in the statement that Egypt would not recognize the right of either the UN Security Council or the International Court of Justice to intervene in the matter. The canal had been Egyptian since its inception, and only Egyptian courts had jurisdiction over it, Nosseir asserted.

Nasser July 31 issued a statement reassuring the world's maritime states of freedom of navigation through the canal. His statement ignored the long-standing Egyptian ban on Israeli shipping. The statement read:

On July 26 the Suez Canal Co. was nationalized. This exercise by the Egyptian government of its right has, however, given rise to some opposition from a few governments, particularly those of France and Britain. Such opposition is devoid of all foundation. The Suez Canal Co. has always been an Egyptian company and, like all other Egyptian companies, liable to be nationalized. This nationalization does not in any way or to any extent affect Egypt's international commitments. We are determined as ever to honor all our international obligations, and both the Convention of 1888 and the assurance concerning it given in the Anglo-Egyptian Agreement of 1954 will be fully maintained. Freedom of navigation on the Suez Canal is neither affected nor involved in any manner or to any degree. Noone could be more interested than Egypt in the freedom of passage through the canal. We are certain that traffic through the canal will in the coming years justify all our hopes and those of the whole world. Egypt is confident of the righteousness of her stand. She will not be deflected from the course she has charted for herself but will proceed in the service of her own interests and those of the world community of nations.

The British government July 27 protested Egypt's move as "arbitrary," but Egypt rejected the protest. Britain July 28 froze the company's assets still in British hands and all Egyptian sterling accounts as well, including about $308 million left from balances deposited for safekeeping in Britain during World War II. Prime Min. Sir Anthony Eden July 30 banned all exports of war materiel to Egypt, including 2 warships of 1,700 tons each that had been bought by Egypt but still had not left British ports.

Within the next 3 days, Britain dispatched 3 aircraft carriers to the Mediterranean and a number of Canberra jet bomber squadrons to Malta and alerted an infantry battalion and a marine commando unit to prepare to move to an undisclosed destination.

France had also protested against the Egyptian move, and Premier Guy Mollet in a press statement July 30 had described Nasser as an "apprentice dictator" whose style was "the policy of blackmail alternating with flagrant violations of international agreements." France Aug. 2 ordered its Mediterranean fleet to sail from Toulon and maintain close cooperation with the British Navy. Britain and France advised all British and French nationals lacking "compelling reasons" for staying to leave Egypt at once.

Soviet Communist Party leader Nikita Khrushchev in Moscow July 31 urged the international community to react calmly to Nasser's takeover of the Suez Canal. He asserted that Egypt's nationalization action was "in the spirit of the times" and "an action that the Egyptian government, as a sovereign government, is entitled to take." He added: "We think that the policy of putting pressure on Egypt is a mistaken one. Rashness and haste in this matter can bring only undesirable consequences for the cause of peace and can only damage the interests of the Western powers themselves in that area. The Suez Canal's nationalization does not affect the interests of the peoples of Britain, France, the U.S. and other countries. Only the former Suez Canal Co., which received high profits from the canal's exploitation, is now being deprived of the possibility of self-enrichment at Egypt's expense. The Soviet Union, directly interested in the maintenance of the freedom of shipping through the Suez Canal and noting the Egyptian government's statement to the effect that the Suez Canal will remain free for all, considers that there are no grounds for alarm and concern over this matter. We are confident that the situation in the Suez Canal will not become aggravated if it is not artificially aggravated from outside."

Khrushchev expressed confidence that the diplomatic "commonsense, experience and political sobriety" of Britain and France would enable those 2 countries to understand "this historic act" and to ignore the counsels of "unreasonable voices." For its part, Khrushchev said, the Soviet Union supported all countries striving to "free themselves from colonial enslavement."

Alone among the leading organs of the Soviet press, the unofficial government daily *Izvestia* attacked what it described as the "threats of war" made by certain Israeli leaders, "aided and abetted by external imperialist quarters," against Israel's "peace-loving neighbors." Some Western observers suggested that the *Izvestia* attack was aimed at Arab opinion, very critical of a Soviet agreement July 17 to sell to Israel in 1957 about $20 million worth of fuel—40% of Israel's projected needs for that year.

The official U.S. reaction to Egypt's move was disapproving—State Secy. Dulles was especially critical—but not condemnatory, unlike the official attitudes of France and Britain. The State Department July 27 issued this 3-sentence statement: "The announcement by the Egyptian government with respect to the seizure of the installations of the Suez Canal Co. carries far-reaching implications. It affects the nations whose economies depend upon the products which move through this international waterway, as well as the owners of the company itself. The United States is consulting urgently with other governments concerned."

Lincoln White, the State Department's chief spokesman, said July 27 that the U.S. was then consulting with Britain and France and that the 3 countries would soon broaden the circle involved in the talks to include other countries affected because of goods transit via the canal.

Dulles returned to Washington July 29 from a visit to Peru and said that the Egyptian government, by its action, had "struck a grievous blow at international confidence."

Pres. Eisenhower, who had conferred on the matter July 27 with his cabinet and Acting State Secy. Herbert Hoover, said at his press conference Aug. 1: "We are manifestly faced with a grave issue, important to every country that has a seacoast." Freedom of navigation in the canal was "vital" to the U.S.' own economy and future welfare.

The U.S. Treasury July 31 had issued under the Foreign Assets Control Statute an order to and through the Federal Reserve banks temporarily "freezing" all Egyptian government and Suez Canal Co. assets in the U.S. "pending determination of their ownership and the existing situation." Private Egyptian funds in the U.S. were not affected by the order.

Deputy State Undersecy. Robert Murphy had gone to London July 29 for the opening of talks on the Suez crisis with French Foreign

Min. Christian Pineau and British Foreign Secy. Selwyn Lloyd. Murphy had a separate meeting July 30 with British Prime Min. Sir Anthony Eden.

Eisenhower sent State Secy. Dulles to London July 31 to conclude the talks. The tripartite discussions ended Aug. 2, and the 3 countries agreed to take part in an international conference of 24 Suez Canal-using countries scheduled to begin in London Aug. 16 on freedom and security of navigation in the canal. The U.S., Britain and France issued a joint communique that said:

The governments of France, the United Kingdom, and the United States join in the following statement:

(1) They have taken note of the recent action of the government of Egypt whereby it attempts to nationalize and take over the assets and the responsibilities of the Universal Suez Canal Co. This company was organized in Egypt in 1856 under a franchise to build the Suez Canal and operate it until 1968. The Universal Suez Canal Co. has always had an international character in terms of its shareholders, directors and operating personnel and in terms of its responsibility to assure the efficient functioning as an international waterway of the Suez Canal.

In 1888 all the great powers then principally concerned with the international character of the canal and its free, open and secure use without discrimination joined in the Treaty and Convention of Constantinople. This provided for the benefit of all the world that the international character of the canal would be perpetuated for all time, irrespective of the expiration of the concession of the Universal Suez Canal Co.

Egypt as recently as Oct. 1954 recognized that the Suez Canal is a waterway economically, commercially and strategically of international importance and renewed its determination to uphold the Convention of 1888.

(2) They do not question the right of Egypt to enjoy and exercise all the powers of a fully sovereign and independent nation, including the generally recognized right, under appropriate conditions, to nationalize assets, not impressed with an international interest, which are subject to its political authority.

But the present action involves far more than a simple act of nationalization. It involves the arbitrary and unilateral seizure by one nation of an international agency which has the responsibility to maintain and to operate the Suez Canal so that all the signatories to, and beneficiaries of, the Treaty of 1888 can effectively enjoy the use of an international waterway upon which the economy, commerce and security of much of the world depends.

This situation is the more serious in its implications because it avowedly was made for the purpose of enabling the government of Egypt to make the canal serve the purely national purposes of the Egyptian government rather than the international purpose established by the Convention of 1888.

Furthermore, they deplore the fact that, as an incident to its seizure, the Egyptian government has had recourse to what amounts to a denial of fundamental human rights by compelling employees of the Suez Canal Co. to continue to work under threat of imprisonment.

(3) They consider that the action taken by the government of Egypt, having regard to all the attendant circumstances, threatens the freedom and security of the canal as guaranteed by the Convention of 1888. This makes it necessary that steps be taken to assure that the parties to that convention and all other nations entitled to enjoy its benefits shall in fact be assured of such benefits.

(4) They consider that steps should be taken to establish operating arrangements under an international system designed to assure the continuity of operation of the canal, as guaranteed by the Convention of Oct. 29, 1888, consistently with legitimate Egyptian interests.

(5) To this end they propose that a conference should promptly be held of parties to the convention and other nations largely concerned with the use of the canal. The invitations to such a conference, to be held in London on Aug. 16, 1956, will be extended by the government of the United Kingdom to the governments named in the annex to this statement. The governments of France and the United States are ready to take part in the conference.

Parties to the Convention of 1888—Egypt, France, Italy, Netherlands, Spain, Turkey, the United Kingdom, the USSR. [The signatories of the 1888 Convention were Great Britain, France, Germany, Austria-Hungary, Spain, Italy, the Netherlands, Russia and Turkey.]

Other nations largely concerned in the use of the canal, either through ownership of tonnage or pattern of trade—Australia, Ceylon, Denmark, Ethiopia, the German Federal Republic [West Germany], Greece, India, Indonesia, Japan, New Zealand, Norway, Pakistan, Persia, Portugal, Sweden, the United States.

Dulles returned at once to Washington and told the country over radio and TV Aug. 3:

This trouble about the Suez Canal started when Pres. Nasser announced that he was going to take over the operation of the canal. He tried to seize the monies, property and personnel of the Universal Suez Canal Co., which is the operating company of that canal. This act by Pres. Nasser goes far beyond a mere attempt by a government to nationalize companies and properties within its territory which are not international in character, because the Suez Canal and the operating company are international in character.

The Suez Canal is an international waterway which was built by the Universal Suez Canal Co. with international funds. . . . In 1888 all the great powers principally concerned with the canal made a treaty providing that the Suez Canal shall be open at all times, in war as well as in peace, to the shipping of all nations on free and equal terms. Egypt is a party to that treaty and has repeatedly recognized it. Indeed, only a couple of years ago Pres. Nasser himself reaffirmed the allegiance of Egypt to that treaty. In all the world there is no international waterway as fully internationalized as is the Suez Canal.

The Universal Suez Canal Co. . . . has been the means of assuring that the canal would in fact be operated as a free and open international waterway as pledged by the 1888 treaty. That company itself is of an international character. Registered in Egypt, it operates under a franchise given it by the government of Egypt. Shareholders are of many nationalities, the board of directors is international, and the canal work—the building of the canal and the keeping of it in good repair—is supervised by an international body of engineers. . . .

In 1955, 14,666 ships passed through the canal. They had a tonnage of over 115 million, flew the flags of more than 40 nations, and carried the products of all the world. There are 187 pilots from 13 nations—56 French, 52 British, 32 Egyptian, 14 Dutch, 11 Norwegian, and so on. 2 of the pilots are Americans. It is by far the world's greatest highway. It has nearly 3 times the traffic that goes through the Panama Canal.

Now, why did Pres. Nasser suddenly decide to take over the operation of the Suez Canal? He has told us about that in a long speech he made. In that speech he did not for a moment suggest that Egypt would be able to operate the canal better than it was being operated. . . . The basic reason he gave was that if he took over this canal, it would enhance the prestige of Egypt. He said that Egypt was determined to score one triumph after another, in order to enhance what he called the 'grandeur of Egypt.' And he coupled his action with statements about his ambition to extend his influence from the Atlantic to the Persian Gulf. He also said that by seizing the Suez Canal he would strike a blow at what he called 'Western imperialism.' And he thought also that he could exploit the canal so as to produce bigger revenues for Egypt and so retaliate for the failure of the U.S. and Britain to give Egypt the money to enable it to get started on the $1 billion-plus Aswan high dam.

Pres. Nasser's speech made it absolutely clear that his seizure of the canal company was an angry act of retaliation against fancied grievances. No one reading that speech can doubt for a moment that the canal, under Egyptian operation, would be used, not to carry out the 1888 treaty better, but to promote the political and economic ambitions of Egypt. . . .

Of course, the government of a free and independent country . . . should seek to promote by all proper means the welfare of its people. . . . But it is inadmissible that a waterway internationalized by treaty, which is required for the livelihood of a score or more of nations, should be exploited by one country for purely selfish purposes, and that the operating agency which has done so well in handling the Suez Canal in accordance with the 1888 treaty should be struck down by a national act of vengefulness. To permit this to go unchallenged would be to encourage a breakdown of the international fabric upon which the security and the well-being of all peoples depend.

The question is not whether something should be done about this Egyptian act, but what should be done about it. There were some people who counselled immediate forcible action by the governments which felt themselves most directly affected. This, however, would have been contrary to the principles of the UN Charter and would undoubtedly have led to widespread violence endangering the peace of the world. At London we decided upon a different approach. We decided to call together in conference the nations most directly involved, with a view to seeing whether agreement could not be reached upon an adequate and dependable international administration of the canal on terms which would respect, and generously respect, all the legitimate rights of Egypt. . . .

We believe that out of this conference will come a plan for the international operation of the canal which will give assurance that the objectives of the 1888 treaty will in fact be realized, and that the canal will continue to be operated by those who feel that it is their duty to serve the international community and not the special interests of any one nation. This plan should give both security to the nations principally concerned with the canal, and also fully protect the legitimate interests of Egypt. Egypt, we believe, should be adequately represented on this operating authority and be assured, also, of a fair and reasonable income for the use of the property, because the canal, although it is internationalized, is on Egyptian territory.

There is every desire that Egypt shall be treated with the utmost fairness. And also, the owners and the employes of the now dispossessed Universal Canal Co. should also be fairly treated. . . .

I have been asked: 'What will we do if the conference fails?' My answer to that is that we are not thinking in terms of the conference's failing. But I can say this: We have given no commitments at any time as to what the United States would do in that unhappy contingency. We assume that the conference will not fail but will succeed. And I believe that by the conference we will invoke moral forces which are bound to prevail. . . . I am confident that out of this conference there will come a judgment of such moral force that we can be confident that the Suez Canal will go on as it has for the last 100 years, to serve in peace the interests of mankind.

The U.S. Treasury Aug. 3 gave U.S. shippers permission to pay canal tolls to the new Egyptian Suez authority provided payment was accompanied by a statement that it had been made "under protest and without prejudice to all rights of recovery." The Aug. 3 Treasury order lifted undisclosed provisions of the July 31 Egyptian assets freeze, which banned all business dealings with the Egyptian government.

It was reported from Paris Aug. 4 that Dulles' TV report had underlined differences in the U.S. and Franco-British policies on Suez, particularly on the use of military force should Egypt refuse to accept international control of the canal. The Paris newspaper *Paris-Presse* said Aug. 4: "We cannot count on the solidarity of Washington in the defense of our Mediterranean positions."

(It had been reported from Paris May 6 that Dulles had urged that the North Atlantic Council [composed of the foreign ministers of the 15 NATO countries] create a permanent high-level NATO cabinet to coordinate political planning among NATO nations, reportedly on problems such as Cyprus, North Africa and the Middle East. Several NATO members were said May 7 to be reluctant to place their international problems in the hands of a NATO cabinet, but the Committee of 3 Wise Men [Canadian External Affairs Secy. Lester B. Pearson, Italian Foreign Min. Gaetano Martino and Norwegian Foreign Min. Halvard M. Lange] was said to be studying the plan.)

(French Foreign Min. Christian Pineau had said May 6 that he, Dulles and Lloyd had agreed that the U.S.-British-French Tripartite Declaration of 1950, guaranteeing Israeli-Arab frontiers, could be used no longer as a basis for action in case of Middle East aggression. Pineau said action could be taken only through the UN Security Council.)

Dulles conferred with Pres. Eisenhower on the Suez dispute Aug. 6, and informed Washington sources reported that he had told the President that Western use of force against Egypt would entail a possible war with the entire Arab world. Saudi Arabian Amb.-to-U.S. Abdullah al-Khayyal met with Dulles Aug. 6 and told reporters that Saudi Arabia "backs" Egypt but believed force could be averted. Syrian Amb.-to-U.S. Victor A. Khouri also saw Dulles Aug. 6 and predicted that Lebanon would "follow the general line of the Arab states."

Dulles Aug. 7 briefed 20 Latin-American ambassadors on the Suez dispute in a closed session reportedly called to insure Latin support for the West should Egypt bring the Suez issue before the UN. Dulles was said to have agreed that Egypt's seizure of the canal might have violated

Article 51 of the UN Charter, but he was represented as implying that the U.S. government did not feel this would justify the use of force at Suez. Dulles reportedly urged economic sanctions against Egypt if the Aug. 16 London parley failed.

U.S. Defense Secy. Charles E. Wilson told reporters Aug. 7 that the Suez crisis was "a relatively small thing" when compared with the total U.S. military program. "We should seek honorable means of reaching a peaceful settlement rather than wave the big stick and threaten people," Wilson said.

The Soviet government Aug. 9 announced its acceptance of the Western Big-3 foreign ministers' invitation to the mid-August conference of Suez Canal users in London and the substance of 2 counter-proposals—(1) that the east European countries, the Arab states and China and other countries (22 more, in all) also should have been invited, and (b) that the conference should have been put off until the end of the month to allow time for better arrangements. The Kremlin also posed 2 preconditions: (a) that the Soviet government did not consider the conference as an international conclave authorized to make any decisions about the canal, and (b) that Soviet participation in the conference would not *per se* commit it to undertake any of the "obligations" foreseen by the Western Big 3 or signify the adoption of any position challenging Egypt's right to nationalize the Suez Canal.

The Soviet note, made public Aug. 9 by Tass, said that Egypt's nationalization move in no way affected freedom of transit through the canal, since Egypt had pledged again to respect the 1888 Convention of Constantinople and to guarantee freedom of navigation and shipping. The Kremlin said it saw "no reason to express any concern in that regard, the more so as Egypt . . . can ensure normal navigation on the canal in a manner not inferior to any private company." The note also said:

The nationalization of the property of enterprises situated in the territory of any country is, according to accepted principles of international law, an internal business of the state concerned . . . The UN General Assembly, in Dec. 1952, passed a special resolution on the rights of peoples to dispose freely of their natural wealth and resources . . . In view of this, the Soviet government considers the decision of the Egyptian government to nationalize the Suez Canal Co. as a fully legal act stemming from the sovereign rights enjoyed by Egypt. . . .

The fact that the Suez Canal has for decades remained in hands other than Egyptian—in the hands of a company in which British and French capital predominated and which used the Canal for its enrichment and interference in the internal affairs of Egypt—cannot serve as a foundation for the preservation of such an abnormal situation in the future. One must take account of the fact that relations created in the past through conquest and occupation . . . do not conform to the principles of cooperation between sovereign and equal states, that is, to the principles and aims of the United Nations. Since the governments of Britain and

France, as well as of the United States, recognize the high principles of the UN and state that they welcome the changes which have taken place in their relations with countries which were formerly in a state of colonial dependence, the governments of these powers should not hinder the realization by these states of their sovereign rights. . . .

. . . The choice of countries invited to the conference has been tendentiously made, with a view to securing a majority of its participants to support the proposals prepared by Britain and France. . . .

Among the signatories of the 1888 Convention were Austria-Hungary and Germany. Austria, Hungary, Czechoslovakia and Yugoslavia are the legal heirs of Austria-Hungary; none of these countries has been invited to the conference. From Germany, only one part of the country has been invited—the German Federal Republic—but not the other part, the German Democratic Republic. . . . There have not been invited to the conference the Arab states whose territories are directly adjacent to the canal and which are vitally interested in the settlement of this question—namely, Syria, Lebanon, Saudi Arabia, Jordan, Sudan, Libya, Yemen, Iraq, Tunisia and Morocco. The majority of the Arab states are the successors of the former Ottoman Empire, which was a party to the 1888 Convention. Nor have there been invited to the conference such maritime powers making extensive use of the canal as the Chinese People's Republic [Communist China], Poland, Bulgaria, Rumania, Burma and Finland.

Thus the projected London conference is a conference of a group of countries which are shareholders of the Suez Canal Co., with another group arbitrarily chosen by these shareholders. The conference has been called in a manner bypassing the United Nations. . . . Without the agreement of the parties to the 1888 Convention, London has been chosen as the venue of the conference, although, if one adheres to the spirit of the 1888 Convention, the discussion of all issues linked with the operation of the canal should take place in Cairo. . . .

The Soviet government regards it as most appropriate to discuss the problems connected with freedom of navigation on canals and straits of international importance within the framework of the United Nations. There are a number of canals and straits which are of international importance. As the tripartite statement raised the problem of internationalization of the Suez Canal, the question logically arises: Why is the Suez Canal singled out from a number of no less important straits and canals? In this matter the Soviet government proceeds from the principle that any solution of the problem of canals and straits possessing international importance must be based on the necessity of respecting the sovereign rights of the states through whose territory these sea-lanes pass.

The Kremlin suggested also that the following countries be invited to the London conference: Austria, Albania, Bulgaria, Burma, Czechoslovakia, Finland, the German Democratic Republic (East Germany), Hungary, Iraq, Jordan, Lebanon, Morocco, Poland, Rumania, Saudi Arabia, Sudan, Syria, Tunisia, and Yugoslavia. The Soviet note said it was also "essential that such a great power as the Chinese People's Republic should take part in the conference."

First London Conference & UN Negotiations

The London conference on the Suez Canal took place at Lancaster House Aug. 16-23, 1956. It produced rival plans for operating the canal—a U.S. plan for international operation and a Soviet-backed Indian plan for Egyptian operation with international advice.

Anthony Nutting reported in *No End of a Lesson*: "Egypt refused to attend the conference on the grounds that its object was to put the clock back and to reinstate the former canal company or its replica. Nasser also declined to negotiate any settlement under the threat of the Anglo-French troop concentrations that were then taking place in the Eastern Mediterranean. Thus the conference . . . met . . . with a built-in majority of the Western powers and their friends and allies. . . . "

Greece, the only other invited country without representation did not send an envoy because Greece was at odds with Britain over Cyprus and also objected to "the conditions in which the London conference was called." A Greek government spokesman in Athens said that the conference had been called without any prior consultation with Egypt as "the main interested power" and in an atmosphere of "war tension and pressure." Greece would have preferred to attend a later-scheduled conference of more enlarged membership somewhere else than in London, the spokesman said.

The heads of the 22 delegations attending the London conference were: Australia—Prime Min. Robert Gordon Menzies (accompanied by External Affairs Secy. Richard G. Casey); Britain—Foreign Secy. Selwyn Lloyd; Ceylon—Sir Claude Corea, high commissioner in London; Denmark—Premier Hans Christian Hansen (also Denmark's foreign minister); Ethiopia—Foreign Min. Tsehafe Tezaz Aklilu Habte-Wold; (West) Germany—Foreign Min. Heinrich von Bretano: France—Foreign Min. Christian Pineau; India—V. K. Krishna Menon, minister-without-portfolio; Iran—Foreign Min. Ali Gholi Ardalan; Italy—Foreign Min. Gaetano Martino; Japan—Foreign Min. Mamoru Shigemitsu; Netherlands—Co-Foreign Min. Joseph M. A. H. Luns; New Zealand—External Affairs Secy. Thomas L. MacDonald; Norway—Foreign Min. Halvard M. Lange; Pakistan—Foreign Min. Hamidul Huq Choudhury; Portugal—Foreign Min. Paulo Cunha; Soviet Union—Foreign Min. Dmitri Shepilov; Spain—Foreign Min. Alberto Martin Artajo; Sweden—Foreign Min. Osten Unden; Turkey—Foreign Ministry Gen. Secy. Nuri Birgi; U.S.—State Secy. John Foster Dulles.

The delegates appointed Selwyn Lloyd as chairman for the duration of the conference.

Dulles opened the conference with a speech outlining the principles under which he thought the canal should henceforth be run. Dulles said that Nasser, by his own admission July 26, had seized the canal for the "grandeur of Egypt." But "the grandeur of a nation is not rightly measured by its ability to hurt or threaten others," Dulles declared, adding that interdependence was as much a characteristic of the modern world as was independence. He said:

> In the Suez Canal, the interdependence of nations achieves perhaps its highest point. The economic life of many nations has been shaped by reliance on the canal system, which has treaty sanction. To shake and perhaps shatter that system, or to seek gains from threatening to do so, is not a triumph, neither does it augment grandeur. . . .
>
> Pres. Nasser . . . says that Egypt will accord freedom of transit through the canal, that operations will be efficient and that tolls will continue to be reasonable. But we are bound to compare those words with other words which have perhaps a more authentic ring. We are also bound to note the difference between what the Treaty of 1888 called 'a definite system destined to guarantee at all times and for all powers the free use of the Suez Canal' and an Egyptian national operation which puts other nations in the role of petitioners.
>
> One thing is certain. Whatever may be the present intentions of the Egyptian government, the trading nations of the world know that Pres. Nasser's action means that their use of the canal is now at Egypt's sufferance. Egypt can in many ways slow down, burden and make unprofitable the passage through the canal of the ships and cargoes of those against whom Egypt might desire, for national political reasons, to discriminate. Thus Egypt seizes hold of a sword with which it could cut into the economic vitals of many nations. . . .
>
> What is required is a permanent operation of the canal under an international system which will, in fact, give confidence to those who wish to use it. Confidence is what we seek, and for this it is indispensable that there should be an administration which is non-political. That, I think, is the key to the problem—an operation which is non-political in character. The canal should not be allowed to become the instrument of the policy of any nation or group of nations, whether of Europe, Asia or Africa.
>
> The United States does not believe that the Egyptian government had the right to wipe out the convention establishing the rights of the Suez Canal Co. until 1968. That arrangement had the status of an international compact. Many nations relied on it. The operating rights and assets of the company were impressed with an international interest. . . .

Dulles, describing himself as convinced that "a fair and equitable plan can be devised which will recognize the legitimate interests of all," enunciated 4 principles for such a plan: (a) that the canal should be run efficiently in accordance with the stipulations of the Constantinople Convention of 1888 as a free and guaranteed international waterway; (b) that its operation should be kept separate from the influence of national politics of any kind; (c) that the Suez Canal Co. should receive fair compensation for the canal, and (d) that all legitimate Egyptian interests and rights in the canal, including an equitable and fair return from its operation, should be recognized and satisfied.

He then put forward this 4-point plan, which, he said, would not infringe on Egypt's sovereignty but would help Egypt avoid confusion in its resolve to continue to recognize the binding force of the Constantinople Convention:

● Operation of the canal would become the responsibility of an international board set up by treaty and associated with the UN. Egypt would enjoy representation on such a board, but no one country would dominate it. It would be so composed as to assure the best possible operation and to preclude favoritism or prejudice.

● The treaty would make adequate provision for the payment of fair compensation to the Suez Canal Co.

● The treaty would entitle Egypt to an equitable return from the canal's operation and take into account Egyptian sovereignty over and all legitimate Egyptian rights in the canal.

● The International Court of Justice at The Hague would be empowered to appoint a commission of arbitration having jurisdiction over all disputes arising from these last 2 points.

Dulles said in conclusion: "We recognize that at this stage any proposal should be flexible, within the limits of such basic principles as we have outlined. Egypt's views should be ascertained. But we believe that the principles set forth, and a plan such as that outlined, contain the basic elements needed to restore confidence and to assure that the Suez Canal will be operated in accordance with the Treaty of 1888."

Dulles' plan received the support of these 18 countries at the London conference: Australia, Britain, Denmark, Ethiopia, (West) Germany, France, Iran, Italy, Japan, the Netherlands, New Zealand, Norway, Pakistan, Portugal, Spain, Sweden, Turkey and the U.S. Ethiopia, Iran, Pakistan and Turkey sought some amendments in the plan's features pertaining to international control of the canal.

Soviet Foreign Min. Dmitri Shepilov said Aug. 17 that the "establishment of an international authority for the operation of the Suez Canal would actually mean the restoration of the former Suez Canal Co., but under a new signboard." Shepilov warned that the Anglo-French "threat to use force with regard to Egypt" could "flame up into a large conflict which could cover the area of the Near and Middle East" and spread beyond those areas. Shepilov charged Aug. 21 that the amended U.S. proposal for international control of the canal was "based on the principle of denying to Egypt her sovereign rights, of establishing under the guise of a concession a colonialist regime" through "foreign operation of the Suez Canal." "Clearly," Shepilov said, "some powers have not yet reconciled themselves to the fact that Egypt has become an independent state."

V. K. Krishna Menon of India Aug. 20 presented an alternative plan calling for the canal's operation by Egypt assisted by an international advisory group representing the canal's users. Menon's plan gained the support of the Soviet Union, Indonesia and Ceylon.

Menon, in presenting the Indian draft proposal, said Aug. 20 that the Suez Canal Co. was "a concessionaire from the Egyptian government" whose status was "derived from the concession granted by Egypt." Although seizure of the firm "was quite within the competence of the Egyptian government," "it is necessary to state that this waterway has an international character," Menon asserted. He said that 3 primary problems had been raised by the seizure of the canal company: freedom of navigation, "which the Egyptian government has to" guarantee under "international law"; security of the canal and of its shipping which "can only be dealt with . . . by the authority of the Egyptian state"; canal tolls and charges, which must remain competitive "if the Egyptian government . . . wants to make a profit."

Speaking of the Egyptian blockade of Israeli shipping through Suez, Menon said that the "right procedure is for the aggrieved party to go to the World Court," and "if the World Court verdict were against the Egyptian government then they ought to abide by it." On differences between the functions of the Suez Canal Co. and the 1888 Convention, Menon said: The company "did not guarantee freedom of navigation. In fact, when the Suez Canal Co. was in ownership, and what is more, when the British troops were in occupation of the Suez Canal, it was at that time that freedom of navigation was obstructed [against Israel]."

Menon Aug. 21 called the amended U.S. proposal "entirely impracticable" and said Egypt would not negotiate on it.

The U.S., France, Britain and the 15 other countries supporting Dulles' plan agreed Aug. 23 to appoint a 5-member committee that would "approach on their behalf the government of Egypt" to ask if it would negotiate a Suez settlement on the basis of the U.S. proposal. The majority, under a statement of intent proposed by New Zealand, named Australian Prime Min. Robert G. Menzies as chairman of the committee. (Other delegates named to the Menzies committee by Aug. 28: U.S. Assistant State Undersecy. Loy W. Henderson, Iranian Foreign Min. Ali Gholi Ardalan, Swedish Foreign Min. Osten Unden, Ethiopian Foreign Min. Aklilu Habte-Wold.)

British Foreign Secy. Selwyn Lloyd had said Aug. 22 that, as conference chairman, he would submit full transcripts of the London meetings to the Egyptian government—the records to include opposing views on internationalization of the canal and both Indian and U.S. proposals made to the conference.

Soviet Foreign Min. Shepilov Aug. 23 submitted a draft communique calling for the negotiation of a Suez settlement "solely by peaceful means" through a committee including the U.S., Britain, France, India and the USSR. The proposal reportedly would have barred the use of force by Britain and France in the event that negotiations failed. The draft was blocked by French Foreign Min. Christian Pineau on the grounds that the USSR had joined in refusing conference voting procedures and thus had prevented the issuance of a final communique. Shepilov told London newsmen Aug. 24 that the U.S. proposal was "based on an unacceptable colonialist position." He charged that the plan was "closely connected with those influential classes" holding interests in the Suez Canal Co. The Menzies committee, Shepilov said, was "outside the conference" and lacked status to negotiate. But, he said, the conference had resulted in a "moral and political defeat" for the "forces" seeking to reimpose imperialism on Egypt.

(Soviet Communist Party First Secy. Nikita Khrushchev had said Aug. 23 that in the event of a Western attack on Egypt, "there would be volunteers" and the Arabs "would not stand alone." The Soviet newspaper *Izvestia* Aug. 25 called the London conference a "fiasco" and said that the "policy of strength" against Egypt had failed.)

Nasser agreed Aug. 28 to discuss the settlement of the Suez Canal dispute. Nasser said that he would meet with the committee representing 18 of the 22 conference nations. Nasser's agreement to discuss the dispute reportedly was drafted and dispatched from Cairo Aug. 26. It followed an Egyptian cabinet session and talks Aug. 26 between Nasser and his London conference observer, Wing Commander Ali Sabry. The Egyptian note, delivered Aug. 28 to the committee chairman, Menzies, said that Nasser had agreed to the committee's desire "to place before me and explain the views of the governments mentioned in your Aug. 24 message concerning the Suez Canal."

Spokesmen for Egyptian Amb.-to-Britain Sami Abdel Foutouh denied Aug. 28 that any additional conditions had accompanied the Egyptian acceptance, but Cairo sources reiterated Aug. 28 that Egypt had made it clear that the discussions would not bind Egypt to any form of international control over the canal. Menzies reportedly proposed to Nasser Aug. 28 that meetings begin in Cairo within a week.

Nasser, in an interview for the *N.Y. Herald Tribune*, had said Aug. 27 that he would be willing to hear the committee's views but did not see how "bright phrases" about internationalization of the canal could lead to any practical settlement. Nasser also denied Aug. 27 that Egypt had become economically or politically dependent on the USSR. "What use to escape one domination to fall to another?" Nasser asked. "Until now," he said, "all Egyptian policy decisions have been made here in this office, not in Moscow, not in Washington."

U.S. State Secy. Dulles said at a press conference in Washington Aug. 28 that he believed Nasser "has sufficient influence and authority to accept a fair" solution on Suez. Dulles said "the 18-nation plan, in its general outlines, is fair." As to whether the U.S. would accept "physical control" of the canal by Egypt under international guarantees, Dulles said that the question was not "primarily of U.S. concern but primarily of concern to the many countries—about 20—whose economies are vitally dependent on the canal."

Dulles said Aug. 28 that "all but one of the countries at the London conference"—the USSR—had sought a genuine Suez settlement. The USSR, he charged, had emitted "vicious propaganda" in Arabic broadcasts calling the conference a manifestation of "colonialism" and "imperialism" and had attacked the U.S. proposal on "the very morning I was . . . explaining" it to Shepilov.

Dispatches from Cairo had said Aug. 25 that the Egyptian government had begun canvassing UN officials on the possibility of a special Security Council session to take up British and French military moves in the Mediterranean. Egyptian leaders were reported still wary of an appeal to the UN for fear it would constitute an admission that the Suez dispute was international.

The negotiations between Nasser and Menzies ended in failure in Cairo Sept. 9. The British and French governments then moved to coordinate military, economic and diplomatic pressure against Egypt to force the acceptance of international operation of the canal.

The U.S., Britain and France Sept. 12 proposed the creation of an international Suez Canal Users' Association (SCUA, or SUA) to supervise pilotage through the canal. The Western powers called Sept. 14 for a new London conference despite its immediate rejection by Egypt. British Prime Min. Eden told an emergency session of Parliament Sept. 12 that:

• The SCUA would "employ pilots" and "undertake responsibility for coordination of traffic through" Suez.
• "Transit dues" would "be paid to the users' association and not to the Egyptian authorities," but Egypt would "receive appropriate payment" for the "facilities provided by her."
• "The government of Egypt" would "have an important bearing on the capacity of the association to fulfill its functions" and would "be requested to cooperate in maintaining" traffic.
• Britain was dependent on Middle Eastern oil, and to boycott the canal "would be very expensive." "There are not the tankers to maintain the supplies we need" though more could be built at "enormous" capital cost.
• The formation of the SCUA did not "exclude" taking the dispute to the UN. Britain and France had addressed a letter to the president

of the Security Council, "informing him of the situation that has arisen."

The U.S. State Department said Sept. 12 that the U.S. would join in the SCUA if it were advanced by Britain or other states and "organized by the 18 nations which sponsored the London proposals" for international control of the canal. The State Department emphasized that backers of the SCUA would "seek such cooperation with Egypt as would achieve" guarantees contained in the 1888 Constantinople Convention.

Dulles said at a news conference Sept. 13 that "we do not intend to shoot our way through" the canal. "If physical force should be used to prevent passage" of SCUA shipping, he declared, "the alternative . . . would be to send our vessels around the Cape [of Good Hope]." Dulles denied that the U.S. had joined in planning a boycott if the canal were closed. Under those conditions, he said, "each country would have to decide for itself what it wanted its vessels to do." Dispatches from Washington Sept. 12 had attributed the basic SCUA plan to Dulles, who reportedly had formulated the proposal in an effort to avert military action against Egypt and delay action before the UN. He was described Sept. 12 as irritated at Eden's presentation of the SUA scheme in terms of "gunboat diplomacy.")

Dulles said of the user's association plan Sept. 13:

• "The idea that this is a program which is designed to impose some regime upon Egypt is fantastic." "It is normal for users" to "work in association when rights which they possess jointly are in jeopardy."

• An SCUA test vessel could approach the canal with an experienced Suez pilot aboard and "hope" to be let through the canal. Should a test vessel be attacked in the canal "if it had any means to defend itself, it would be entitled to use those means."

• "The question of oil" had been studied and "the loaning capacity of the Export-Import Bank" "could be made available" for SCUA purchases of Western Hemisphere oil.

• Shipping via the Cape of Good Hope had been considered and would not "be catastrophic or beyond the capacity to deal with it." Some tankers of the Maritime Administration and Military Sea Transport Reserve fleets would "be taken out of mothballs."

• The SCUA "should be developed by the group" of 18 nations that backed international control for the canal at the London conference, but if some refused "then we would go along on a 3-party basis."

(It was reported in Washington Sept. 16 that the U.S. would offer $500 million in credits for oil purchases, that 35 to 40 tankers had been ordered reactivated and reconditioned at a cost of $350,000 each and that 14 U.S. oil firms had agreed to supply 450,000 barrels of the 2½ million barrels of oil needed daily by Europe. Dulles Sept. 17 denied any knowledge of the $500 million credit but said the Export-Import Bank was ready to offer loans.)

The Egyptian government had already showed signs of the strain of withstanding international pressure. It called Sept. 10 for the formation of a new "negotiating body" "representative of the different views held among the states using the Suez Canal." A note, sent to all nations having diplomatic relations with Egypt, urged immediate talks on "the freedom and safety of navigation of the canal," "development of the canal" and "establishment of just and equitable tolls and charges." A new conference, Egypt said, could be "entrusted the task of reviewing the Constantinople Convention of 1888." The Egyptian note, which reviewed the Suez crisis, protested "displays of force" against Egypt and "inducements from certain quarters to cause defection of technical personnel with the intention of hampering the navigation in the Suez Canal." Egypt "wishes now to declare that it believes . . . solutions can be found," the note said.

The British Foreign Office said Sept. 10 that the Egyptian offer did "not appear to suggest any basis for negotiations." British spokesmen charged Egypt with "unqualified refusal" of the proposals offered by the Menzies committee. Pres. Eisenhower said at a news conference Sept. 11 that he saw "no substantive point on which to base" a new Suez conference.

The USSR charged Sept. 15 that the Western SCUA plan was "a great provocation against Egypt" and that attempts to impose it by force "would lead to immense destruction in the Suez Canal and in the oil fields" of the Middle East. A lengthy Soviet statement broadcast by Moscow Radio said that the Anglo-French military build-up on Cyprus was "an act of aggression" against Egypt, and that the withdrawal of non-Egyptian Suez pilots "aimed at disruption of normal work in the canal." The statement said that "the USSR, as a great power, cannot stand aside from the Suez problem" and "consider that the UN cannot but react to the existing situation." The Soviet government warned that "in the age" of the "atomic and hydrogen weapon, one cannot threaten and rattle the saber." It said the USSR considered "any violation of peace in the Near and Middle East" to be linked to "the security of the Soviet state." The statement criticized Eisenhower for not protesting British and French military policy at his Sept. 11 press conference. The Russians said that they would attend the Egyptian-sponsored Suez conference.

Nasser told an Egyptian Air Force College graduating class at Bilbeis Sept. 15 that the Suez Canal Users' Association scheme was "in truth one for declaring war" on Egypt. Nasser reiterated that Egypt would not "discriminate between canal users" and would defend the nationalized canal. Nasser said: "Those who attack Egypt will never leave alive"; "we shall fight a regular war, a total war, a guerrilla war"; "he who attacks Egypt, attacks the whole Arab world"; "they do not know how strong we really are." Nasser said in an interview with the Press Trust of India Sept. 16 that Egypt would "not allow the Western-proposed canal users association to function through the canal." "We Egyptians shall run the canal smoothly and efficiently," Nasser declared, "and if, in spite of this, the canal users association forces its way through the Suez Canal, then it would mean aggression and would be treated as such." (Col. Mahmoud Yunes, deputy director of the Egyptian Suez Canal Authority, warned Sept. 18 that if an SCUA vessel approached the canal, "regulations say they must ask us for a pilot." Asked what would happen if an SCUA vessel tried to pass without an Egyptian Authority pilot, Yunes said, "Let them try.")

By mid-Sept. 1956 pressures were mounting among canal-using countries in the West and elsewhere for a UN solution to the nearly 2-month old dispute. The foreign ministers of Norway, Sweden and Denmark, meeting in Stockholm Sept. 16, reportedly criticized the SCUA plan and recommended referral of the dispute to the UN. Pakistan was said Sept. 17 to be opposed to the users association scheme and to have accepted an invitation to the Egyptian-sponsored Suez conference. Spanish Foreign Min. Alberto Martin Artajo reportedly urged Sept. 17 that other Western governments attend the Egyptian-proposed conference. Italy indicated Sept. 17 that it was doubtful of the value of SCUA plan, West Germany was uncommitted and Australia divided on it. Indian Prime Min. Jawaharlal Nehru conferred on the Suez dispute Sept. 15 with envoys of the Colombo Powers (Pakistan, Indonesia, Burma, Ceylon) and ordered his political adviser, V. K. Krishna Menon, to Cairo for talks with Nasser. Menon met with Nasser Sept. 17 and Wing Commander Ali Sabry Sept. 18, reportedly in an unsuccessful attempt to press Egypt into a public statement of terms for a Suez compromise. Indian reports had said Sept. 14 that Egypt would be willing to agree to international control of Suez transit fees. Nasser continued talks Sept. 19-20 with Menon, who was said to be attempting to establish contact with U.S. diplomats for a joint mediation effort between Egypt and the West. Menon flew to London Sept. 22 and conferred with British Foreign Secy. Selwyn Lloyd Sept. 24 on his Cairo talks.

Nehru said in New Delhi Sept. 23 that India backed Egypt's ownership of the Suez Canal, "but India would not have followed the same
procedure by which Egypt nationalized the canal." He repeated warnings against a Western-imposed settlement by force. Nehru flew to
Dhahran, Saudi Arabia Sept. 23-24, saying he was "a pilgrim in search
of peace and friendship," and conferred with King Saud in Riyadh
Sept. 25-28. On the conclusion of the talks, the 2 leaders said in a joint
communique that there "can be no settlement of the [Suez] dispute by
methods of conflict or by the denial of the sovereign rights of Egypt
over the Suez Canal." The communique urged a negotiated settlement
and expressed "the hope that there will be no recourse to political and
economic pressure."

Nasser had conferred with King Saud and Syrian Pres. Shukri al-
Kuwatli Sept. 22-24 in Dammam and Riyadh. The meetings were held
amid reports that Saudi Arabia, dependent on full operation of the Suez
Canal for continued high oil royalties, had pressed for Egyptian modera-
tion on the problem. (The historically antagonistic Hashemite King
Faisal of Iraq and Saudi Arabian King Saud had met Sept. 18-20 in
Saudi Arabia. The Suez crisis was believed to have been the central
topic of their talks.) A joint communique issued by Nasser, Saud and
Kuwatli in Cairo Sept. 24 supported Egypt "in every attitude she takes"
on the Suez question. The 3 leaders pledged "unbreakable Arab solidarity" and backed "Egypt's declared readiness to reach a peaceful settlement that would safeguard Egypt's national interests and conform
with the aims of the UN." They urged a settlement through "negotiations with Egypt, the owner of the canal," "free from pressure" or intent "to impose any unilateral solution." (The communique also said
that the 3 conferees had given "attention to consolidating Arab security,
warding off the Israeli threat" and steps to "complete the Arab policy
drawn up in Cairo" at the first meeting of the 3 rulers Mar. 7.)

Soviet Premier Nikolai A. Bulganin had said Sept. 19 that the USSR
would be "prepared to take part in a meeting of the heads of government of Egypt, India, France, Britain, the U.S. and the Soviet Union"
to seek a "just and peaceful solution of the Suez Canal issue."
Bulganin, replying to questions submitted to him Sept. 13 by J. Kings-
bury Smith, general manager of the Hearst newspaper chain's International News Service, said that an "agreement on freedom of navigation
in the canal must in the end be reached" by a "wide international conference" and that the USSR "would have no objection to handing"
any Suez agreement "to the UN" for ratification.

At that point, however, Britain and France—the 2 most "aggrieved
parties"—were still opposed to any direct UN role in the dispute.

Delegates-to-UN Sir Pierson Dixon of Britain and Louis de Guiringaud of France had charged in a joint letter to UN Security Council Pres. Emilio Nuñez-Portuando Sept. 12 that the Egyptian refusal to negotiate a "just and equitable solution" to the Suez dispute had aggravated "the situation, which, if allowed to continue would" be a "danger to peace and security." But Nuñez said Sept. 12 that the letter had requested no action and that a Security Council meeting "is not considered necessary."

Egyptian Rep.-to-UN Omar Loufti said in a letter to Secy. Gen. Dag Hammarskjöld Sept. 13 that "the former Suez Canal Co." had with British and French "indorsement," ordered Suez pilots to leave their posts, "an act of intimidation." Loufti wrote that Egypt wished "to assure the continuation of normal passage through the canal" and that if navigation were hampered, "the responsibility" "would lie with those" who had attempted to obstruct "the so far unaffected" canal traffic.

Sir Pierson Dixon, in a 2d note circulated to UN members Sept. 14, criticized "the inaccuracy of [the Egyptian] statements." Dixon reviewed British and French requests to pilots to stay at their posts and Egyptian threats to imprison those quitting. He quoted Prime Min. Eden as saying Sept. 12 that "if these pilots decide to leave Egypt, it will clearly, in our view, be the responsibility of" Egypt.

Loufti transmitted a 2d Egyptian letter to the Security Council Sept. 17. It charged that the Western SCUA plan was "incompatible with the dignity and sovereign rights of Egypt" and in "flagrant violation" of the UN Charter and 1888 Constantinople Convention. The SCUA scheme, Egypt said, "would seek to establish in an unprecedented manner an organization within the territory of a sovereign state member of the UN without the consent of that state." (Loufti said Sept. 17 that an average of 42 ships per day had passed through the canal since the Western pilot walkout. This made a total of 2,216 vessels since July 26, compared with 2,103 for the equivalent period of 1955.)

A Soviet note to the Security Council Sept. 17 said that the SCUA plan was a "provocation" and could only be enforced by "an act of aggression." A joint Syrian-Lebanese letter to the Security Council charged Sept. 17 that the dispatch of French troops to Cyprus was "a threat" to "peace and security" in "the immediate vicinity" of Syria and Lebanon.

The British and French governments, under increasing U.S. pressure, finally asked UN Security Council Pres. Nuñez-Portuando Sept. 23 to call the Council into session Sept. 26 to consider the "situation created by the unilateral action" of Egypt in ending "the system of international operation of the Suez Canal" as "completed by the Suez Canal Convention of 1888."

Omar Loufti countered Sept. 24 with the request that the Security Council be "urgently convened to consider" the "actions against Egypt" by "some powers," particularly Britain and France. Loufti's letter to Dr. Nuñez charged that Anglo-French moves in the Mediterranean were "a danger to international peace and security" and were "serious violations of the charter of the UN." Loufti was reported Sept. 24 to have agreed to prior action on the British-French request, with Egypt to be given a non-voting seat during the debate.

Britain and France Sept. 25 rejected Egypt's complaint to the Security Council. British Foreign Office spokesmen said that Britain would "not accept that any moves made by us could be described as a threat to peace." French Rep.-to-UN Bernard Cornut-Gentille said Sept. 25 that "we definitely cannot accept" Egypt's charges of UN Charter violations.

The Security Council voted unanimously Sept. 26 to debate (starting Oct. 5) the Anglo-French complaint against Egypt's nationalization of the Suez Canal. The Council then agreed by 7–0 (U.S., Nationalist China, Cuba, Iran, Peru, Yugoslavia and the USSR in favor; Britain, France, Australia, Belgium abstaining) to consider Egyptian counter-charges that a joint British-French military buildup in the Mediterranean was endangering peace and a violation of the UN Charter. The Council Sept. 26 rejected a Yugoslav motion for simultaneous debate on the 2 complaints. It agreed that the prior Anglo-French charge would be heard first. The Council adopted a British-French proposal that Egypt be invited for non-voting participation in the Suez debate. It approved an Australian resolution delaying action on Israeli requests for inclusion until the next Council session.

The Security Council, before adjournment Sept. 26, heard Soviet UN delegate Arkady A. Sobolev attack Britain and France for having used "crude pressures" against Egypt. U.S. Amb.-to-UN Henry Cabot Lodge Jr., who cast the decisive vote on inclusion of the Egyptian complaint, told the Council that the U.S. did not agree with Egypt's charges but "generally" followed a "liberal policy" on UN agenda items.

It was reported from Washington Sept. 29 that the U.S., Britain and France were conferring on a possible joint resolution to be presented to the Security Council. U.S. officials reportedly advocated a text that would embody international control over the canal but characterize it as international "participation" in the canal's operation. British Foreign Secy. Lloyd, arriving in the U.S. for pre-UN session talks Oct. 2, reasserted that the interests of underdeveloped nations could not "be assured if the canal" remained "under the control of one man or one government."

2d & 3d London Conferences on Suez

The British government had invited the U.S., France and 13 other nations Sept. 14, 1956 to discuss the creation of the Suez Canal Users' Association at another conference in London. Pres. Eisenhower ordered State Secy. Dulles Sept. 14 to attend the parley with the other representatives of the 18-nation majority of the Aug. 16–23 conference on Suez.

Dispatches from London said Sept. 15 that a proposed conference agenda included in the invitations had slated discussions on (a) action to be taken following Egypt's Sept. 9 rejection of negotiations on international control of the canal, (b) Egypt's Sept. 10 counterproposal to renew negotiations with enlarged participation and (c) the establishment of the proposed Suez Canal Users' Association.

Representatives of the 18 nations held their 2d London conference Sept. 19–21. An agreement on basic SCUA aims was reached after much debate and substantial revision, but France at once rejected the revised scheme. The 2d conference had opened with the 18 invited countries openly divided on the SCUA plan, on measures envisaged against Egypt and on the possibility of UN action. A bloc of SCUA supporters, led by the U.S., Britain and France, included West Germany, Australia and New Zealand. Pakistan Sept. 19 refused membership in the SCUA. Spain urged new talks with Egypt. Norway, Sweden, Denmark and the Netherlands pressed for UN consideration of the dispute.* Japan, Ethiopia, Iran, Turkey and Portugal were said Sept. 19 to be uncommitted on the SCUA.

Dulles told the conferees Sept. 19 that the "great restraint" exercised by the West toward Egypt could not last indefinitely. He said that the Suez crisis, "a problem of great peril which could have been solved by force by nations sitting here," demanded the unity of the 18 conferring powers and a just solution in accord with international law. "If we emphasize just one side—trying to prevent the use of force—the effort will be doomed," Dulles said. Dulles suggested that the SCUA would:

---

*A resolution submitted to the conference Sept. 19 by Italian Foreign Min. Gaetano Martino with the support of the Netherlands, Denmark and Norway sought to limit SCUA functions to the negotiation of a new canal convention with Egypt. The resolution called for bringing the Suez dispute before the UN and opening the SCUA to all nations using the waterway.

• "Continue our present association" and stand on "our joint state-ment of Aug. 23, 1956" as "a basis for the negotiation of a permanent solution" of the Suez dispute.

• Need "a small operating staff which would be ready to assist our ships" in "operating through the canal" under an administrator acting "on behalf of the ships of the members."

• Depend on the administrator to "make available experienced pilots," to "assist" SCUA "participation in the pattern of traffic through the canal" and to "help coordinate routes through or around the canal."

• Authorize the administrator to act as "agent of the owners" and to "collect and pay out" money for the "maintenance of and transit through the canal."

• Be controlled by a "small governing board" formed to "appoint the administrative agent and fix his authority" and to maintain liaison with planning affecting dependence on the canal.

• "Suggest a provisional solution which the UN might find it useful to invoke while the search for a permanent solution goes on."

"Membership" in the SCUA "would not involve the assumption by any member of any obligation," Dulles said, although he expressed the hope that "members . . . would voluntarily take such action with respect to their ships and the payment of canal dues as would facilitate the work of the association." Dulles told Japanese Amb.-to-Britain Haru-hino Nishi that under the SCUA plan, Egypt would continue to operate the canal and its installations and that cooperation with Egypt would permit SCUA members to bar Soviet pilots from their ships.

(Moscow Radio had said Sept. 4 that a number of Soviet Black Sea pilots had agreed to join the Suez Canal force. Egypt had been per-mitted to place ads for pilots in Soviet newspapers Sept. 2.)

Dulles stressed in his Sept. 19 statement that Egyptian cooperation would be necessary under any canal plan. "Obviously," he said, "if Egypt makes it obligatory to use only pilots that are chosen and as-signed [by] it, then I do not see that pilots of the association would practically have very much to do and that part of the [SCUA] plan would have collapsed." The SCUA could, in this event, constitute "a bargaining body" "*vis a vis* Egypt."

The British leadership was quite dissatisfied with this turn of events, according to Anthony Nutting, then British minister of state for foreign affairs. Nutting, who disagreed with Prime Min. Eden's policies in the crisis and ultimately resigned in opposition to them, later wrote in *No End of a Lesson*:

On Eden's instructions, [British Foreign Secy.] Lloyd [had] made it clear that Britain looked to the SCUA as a means of denying canal dues to Egypt and, to this end, he [had] tried hard to get words written into the association's terms of reference which would bind all members to pay their dues to its account, and not to the Egyptian Canal Authority. . . . Far from making things tougher for Nasser, as Dulles had contended was his purpose, this new American approach suggested that the Users' Club would do no more than crystallize the *status quo* and would not be empowered to bring any further pressure on Egypt. . . . Although Nasser denounced . . . [the SCUA] as an 'association for waging war' and an unjustifiable attempt to infringe [on] Egypt's sovereign rights, it was . . . a feeble project. . . .

Dulles, in a letter to London Conference Chairman Lloyd, said Sept. 21 that he would confer with U.S. Treasury officials and "owners of American-flag vessels" to assure U.S. alignment with SCUA "operating practices." Reports Sept. 21 said that much U.S. shipping, under Panamanian and Liberian registry, could not be compelled to stop paying Suez tolls to Egypt. But U.S. Treasury spokesmen said Sept. 25 that American trade and currency regulations applied to American-run vessels "irrespective of registry" and that Treasury and State Department lawyers were "checking."

The SCUA scheme had undergone revision Sept. 20 in an effort to reach a formula acceptable to a majority of the 18 nations present. Dispatches from Washington said Sept. 21 that the U.S. had abandoned the organization of a boycott of the canal in the face of European opposition and continued Egyptian success with canal operations. Other reports said Sept. 21 that Egypt, currently receiving little of the canal's income, would not suffer from a boycott as much as European shippers, who, it was estimated would have to spend $500 million yearly for increased shipping costs via the Cape of Good Hope.

The 2d London conference ended Sept. 21 with a joint Suez policy statement and declaration of SCUA aims. The statement noted "with regret" Egypt's rejection of the first London conference's proposals for international control of the canal and the Egyptian failure to "make any counter-proposals to the 5-nation committee" headed by Robert G. Menzies. The statement rejected Egypt's Sept. 10 call for a new Suez conference as "too imprecise to afford a useful basis for discussion."

The Sept. 21 declaration said that the SCUA would aim to: "facilitate" a "final or provisional solution"; "promote safe . . . transit of the canal" and "seek the cooperation of the competent Egyptian authorities"; "extend its facilities" to "non-member nations"; "receive, hold and disperse the revenues accruing from [canal] dues" "pending a final settlement"; "consider and report to members" on "developments" affecting the canal; "assist" with "problems arising from [any] failure of the Suez Canal" and study means "to reduce dependence on the canal"; and "facilitate" any "provisional solution of the Suez problem that may be adopted by the UN."

The SCUA declaration provided for a council of all members, a council "executive group" to which the council might "delegate such powers as it deems appropriate," and an administrator to "make the necessary arrangements with shipping interests" and "serve under the direction of the council through the executive group."

The U.S., British and Italian governments formally accepted the SCUA declaration Sept. 21.

French Foreign Min. Christian Pineau rejected the SCUA declaration on direct orders of Premier Guy Mollet and returned to Paris Sept. 21. The Mollet cabinet, weakened by the conference's failure to require toll payments to the SCUA, was reported split with one faction demanding outright rejection of the SCUA scheme, another seeking the Mollet government's resignation. The cabinet met Sept. 22 and agreed to join the SCUA with the "express reservation" that "international operation of the canal, defined by the first London conference," remained subject to "no transaction." The cabinet said that "France intends to retain its freedom of action and refuses to collaborate in any measure which" may "be contrary to its essential interests." Mollet said Sept. 22 that, with regard to the SCUA, "the reservations of the English are the same as our own." He expressed "bitterness and anxiety" Sept. 23 that "the free peoples are not all aware, as we are, of the danger" posed by Egyptian-led Pan-Arabism. Mollet stressed that the Western division lay between U.S. and Anglo-French views on how to counter Egypt.

British Foreign Secy. Lloyd Sept. 22 invited the 18 London conference member-countries to meet in London Oct. 1 for a 3d conference on the ambassadorial level to organize the SCUA.

The Suez Canal Users' Association was formally inaugurated Oct. 1 by Lloyd at the opening session of the 3d London conference on the Suez dispute. The conference, attended by ambassadors of the 15 SCUA member states,* divided Oct. 1 into 3 committees—on organization, operations and finance—to begin drafting a formal SCUA constitution.

U.S. State Secy. Dulles had said at a news conference Sept. 26 that the U.S. would practice "patience and resourcefulness" to reach an

---

*Nations that had indicated their acceptance of the SCUA plan before the open-of the 3d London Conference Oct. 1: Australia, Denmark, France, West Germany, Iran, Italy, Netherlands, New Zealand, Norway, Portugal, Spain, Sweden, Turkey, U.S., Britain. Denmark, Norway and the Netherlands were reported to have made membership conditional on ratification of the SCUA Charter by their parliaments. Iran was said to have insisted on an SCUA pledge against the group's resort to force. Pakistan, Ethiopia and Japan remained uncommitted to the SCUA and were represented at the 3d London Conference by observers.

"agreed settlement" with Egypt on the Suez problem. Dulles warned that Egypt would find that "foreign markets and foreign sources of credit" were "not readily available to a nation which rejects" "interdependence" with its neighbors. Dulles said that the U.S. "would expect to be in accord" with Britain and France in the presentation of the West's case to the UN Security Council. He said that under plans for the operation of the Suez Canal Users' Association:

• It was "quite likely" that an SCUA-piloted vessel would attempt to use the canal and, if refused entry, "we assume" it would bypass the canal, although "we have no" "power to direct ships."

• Use of either SCUA- or Egyptian-controlled pilots would be "primarily for the master of the ship to decide." "If he wanted to take the Egyptian pilot, he is entitled to do so."

• There "is no obligation which results from joining the users association to act in unison." "Each vessel" and "each country" would "decide for itself"—we "cannot create" a "universal boycott of the canal."

• The U.S. "would not expect" that "U.S. flag vessels" would continue to make Suez toll payments to Egypt, although "there is no authority to compel payments" to the SCUA, and "we do not have in mind" restrictions on non-U.S. flag vessels.

• The "amount of money which Egypt gets out of the Suez Canal is not a major factor," and "the pressure which could be exerted by going around the canal would be relatively little."

• "Israel would not be eligible" for SCUA membership under requirements proposed in London, but "Israeli ships" "would have all the facilities of the association."

(Pres. Eisenhower said at his press conference Sept. 27 that the "great hope" of the user nations would be their "unanimity in what they believe should be a proper" settlement. The President expressed the belief that "Egypt will see that her own best interests" would be served by such a settlement and that if user nations were successful in winning "a provisional method of operation," the Israeli canal blockade could be "cured" simultaneously.)

Dulles conceded at a 2d press conference Oct. 2 that there "has been some difference" with Britain and France "in our approach to" the Suez problem. In an amended State Department transcript released Oct. 2, Dulles commented that "this is not an area where we are bound together by treaty." He cited "other problems where our approach is not identical," with one being "the so-called problem of colonialism" toward which "the U.S. plays a somewhat independent role" and tried to assure the country that the "process moves forward" constructively.

(In a paraphrase of Dulles' original remarks published Oct. 2, the *N.Y. Times* reported: Dulles denied a "detectable change" in the SCUA plan; he said that "there is talk that the teeth were pulled out of it—there were no teeth in it"; he asserted that differences with Britain and France over Suez policy were related "to some rather fundamental things." It was then that he had mentioned "the so-called problem of colonialism," on which the U.S. maintained an "independent role.")

British Prime Min. Eden was incensed by Dulles' statement, according to Anthony Nutting, who reported in *No End of a Lesson*: "I was at . . . [Eden's official residence] when the news-flash of Dulles' press conference came across the tapes. Eden's private secretary brought it in at the very moment when I was pleading with the prime minister not to get too far out of step with the U.S. and not to despair of carrying them with us in the Security Council and subsequently. Eden read the Dulles statement quickly and then, with a contemptuous gesture, he flung the piece of paper at me across the table, hissing as he did so, 'And now what have you to say for your American friends?' "

The French leadership, too, was known to have been angered by Dulles' statements. Reports from Paris Oct. 2 said that French officials had been troubled by Dulles' dissociation of the U.S. from the major colonialist powers. French sources were said to believe that Dulles' statement had been intended to delineate long-term U.S. policy, rather than its policy on the Suez crisis and that it particularly applied to the French problem in Algeria.

Anglo-French Alliance & UN Debate

French and British disagreement with the U.S. over the most effective policy to take toward Egypt brought Paris and London into close cooperation. By mid-Oct. 1956, the 2 countries sealed this cooperation with an alliance.

The British press Sept. 21 had viewed the final SCUA plan as a setback for Prime Min. Sir Anthony Eden's "firm" Suez policy. The London *Times* charged Sept. 21 that the SCUA scheme had "been changed and weakened out of all recognition." The Conservative *Daily Telegraph* said Sept. 21 that "we cannot tag along indefinitely behind any ally, however important." The weekly *Economist* said Sept. 21 that "the original decision personally to bring down Nasser has dictated the subsequent . . . events."

Eden and Foreign Secy. Lloyd conferred in Paris with French Premier Guy Mollet and Foreign Min. Pineau on the Suez dispute Sept. 26–27. Mollet and Eden, appearing together on TV Sept. 26, indicated that they had established Anglo-French solidarity on the issue.

Pineau said Sept. 26 that his first talks with Eden had "very clearly shown" a "desire for common action." A joint communiqué issued Sept. 27 said that France and Britain had "defined their common position" on "the recent British decision to place the question" before the UN and on "the line to be followed by them in the forthcoming debate."

Paris sources reported Sept. 27 that Britain and France had agreed to maintain their Mediterranean force on standby alert, to consult closely on Middle Eastern policy and to discuss French objections to the Baghdad (METO) Pact linking Britain with Pakistan, Iran, Iraq and Turkey. The British carrier *Albion* arrived at Malta Sept. 27 with operational air units transferred from Britain. A fleet of French landing craft reportedly left Malta the same day for the Eastern Mediterranean.

British Foreign Office spokesmen Sept. 26 had rejected an absolute prohibition on the use of force against Egypt. A Foreign Office statement that day indorsed Australian Prime Min. Robert G. Menzies' Sept. 25 defense of the user nations' right to "impose sanctions." The London statement reiterated that "the use of force in settling [the Suez dispute] would be a last resort." French Premier Mollet said Sept. 30 that Britain and France had achieved "unshakeable" unity on the Suez issue and that "the responsible men" of the U.S. were "profoundly in agreement with us on the objectives to be reached."

Speakers at the British Liberal Party Conference Sept. 27 had urged the Eden government to end "gunboat diplomacy" and seek a peaceful settlement of the Suez question. British Laborite leader Hugh Gaitskell said at the final session of the Labor Party's 55th annual conference Oct. 1 that Britain had not yet given a clear assurance against the use of force without prior UN consent. The Labor Party Conference Oct. 1 approved resolutions condemning the Eden government's "lamentable" handling of the Suez dispute and lauding Laborite success in pressing for action before the UN.

The UN Security Council opened debate Oct. 5, 1956 on a complaint of France and Britain against Egypt's nationalization of the Suez Canal. The session was convened by French Foreign Min. Pineau, Council president for October, after Western, Soviet and Egyptian diplomats had conferred with other UN members and UN Secy. Gen. Dag Hammarskjöld Oct. 3-4 on policies to be presented in the Council's Suez debate.

A joint Anglo-French draft resolution on the Suez question was submitted to the Council Oct. 5 by Pineau and British Foreign Secy. Lloyd. It charged Egypt with subjecting "the operation of an international public service" to "the Egyptian national interest and to exclusive

Egyptian control." Egypt, the resolution said, had seized the waterway "contrary to the principles of respect for international obligations" and had endangered "international peace and security." The British-French draft called on the Security Council to:

- Reaffirm "the principle of the freedom of navigation" through the waterway in "accordance with the Suez Canal Convention of 1888."
- Consider that the rights of "all users of the Suez Canal" should "be safeguarded and the necessary guarantees restored."
- Indorse "the proposals of the 18 states" at the first London conference as "designed" to solve "the Suez Canal question."
- Recommend that "Egypt should cooperate by negotiation" of a "system of operation to be applied to the Suez Canal."
- Recommend that "Egypt should, pending the outcome of such negotiations, cooperate with the Suez Canal Users' Association."

State Secy. Dulles told the Security Council Oct. 5 that "the U.S. adheres" to "the 18-nation proposals" and "intends to vote for the [Anglo-French draft] resolution." UN reports said Dulles had met with Lloyd and Pineau earlier Oct. 5 in an effort to soften the wording of the draft and to enable the U.S. to join in the sponsorship of the resolution. UN informants said Oct. 5 that, pressed by Dulles, Lloyd and Pineau had agreed to direct negotiations with Egyptian Foreign Min. Mahmoud Fawzi before the Council vote on the draft resolution.

The Council seated Fawzi Oct. 5 as a non-voting participant in the Suez debate but indefinitely postponed action on similar permission for Israel and other Arab states. Israeli Amb.-to-U.S. Abba Eban had promised Oct. 4 that Israel participation would, if granted, be limited to the Suez question. (Non-voting seats had been requested Oct. 4 by 7 Arab nations—Iran, Jordan, Lebanon, Libya, Saudi Arabia, Syria and Yemen.)

Fawzi charged in the Security Council Oct. 6 that Britain and France had attempted to insure "that the Suez Canal be finally amputated and severed from Egypt." Fawzi said Britain and France had continued their threats of "military and economic measures" against Egypt despite "standing offers to negotiate a peaceful settlement." Egypt, he said, had refused the "ultimatum and insult" surrounding invitations to the London conference and would continue to resist "dictation of a solution" for the canal crisis. Fawzi told the Council that the Menzies committee talks in Cairo Sept. 3–9 had been conducted on a "take it or leave it" basis and that Australian Prime Min. Menzies had confined the talks to the "presentation of the 18-power proposals." Fawzi charged that the "sudden withdrawal" of U.S. and

British aid offers for the Aswan high dam had been accompanied "by a vicious campaign against the Egyptian economy." He called for new Suez talks through "a negotiating body of reasonable size."

Fawzi informed the Council Oct. 8 of offers to compensate Suez Canal Co. shareholders on "the average value of the shares during the 5 years preceding nationalization" or to submit the case to international arbitration. Fawzi Oct. 8 urged a Suez settlement based on: a "system of cooperation" between Egypt and the user nations; a toll system "which guarantees . . . fair treatment free from exploitation"; a "reasonable percentage of the revenues" for development of the canal.

Soviet Foreign Min. Dmitri T. Shepilov told the Council Oct. 8 that efforts to internationalize the canal were the work of "reactionary elements" attempting "to force Egypt to her knees" and to "serve a lesson to other peoples of the East." Shepilov charged that, according to press reports, "major oil and shipping companies" in the U.S. were planning a consortium aimed at "taking over the Suez Canal" and dislodging their "French and British rivals from the positions they now hold." Shepilov proposed that "an authoritative committee of the Security Council," including Egypt, Britain, France, the U.S., India and the USSR, "be set up for [Suez] negotiations." The committee should "be balanced in such a way as to forestall the prevalence of some one point of view" and could include other nations, Shepilov said. It "could also be instructed to draw up the draft of a new convention" and "be entrusted with the preparations for a broad international conference to be attended by all countries using the Suez Canal to consider and approve the new convention."

Dulles Oct. 9 rejected the Soviet call for a new negotiating body. He told the Council that the Shepilov plan was designed to "perpetuate controversy" by "establishing a committee which is so constituted that we can know in advance that it will never agree." "The U.S.," he repeated, "intends to vote for [the Anglo-French] resolution." Dulles stressed the need for insulation of the canal from politics and said that "if Egypt accepts that simple and rudimentary principle of justice, then I believe that the subsidiary problems can be resolved."

British Foreign Secy. Lloyd, French Foreign Min. Pineau and Egyptian Foreign Min. Fawzi met privately with UN Secy. Gen. Hammarskjöld Oct. 9 in an effort to reach a compromise settlement. The private talks followed a closed Security Council session earlier Oct. 9 at which Fawzi reportedly rejected the principle of international control over the canal. Hammarskjöld refused to comment on the private talks Oct. 9 but said that he would continue talks with the 3 diplomats.

It was reported from the UN Oct. 9 that the Western powers were shifting toward acceptance of a proposed British solution similar to that advanced by India at the first London conference. Under the British plan, it was reported, an international commission would oversee canal operations and rule on alleged toll or priority discrimination against shippers. The commission could impose sanctions by forcing Egypt to give victimized vessels free canal passage and withholding Suez development funds. A U.S. version of the plan was said Oct. 9 to provide for appeal of violations directly to the UN.

(Reports said Oct. 9 that the British plan would permit Egypt to continue the Suez Canal blockade against Israeli shipping and Israel-bound cargoes. The Israeli UN delegation Oct. 8 had charged Egypt with blacklisting and blockading 103 vessels from 14 nations. Israel said the Egyptian blacklist had in Feb. 1956 included 45 British and 8 U.S. ships plus smaller numbers from Sweden, Greece, Morocco, Denmark, Italy, the Netherlands, Liberia, Costa Rica, Switzerland and the USSR.)

Egypt, Britain and France continued direct negotiations toward the settlement of the dispute Oct. 10-12. Foreign ministers of the 3 powers, meeting in private with Hammarskjöld, moved from the deadlock Oct. 10-11 to agreement Oct. 12 on 6 principles to govern future operation of the canal. The 6 principles, first presented by Lloyd at the outset of the Security Council debate, were accepted as a basis for further talks Oct. 12 by Mahmoud Fawzi, Lloyd and Pineau. The 6 principles, made public following their presentation at a closed session of the UN Security Council by Hammarskjöld Oct. 12, were:

(1) "There shall be free and open transit through the canal without discrimination, overt and covert."

(2) "Egypt's sovereignty shall be respected."

(3) "The operation of the canal shall be insulated from the politics of any country."

(4) "The manner of fixing tolls and charges shall be decided by agreement between Egypt and the users."

(5) "A fair proportion of the dues shall be allotted to development."

(6) "In case of dispute, unresolved affairs between the Suez Canal Co. and the Egyptian government shall be settled by arbitration. . . ."

The direct negotiations were recessed by Egypt, Britain and France Oct. 12 amid reports that they had failed to agree on enforcement of the 6 principles. According to Anthony Nutting in *No End of a Lesson*. these reports were false and the result of an announcement by Pineau to the press that "no progress was being made in the talks and that there was no basis for negotiation with Egypt." Pineau acted in bad faith in doing this, Nutting alleged, because Pineau was attempting "to ensure that continuing state of deadlock which France wanted in order to fulfill her plans with Israel" for military action against Egypt. Nutting reported, however, that, in the private talks, Fawzi had offered (a) a system of cooperation between Egypt and the canal's users that would recognize both Egypt's rights and the users' interests; (b) a fair program of tolls and charges; (c) the use of a rational amount of the canal's revenues for the improvement and development of the canal, and (d) an agreement to consider the question of user participation in the canal's operation.

The UN Security Council met in open session Oct. 13 to consider a revised Anglo-French draft resolution on Suez. Lloyd told the Council that while "no basis for negotiation" had been found in talks with Fawzi, the 6 principles could "provide a framework" for future negotiations. France and Britain, he said, while not abandoning the intent of their earlier draft Suez resolution, had submitted this softened version to attempt a settlement "by a different road." The revised Anglo-French resolution:

● Urged "that any settlement of the Suez question" should meet conditions of the 6 principles agreed on by Britain, France and Egypt.
● Considered "that the proposals of the 18 powers" were "designed to bring about a settlement" by "peaceful means in conformity with justice."
● Noted that Egypt had accepted "the principle of organized collaboration" with the users but had not yet "formulated . . . precise proposals."
● Urged continued "interchanges" and invited Egyptian "guarantees to the users" and cooperation with the Suez Canal Users' Association pending an agreement.

The Council voted 11-0 Oct. 13 to approve the first part of the draft resolution. A Soviet veto, backed by Yugoslavia, blocked acceptance of the draft's operative clauses, beginning with reference to the 18-power declaration.

Following the vote, Dulles urged Hammarskjöld to continue talks with British, French and Egyptian envoys, "a procedure which has already yielded positive results." Hammarskjöld agreed Oct. 14 to "be of assistance" in obtaining an Egyptian counter-offer based on the 6 principles.

Lloyd met with Dulles Oct. 14 and urged the U.S. to join in launching SCUA operations. Lloyd asked the U.S. to back initial SCUA moves and divert Suez Canal tolls from Egypt to the SCUA before the final agreement on the organization of the users' group. Dulles promised to answer the Lloyd request through "normal diplomatic channels." British UN sources said Oct. 14 that a U.S. agreement would be followed by a British attempt to force the opening of the canal to SCUA vessels in the event that Egypt refused cooperation.

Soviet First Deptu Premiery Anastas I. Mikoyan told newsmen at an Afghan embassy reception in Moscow Oct. 15 that "absolutely all states should have equal rights in the canal." Mikoyan, said to be the first Soviet official to acknowledge publicly the Suez blockade of Israel conceded that "for a long time they [the Israelis] have not been able to use it and nothing has been said about it." Dispatches from Moscow said Oct. 15 that all mention of the blockade had been deleted from Soviet press accounts of the Suez crisis.

British Prime Min. Eden had taken his case before his own political party. Eden, at the Conservative Party's annual conference in Llandudno, Wales Oct. 13, cited as a "happy consequence" of the Suez problem a growing "sense of partnership" with Europe and unity with "our French allies." He conceded there had been "a little progress" toward solving the dispute in the UN. He credited it "to the firmness and resolution which we and those who think like us have been showing throughout the crisis." Eden repeated that no acceptable Suez settlement could "leave it [the canal] in the unfettered control of a single power." He asserted that Britain had "always said that with us force is the last resort, but it cannot be excluded." "No responsible government could ever give such a pledge," he said. Eden said that Britain would continue her military buildup in the Eastern Mediterranean because "to relax now before a settlement is reached would be fatal."

Dispatches from Paris Oct. 10–16 cited continued French bitterness against U.S. Suez policy and the repeated instances of calls in the press for firm action against Egypt. Foreign Min. Pineau, answering critics at the opening of a National Assembly debate on Suez Oct. 16, conceded that U.S. policy had been "very difficult for us to follow." Pineau, defending the effectiveness of NATO with respect to the Suez problem, said that France "often has the impression that the U.S. does not understand, as we do, the obligations of the Atlantic Alliance."

Egyptian Foreign Min. Fawzi, in a letter to the Security Council Oct. 15, had said that Eden's reference in his Llandudno remarks to a possible use of force over the canal had been "extremely unfortunate" and "a matter of deep regret." Fawzi charged that France and Britain were "persevering in the military and economic measures which they initiated" after the canal seizure July 26. "These statements," Fawzi said, did not insulate the canal from politics but "throw this question into the turmoil of politics."

U.S. State Secy. Dulles warned at a press conference in Washington Oct. 16 that, "within constitutional means," the U.S. would carry out an Apr. 9, 1956 White House declaration and "assist" and "give aid to any victim of aggression" in the Middle East. Dulles attributed mass Israeli reprisal raids against Jordan to "deterioration of the situation" and "failure of the efforts" by UN Secy. Gen. Hammarskjöld.

It is generally agreed that a low ebb in Anglo-U.S. relations was reached during and immediately after the Suez crisis. Dulles and Eden were at odds and, according to Mohammed Heikal, certain Americans informed Nasser of the plan for an armed attack against Egypt. In *Nasser: The Cairo Documents,* Heikal wrote: "In their efforts to persuade Egypt of the dangers of the situation and to agree to the 6 Principles, the Americans had leaked to Ahmed Hussein the news that Gen. Keightley had been chosen to command an invasion of Egypt and ... [was] training his men in Cyprus. This was one of a number of warnings about Britain and France's determination on military intervention."

In *No End of a Lesson,* Anthony Nutting recorded the following information, held in strict confidence until the publication of his book early in 1967:

● French Premier Guy Mollet telegraphed Eden the morning of Oct. 13 to say that he was sending Labor Min. Albert Gazier (the acting foreign minister while Pineau was in New York) and Gen. Maurice Challe, deputy chief of staff of the French air force, to Eden's summer residence at Chequers Oct. 14 "with a message of the utmost importance."

● British Amb.-to-France Sir Gladwyn Jebb returned to London Oct. 13 with a report that "the French government had recently delivered to Israel no fewer than 75 of the latest French Mystere fighter aircraft."

● Gazier and Challe met Eden, Eden's private secretary and Nutting at Chequers at 3 p.m. Sunday, Oct. 14. Gazier asked Eden whether Britain would intervene if Israel attacked Egypt. Nutting interposed that Britain was bound to do so under the Tripartite Agreement of May 25, 1950 with the U.S. and France. Gazier thereupon noted that Egypt "had recently contended that the Tripartite Declaration did not apply to Egypt."

Eden's secretary, at Gazier's and Eden's insistence, stopped taking notes. Challe then outlined "a possible plan of action for Britain and France to gain physical control of the Suez Canal." The plan called for Israel to attack Egypt across the Sinai Peninsula and for Britain and France, "having given the Israeli forces enough time to seize all or most of Sinai," then to order "both sides" to withdraw their forces from the

Suez Canal. (This would put Egypt back to the west of the Canal and Israel on its eastern bank.) An Anglo-French force would then intervene and occupy the canal "on the pretext of saving it from damage by fighting."

● Eden and Foreign Secy. Lloyd, who had returned to London Oct. 15, went to Paris the afternoon of Oct. 16 and accepted the French proposal. When Lloyd returned Oct. 17, he told Nutting that "the French had clearly been in cahoots with the Israelis for several weeks."

● Lloyd met Israeli Premier David Ben-Gurion secretly outside Paris Oct. 22 and learned from Ben-Gurion that Israel would not proceed without assurance that Britain and France "would 'take out' the Egyptian air force as soon as Israeli forces began their attack." Israel had no bombers and feared that Egypt would raid Tel Aviv and other Israeli cities with their Russian-made bombers.

● Eden received French Foreign Min. Pineau in London late Oct. 23 and held unrecorded talks with him. Lloyd, who had been present, conferred with Nutting the morning of Oct. 24, and Nutting gathered that Pineau had received Eden's assurance that Britain would give Israel the requested support. Lloyd told Nutting that Israel would attack the evening of Oct. 29, that Britain and France would issue their ultimatum early Oct. 30 and that, when Egypt refused it, the British and French would start bombing Egyptian airfields.

A joint Anglo-French communique said Oct. 17 that France and Britain were "ready to consider together" any new Egyptian proposals for a Suez settlement. The communique, issued following talks in Paris Oct. 16–17 among Mollet, Pineau, Eden and Lloyd, said that Britain and France were "resolved to adhere to the requirements" of the UN Security Council resolution on Suez but also would "stand by the 2d part of the resolution . . . vetoed by the Soviet Union."

The joint communique said that Britain and France would continue to consider "the 18-power proposals, including the international operation of the canal," as "the basis for settlement." Any acceptable Egyptian proposals would have to meet the requirements of the 18-power proposals and afford "equivalent guarantees to the users," the communique said.

Egyptian Pres. Nasser was interviewed by Hanson W. Baldwin of the *N.Y. Times*. In the interview, which appeared in the Oct. 18 editions, Nasser maintained that Egypt was ready for "any form of consultation or cooperation" with the canal users toward a solution of the crisis but would not accept foreign "domination" of the canal.

The Suez Canal Users' Association Council, meeting in London

Oct. 19, appointed Eyvind Bartels, Danish consul general in New York, as chief SCUA administrator. From Washington Oct. 19 came reports of Western disagreement on the payment of Suez tolls into SCUA accounts. Britain and France were said to feel that the funds should be blocked and that the SCUA should be used to coerce Egyptian cooperation in the absence of a firm canal agreement. The U.S. was reported to be backing the distribution of a share of SCUA tolls to Egypt and the use of the SCUA as an instrument of cooperation with Egyptian Suez officials.

Nasser conferred on the Suez question Oct. 19-20 with Indian diplomat V. K. Krishna Menon, who had arrived in Cairo from talks in London Oct. 19. Before leaving for New Delhi Oct. 20, Menon said he had "put various plans" before Nasser "for consideration." The Cairo newspaper *Al Goumhouria* reported Oct. 21 that Menon had proposed a new Suez plan under which Egypt would "recognize" the Suez Canal Users' Association, which would "function in an advisory capacity." The plan would provide for UN appointment of chiefs for the 3 divisions of the Egyptian Suez Canal Authority during the first 3 years of the plan's operation. Egyptian spokesmen said Egypt expected to begin talks with Britain and France in Geneva.

After French Foreign Min. Pineau's meeting with British Prime Min. Eden in London Oct. 23, however, Pineau said that Britain and France had agreed that they could not consider "seriously" a new Egyptian offer of direct negotiations on a possible Suez settlement. The British and French leaders reportedly had been informed Oct. 23, through UN sources, of an Egyptian bid to discuss guarantees for unrestricted use of the canal. UN Secy. Gen. Hammarskjöld had met with Egyptian Foreign Min. Fawzi and British UN delegation chief Sir Pierson Dixon at UN headquarters in New York Oct. 19 in an effort to renew direct 3-power Suez negotiations.

Anthony Nutting reported in *No End of a Lesson* that Eden and Lloyd sent "a senior Foreign Office official [to Paris Oct. 24] with further assurance for the French to pass on to the Israelis that we . . . would do all that the Israelis required in the way of air strikes against Egyptian airfields to forestall the bombing of their cities. These assurances turned the scale, and on Thursday, Oct. 25th, Eden learned that the Israelis had decided finally to play their part in the Sinai campaign. That afternoon the [British] cabinet came to its final . . . decision" to commit Britain to full cooperation in the Franco-Israeli plans.

In Israel, meanwhile, Premier Ben-Gurion Oct. 15 had opened a general debate in the Knesset on Israeli defenses and foreign affairs by attacking British support for a plan to have Iraq, a Baghdad Pact partner, send a battalion of troops to Jordan in accordance with the Jordanian-Iraqi defense treaty. Israel would consider itself free to act in keeping with its own standards of self-defense if Iraqi troops entered Jordan, Ben-Gurion said. (Israeli infantry and Jordanian police, army and national guard contingents had fought in the Qalqilya area Oct. 4. Israel later admitted losing 18 soldiers in the battle, and UN observers put Jordanian losses at 45 servicemen and 3 civilians killed.) Ben-Gurion denounced as "a disguised attack on the integrity of our borders" a proposal by Iraqi Premier Nuri es-Said that Israel settle its border disputes on the basis of the UN General Assembly's partition resolution of Nov. 29, 1947.

Ben-Gurion, replying in the Knesset Oct. 17 to right-wing and left-wing attacks on his position, refused to go any further than his statement of Oct. 15 in regard to the projected Iraqi troop movements. He said that "a number of favorable developments in the last few days" with respect to both the Iraqi threat and the Suez crisis had underscored to him the advantages of patience, but he cautioned against overoptimism and excessive reliance on "verbal promises." The greatest danger of all, he told the Knesset, rested with "the Egyptian dictator," who had repeatedly expressed an intention to destroy Israel. Ben-Gurion won from the Knesset a 76–13 vote of confidence Oct. 17.

Suez Campaign: U.S. Seeks to End Invasion

An Anglo-French-Israeli move to seize the Suez Canal began Oct. 29, 1956 when Israeli armed forces thrust deep into Egypt's Sinai Peninsula and drove toward the canal.

Britain and France issued a 12-hour ultimatum to Israel and Egypt Oct. 30 demanding that hostilities cease and announcing plans to reoccupy the Suez Canal Zone. The Anglo-French message demanded that Egypt and Israel withdraw their forces from the vicinity of the canal.

The Israeli forces reached the canal Oct. 31 and then pulled back to the 10-mile limit specified in the Anglo-French ultimatum.

Anglo-French military operations opened with air attacks on Egyptian and Suez Canal installations and airfields Oct. 31. They were climaxed by commando and paratroop landings at key points of the canal Nov. 5-6.

Officially, the Eisenhower Administration took the position that the U.S. was caught almost completely by surprise. According to Eisenhower Administration sources, it wasn't until late October that American intelligence sources had begun reporting to the Eisenhower

Administration on growing evidence of a Franco-Israeli arms arrangement and an increasing Israeli military buildup.

Pres. Eisenhower, campaigning for reelection, had told TV interviewers Oct. 24 that no one could challenge Egypt's legal right to nationalize the Suez Canal. Eisenhower revealed Oct. 28 that he had sent Israeli Premier David Ben-Gurion a message Oct. 27 noting "disturbing reports from the Middle East," including word of "heavy mobilization" of Israeli armed forces, and urging that "no forceful initiative be taken which would endanger the peace." Eisenhower said the U.S. had not heard of "largescale mobilization in countries neighboring Israel which would warrant such Israeli" action. He said he would send "a further urgent message" to Ben-Gurion and similar notes to the Arab states concerned.

Following the Israeli thrust into Sinai, U.S. Amb.-to-Britain Winthrop Aldrich visited Foreign Secy. Selwyn Lloyd at the British Foreign Office in London early Oct. 30, but learned nothing there to prepare him for the Anglo-French move that started a few hours later.

Eisenhower appealed to British Prime Min. Eden and French Premier Mollet Oct. 30 to cancel the then projected British-French military action. A White House statement said that Eisenhower's appeal had been sent "as soon as the President received his first knowledge, through press reports of the ultimatum." The statement said Eisenhower had requested that "full opportunity" be given the UN to settle the crisis "by peaceful means." Press reports Oct. 30 said the President was "disturbed" over the lack of Western coordination of policy on the Egyptian situation.

State Secy. Dulles called in the British and French envoys Oct. 30 to express "extreme displeasure" at the Anglo-French failure to inform the U.S. of the impending ultimatum. British diplomatic sources asserted Oct. 30 that U.S. Amb.-to-Britain Aldrich had been informed of the Anglo-French move at least 7 hours before the first news reports of the ultimatum. (Anthony Nutting contradicted this in *No End of a Lesson*.) The British and French envoys reportedly denied State Department suspicions of Israeli-British-French "collusion" to provoke military action against Egypt.

A White House statement issued Oct. 29 had said that the U.S. would refer the Israeli attack on Egypt to the UN Security Council. The decision was said to be based on the Tripartite Declaration of 1950, in which the U.S., Britain and France had pledged to guarantee existing Arab-Israeli borders. The statement disclosed that Eisenhower, in a meeting with State Secy. Dulles, Defense Secy. Charles E. Wilson, Joint Chiefs of Staff Chairman Arthur W. Radford, CIA Director Allen W.

Dulles and other Administration leaders Oct. 29, had "recalled that the U.S." had "pledged itself to assist the victim of any aggression in the Middle East." "We shall honor our pledge," the statement said.

Eisenhower Administration officials showed amazement and anger when, in an emergency session of the UN Security Council Oct. 30, Britain and France vetoed a U.S.-authored resolution against the new military activities in Egypt. This was the first time that Britain had used the veto and the first instance of the U.S. and USSR being aligned against Britain and France on a major issue before the council.

The action in the Security Council was on an American-sponsored resolution calling for: (1) "Israel and Egypt immediately to cease fire"; (2) Israel to "withdraw its armed forces behind the established armistice lines"; (3) "all members" to "refrain from the use of force or threat of force in the area" and "refrain from giving any military, economic or financial assistance to Israel so long as it has not complied with" the resolution. The vote on the resolution was 7-2 (Australia and Belgium abstaining), but Britain and France—permanent members with veto power—cast the 2 negative votes. British delegate Sir Pierson Dixon held that the UN could not act quickly enough to affect the situation.

U.S. Amb.-to-UN Henry Cabot Lodge Jr. said that the UN had a "clear and unchallenged responsibility" to maintain the Palestine armistice agreements. Soviet delegate Arkady A. Sobolev charged that Britain and France were trying to use "Israeli aggression" as an excuse for seizing the Suez Canal in another act of "aggression against Egypt."

Eisenhower Oct. 31, in the closing days of his 2d Presidential campaign, told Americans in a TV address on the Middle Eastern crisis:

The Middle East was, as we all know, an area long subject to colonial rule. This rule ended after World War II, when all countries there won full independence. Out of the Palestinian mandated territory was born the new state of Israel. These historic changes could not, however, instantly banish animosities born of the ages. Israel and her Arab neighbors soon found themselves at war with one another. And the Arab nations showed continuing anger toward their former colonial rulers, notably France and Britain.

The United States . . . has labored tirelessly to bring peace and stability to this area. We have considered it a basic matter of U.S. policy to support the state of Israel and at the same time to strengthen our bonds both with Israel and with the Arab countries. But unfortunately, through all these years, passion in the area threatened to prevail over peaceful purpose, and in one form or another there has been almost continuous fighting.

This situation was recently aggravated by Egyptian policy, including rearmament with Communist weapons. We felt this to be a misguided policy on the part of the Egyptian government. Israel, at the same time, felt increasing anxiety for her safety. And Britain and France feared more and more that Egyptian policies threatened their lifeline of the Suez Canal.

These matters came to a crisis on July 26 of this year when the Egyptian government seized the Suez Canal Co. For 90 years, ever since the inauguration of the canal, that company had operated the canal, largely under British and French technical supervision. There were some among our allies who urged an immediate reaction to this event by use of force. We insistently urged otherwise, and our wish prevailed, through a long succession of conferences and negotiations, for weeks—even months—with participation by the United Nations. There in the UN only a short while ago, it seemed that an acceptable accord was within our reach on the basis of agreed principles. But the relations of Egypt with both Israel and France kept worsening to a point at which first Israel, and then France and Britain, determined that, in their judgment, there could be no protection of their vital interests without resort to force.

Upon this decision events followed swiftly. On Oct. 28 the Israeli government ordered mobilization. On Oct. 29 their armed forces penetrated deeply into Egypt and to the vicinity of the Suez Canal—nearly 100 miles away. On Oct. 30 the British and French governments delivered a 12-hour ultimatum to Israel and Egypt, now followed up by armed attack against Egypt. The United States was not consulted in any way about any phase of these actions. Nor were we informed of them in advance.

As it is the manifest right of any of those nations to take such decisions and actions, it is likewise our right, if our judgment so dictates, to dissent. We believe these actions to have been taken in error, for we do not accept the use of force as a wise or proper instrument for the settlement of international disputes. To say this, in this particular instance, is in no way to minimize our friendship with these nations nor our determination to maintain those friendships.

We are fully aware of the grave anxieties of Israel, Britain and France. We know that they have been subjected to grave and repeated provocations. The present fact nonetheless seems clear. The action taken can scarcely be reconciled with the principles and purpose of the UN, to which we have all subscribed. . . .

Now we must look to the future. In the circumstances I have described, there will be no U.S. involvement in these hostilities. I have no plan to call Congress in special session. . . . At the same time it is—and will remain—the dedicated purpose of our government to do all in its power to localize the fighting and to end the conflict.

We took our first measure in this action yesterday. We went to the UN with a request that the forces of Israel return to their own lines and that hostilities in the area be brought to a close. This proposal was not adopted because it was vetoed by Britain and France. It is our hope and intent that this matter will be brought before the UN General Assembly. There, with no veto operating, the opinion of the world can be brought to bear in our quest for a just end to this tormenting problem. . . .

. . . I am ever more deeply convinced that the UN represents the soundest hope for peace in the world. For this very reason I believe that the processes of the UN need further to be developed and strengthened. I speak particularly of increasing its ability to secure justice under international law. In all the recent troubles in the Middle East there have been injustices suffered by all nations involved. But I do not believe that another instrument of injustice—war—is a remedy for these wrongs.

There can be no peace without law. And there can be no law if we work to invoke one code of international conduct for those who we oppose and another for our friends. . . . The peace we seek and need means much more than mere absence of war. It means the acceptance of law and the fostering of justice in all the world. . . .

Eisenhower defended his Middle East policy at a GOP rally in Philadelphia Nov. 1. The Middle East crisis, the President said, was "a much sterner test of our principles. . . . We cannot and we will not condone armed aggression—no matter who the attacker and . . . who the victim. We cannot . . . subscribe to one law for the weak, another law for the strong; one law for those opposing us, another for those allied with us." He asserted that "we value—deeply and lastingly—the bonds with . . . those great friends [Britain and France] with whom we now so plainly disagree." But he insisted that "there are some firm principles that cannot bend—they can only break. And we shall not break ours."

Soviets Condemn Suez Invasion

The Soviet Union Nov. 1, 1956 strongly condemned the Anglo-French military action in Egypt and said that it would urge the "Bandung [Afro-Asian] powers" to demand that British, French and Israeli forces quit Egypt immediately. Soviet Foreign Min. Dmitri Shepilov described the Anglo-French air operations against Egyptian airfields Nov. 1 as an "act of gangsterism."

The Kremlin Nov. 2 sent notes to Britain and France in which the Soviet government accused the 2 countries of violating the 1888 Constantinople Convention guaranteeing freedom of navigation in the Suez Canal. Britain and France had set up a "naval blockade" in Egyptian waters of the eastern Mediterranean and the Red Seas and bore full responsibility for "acts of aggression affecting not only Egypt but other states as well," the Soviet note charged.

At the height of the Suez crisis, the USSR Nov. 4 crushed the Hungarian revolution of Oct. 23, 1956 with a massive deployment of Soviet troops to Budapest and other Hungarian centers of rebellion against Soviet control of Hungary. The Anglo-French role in Suez had already diverted much of the force of international condemnation in the UN of the Soviet action in Hungary.

Soviet Premier Nikolai A. Bulganin warned Britain, France and Israel Nov. 5 that the USSR was fully prepared "to crush the aggressors and restore peace in the East through the use of force." Bulganin the same day proposed in an open letter to U.S. Pres. Eisenhower a joint Russo-American military action that would end the fighting and remove the Anglo-French threat to Egyptian sovereignty. Bulganin told Eisenhower that the U.S. and the USSR, as Security Council members and possessors of "all modern types of arms, including the atomic and hydrogen weapons," bore "particular responsibility for stopping war." He proposed that American and Soviet air and naval forces be combined in the Middle East, "backed by a UN decision," as a "sure guarantee of ending the aggression against" Egypt. Bulganin wrote British Prime Min. Eden of his proposal for U.S.-Soviet action and told French Premier Guy Mollet to consider "the position of France if she were attacked" by "states having . . . modern and terrible" weapons. Bulganin warned Israeli Premier Ben-Gurion that Israel's attack on Egypt was "sowing such hatred" for Israel as to "place in jeopardy" its "very existence." The USSR Nov. 4 had sent Britain and France notes of formal protest against the bombing of Egypt and closure of the Suez Canal. Moscow recalled Amb.-to-Israel Aleksandr N. Abramov; Israeli Amb.-to-USSR Joseph Avidar, visiting Tel Aviv, canceled plans to return to Moscow Nov. 5.

A White House statement Nov. 5 rejected Bulganin's suggestion of joint U.S.-Soviet intervention by force in Egypt as "unthinkable" and "an obvious attempt to divert world attention from the Hungarian tragedy." The statement said further intervention in Egypt would contravene the UN General Assembly's action to establish a UN peace force.

Ben-Gurion replied to Bulganin Nov. 8 that "some of your arguments are based on incomplete and incorrect information." Ben-Gurion said:

. . . More than 2 years ago the ruler of Egypt [Gamal Abdel Nasser] organized a special force, under the name of *fedayin*, whose purpose was to penetrate surreptitiously within the boundaries of our country and to murder our citizens. . . . At the beginning, these groups operated only from areas occupied by Egypt, such as the Gaza Strip. Lately, he has organized such groups of murderers in Jordan, Lebanon and Syria, and the lives of our farmers along the borders are subject daily to their murderous onslaught. During the Suez crisis, the activity of these groups ceased. 3 weeks ago, however, their activity was intensified.

In an order dated Feb. 15, 1956, by the commander of the 3rd Egyptian Division in Sinai, Maj. Gen. Ahmed Salem, . . . it is written *inter alia*: 'Every commander is to prepare himself and his subordinates for the unavoidable war with Israel for the purpose of fulfilling our exalted aim — namely the annihilation of Israel and her extermination in the shortest possible time and by fighting her as brutally and cruelly as possible.'

The ruler of Egypt . . . organized an economic boycott against Israel. He established a blockade against our freedom of the navigation in the Suez Canal and the Straits of Eilat [Strait of Tiran] and for 5 years violated a decision of the Security Council concerning freedom of passage of Israeli shipping in the Suez Canal. After the Security Council, on 13 October this year, again forbade discrimination with regard to freedom of navigation on the Suez Canal, Egypt's ruler announced that discrimination against Israel would be continued.

About 2 weeks ago the Egyptian ruler concluded a military pact with Jordan and Syria against Israel. Therefore the action that we carried out at the end of October was necessitated by self-defense and was not an action dictated by foreign wishes as you allege. In response to the appeal of the special UN Assembly of the United Nations, we ceased fire. . . .

Yesterday I stated in the Knesset that we are willing to enter immediately into direct negotiations with Egypt to achieve a stable peace without any prior conditions and without any compulsion. . . .

I am constrained, in conclusion, to express my surprise and sorrow at the threat against Israel's existence contained in your note. . . .

The Soviet delegation to the UN Nov. 5 had put before the Security Council a resolution proposing that Britain, France and Israel "immediately, and not later than 12 hours after the adoption of this resolution, cease all military operations against Egypt and withdraw their troops from Egyptian territory within 3 days." The resolution also proposed that, acting in conformity with UN Charter Article 42, the U.S., the Soviet Union and other UN members with "powerful air and naval forces . . . give armed and other aid to the victim of aggression—the republic of Egypt—by sending naval and air forces, military units, volunteers, military equipment and other types of aid" if Britain, France and Israel failed to comply "by a fixed date" with the terms of the resolution. The Soviet government, the resolution said, was "ready to make its contribution toward the task of curbing aggression and reestablishing peace by sending to Egypt the air and naval forces needed for that purpose."

U.S. Amb.-to-UN Henry Cabot Lodge told the Security Council that the Soviet plan "would convert Egypt into a still larger battlefield" and went counter to "everything the General Assembly and Secretary General are trying to do" to win a UN-policed cease-fire. Lodge attacked Soviet "cynicism and disregard of the values of international morality" in decrying the attack on Egypt while practicing "butchery . . . against the people of Hungary." The Soviet resolution was defeated by a vote of 4 (the U.S., Britain, France and Australia) to 3 (the USSR, Yugoslavia and Iran), with 4 abstentions (Belgium, Cuba, Nationalist China and Peru).

Pres. Eisenhower ordered a global alert of U.S. armed forces Nov. 6, the U.S. Presidential election day. Israel and Britain Nov. 6 agreed to halt their advance. (Israel had already cut off the northern Sinai and captured Gaza.) The Anglo-French force by then had control of the Suez ports, but ships already sunk in the canal rendered the occupation futile.

The General Assembly had reconvened Nov. 4–5 to hear Hammarskjöld report on the proposed UN emergency force. The Assembly voted 57–0 early Nov. 5 to approve a resolution creating a UN Command Force and naming Maj. Gen. Eedson L. M. Burns of Canada, UN Truce Supervision Organization head, as chief of the UN force. Approval of the resolution, submitted by Canada, Norway and Colombia, came after Hammarskjöld had urged the Assembly late Nov. 4 to act without waiting for his full report on the project. Hammarskjöld reported that Colombia, Norway and New Zealand had pledged participation in the force and that other nations had submitted the question to their parliaments. He urged that Burns be named UN force chief "on an emergency basis" and be authorized to recruit a "small staff" of officers from UN truce supervision teams in the Middle East and additional officers "directly from various member states"—none from the permanent members of the Security Council (U.S., Britain, France, USSR, Nationalist China). U.S. Amb.-to-UN Lodge said Nov. 5 that the U.S. would aid the UN force "as regards airlifts, shipping transport and supplies."

Eisenhower Nov. 7 approved Defense Department orders to tighten U.S. defenses and subject the Atlantic fleet to "readiness" tests. The Navy Department disclosed Nov. 9 that the 60,000-ton carrier *Forrestal* would be transferred to Mediterranean service in Jan. 1957 to be followed by the 45,000-ton carrier *F. D. Roosevelt* in April. The Navy had ordered a submarine "hunter-killer" group to break off a visit to Rotterdam Oct. 30 and sail to reinforce the U.S. 6th Fleet in the Mediterranean.

Well-organized demonstrations took place in Moscow Nov. 5 and 6 outside the British, French and Israeli embassies. The demonstrators, most of them students and factory workers, shouted demands for the withdrawal of the 3 countries' forces from Egypt and submitted petitions to the effect at the British and French embassies, forcing their way into the British embassy to do so.

Britain's and France's determination to keep up their invasion of the Suez had already evoked Soviet threats of intervention on the side of Egypt. The official Soviet news agency Tass reported Nov. 10 that "great numbers of Soviet air force pilots, tank personnel, artillerymen and officers" who were World War II veterans had "asked to be allowed to go to Egypt as volunteers in order to fight together with the Egyptian people to throw the aggressors out of Egypt." "The Soviet people will not stand idly by at the spectacle of international banditry," Tass declared. It quoted "leading Soviet circles" as having warned that "the USSR will raise no obstacle to the departure of Soviet volunteers" for Egypt "if Britain, France and Israel, contrary to UN decisions, do not withdraw . . . and delay the implementation of the decisions."

The Egyptian ambassador in Moscow was reported Nov. 12 to have told journalists at a Swedish embassy reception that more than 50,000 Soviet reservists had volunteered for duty in Egypt. He also said that Communist China had offered Egypt 250,000 volunteers and that Indonesia, the host of the Bandung Conference in Apr. 1955, was prepared to send Egypt 50,000 fighting men.

Pres. Eisenhower said at a White House press conference Nov. 14 that "it would be the duty of the UN, including the U.S., to oppose" the introduction of or any intervention by Soviet or Chinese volunteers into the Middle East on Egypt's behalf. The President said that the UN was "not by any manner of means limited to resolutions" when confronted with such emergencies. He termed the Soviet gesture toward Egypt an attempt to "woo for the moment" a susceptible Arab state.

The Syrian minister to West Germany called attention to the irrelevance of the dispute over potential Soviet volunteers by asserting Nov. 15 that there were no Soviet volunteers in the Middle East, that Egypt no longer saw any need of such volunteers in the light of the existing cease-fire and that he had been authorized by Egypt, Syria, Jordan, Iraq and Yemen to make his statement.

Soviet Premier Bulganin Nov. 15 opposed the stationing of UN forces in the Suez Canal Zone and demanded that Egypt be consulted on the deployment of UN troops elsewhere on Egyptian territory. In notes to British Prime Min. Eden, French Premier Mollet and Israeli Premier Ben-Gurion, Bulganin renewed Soviet demands for the withdrawal of their troops from Egypt. He also urged the payment of compensation to Egypt for the loss of life and property damage inflicted by the invading foreign forces. Bulganin told Eden and Mollet that the continued presence of Anglo-French forces and the planned deployment of UN troops to the Suez Canal Zone "would be contrary to the [Suez] Convention of 1888." Bulganin said that the evacuation of Egypt by British, French and Israeli forces would render UN troops unnecessary. He conceded that with Egyptian permission, UN forces "could be stationed on the 2 sides" of the 1949 Israeli-Egyptian armistice line.

Diplomats from NATO countries and Israel walked out when Soviet Communist Party First Secy. Nikita S. Khrushchev denounced their policies during talks at receptions in Moscow Nov. 17–18 in connection with a Polish-Soviet conference. He said during a Kremlin affair for the Polish delegates Nov. 17 that the Anglo-Egyptian attack on Egypt was "piratic" and that Israel was a "puppet" of "imperialists" in their "hopeless attempt to restore lost colonial bastions." He addressed this warning to capitalists: "History is on our side. We will bury you." He repeated the denunciation at a Polish embassy reception Nov. 18 and said that Egyptian Pres. Nasser, although not a Communist, "he has even put Communists in jail", was "fighting for national independence, . . . is the hero of his nation and our sympathies are on his side."

The USSR disclosed Nov. 17 that it was sending 15 million rubles [$3¾ million] worth of food and medical supplies to Egypt. A large group of Soviet military experts passed through Rome en route to Moscow from their Egyptian posts Nov. 16. British informants reported

Nov. 20 that Egypt had begun negotiations with the USSR for the replacement of the tanks, jets and artillery lost to the Israelis.

Suez Campaign's Aftermath

The U.S. by mid-Nov. 1956 was faced with the necessity of fashioning an entirely new policy formulation to meet the greatly changed circumstances. The Tripartite Declaration of May 25, 1950, hitherto the basis of Washington's foreign policy in the Middle East, had been rendered extinct by the Anglo-French invasion of Suez. More immediately urgent to U.S. leaders, however, was the necessity of keeping the Soviet Union from obtaining a greater bridgehead in the Middle East than it had already gained with the introduction into Egypt of some 2,000 Soviet-bloc technicians, diplomats and propagandists.

The threat of armed Soviet intervention in the Middle East apparently waned Nov. 15-16 following the warning by Pres. Eisenhower that the U.S. would oppose the dispatch of Russian "volunteers" to aid Egypt. UN Emergency Force units landed in Egypt Nov. 15 and were ordered to take up truce supervision positions in the Port Said area Nov. 20.

Acting U.S. State Secy. Herbert Hoover Jr. told the UN General Assembly in New York Nov. 16 that "the UN would be obligated" to take action against the introduction of "so-called "volunteers" into the Middle East." Hoover warned that the prohibition on the reinforcement of Egyptian, British, French and Israeli forces applied to "all" powers, including those engaged in hostilities." The introduction of "external" forces, he said, would be "a threat to the UN Force now entering the area."

The Eisenhower Administration had already begun to consult with U.S. Congressional leaders in its effort to shape a new policy. Eisenhower met Nov. 9 with officials of his Administration and 23 Congressional leaders for a review of the Middle Eastern situation. Senate Democratic leader Lyndon B. Johnson (Tex.) said after the meeting that "no commitments were asked or given." Washington sources said Nov. 9-11 that the White House assessment had showed that no shift in U.S. policy on the Middle East was required then and that Soviet forces would not intervene in Egypt. A general review of Middle Eastern policy was reported under way Nov. 13 as pressure mounted for U.S. action to counter Soviet threats of intervention by "volunteers."

Several Congressional leaders asked for a reassessment of U.S. Middle East policy. Sen. Mike Mansfield (D., Mont.) Nov. 10 urged an Israeli-Egyptian non-aggression pact and the patrolling of the Israeli-

Egyptian frontier by UN forces.   Senate Republican leader William F. Knowland (Calif.) Nov. 11 recommended U.S. support for UN economic sanctions against Britain, France and Israel if they refused to leave Egypt.   Senate majority leader Johnson said Nov. 13 that the UN force would be only "a temporary expedient." He urged a new long-range U.S. policy for the Middle East.   Sen. Hubert H. Humphrey (D., Minn.) Nov. 13 proposed a 25,000-man UN Middle Eastern peace force.

State Secy. John Foster Dulles, in a statement issued as he left Walter Reed Army Hospital in Washington Nov. 18, said that it would be a "grave mistake" to think that the cease-fire could result in permanent Middle East stability.   Dulles, leaving for Key West, Fla. to recuperate from intestinal surgery, said that a "just and durable" Middle East peace must include permanent Arab-Israeli frontiers and the resettlement of 900,000 Arab refugees.   Dulles assailed the USSR for its attempted intervention in the Middle East and for the "promiscuous slaughter" brought by its intervention in Hungary.

U.S. officials expressed concern Nov. 24 at reports of deepening Soviet penetration in Syria.   They cited French reports that Syria was receiving 2 shiploads of Russian arms weekly under a Syrian-Soviet agreement negotiated by Syrian Premier Shukri al-Kuwatli during a Moscow visit Nov. 3–4.   An Arab diplomatic courier arriving in Iraq from Syria said Nov. 27 that Soviet-built jet planes were arriving in Syria daily and that Syrian roads were "lined" with Russian tanks, artillery and matériel.   The British Foreign Office Nov. 24 confirmed as "quite likely correct" reports that Syria was under the control of a pro-Soviet and pro-Nasser army intelligence chief, Lt. Col. Abdel Hamid Sarraj.   Tension had been reported between nationalist pro-Soviet army units and pro-Western government factions in Syria since the proclamation of a state of emergency following Israel's invasion of Egypt Oct. 29. Tank units were reported massing near Damascus Nov. 17 and Sarraj was reported firmly in control of Syria Nov. 18.

The U.S. State Department announced Nov. 29 that the U.S. would view "with the utmost gravity" any threat to the territorial integrity or political independence of Turkey, Iran, Iraq or Pakistan, the 4 Middle Eastern members of the Baghdad Pact.

Eisenhower Doctrine

Pres. Eisenhower reportedly decided Dec. 27–29, 1956 to ask Congress to join him in announcing that the U.S. would oppose—with military might if necessary—any armed Soviet aggression in the Middle East. This declaration was to be part of a proposed new "Eisenhower Doctrine" that would include increased U.S. economic aid to counter Soviet economic penetration in the Middle East and to help in the settlement of the area's problems.

The fact that Eisenhower and State Secy. Dulles were considering this plan—which Dulles was said to have originated—was made known to *N.Y. Times* writer James Reston by an unnamed "reliable source" Dec. 27. The President, it was reported, had discussed it with Dulles that day and intended to broach it to Congressional leaders Jan. 1, 1957. Observers labeled this and subsequent "leaks" to the press a "trial balloon" to test reaction in the U.S. and abroad. By Dec. 29, it was reported, the Administration had adopted the plan.

Dulles and U.S. Amb.-to-UN Henry Cabot Lodge conferred with UN Secy. Gen. Dag Hammarskjöld in New York Dec. 31 and were said to have discussed the new U.S. plan. Dulles Dec. 31 issued a statement saying U.S. policies had not "yet been finalized" and must "reinforce and fit into United Nations policies." A 2d Dulles statement Dec. 31 asserted that the U.S. "has a major responsibility to help prevent the spread to the Middle East of Soviet imperialism" and would "have to accept" during 1957 "an increasing responsibility to assist the free nations of the Middle East, and elsewhere, to maintain their freedom and to develop their welfare."

The new Eisenhower Doctrine was criticized by Democratic leaders, but many Republicans seemed ready to support it. Foreign diplomats gave it a mixed reception.

Sen. Alexander Wiley (Wis.), ranking Republican of the Senate Foreign Relations Committee, said Dec. 28 that Congress would act "in the interest of peace" if it gave the President standby authority to use U.S. forces in the Middle East. He said he considered the situation similar to that in 1955, when Congress gave Eisenhower such authority in the case of Formosa. But Sen. Mike Mansfield (D., Mont.) of the Senate Foreign Relations Committee said he saw no parallel. He pointed out Dec. 28 that before Congress acted in 1955, Eisenhower had "committed" the U.S. "to defend Formosa against any major assault" and there was "an already negotiated American-Nationalist Chinese security pact." But, he said, in the Middle East "we have already gone to the UN with the matter. Why ... authorize the President to get us, alone, stuck out there?" Wiley denied Dec. 30 that the plan meant a break in the Eisenhower policy of working through the UN. He said he was sure the President would not use the authority requested "except in conjunction" with the UN.

Sen. Hubert H. Humphrey (D., Minn.) of the Senate Foreign Relations Committee charged Dec. 30 that the Eisenhower Administration had proposed an "adolescent and shocking" shift in position after, "in effect," it had "renounced the use of force." He said it would be wiser to come out for a strong UN police force for the Middle East. Humphrey also accused the Administration of "insulting" Democratic Senators by telling the press about its plans before informing any members of the Senate majority. He called it "a rather peculiar and unorthodox way of announcing a new policy." Sen. John J. Sparkman (D., Ala.) of the Senate Foreign Relations Committee said Dec. 30 that he saw no need to give Eisenhower "advance authority" since Congress would be in session and immediately available if emergency action were required.